Asia's New Little Dragons

Asia's New Little Dragons

The Dynamic Emergence of Indonesia, Thailand, and Malaysia

STEVEN SCHLOSSSTEIN

CB

CONTEMPORARY
BOOKS

CHICAGO

Library of Congress Cataloging-in-Publication Data

Schlossstein, Steven.
  Asia's new little dragons : the dynamic emergence of Indonesia,
Thailand, and Malaysia / Steven Schlossstein.
      p.   cm.
  Includes bibliographical references and index.
  ISBN 0-8092-4038-6
  1. Indonesia—Economic conditions—1945-   2. Indonesia—
Economic policy.   3. Indonesia—Politics and government—1966-
4. Thailand—Economic conditions.   5. Thailand—Economic
policy.   6. Thailand—politics and government.   7. Malaysia—
Economic conditions.   8. Malaysia—Economic policy.
9. Malaysia—Politics and government.   I. Title.
HC447.S367   1991
338.959—dc20   91-2661
                                                                                      CIP

Published by Contemporary Books, Inc.
180 North Michigan Avenue, Chicago, Illinois 60601
Manufactured in the United States of America
International Standard Book Number: 0-8092-4038-6

For the people of Southeast Asia—
whose hard work and arduous effort under often
adverse conditions have produced dramatically
higher living standards for their children and created
a model of inspiration and hope for developing
countries everywhere

CONTENTS

PREFACE

Thirty years ago Japan first caught the world's attention through its high-quality consumer goods, its near-neurotic attention to manufacturing detail, and its now-famous "economic miracle." Then, not long thereafter, came the so-called Little Dragons—Korea, Taiwan, Singapore, and Hong Kong—which replicated many of Japan's own commercial and economic successes. Their stories are now familiar, and most Americans have become aware of them—through popular products, new books, and TV.

Less familiar, however, are the stories of Indonesia, Thailand, and Malaysia, three nations that are laying a solid foundation for economic takeoff, yet to appear on the horizon, but already they are registering some of the highest rates of real economic growth in the world. Far removed from the fallout of the Cold War and untouched by America's public policy debates over mainly domestic issues—tax policy and the federal deficit, public education reform, the war on drugs, family policy and welfare reform, urban redevelopment, the repair and upgrading of our infrastructure, affordable housing, health care, the environment—these countries are fighting a quieter battle for higher living standards, for faster economic growth, for the creation of new wealth.

Can another group of countries in East Asia repeat the successes of Japan and the Little Dragons? And why have all the economic achievements by developing countries been in Asia? What policies are being created, and implemented, that consistently enable these Asian nations to succeed? Are there valuable lessons for their counterparts in Latin America and Africa? How much of their success is attributable to indigenous factors—political, social, cultural, educational—and how much to external developments? Why is Japan giving them such priority attention, while America is not? Will these three potential new Little Dragons, a few years from now, be as familiar to Americans as the four old Little Dragons are today? Or have we seen the end of the phenomenon called newly industrializing countries—the NICs? And what are the implications for American foreign and economic policy—in both the public and the private sectors—if these three nations do continue their explosive growth? Will they have a meaningful role to play in the new information age, and will they be our partners or our foes?

This book is an attempt to answer these and other related questions. It is an outgrowth of several months of research in the field, in the summer of 1989, when I was a visiting fellow at the Institute of Southeast Asian Studies (ISEAS) in Singapore, and its sister institutions in Jakarta, Bangkok, and Kuala Lumpur. During this period of time, from late May through early September, I conducted more than 200 background interviews with senior government officials, local business executives, educators, economists, taxidrivers, and shopkeepers, as well as with American and Japanese expatriates in each of these countries. Without their close cooperation and support, simply put, this project would have been impossible to complete.

Many of the issues raised in this book are not without controversy—opinions expressed about American and Japanese attitudes or policy or personal behavior, insights into sensitive cultural concerns like religion or prostitution or corruption, and observations on the efficacy of the local policy formulation process and the personal chemistry of government leaders involved therein. Understandably many senior Indonesian, Thai, and Malaysian informants preferred to speak off the record or without attribution. But I would like very much to acknowledge their invaluable assistance, as they were helpful in countless confidential, clandestine, and often controversial ways (with interviews, with information, or with introductions). Without their help this book would have been remarkably thin.

On the other hand, many people generously shared their time, their convictions, and their thoughts with me on the record. They are reflected (and named) in the many interviews that follow in the text;

space limitations prevent listing them all here, but they must take credit for making the narrative so human and so lively. They know they have my heartfelt thanks and gratitude, for without their participation, interest, and effort this book would not have been possible.

To the trustees and staff of the Institute of Southeast Asian Studies in Singapore, and to its executive director, Kernial Sandhu—whose friendship, support, and constant encouragement I will always treasure—a special note of appreciation and thanks. ISEAS was (and will forever be) a "home away from home" for me, and I have only the highest praise for its professional standards and achievements.

To the Center for Strategic and International Studies (CSIS), Japan's Ministry of International Trade and Industry (MITI) representatives (and their voluminous background materials, in Japanese, always detailed and incredibly thorough), the U.S. embassy commercial and political staffs, and the Asia Foundation office, in Jakarta; to the Thailand Development Research Institute, the Institute for Strategic and International Studies, the MITI representatives, both the American and Japanese embassies and Chamber of Commerce staffs, and the Asia Foundation office, in Bangkok; to the Institute for Strategic and International Studies, the Malaysian Institute for Economic Research, the MITI representatives, the American and Japanese embassies and Chamber of Commerce staffs, and the Asia Foundation office, in Kuala Lumpur—my thanks for all their help in arranging introductions, providing valuable background data, and suggesting useful new sources that added considerable depth and perspective to the text.

To Hadi Soesastro of CSIS in Jakarta, Patcharee Sororos at Thammasat University in Bangkok, and Paul Low, chairman of Malaysian Sheet Glass Berhad in Kuala Lumpur, each of whom commented helpfully on early drafts of the manuscript, my grateful appreciation. They know that the opinions and ideas expressed herein are totally mine, and they are absolved of any responsibility for the positions taken (or predictions made) in the text.

To the research staff at the ISEAS Library (whose Xerox copiers achieved new levels of output during my stay), to the staff at Princeton University's Firestone Library, and to the reference librarians at the Princeton Public Library—especially Jane Clinton and Eric Greenfeldt—special thanks, as ever, for special help.

To my agent, Dominick Abel, who is a gentleman in an often curmudgeonly business; to my publisher, Harvey Plotnick, a man of vision who senses trends (and leverages them) as well as anyone in the industry; to my editors, Bernard Shir-Cliff and Kathy Willhoite, who offered valuable suggestions that have made the text more accessible to the general reader; and to my manuscript editor, Christine M. Benton, who brought her usual high standards of professional performance to bear on both style and content—you each played a strong role in making this production successful, and you have my most grateful appreciation and deepest thanks.

Finally, to my wife, Marty, and our children, Claire and Peter, who shared so many of these experiences during our lengthy stay in Southeast Asia, my heartfelt gratitude and love for making our peripatetic family so strong, so flexible, and in the end analysis so durable.

Despite the generous assistance, advice, and guidance I have received from one and all, including those who preferred to remain anonymous, I alone remain responsible for the interpretations, opinions, and judgments rendered throughout the text, and any errors resulting therefrom are of course my own.

Princeton, New Jersey
January 1991

Asia's New Little Dragons

1
INTRODUCTION
Of Dragons Old and New

The copycat days are over. Japanese industry is well on the way to becoming not just self-sufficient in technology, but a big exporter of know-how, as well. Its engineering laboratories are brimming with ideas that have been cultivated entirely at home. Japanese firms now have a virtual stranglehold on the technologies for making cars, cameras, semiconductor memory chips, video equipment, fiber optics, machine tools, industrial robots, flexible manufacturing systems, quality steels, and composite materials. Japanese firms are responsible for almost half of the patents being filed around the world. All this, and they are only just getting into their stride.

In the process, Japanese industry is being remade. Since 1986, Japan's economic growth has come exclusively from domestic demand; net exports have [declined as] imports have risen on the back of a soaring yen. Japanese firms have hastened the process along by exporting their know-how to subcontractors in South Korea, Thailand, and Taiwan, who then manufacture the goods for them and stick on Japanese labels. [This] new direction suggests a shift from the export of products to the export of software and services, centering on advanced technology.

—Nicholas Valéry, "Japanese Technology:
Thinking Ahead," *The Economist*

During the past two decades, close on the heels of Asia's economic miracle—Japan—the world has witnessed the explosive growth of South Korea, Taiwan, Singapore, and Hong Kong, East Asia's so-called Little Dragons, whose aggressive export strategies, close government/business cooperation, strong public education systems, high rates of savings and capital formation, and soaring personal incomes have put American firms under increasing competitive pressure and have caused the United States to rethink its own neoclassical economic theory and free-trade philosophy.

For the past twenty years the Little Dragons have generated the highest rates of growth in the world, with the annual average at 9 percent compared with nearly 5 percent in Southeast Asia, less than 4 percent in Latin America, under 3 percent in Africa, and just over 2 percent for the United States. Most recently, for the five years from 1983 to 1988, their average growth rates were nearly in double digits: 10.2 percent for Taiwan, 9.5 percent for Korea, 9 percent for Singapore, and 8.1 percent for Hong Kong. What's more, these four countries *alone* accounted for almost two-thirds of *all* manufactured goods exported during that time. Together with the front-runner, Japan, two of them—Korea and Taiwan—had amassed nearly $200 billion in official foreign exchange reserves by 1988, around four times the U.S. level and nearly half the world's total, and the same three countries accounted for about two-thirds of America's total global trade deficit.

In fact the economic growth rates of the Little Dragons have been so strong—with their export strategies so aggressive and their per-capita incomes so high—that Washington has taken an increasingly harsh view, reacting with protectionist sentiment rather than attempting to adjust and adapt to these new forms of Asian-Pacific dynamism. But contrary to popular perception, the Little Dragons were not exporting just to America. By 1988, while some 30 percent of Korea's trade was with the United States, more than 25 percent was with Japan; Taiwan was shipping about a third of its exports to America but more than 20 percent to Japan; Hong Kong was sending 18 percent of its exports to the United States, but 12 percent to Japan; and 19 percent of Singapore's exports were going to the United States, but 15 percent to Japan. The best-kept secret of East Asian growth is that trade *within the region* now constitutes nearly half of its total: intraregional trade among the Little Dragons themselves exploded by almost 50 percent in 1988.

By early 1988 Washington had graduated all four countries from its Generalized System of Preferences (GSP), which previously gave certain of their exports preferential tariff treatment. In mid-1988

Representative Richard Gephardt of Missouri, an early Democratic candidate in the presidential primaries (and now majority leader of the House), called for punitive tariffs against Korea's automobile exports to reduce their price competitiveness in the United States. And throughout 1989 America's trade officials pressed both Korea and Taiwan to "open" their markets further to American products, such as cigarettes and farm goods, creating an unprecedented amount of anti-American sentiment in these countries.

In the meantime some observers of these trends have argued that the strategies and tactics used by the Little Dragons cannot be sustained. That their success is a limited, one-shot achievement that cannot be replicated. That America will not be able to keep its market as open as it has in the past if these sorcerer's apprentice economies cannot learn to control their aggressive behavior. "It is time to ask," one analyst noted, "whether any more developing countries can really hope to become the South Korea of the late 1980s or the Hong Kong of the early 1990s."

But right behind the four Little Dragons are three *more* East Asian economies—Indonesia, Thailand, and Malaysia—sitting on the runway revving up for takeoff, expanding at double-digit rates of growth since 1986 or 1987. Thailand's growth has been so rapid that its physical infrastructure—roads, highways, and port facilities—has become saturated to the point of gridlock as more and more Thai manufactured exports head for foreign markets. Indonesia, in a period of less than three years, had a *higher* percentage of exports in manufactured goods by 1989 than it did in gas and oil, and this from a country which is a member of OPEC. Malaysia, in addition to being the world's number-one exporter of palm oil, rubber, and tin, is today the world's leading exporter of computer chips and the third-largest manufacturer of semiconductor devices overall after Japan and the United States.

Why has this been happening? How have three more East Asian nations been able to achieve rapid economic development so closely on the heels of their northeastern neighbors, while the sluggish economies of Latin America and Africa remain heavily burdened with debt, severely shackled by inflation, deeply mired in socialist ideology, and firmly entrenched as spectators of rather than participants in the international trading system that the dynamic nations of East Asia have so successfully mastered?

THE ALPHABET SOUP

In the "old days," going back some thirty years, there were essentially just two categories of economic development: the industrialized (or developed) nations of the West (and Japan), and the developing nations, called lesser developed countries, or LDCs. Beginning around 1970, however, as the pace of economic growth in East Asia began to quicken, countries like Korea and Taiwan chafed at being categorized as "lesser developed"—especially since the noneconomic sides of their cultures, such as their social organization and rich historical traditions, were in fact highly developed—so they collectively became known as newly industrializing countries, or NICs, instead. Then, as their economic growth rates exploded throughout the 1970s and 1980s, the four East Asian NICs earned their popular nicknames—the Little Dragons. They quickly left the Philippines behind, even though that country had had the region's highest per-capita income a generation earlier.

Culturally, of course, China was the Big Dragon, even though its economy was wedded to the failing ideology of communism and concepts more appropriate to the nineteenth century. But economically Japan, too, was a Big Dragon since its GNP comprised about 80 percent of the total East Asian output of goods and services. Still, the four Little Dragons owed much if not all of their own cultural heritage to China: Taiwan was itself a former Chinese province, occupied and governed by mainlanders since 1949 as the Republic of China; the population of Singapore was three-quarters Chinese, although its society and government were characterized by strong multiracial interaction based also on Malay and Tamil traditions; Hong Kong was by origin virtually a Chinese city, despite its heritage as a British colony; and Korea had adapted its own Confucian traditions from China. All four of the Little Dragons were quintessentially chopstick cultures: like chopsticks, individually the people would break, but together they were strong and durable.

But by the mid-1980s, as the three Southeast Asian economies began accelerating, the terminology started getting a bit confused. Thailand, Indonesia, and Malaysia were being called the new NICs, to distinguish them from the Little Dragons, which had now become the old NICs, so a new designation clearly was needed.

Enter the newly industrializing economies, or NIEs (pronounced *knees*). But the NIEs clearly weren't yet industrializing as rapidly as the NICs. Whatever the yardstick, NIEs were by no means clones of NICs.

But the designation seems to have survived, so throughout this text the Little Dragons of Korea, Taiwan, Singapore, and Hong Kong are NICs, while the now rapidly growing economies of Indonesia, Thailand, and Malaysia are referred to as NIEs.

THE DESCRIPTIVE CHARACTERISTICS

Economists, businesspeople, and journalists tend to use just two or three simple yardsticks when measuring a country to see if it qualifies as a NIC: per-capita income, manufacturing as a percentage of total GNP, and manufactured goods as a share of total exports.

If we use these three conventional parameters of economic performance alone, how do Japan and the NICs fare?

ECONOMIC PERFORMANCE OF JAPAN AND THE NICs
(As of December 31, 1989; US$, %)

Category	Japan	Korea	Taiwan	Singapore	Hong Kong
Per-capita income	23,539	4,968	6,889	10,810	10,918
Manufacturing as % of GNP	30.9	34.5	35.6	30.1	26.7
Manufactured goods as % of total exports	86.7	94.5	96.8	81.3	88.0

The price of admission for joining the NICs' club is generally considered to be a per-capita income of at least $3,000, manufacturing equal to 25 percent or more of GNP, and manufactured goods comprising not less than 25 percent of total exports. All the Little Dragons qualify easily.

But while these three characteristics may represent a statistical snapshot of an economy's overall performance at any time, they overlook a number of more complex economic, historical, and cultural factors that are crucial in determining whether a country may in fact be called a NIC.

These factors—and there are about a dozen of them that are key—have played a seminal role in the impressive development of the NICs and, before them, Japan (though Japan had emerged as an industrial powerhouse long before the NIC terminology became popular). These twelve characteristics—with the first five or six being the most important—are discussed on the following pages in descending order of relevance.

1. An Authoritarian Political System

Perhaps the most frequently overlooked factor in the recent rise of East Asian economies, political authoritarianism has created a solid base of stability from which economic growth could proceed. *None* of these countries (Japan included) has picked representative democracy as the political model on which to base its economy. Since 1955 Japan has been dominated by a single-party system, controlled by the Liberal Democratic Party (the LDP), a group of conservatives whose primary policy focus has always been to maximize Japan's national economic interests by benefiting producers at the expense of consumers. Similarly, Singapore's politics have been controlled by Lee Kuan Yew's Political Action Party (the PAP) since well before the Lion City became an independent nation in 1965. These two systems have employed what some analysts call "soft" authoritarianism, in contrast to the "hard" variety of authoritarianism practiced until only very recently by South Korea and Taiwan.

From the time Park Chung-hee took control of South Korea in 1961 until his successor, Chun Doo-hwan, stepped down in 1987, the country's political system was virtually dominated by the army— a kind of martial law in mufti. Taiwan was literally ruled by the military from the time Generalissimo Chiang Kai-shek fled from the mainland in 1949 until his son, Chiang Ching-kuo, canceled the martial law order in September 1987, shortly before his death a few months later.

Both countries have now planted the delicate seeds of democracy, but their political economies were dominated by firm authoritarian rule for nearly three decades, the decades underpinning their rapid economic growth. Taiwan's political system is still controlled by a single party, the Kuomintang, despite recent liberalization that permits the participation of opposition parties. And by early 1990 Korea had merged two of its own opposition parties into the government party, forming a new Democratic Liberal Party (DLP), cloned from the Japanese model.

Hong Kong, of course, has been a British colony since the mid-nineteenth century, with little participation by the people in their system of government, however benign or beneficent it may have been with its growth-supporting economic policies. In fact the *only* country in East Asia that has had a functioning system of American-style democracy since the end of the Pacific War is the Philippines (not counting the fifteen years of "constitutional authoritarianism" under the late Ferdinand Marcos), and it is still the only nation in the region that is more characteristic of anemic African economies than of the more robust, vigorous economies of Northeast Asia.

One further distinction needs to be made: while the NICs may have put authoritarian political systems in place, they are by no means totalitarian. Unlike the central command systems of the Soviet Union and China, all the Little Dragons encourage the growth of private ownership and permit a remarkable degree of personal freedom. And their institutions, both public and private, are much more highly developed than those in either the Soviet Union or China.

So while American thinking suggests that economic development promotes political stability, the Little Dragons have turned this theory on its head and demonstrated just the reverse. As Harvard political scientist Samuel Huntington put it in his classic work *Political Order in Changing Societies*, "The primary problem is not liberty but the creation of a legitimate public order. Men may have order without liberty, but they cannot have liberty without order. Authority has to exist before it can be limited, and it is authority that is in scarce supply in modernizing countries where government is at the mercy of alienated intellectuals, rambunctious colonels, and rioting students."

2. New Forms of Government/Business Cooperation

Years ago the expression "Japan, Inc." was coined to convey the way in which Japanese government and business interests worked together to achieve a common goal: conquering global markets through aggressive, mercantilistic practices while simultaneously keeping the domestic Japanese market relatively immune to foreign penetration.

The Japanese ministry with frontline policy responsibility for the nation's economic growth during the catch-up years was MITI—the famed Ministry of International Trade and Industry—which in the early years of Japan's industrialization nearly a century ago had created the concept of industrial policy. By focusing on strategic industries, disaggregated incentives, and sectoral targeting, the state (via MITI) played a key role in Japan's industrialization and modernization process, with a success that has since been more than amply documented.

Japanese industrial policy virtually ignored Western economic theory—especially the neoclassical school of Adam Smith and his "invisible hand of the market"—in hammering out its tactical policy tools: tax and depreciation benefits disaggregated by industry to strengthen those industrial sectors targeted for growth and development, incentives to stimulate exports of manufactured goods and to ensure that manufacturing moved progressively up the ladder of value-added production, aggressive R&D credits for selected sectors, encouragement of export cartels to harness and direct the fierce competitiveness of Japan's small and medium enterprises, and development of aggressive strategies for the predatory penetration of overseas markets.

This process has been called *capitalist developmental economics*, to distinguish it from the more familiar Western version known as *capitalist regulatory economics* (as practiced primarily in the United States and Europe). It relies heavily on what the Japanese themselves call "the visible hand of the market" and has resulted in a dynamic economic system that I have termed "turbocharged capitalism."

While the term "Japan, Inc." tends to overstate the nature of the government/business relationship in Japan, it connotes an appropriate flavor; I have called it an "equal partnership" because the policies MITI and the Ministry of Finance have created have been market-*conforming* rather than market-*determining*. In Korea, because of the more pronounced role of the government, I have called the government/industry relationship a "senior partnership," and in Taiwan, given the more subliminal (but no less important) position of government, I have termed the relationship a "silent partnership." Singapore is closer to the Japanese model (without its more mercantilist, predatory practices), and Hong Kong is closer to Taiwan. But in each case the evidence is clear: government works *with* business in a positive, mutually reinforcing relationship rather than *against* business in the adversarial, confrontational manner more characteristic of Western political economies.

3. An Outward Economic Orientation

Japan and the Little Dragons all figured out rather early on that the traditional system of import substitution had more limitations than benefits, so they turned their attention to exports instead.

When Japan embarked on former prime minister Ikeda's "income-doubling" plan in the late 1950s, it was the rapidly expanding domestic economy that had fueled this growth. But the primary actors involved—Japan's public and private sectors—were tuned to international markets to an extraordinary degree, licensing technology, setting prices, and establishing product quality standards that used global standards as a benchmark for performance. Thus was the launchpad built for takeoff of Japanese exports a decade hence.

Similarly, by the early 1960s the NICs were laying the groundwork for their own export-led growth, forsaking the conventional economic theory that stressed import substitution and replacing it with a more outward-looking focus on exports. It is hard to remember now that in those days the conventional wisdom held that India and Argentina would grow two to three times as fast as Korea or Singapore because they had put in place large petrochemical complexes and steel mills. Nobody expected Asia to do well, but by 1980 Korea's per-capita income had reached that of Argentina and Brazil, and by 1987 it had outstripped them both, yet it was still only *fifth* in Asia after Japan, Singapore, Hong Kong, and Taiwan.

For the five-year period from 1978 to 1983 Korea's export-driven economy grew at an average rate of 9.7 percent a year; Singapore's at 8.9 percent, Taiwan's at 7.5 percent, and Hong Kong's at 9.4 percent. During the same period total foreign trade comprised 91 percent of Korea's GNP, 345 percent of Singapore's (because of its emphasis on reexports), 98 percent of Taiwan's, and 172 percent of Hong Kong's. So by the early 1980s the Little Dragons had caught the attention of economists and businesspeople alike.

For the next five-year period, from 1983 to 1988, the NICs maintained their world-class performance: Korea's GNP expanded at an average annual rate of 9.5 percent, Singapore's at 9 percent, Taiwan's at 10.2 percent, and Hong Kong's at 8.1 percent. For the same period Korea's total trade was equal to 95 percent of its GNP, Singapore's 307 percent, Taiwan's 93 percent, and Hong Kong's 262 percent. The previous generation's conventional picks, India and Argentina, had long since been left in East Asia's dust.

4. Massive Incentives to Increase Private Savings

Korea was the only Little Dragon to have gone extensively into debt during the heyday of rapid economic growth, having borrowed, at its peak, about $45 billion from foreign private banks and international institutions like the World Bank. By the end of 1987 Korea still owed nearly $35 billion to foreign lenders, but practically *all* of the principal and interest due was being financed by its merchandise trade surplus with the United States, which alone was generating about $9 billion a year.

Still, taking their cue from Japan, Korea and the other NICs had put in place aggressive incentives to generate private savings and increase capital formation at the highest rates in the world. Japan had long before created a tax system that favored producers over consumers and implemented policies that exempted high levels of interest income from tax to encourage its people to save. Dividends were subject to double taxation, as in the United States, but capital gains bore no tax at all. As a consequence Japanese firms rarely declared dividends, preferring to reinvest their retained earnings rather than distribute them to shareholders.

Mortgage interest (as well as interest on other personal loans) was (and is) not deductible for tax purposes in Japan. And to make it convenient for Japanese depositors, the Japanese government opened savings windows at every post office nationwide as part of its postal savings system, the proceeds of which were (and still are) the core of its Fiscal Investment Loan Program (FILP), which the Ministry of Finance channels into key off-budget strategic investments every year. (If the Japanese postal savings system were a bank, it would be the largest financial institution in the world, with total deposits of nearly $1 trillion.) Thus it was no mystery why Japan's capital formation rate had been one of the highest in the world, at close to 30 percent of GNP, during the years of rapid economic growth.

The Little Dragons all utilized similar tax incentives to favor producers over consumers and to generate high rates of personal savings and capital formation. Singapore, for example, created its vaunted Central Provident Fund (CPF) scheme, which was like a turbocharged Individual Retirement Account (IRA): employees as well as employers were required to make regular monthly contributions to the account (up to, at times, as much as a third of gross salary), which could be invested, tax-free, in any number of government-approved plans but could not be withdrawn until age fifty-five. Borrowings could be made against principal, however, to finance a primary residence or for emergency medical expenses. But each account was established and administered separately, in an individual's own name and for his or her own future, rather than pooled together as is the case with America's social security system.

These tax policies generated extremely high rates of savings and capital formation. By 1988 Korea's gross capital formation as a percent of GNP was nearly 30 percent, Hong Kong's was 24 percent, Taiwan's 20 percent, and Singapore's 36 percent (compared to the much lower rate of around 12 percent in the United States). While these policies may have penalized the individual as consumer, they have rewarded the individual as saver, thus creating enormous personal financial power by eliminating the burden of personal debt that so weighs the American consumer down.

5. An Unswerving Commitment to Public Education

From barren Korea in Northeast Asia to the densely populated island of Singapore in Southeast Asia, including the colorful colony of Hong Kong and the small island of Taiwan in between, the NICs are totally bereft of natural resources. Japan, too, has to import virtually all of its own petroleum and the raw materials it needs to produce its higher-value-added exports.

Unlike the United States, which has abundant natural resources, these nations have had to rely entirely on their *human* resources—

their people—for economic growth and development. And this means essentially two things: rigorous and successful efforts to curtail population growth and the creation of public education systems that are intensely competitive, push meritocracy to new limits, and ensure that the best and brightest are channeled into society's two most productive and important sectors—private manufacturing and government service.

It should come as no surprise, then, that the students of East Asia today consistently score highest on international tests of academic achievement. Or that they comprise the single largest group of foreign graduate students in the United States—again, not surprisingly, they make up nearly 50 percent of all postgraduate students of science and engineering at American universities. Or that the literacy rates of the East Asian countries are the highest in the world. Or that incentives exist in each of these countries to exalt teaching as a highly respected profession.

Neither Japan nor the Little Dragons accept the thesis that the world is moving into a so-called postindustrial age. Rather they maintain that it is entering an information age, in which it no longer matters how amply endowed with natural resources a nation may be. What matters is how advanced the development of a nation's human resources are, to benefit from (if not control) those industries—such as computers and telecommunications and semiconductor technology—that are to the world's knowledge-intensive future as automobiles and iron and steel were to its industrial past.

6. A Strong Emphasis on Applied R&D

The Western concept of research and development (R&D) emphasizes a "breakthrough" approach to discovery, which puts a great premium on basic (as opposed to applied) research and rewards the invention of new processes rather than the development of new applications for existing ones.

Japan has turned the art of applied R&D into a veritable science. Called *kaizen*, it refers to the incremental, step-by-step process that stresses commercial and technical applications of existing discoveries. Thus most Japanese R&D is funded neither by academic institutions nor by the central government but by private organizations, mostly concentrated in the manufacturing sector. By 1989 nearly two-thirds of Japan's total R&D expenditures were being funded by Japanese companies, with 94 percent of this private sector total concentrated in manufacturing, spending on average more than 3 percent of gross sales.

The NICs have followed in Japan's footsteps, emphasizing applied rather than basic research and focusing on technical and commercial development. They have benefited enormously from trade in technology—from the West, to be sure, but also from Japan. By 1988 Japan was exporting technology (technical applications and know-how) worth a total of nearly $2 billion a year, of which about 40 percent went to other nations in Asia (including the Little Dragons) and was concentrated overwhelmingly—more than 96 percent—in the manufacturing sector.

Each of the NICs has put strong emphasis on applied R&D. As part of its industrial infrastructure and to serve as the focus of its industrial R&D, Singapore has created its own Science Park, which by 1987 had twenty-one on-site firms conducting research in advanced industrial technologies and software development. By 1986 Singapore was spending just under 1 percent of GNP on R&D (the United States spends about 2.5 percent of GNP overall) and in less than five years' time had doubled the number of its research scientists and engineers. Taiwan, too, had developed its own science city at Hsinchu, the nation's focal point for new advances in information and chip technology. By 1987 Taiwan had already begun to experience a "reverse brain drain," whereby the number of talented scientists and engineers returning to the country was greater than the number leaving.

The upshot of this concentration on applied R&D was that Japan and the Little Dragons were consistently able to move high-quality manufactured products from design to market in about *half* the time of their American competitors—a clear commercial advantage in an age of growing globalization, market-share orientation, and knowledge-intensive industrialization.

7. A Consistent Focus on Value-Added Production

There are nations in the world that, applying the free-trade and comparative-advantage theories of Adam Smith and David Ricardo, started out exporting coffee beans and bananas and today, centuries later, still export coffee beans and bananas. Central American "banana" republics come to mind here, as do many countries in Africa and Latin America.

But Japan and the NICs were never content to rely on commodities exports, not only because they had so few natural resources to begin with but also because they knew that they could add better value (and generate greater wealth) by focusing on the production and export of manufactured goods. Thus was their industrial policy geared toward what they called the strategic industries, with a clear focus on manufacturing.

In the 1950s Japan's strategic industries were petrochemicals, shipbuilding, and steel, but by the 1980s they had shifted up the value-added ladder to semiconductors, telecommunications equipment, and numerically controlled machine tools. Similarly, Korea's early export industrialization was built on a large supply of cheap labor (relative to Japan), so it stole market share in chemicals, ships, and steel from the Japanese. Singapore established its reputation as Asia's financial services and telecommunications center. The smaller, more entrepreneurial firms in Taiwan, long known as the Land of the Order Taker, had established a reputation for excellence in manufacturing electronic and consumer products, and Hong Kong gradually became known as the toy capital of the world.

All the Little Dragons used policies consciously designed to move their products higher up in the value-added hierarchy, build on their close government/business relationships, apply a "visible hand of the market," and strengthen industrial policy formation. By putting the focus on manufacturing, they could deal more directly with the process of industrial restructuring—shifting human and financial resources away from declining industries to emerging ones.

8. A Marked Absence of Natural Resources

Again, Japan and the Little Dragons are virtually devoid of natural resources. Japan imports virtually all of its crude oil, iron ore, and food grains. South Korea lacks the iron ore, oil, and coal that exist in the North. Singapore depends totally on its neighbors for food and water. Hong Kong, too, depends on China for all of its water and most of its food. Taiwan is self-sufficient in rice and grows most of its own food but has no natural resources it can export.

These resource-poor nations could have decided long ago, as most developing countries have done, to lock themselves into foreign dependence, but they did not. Knowing it had no natural resources on which to rely, each in its own way discovered a fundamental rule of survival: no law of nature provides that life will get better year after year; its people would have to work to make it better. So these East Asian nations created a kind of capitalistic Darwinism: survival of the industrial fittest. And, as discussed earlier, to ensure that survival they have made the most of their human resources.

9. The Relative Neutrality Role of Religion

From Buddhism and Shintoism in Japan to a kind of secular Confucianism in the Little Dragons, religion has served these nations best by getting out of the way. It is, in the end analysis, "business-friendly." Historically there have been no conservative religious movements in East Asia that, like Protestant fundamentalism in the United States, have impeded either the process of rapid economic growth or the business of making money.

Religion in East Asia, at least in its organized sense, occupies itself solely with life's rituals: from birth and marriage to death and burial, whether for individuals or for corporate institutions. As such, its preoccupation remains very much this-worldly and concerns itself not in the least with the afterlife. It does not intrude or interfere; it is compartmentalized, separate, and neutral.

Ethics, as a subbranch of religion, does not really exist; behavior is governed by powerful peer pressure and by conformity to traditional social norms, based on deeply ingrained cultural values such as personal obligation, duty, and loyalty.

East Asian social norms also create a different attitude toward corruption from what is typically observed in the West. Corruption of government officials in Japan, Korea, and Taiwan, while stoutly denied by all, has typically taken the form of gift giving in the traditional Confucian pattern.

Hot stock tips are often passed to powerful politicians; unlisted shares of stock are routinely given to key politicians prior to public issue by individual or corporate constituents seeking special favors; predetermined portions of foreign loan proceeds are skimmed off by key government officials and paid to important supporters, junior officials, or other individuals to ensure continued loyalty and to reinforce duty or obligation.

Alone among the Little Dragons, Singapore as a country and its government officials as a group have a reputation of being practically squeaky clean, followed by the British colony of Hong Kong. But Japanese prime ministers and other senior officials have been thrown out of power (Tanaka in the Lockheed scandal) or forced to resign (Takeshita and Uno following the Recruit affair) and Korean presidents either assassinated (Park) or relegated to a life of monastic ostracism in retirement (Chun) as partial penance for excesses committed in office.

10. Sacrificing the Individual to the Group

The family unit remains remarkably strong throughout East Asia, having withstood the winds of social change that have swept through so much of the world in recent years. Divorce rates are low, less than one-quarter of those prevailing in America, where they are the highest in the industrialized world. The incidence of single-parent families is equally low, stemming from the fact that Asian societies have yet to be overwhelmed by the role confusion so prevalent in the West; role differentiation is still the norm. Young people in East Asia marry less to seek self-fulfillment than to rear a family, so marriage is focused less on the individual spouse than on children and the creation of a functioning family unit.

In both Japan and the Little Dragons social stability has played a key supporting role in rapid economic growth. The needs of individuals have been sacrificed to those of the group—child to family, student to class, worker to company. This process, combined with the financial incentives discussed earlier, has brought with it a willingness to sacrifice present fulfillment for future rewards—the kind of deferred gratification that is reflected in East Asian adults' heavy investment in their children's future, both in economic terms (via high savings rates) and through education. While quality of life suffers as a result (fewer miles of paved roads and less-developed urban sewage systems), that is a burden shared equitably by all.

Confucius is the intellectual godfather of this process. All of these societies, especially Japan, have adapted Confucius's teachings on human interrelationships, emphasizing the importance of hierarchy, social order, and proper behavior. These values in turn have reinforced the principles of thrift, discipline, and hard work—values associated with American society in an earlier, more puritanical stage of its development. And they have complemented, of course, the underlying systems of political authoritarianism.

11. Cultural Homogeneity

Japan and the Little Dragons each have a culturally homogeneous population. Japan takes pride in its cultural purity, often (in its extreme form) bordering on a kind of racial exclusivity. As a people the Japanese are remarkably uniform in physical appearance as in their allegiance to national economic goals. Hence the expressions "125 million hearts beating as one" and "the nail standing up gets hammered down." In Japan conformity to social norms and standards is relentlessly enforced, in the family, in school, and in the workplace, with severe penalties (shame and banishment from the group) for nonconforming behavior.

Korea is distinctly Korean, with its own language, its own social mores, and its own homogeneous population. Taiwan and Hong Kong are ethnically Chinese in cultural makeup, and Singapore is 75 percent Chinese. Of all the NICs Singapore comes the closest to having a pluralistic society, but its government, its institutions, and its work force are dominated by the Chinese.

In each case cultural homogeneity makes the policy formulation process smoother, its implementation easier, and its enforcement "cleaner." Absent are the diverse, pluralistic pulls characteristic of either American or Western European culture.

12. A Favorable Climate and Infrastructure

Weather, while a minor factor in the process of industrialization and rapid economic growth, nonetheless does play a role. Japan and Korea have the coldest climates in the region outside China; their winters are cold, their summers warm, and their transition seasons moderate, not unlike the American Northeast. Taiwan and Hong

Kong both have moderate climates, with hot and very humid summers but cool winters. Singapore lies in the tropics, practically straddling the equator.

The NICs have also distributed their industrial and manufacturing sites rather equitably rather than simply concentrating them in and around their capital cities. Major cities in Japan, such as Osaka and Nagoya and Kobe, have kept abreast of Tokyo by balancing industrial growth along the full sweep of the Tokaido region between eastern and western Japan. Today that growth is being orchestrated south to Fukuoka and Kitakyushu and north to Akita, Morioka, and Sendai.

In Korea, while Seoul is undeniably the industrial center, satellite cities such as Inchon, Ulsan, and Pusan have played a major role. On Taiwan the port cities of Keelung to the north and Kaohsiung in the south have complemented the capital city, Taipei, drawing manufacturing-related investment to the huge export-processing zones located there. And both Hong Kong and Singapore have pioneered the development of industrial estates, using tax and other incentives to lure new investment to strategically targeted areas such as Tai Po and Jurong, thus avoiding dangerous overconcentration in any one sector of the city—dangerous because overdevelopment at the core, as we shall see, can lead to infrastructure gridlock and practically paralyze the economy.

THE NIEs: INDONESIA, THAILAND, AND MALAYSIA

Contrasting the performance figures for Japan and the NICs on page 5, how do Asia's new Little Dragons—the NIEs—measure up?

ECONOMIC PERFORMANCE OF THE NIEs
(As of December 31, 1989; US$, %)

Category	Indonesia	Thailand	Malaysia
Per-capita income	500	1,238	2,092
Manufacturing as % of GNP	27.6	25.4	26.9
Manufactured goods as % of total exports	49.7	69.0	59.3

Using per-capita income alone as a benchmark, none of the three NIEs really qualifies as a Little Dragon: the figures, especially in the case of Indonesia, fall far short of the $3,000 floor. Only Malaysia comes close.

The figures for manufacturing as a percent of GNP are somewhat better. While none of the three countries fails this litmus test, they all barely make the threshold mark of 25 percent. Indonesia's case is perhaps the most surprising because, as we shall see, the government has implemented a number of industrial policy measures and economic incentives to stimulate its value-added manufacturing sector.

The figures for manufactured goods as a percent of total exports come closest to qualifying the NIEs as NICs. Though none of the three approaches the performance of the NICs in this category, all three countries come in well over the 25 percent mark. Again, Indonesia's performance is quite stunning for a nation so well endowed with natural resources. (Later, when we analyze the composition of this category more closely, we will see some rather startling anomalies, especially regarding the rates of growth.)

Still, as we know from examining the cases of Japan and the NICs, these criteria alone do not a Little Dragon make. So we need to take a closer look at the other noneconomic parameters of performance to determine whether the three NIEs can fulfill their apparent potential and become Asia's next Little Dragons—the issue that will be addressed in detail throughout the book.

1. A System of Political Authoritarianism

Of the three NIEs only Indonesia has a bona fide authoritarian political system, a necessary (but insufficient) condition for economic takeoff. Since independence in 1945, Indonesia has had only two presidents, Sukarno (1945–1967) and Soeharto (1967 to the present). The nation has suffered through some rather remarkable political gyrations just in the past half-century alone: from colonial control by the Dutch to occupation by another foreign power, Japan, in the 1940s; from parliamentary democracy to Sukarno's "Guided Democracy" in the 1950s; from chaos and crisis in the 1960s to Soeharto's "New Order" democracy today.

President Soeharto and the Indonesian armed forces (through *dwi fungsi*, their dual military and political function) dominate Indonesia's political system. Indonesia has created a solid foundation for political stability and faces a bright future, *provided* it gets enough of the other noneconomic factors right.

Thailand, the only major nation of Asia besides Japan never to have been colonized, has had a constitutional monarchy since 1932. The armed forces play a major role in Thai politics, having engineered more than a dozen coups d'état and at least as many constitutional revisions in the past half-century. Thailand's economic system seems to survive in spite of its frequent political turbulence, anchored securely to a strong tradition of loyalty to the king. The question is whether future economic growth can be sustained by the civilian parliamentary democracy that controls the political economy today.

Malaysia, of course, was a British colony until after World War II, when it became first the Federation of Malay States and then, in 1957, the Federation of Malaya, followed in 1963 by independence as Malaysia, booting Singapore out of the federation in 1965. Malaysia's political system has been controlled by the United Malay National Organization (UMNO), which with two obsequious minority parties, the Malaysian Chinese Association (MCA) and the Malaysian Indian Congress (MIC), dominates Parliament. Malaysia is a cutaneous democracy; elections define its form, but its content is clearly dictated by its current prime minister, Mohamad Mahathir. Malaysia may be the conventional pick as the next NIC, followed closely by Thailand, but Dr. Mahathir's political machinations could well keep the ship off course if in fact they don't sink it.

2. Forms of Government/Business Cooperation

None of the three NIEs has anywhere near the degree of public/private cooperation achieved by the Little Dragons. Again, Indonesia comes closest, separated from Thailand by a hair, with Malaysia a distant third.

In Indonesia two prominent groups—the army and the Chinese—define the process. In fact it is often difficult to draw the line between public and private interaction, so involved is the army in positions of both corporate management and government control. The Chinese have dominated the entrepreneurial sector for generations, going back to early Dutch colonial rule nearly three centuries ago. Rather than viewing the Indonesian political economy as a bipolar partnership, as in Korea or Japan, it is perhaps more meaningful to describe it as a *triangular* partnership among President Soeharto, the armed forces, and the Chinese ethnic entrepreneurs.

Thailand has achieved Southeast Asia's most impressive assimilation of ethnic Chinese into the host culture, and for that reason it is often hard to delineate the public/private partnership. The armed forces play a dominant role in managing Thailand's numerous state authorities, such as Thai International Airways and the Electrical Generating Authority of Thailand (EGAT). The ethnic Chinese, fully integrated, tend to run the private sector, with dominant positions in banking, manufacturing, construction, and retail services. As such Thailand has what I would call a *parallel* partnership between government and business, with a dotted line to the king.

Malaysia more closely resembles a scattergram in comparison with Indonesia and Thailand. The Tamil minority is passive, but the ethnic Chinese minority dominates the private commercial sector overwhelmingly, while the native Malay majority enjoys exclusive access to positions of public sector leadership via aggressive affirmative action programs created by them in their own interest. This imbalanced relationship leads, not unexpectedly, to much friction, a waste of talent and energy, and a system of institutionalized corruption. So the government/business relationship in Malaysia can only be called a *feuding* partnership.

3. External Orientation

Here all three of the Southeast Asian NIEs unarguably qualify. Since colonization by the Dutch and the British, respectively, Indonesia and Malaysia have both been intensely involved in international trade. And Thailand, given its historical desire to avoid colonization by the West, has economic antennae that are finely tuned to external markets.

Indonesia has long been known as the Spice Islands by virtue of its immense concentration of riches. Since early trading visits by the

Portuguese, then later by the Arabs sailing from Malacca, and finally colonization by the Dutch, Indonesian wealth has been the target of Western traders. That tradition of access to external markets continues today. Thailand, too, has enjoyed a reputation as a trader of agricultural goods, having built a network of trading contacts not only in the West but throughout Asia as well. And Malaysia's ties to Britain via membership in the commonwealth have helped it retain an important outward economic orientation.

4. Savings and Gross Capital Formation

Because of the more dominant role played by foreign direct investment in each of the three NIEs, incentives to stimulate private savings and to generate higher levels of capital formation are nowhere near as high as among the NICs. This is a serious deficiency that has led to a significant savings-investment gap in each country, particularly in Thailand and in Indonesia but also in Malaysia, and could well deter subsequent levels of both foreign and domestic investment.

Because of its higher percentage of ethnic Chinese, who generate fairly high levels of private savings for historical reasons relating to outward remittances to relatives and family in China, Malaysia tends to have better capital formation rates than either Thailand or Indonesia. But because of the persistent and volatile political tension between Malay and Chinese ethnic groups, flight capital from Malaysia has been increasing in recent years, most of it from the very high-saving Chinese.

A further risk factor for the NIEs is the degree to which their economies may become overly dependent on foreign capital (especially from Japan) to finance their growth. This is particularly true for Indonesia, which by 1990 had nearly $60 billion outstanding in external debt, compared to less than $20 billion each for Malaysia and Thailand. By 1989 Japan had become the leading foreign investor in each of the three NIEs (in fact Japan is the leading foreign investor in every country in Asia except America's former colony, the Philippines, where the United States is still number one), causing some observers to speculate that Japan had creatively gained the benefits of colonization without its administrative burden—in other words, a kinder, gentler co-prosperity sphere.

Political leaders in Indonesia and Thailand are aware of this growing overdependence, but whether they can develop the incentives necessary to generate more domestic sources of capital (or alternative sources of foreign investment) remains to be seen. The stunning difference is that, with the sole exception of Korea, all the NICs financed their rapid economic growth entirely through domestically generated savings, thus avoiding the political risk of foreign capital dependence.

5. Development of Human Resources

All three of the Southeast Asian NIEs have made great strides toward curtailing population growth—Indonesia and Thailand have both been recognized for their successful efforts, and Malaysia's population base is small, only 17 million, to begin with, though growing at well over 2 percent a year. Thailand's population now numbers about 55 million, but its rate of growth is well under 2 percent a year. And as the world's fifth-largest country with nearly 190 million people, Indonesia has brought its population growth down to 1.7 percent a year.

But none of the NIEs has yet committed the resources to public education that, say, Japan historically has or Singapore. In part this may be due to their abundant endowment of natural resources, which has mitigated the necessity to commit scarce financial and human capital to education. A lack of natural resources tends to make human resources development a priority, so the NIEs lack that unwavering commitment to education shared by their Northeast Asian counterparts.

Though it remains a publicly stated priority in each country (as everywhere in the world except perhaps the hermit nations of Burma and North Korea), education in the NIEs has yet to be elevated from rhetoric to reality. Thailand has the highest adult literacy rate of the three (an estimated 86 percent of the population), but none of the NIEs even comes close to the 98–99 percent levels attained in the Little Dragons (the comparable U.S. level is about 93 percent). Malaysia's literacy rate is only 76 percent—stunningly low for a former British colony—and Indonesia's is alarmingly low at 26 percent.

Spending on education as a percent of national budget also lags behind the NICs, which spend anywhere from 9 percent (Japan) to 21 percent (Korea), with Singapore, Taiwan, and Hong Kong near the median of about 13 percent. Thailand spends 16 percent of budget on education, but Indonesia only 6.7 percent and Malaysia just 5.3 percent. As the industrialized world accelerates into the information age, can the NIEs compete effectively without a more substantial commitment to education?

6. Research and Development

As with capital, so with technology: the NIEs are overwhelmingly dependent on Japan and Japanese commercial R&D. With Japan now the number-one foreign investor in each of the three NIEs, Japan's technology is pouring into Southeast Asia on the heels of its direct investment. The risk for the NIEs is that dependence creates potential addiction and gives Japan a powerful political lever that could be more beneficial to itself than to the recipient nations.

In 1987 Japan licensed about $625 million worth of its technology throughout Asia; Thailand, Indonesia, and Malaysia accounted for 16 percent of the total. Cumulatively, for the four years from 1984 to 1987, Japan licensed nearly $3 billion worth of its technology in Asia, of which the three NIEs accounted for some 15 percent, so their share has been relatively constant. Again, of primary importance is the concentration of Japan's technology—99 percent of it— in manufacturing.

Part of the NIEs' problem is financial—not enough capital is being generated to satisfy infrastructure needs, let alone to fund more sophisticated research projects—and part is educational. Japan has some 2 million full-time students enrolled at the university level, Korea 1.1 million, Taiwan nearly 500,000. In the NICs, on average, about 2 percent of the population is engaged in tertiary education. By comparison, Indonesia has less than 1 percent of its population studying at university levels, Thailand and Malaysia each only about 0.3 percent. With insufficient capital to support indigenous R&D and proportionately fewer students attending universities, the NIEs have some fairly serious cracks in the foundation necessary for sustained economic growth.

7. Value-Added Production

This category makes the performance figures for the NIEs highly transparent. As the table on page 18 shows, Thailand and Malaysia both report fairly high percentages of manufacturing as a composite of total GNP (25 and 27 percent respectively) and considerably higher percentages of manufactured goods as a percent of total exports (69 and 59 percent respectively). But Indonesia's comparable percentages of 28 and 50 percent probably reflect a more accurate accounting.

Much depends on what a country chooses to include in its "manufacturing sector"—what products it chooses to call "manufactured goods." The list of manufactured products exported by Korea or Taiwan, for example, reads like a Who's Who in Machinery and Equipment. Korea exports automobiles, ships, engine components, electrical machinery, consumer electronics equipment (TVs, videocassette recorders, stereos), IBM-compatible computers, and microwave ovens. Taiwan exports everything from machine tools to power lawn mowers, and Japanese manufactured exports, the granddaddy of them all, are now themselves *American* household words.

But a similar list of Thai or Malaysian so-called manufactured exports reflects quite a different interpretation of the term. Thailand exports canned shrimp, jewelry, cement, textiles, maize, hardwood lumber, paper and paper products, plus miscellaneous manufactured goods and machinery. While the *total* for manufactured goods in 1987 was just over 24 percent of total exports, when *processed* as opposed to *manufactured* goods are netted out, the ratio drops by about half, to just over 12 percent.

Malaysia fares somewhat better, but there too the anomalies are apparent. In 1988 more than half of Malaysia's manufactured exports (56 percent) were *Japanese* electrical appliances and parts, shipped either directly to third markets or back to Japan. The remaining products included food and beverages, clothing and footwear, wood and rubber goods, and petroleum and chemicals. Where, one might reasonably ask, is any indigenous Malaysian machinery and equipment?

The difference, of course, relates to the degree of value added in the production process. Exporting canned shrimp may be a step above exporting raw shrimp, but exporting gourmet microwave shrimp dinners would represent still more value added. Lumber and hardwood exports are one thing, but manufactured office furniture products would be quite another. In Thailand's case, textiles come the closest to representing value-added manufactured goods, but the balance of its products should more realistically be classified as processed and not manufactured.

Indonesia's figures not only are more realistic—because Indonesia makes a clear distinction between processing and manufacturing—but they actually tally better than those of Malaysia and Thailand because the country has made a more concerted effort since the early 1980s to develop its value-added manufacturing sector. As a priority, government policies have stressed incentives to produce manufactured goods for export, so instead of shipping raw rubber or rattan, Indonesia now exports running shoes and furniture.

Can the NIEs realistically expect to be competitive in value-added production without generating the necessary capital, without raising the level of education, and without ending their dependence on Japan's foreign direct investment?

8. Natural Resources

The NIEs boast some of the richest natural resources in the world: Indonesia is a major exporter of coffee, tea, pepper, tapioca, cloves, rubber, tin, copra, palm oil, and untold varieties of natural hardwoods. Malaysia is the world's leading exporter of palm oil, rubber, and tin. And Thailand has long been Southeast Asia's primary provider of rice, maize, and corn.

In an industrial age that depended on abundant natural resources, these commodities would have constituted a distinct comparative advantage. But how advantageous will they be in an intensely competitive information age, which depends more on the quality and skills of human resources? As the NICs' dearth of natural resources has spurred its development of human resources, will the NIEs' natural bounty stymie that evolution? While the NIEs cannot ignore their natural factor endowments, the question is whether they will be stuck in the role of simple commodities exporters—and generate less wealth as the prices of their commodities continue to decline in real terms—or will be able to add more value to the production process.

9. Religion and Corruption

Each of the NIEs has a dominant religion that could be less tolerant of rapid economic growth than the religious institutions of the NICs have been.

Thailand is unabashedly a Buddhist country. Buddhism dominates Thai social life and customs, and Buddhist architecture dots the urban landscape; the focal point in every community is the *wat*, or temple, and the saffron-robed monks are ubiquitous. Buddhism is normally a tolerant faith, but it also has purer, more ascetic, less tolerant strains. Could Thai Buddhism revert to a phase of extreme fundamentalism, and possibly hold the country back, if Thailand achieves material success as a NIC?

Indonesia and Malaysia are Islamic nations. With its 190 million people, Indonesia is the most populous Islamic nation in the world. Malaysia's political economy is already fractious and strife-ridden. Will Islamic fundamentalism, which has been linked to so much violence and unrest in the Middle East, also become a destabilizing force in these two NIEs, especially if rapid economic growth causes the gap between rich and poor to spread still wider?

Corruption seems more noticeable by an order of magnitude in the NIEs than in the Little Dragons. It is the frequent subject of newspaper accounts, idle cocktail conversation, and local gossip in all three countries. But it is more an acknowledged practice than a cultural constraint, economic or political. The ethical question thus tends to revolve around what constitutes "excessive" corruption rather than the mere criticism of its existence.

In Washington the Abscam scandals of the early 1970s and the uproar over influence buying by S&L owners in the late 1980s suggest that corruption American-style is more a matter of out-and-out wrongdoing, aided and abetted by the structure of the political system in the United States, given the greater degree of power held by special-interest groups and their financially influential political action committees.

But in Southeast Asia corruption is tied more to traditional peer group behavior and accepted cultural norms than to the structure of the political system per se. So it tends to be viewed simply as a fact of life, albeit in many instances a distasteful one, and not as a constraint on economic growth or development. This having been said, there is often considerable economic "leakage," not to mention excess, as we shall see when examining the NIEs in further detail, though by no means as dramatic as in the Philippines, which suffers from extraordinarily high levels of capital flight.

10. Individual vs. Group

None of the NIEs has anything like the group-oriented social systems of the NICs. Indonesia perhaps comes closest, followed by Thailand; Malaysia is a distant third, with the highest divorce rates in the region. But the shared concepts of individual sacrifice and deferred gratification so prevalent in the NICs seem strangely absent in the NIEs, possibly because the climate is so benign, possibly because all three nations are still so close to their agricultural roots. But can the NIEs compete successfully in an age of rising economic nationalism *without* creating a sense of national cooperation and greater group effort?

11. Cultural Homogeneity

Unlike the NICs, the NIEs are anything but homogeneous. Thailand may come closest, having assimilated its ethnic minorities (primarily Chinese and Khmer) so successfully that they are now practically indistinguishable from native Thais. But Indonesia has literally hundreds of diverse ethnic groups scattered throughout its more than 13,000 islands; that diversity is reinforced by pronounced linguistic differences that were resolved only after independence in 1945, when one national language, Bahasa Indonesia, was adopted. And Malaysia has the Southeast Asian equivalent of the Hatfields and the McCoys, with irreconcilable fissures between the native Malays and the ethnic Chinese, who today still retain their own language, newspapers, and schools. So cultural heterogeneity tends to characterize the NIEs, and it may continue to be an impediment to growth.

12. Climate and Infrastructure

The NIEs are all tropical countries. They are not just hot; they *steam*. In an average year temperature highs and lows may not vary more than a few degrees; the thermometer seems stuck in the low nineties, day and night. Transition seasons are nonexistent, and winter is a concept taught in science class. There are but two distinct seasons—wet and dry—both extremely hot.

Industrial development in the NIEs also tends to be concentrated in and around their capital cities. Bangkok alone has nearly 20 percent of Thailand's population of 55 million, and its infrastructure is near meltdown; it now takes an average container truck nearly four hours to travel the thirty kilometers from Nava Nakorn industrial estate to Klong Toey port, so clogged are the roads. Thailand has abundant plans for expansion outside Bangkok, with incentives for investors to site there, but that will all take time.

Malaysia possesses a somewhat better physical infrastructure, a distinct throwback to its colonial background and related to its smaller population. But with the sole exception of Malaysia's semiconductor production, on the island of Penang, its industrial development is situated primarily in the state of Selangor, around the capital city of Kuala Lumpur.

Indonesia's industrial development is the most diversely scattered of all the NIEs, from major oil and gas projects on Sumatra, to new manufacturing sites in and around Jakarta, to the productive and neatly manicured agribusiness plots on Java, to massive lumber and logging operations on Kalimantan. And its transportation system—the interisland waterways and the road networks—is impressive. Again, Indonesia, with its natural geographic endowment and the legacy of the Dutch colonial system, appears to have a significant advantage.

THE EXTERNAL ENVIRONMENT

In addition to the twelve country-specific considerations discussed so far, there are a number of factors that did not inhibit the NICs (because they are more recent developments) but could well deter the NIEs as the post–Cold War external environment continues to change. The NICs had the advantage of "coming of age" in an era of unparalleled prosperity, with unprecedented rates of economic growth in the world economy, peace in the region, and a widespread commitment to free trade—in effect, a "window of opportunity" that they exploited well but that no longer exists for the NIEs.

1. Regional Security

Japan and the Little Dragons have enjoyed a period of unprecedented prosperity and rapid economic growth in part because the United States has provided—and paid for, at a cost to American taxpayers of around $50 billion a year—an umbrella of strategic security in East Asia. Until 1975 U.S. forces were still deployed in Southeast Asia too, but that all changed with the American withdrawal from Vietnam. Now, partly because of continuing federal budget deficits and partly due to much stronger local economies, it is no longer possible or appropriate for America to maintain such a strong security presence in the region.

Will a reduced American presence create greater regional instability and unrest? The domino theory—which predicated the fall of Thailand and Malaysia after North Vietnam defeated the South—proved to be baseless, but the nations of Southeast Asia have a history of nettlesome relations all their own: border disputes between Indonesia and Malaysia (called *Konfrontasi* under Sukarno in the 1960s), armed confrontation between Thailand and Burma (and between Thailand and Cambodia), contentious land claims between Malaysia and the Philippines, hostility between Singapore and Malaysia. The archipelagic states of Indonesia and the Philippines have the highest ratio of water to land in the world, which leads to definitional conflicts with their neighbors regarding territorial waters issues.

Intraregional relationships are of greater importance in Southeast Asia—among the NIEs—than in Northeast Asia among the NICs. One reason is that the NIEs share many more common borders (Thailand and Cambodia, Thailand and Malaysia, Malaysia and Singapore). Another is that geographic distances are shorter. Korea, Taiwan, and Singapore had the luxury of distance, cultural as well as geographic. And Hong Kong always had its British colonial cocoon. But the two "unifying" influences in Northeast Asia, Japan and China, historically supplied either a military hegemony or an underlying cultural leverage that is lacking today in Southeast Asia. Then, too, the NICs were not so much competing against each other economically as complementing each other in entering overseas markets, like the United States or Japan. And as economic competition escalates, so can political tension.

The phased withdrawal of Vietnamese troops from Cambodia beginning in late 1989 gave a glimmer of hope that stability might return to the Indochinese Peninsula, but the slow progress of multilateral negotiations by mid-1990 dimmed that prospect. The Association of Southeast Asian nations (ASEAN) which in 1967 brought together Singapore, Thailand, Indonesia, Malaysia, and the Philippines (and later Brunei), was created primarily as a response to these perceptions of external threat stemming from the Vietnam War. But could the growing economic tugs and pulls among its individual members slowly tear it apart?

Today, with the exception of the precarious peace in Cambodia, it is safe to say that relations among the ASEAN member states suffer no more (or no less) irritation than would characterize dealings among Organization for Economic Cooperation and Development (OECD) nations. Singapore, two-thirds of whose population is Chinese, and Malaysia, a majority of whose population is Malay, are constantly at each other's intellectual throats: in Singapore you hear it said that Malaysia's best exports are Singaporeans, and in Kuala Lumpur they say that the best Singaporeans are Malay. (The humor is tense, as are the bilateral relations; Singapore was born in a crucible of racial riots, labor strikes, and social unrest.)

Thailand has perennial border problems with its traditional antagonists, Burma and Cambodia, and had a rather unpleasant diplomatic imbroglio with Singapore in 1989 over illegal Thai construction workers there. Indonesia and Singapore had a testy time in the mid-1970s when four Indonesian sailors were hanged on espionage charges, but Lee Kuan Yew later uncharacteristically ate humble pie by planting flowers on their graves during a state visit to Jakarta; relations are normal today. And the Philippines tends to wind up on the bottom of everybody's list for practically any issue; it is the only ASEAN member today with a festering Communist insurgency— typically a day late and a dollar short.

2. The Role of Japan

Given the creation of a United States–Canada free-trade agreement in 1988 and the fact that Europe is moving tentatively toward economic union in 1992, it appears that the world may be evolving into three separate trading blocs: North and South America, with the United States as its hub; continental Europe, with Germany as its anchor; and Asia-Pacific, centered on Japan. Will these developments help or hinder the NIEs in their efforts to replicate the successes of the Little Dragons?

With intraregional trade in East Asia growing at increasingly faster rates, Japan's role in the economic development of the region has become key. Japan, as we have seen, is already the leading foreign investor in every regional economy except the Philippines, the "sick man of Asia"; nine of its ten largest foreign aid recipients are located in East Asia; Japan exports more technology to Asia than anywhere else; and the trade ties between the NIEs and Japan are growing stronger.

In the flying geese formation of the East Asian economies, with the more advanced NICs toward the front and the NIEs close behind, Japan has traditionally regarded itself as being at the apex. But Asian leaders are concerned that the NICs' and NIEs' satisfaction with the comfort of this formation may lead to a dangerous degree of overdependence on Japan and ask whether (and how) the United States expects to play a more visible economic role in East Asia in the future.

3. Heightened Competition

The NIEs are poised for initiation into Little Dragonhood at precisely the time when conditions in the global economy are becoming more competitive, when the NICs themselves are looking carefully over their shoulders to make sure their own hard-won positions are not lost to the new challengers.

America, for its part, is also rapidly adjusting to the new economic realities: private firms are shedding unneeded layers of management to become leaner and more competitive; public schools are gradually being restructured to reflect the changing needs of the marketplace; tax and other incentives are being implemented to revive America's strength in manufacturing; science and technology are getting a much-needed boost; and political leadership is shifting from the federal to the state and local levels. In short, America represents not just a market for the NIEs but a more serious competitor as well.

4. Increasing Protectionism

As the American private sector adjusts and adapts to Asian-Pacific dynamism, a cloud hangs over its head—the cloud of protectionism. Washington has shown a greater propensity to protect vested economic interests than to let them live or die in the new, more competitive international order.

During the past decade so many new import quotas, voluntary export restraints, and orderly marketing arrangements were imposed on Japanese products by Washington that now fully two-thirds of Japan's manufactured goods come under some form of managed trade. If that trend continues, the NIEs could find it increasingly difficult to sell into the American market. Yet they may need the huge North American market to create economies of scale for their manufacturing sectors, just as the aggressive Little Dragons did before them.

5. The Death of Communism and the Rise of Hostility

Contrary to conventional wisdom, history did not come to an end when the dirge was sung at communism's funeral in late 1989 and put the Soviet Union at political risk. As the British philosopher John Gray recently put it, "If the Soviet Union does indeed fall apart, that beneficent catastrophe will not inaugurate a new era of post-historical harmony, but instead a return to the classical terrain of history, a terrain of great-power rivalries, secret diplomacies, and irredentist claims and wars."

But while the risk of regional military conflict may have been reduced during the Cold War, the risk of regional *economic* confrontation would now certainly appear to be much greater. It has become apparent to the superpowers that the fine line between their economic interests and their national security interests is rapidly disappearing. So the NIEs may well have to plan for greater economic contentiousness between and among the great powers (the United

States and Japan, for example, or the Soviet Union and Germany) if they want to steer their rapid-growth economies along the aggressive path previously set by the NICs.

6. Exit Moscow, Enter Tokyo

The demise of communism will bring with it yet another development, as yet unrecognized by the world's markets. In the postwar era of unprecedented economic growth Washington and Moscow have been the focal points of conflict in the bipolar world. Communism and capitalism have been the two contenders for acceptance by the developing world. As the Soviet Union proceeds with its efforts at *perestroika* (restructuring) and *glasnost* (openness), conventional wisdom again suggests that prospects for global harmony may be greater because Moscow will be preoccupied with its predominantly domestic (and economic) concerns.

But as Moscow exits the world stage, Tokyo may want to enter. The major foreign policy conflicts for America in the decades ahead may not be with Russia but with Japan, for two reasons. First, there is a fundamental clash of values between the two countries; America's principal underlying values are freedom, liberty, and justice, but Japan's are obedience, loyalty, and order. Second, Japan's mutant model of turbocharged capitalism, based on its authoritarian industrial policy machine, could well replace America's model of free-enterprise capitalism among the developing nations of the world. So the principal ideological conflict in the future could likely be between America's democratic, free-enterprise capitalism and Japan's authoritarian, turbocharged capitalism, which could fill the void left by the death of communism.

For their part the Japanese realize they are moving into a period of delicate transition and considerable uncertainty. No longer content to be subservient to Washington's policy initiatives, Tokyo will increasingly contest them as it ruthlessly defends its own national economic interests. Will the fallout from this conflict help or hinder the NIEs? Their close ties to Japan could create economic opportunity with Asia's dominant leader, but they could also find themselves increasingly alienated from the United States as a result.

7. Environmental Issues

As concern about "global warming" rises, with often irrational fears of "ozone depletion" or a "greenhouse effect" in the atmosphere, the liberal Western democracies are paying more attention to environmental issues. This political trend is understandable, given the shift in emphasis from untrammeled economic growth and near total disregard for the environment a generation ago to concern for responsible environmental stewardship by major corporate and political leaders today. Environmentalism may thus be a powerful driving political force in the decade ahead, with its own agenda, significant momentum, and major implications for U.S. foreign policy.

Environmental issues must now be taken seriously, from hazardous waste disposal to purer water and cleaner air. But there is the danger, as we have seen so clearly from irrational Islamic behavior in the Middle East or Hollywood's role in the recent alar scare, that emotions can provide a powerful fuel for very passionate politics. It seems clear that reason, logic, and a healthy dose of cost-benefit analysis are more important ingredients in our solutions to environmental problems, because they are increasingly technologically derived. The issue is thus one of achieving an appropriate balance between growth and environmental protection: environmental solutions that preclude growth fail to produce adequate jobs for an expanding population, but development that disregards the environment is no longer politically acceptable (the growth-protection complex).

So as the NIEs exploit their natural resource base for export or create raw materials and intermediate goods for production, they are being subjected to increasing criticism from a hypocritical West for engaging in practices destructive to the environment today—just as the West itself did during earlier stages of its own development. Despite this irony, as natural rain forests disappear from the Indonesian island of Kalimantan (previously Borneo) or the Malaysian state of Sarawak—with the connivance and insensitivity of major Japanese trading companies—or as Amazon fires scorch greater acreage in the world's largest forest, Western scorn continues to mount.

Thus it appears that the NIEs will have to contend with a kind and a degree of criticism that the NICs were able to avoid. What impact is this likely to have on their economic growth and development plans?

8. Regional Isolationism

America is becoming increasingly preoccupied with a long list of domestic political concerns: drugs, crime, high-cost housing, inadequate public education, deteriorating physical infrastructure, higher taxes. These internal issues will put even greater demands on limited resources and require a reordering of priorities from global, multinational, or foreign policy concerns to local, national, and domestic policy concerns.

America has a dark streak of isolationism in its history too, coupled with a dangerous tendency toward anti-intellectualism. Should this trend revert, America's turning inward could hurt the NIEs at precisely the time they expect the United States to keep its enormous market open and remain receptive to exports from its strategic allies. During the past thirty years Japan and the NICs have benefited tremendously from a strong and open America. Will the NIEs be as lucky?

These changing external conditions are pressing issues with which the NIEs will have to contend. How will they fare? Let us begin our consideration by taking a long look at the world's fifth-most-populous nation. There is perhaps no country as dynamic or as strategically important—and about which Americans know so little—as Indonesia.

2
INDONESIA
Unity in Diversity

For [Indonesia], the obvious comparative case is Japan. Much differs between them: geography, history, culture, and of course, per capita income. But much, too, is similar. Both are heavily populated. Both rest agriculturally on a labor-intensive, small-farm, multicrop cultivation regime centering on wet rice. Both have managed to maintain a significant degree of social and cultural traditionalism in the face of profound encounter with the West and extensive domestic change. In fact, in agriculture, the further back one goes toward the mid–nineteenth century the more the two resemble one another. . . .

Given, then, all the admittedly important background differences, one can hardly forbear to ask when one looks at these two societies: "What has happened in the one which did not happen in the other?"
—Clifford Geertz, *Agricultural Involution*

THE LOOSELY LINKED CHAIN

As a nation we Americans tend to lack empathy—the ability to put ourselves in the shoes of foreigners and imagine the world as *they* see it, from their perspective, with their own limitations, cultural and geographic. This is especially true for countries like Indonesia, which are marginal to most Americans, whose geopolitical views of the world are (or have been) shaped primarily by the influence of Europe or the Soviet Union.

So consider Indonesia in the first person, to get a more realistic sense of what the world's fifth-most-populous nation might be like. Two caveats: First, imagine America as an archipelago; put yourself on an island, any island, to divorce yourself from a "continental" viewpoint. Second, imagine this island as your home; you have always lived there.

Your home island is one of 13,500 in a great archipelago—the world's largest—that spans five time zones and a distance equal to that from Los Angeles to Puerto Rico. In the group are seven principal islands: Sumatra, with huge reserves of oil and natural gas and enormous rubber plantations; Java, where two-thirds of your nation's total population of 190 million lives a distinctly rural life of wet-rice agriculture (as an analogy, imagine 150 million Americans crammed into the state of California); Kalimantan, the largest island in the group, with huge hardwood rain forests inhabited primarily by native Indians; Timor, until 1975 a Portuguese colony; Sulawesi (formerly Celebes), a cornucopia of spices; Irian Jaya, blessed with untold mineral resources; and Bali, a world-class resort island with flawless beaches. The thousands of remaining islands, tiny and for the most part uninhabited, lie scattered throughout the immense archipelago.

Jakarta, your home, is your nation's capital, with a population of 8 million. You are a fruit merchant, and you earn an average income of $400 a year. Bahasa Indonesian is your national language, although you speak Javanese at home and with friends. To get to other major islands you must either fly, which is prohibitively expensive, or travel by boat, which is cheap but a three-day trip. Your nation's newspapers and magazines are published in Jakarta in Bahasa and airlifted to the other islands. You have one government-owned television channel that connects all the major islands by satellite—the only national link in an otherwise unconnected insular chain.

Your country has a long and proud history, dating back thousands of years, and your ancestors were indigenous traders, selling a wealth of spices to European buyers. But for three centuries until 1945, your people lived as pawns of a powerful Dutch colony, exporting your nation's wealth to support the advanced lifestyles of Europe: oil and rubber from Sumatra; coffee, tea, and rice from your home island of Java; hardwoods, rattan, and corn from Kalimantan; pepper, vanilla, and sage from Sulawesi; copper and tin from Irian Jaya. Because the Dutch had no interest in training your forebears, they brought in thousands of Chinese, who became local merchants and entrepreneurs.

From 1942 to 1945 your country was occupied by Japan, which needed natural resources and raw materials for a growing industrial base. During the Japanese occupation your national leaders drafted a constitution and prepared for independence, but the Dutch refused to abandon their rich source of wealth; they continued to fight against your revolutionary army in protracted and inconclusive wars of attrition. In 1949, under pressure from the United Nations and worldwide public opinion, the Dutch relinquished control, and your country became an independent republic for the first time in its history.

Throughout the 1950s the developing world was caught in the cross fire between two global ideologies, communism and democracy. Your nation tried to graft a system of representative democracy onto a diverse, politically inexperienced, insular people. The result was chaos, and it lasted until 1965, when the Communists attempted an unsuccessful coup, assassinating six of your top military leaders. A young general, Soeharto, took charge, and the army took revenge on the Communists, slaughtering more than half a million throughout the archipelago.

The rivers on your island turned crimson, choked with dead bodies as they flowed into the sea. In 1968 General Soeharto was installed as president. He ushered in an era called "New Order" democracy, dominated by his own authoritarian rule, supported by the army's dual role as military defenders and technocrats, and based on a political relationship with the Chinese. This triangular partnership has remained in place ever since, bringing a period of unprecedented political stability to your country, creating a consistently rising standard of living, and generating a spirit of optimism and hope for the future.

CULTURAL AND HISTORICAL ROOTS

A glimpse at least of what Indonesia has gone through in its brief life as an independent nation is instructional. Compared with America's own political history—more than two centuries with the same form of stable, democratic government on a continent historically immune to control from abroad—Indonesia is a study in stark contrasts.

It is the nation in Southeast Asia about which Americans know the least, greatly overshadowed by America's preoccupation with its nearby former colony, the Philippines, and by the war in Vietnam. As an archipelago it does not lend itself to a clear, crisp image in the mind. "Indonesia," one friend at a major American corporation recently mused. "Isn't that a province of China?"

For centuries traders and colonizers fought over the islands of Indonesia to exploit their unlimited natural wealth, or to take advantage of their strategic location along the Lombok and Sunda straits on the sea route between Japan and India. In the third century A.D. Indian sailors bound for China landed on the main islands of Sumatra, Java, Borneo (now Kalimantan), and Celebes (now Sulawesi), bringing Hindu and Buddhist beliefs to the native rulers and giving them an ideology to support a hierarchical political system. The Sanskrit language also brought literacy and literature to Indonesia.

By the seventh century this Indian influence had produced the Srivijaya Empire, which became a major sea power for more than 600 years. Srivijaya generated great wealth from its entrepôt trade with China, was a haven for Buddhist pilgrims in Southeast Asia, and created the first architectural monument in Indonesia, a huge stone temple complex at Borobudur, near Yogyakarta, in central Java.

In the thirteenth century a new dynasty called Singhasari took control of the spice trade and established a new capital at Majapahit, which became the center of the greatest of all Javanese empires. Its expansion was orchestrated by Gadjah Mada, a brilliant administrator who codified native law, wrote epic poems, and for the first time brought the entire Indonesian archipelago under unified control. Gadjah Mada was Indonesia's George Washington, its most famous historical leader. A major university was created in his name in Yogyakarta in 1946.

But the prosperity and stability of Majapahit rule was relatively short-lived. By the fifteenth century Indonesia was being threatened by the Malay kingdom nearby, which had already adopted Islam and was prepared to wage a holy war on behalf of the prophet Muhammad and his one god, Allah. Muslim traders had come all the way from Arabia, invading Indonesia from Malacca, the immense port city on the Malay peninsula that now controlled the straits trade. The Muslims persecuted adherents of the competing Hindu and Buddhist religions; in the interest of self-preservation most Indonesian rulers converted to Islam, from Banda Aceh at the westernmost tip of Sumatra (which remains a hotbed of Islam fundamentalism today) to Surabaya at the eastern end of Java.

By 1600 the first Europeans had arrived, led by Portuguese traders who had discovered Indonesian peppers, nutmeg, and cloves—spices used to cure meat before refrigeration. Portuguese control of ocean shipping decimated the Islamic trading network, spread Catholicism to Southeast Asia, and brought huge profits to the Continent: spices bought for next to nothing in the archipelago could be sold for a prince's ransom in Europe, establishing a pattern that would last well into the twentieth century, enriching Europe and impoverishing Indonesia.

But the Portuguese had to contend with the Dutch. Holland emerged as Europe's preeminent merchant power, with Amsterdam the center of international finance and commerce. In 1602, the Dutch parliament created the United East India Company, giving it military as well as commercial power. The company challenged the Portuguese (who had joined forces with Spain in the nearby Philippines) and won, displacing them by creating alliances with the local rulers. (Timor, in the Lesser Sunda Islands, was the sole exception; Portugal kept control until 1975, when the last vestiges of its rickety overseas empire finally withered away.)

When they saw the British build up their own power in the area to compete for the spice trade, the local rulers thought they had the best of all possible worlds: a seller's market with new, aggressive buyers who could bid up the prices of their precious spices. But their contentment was premature. The Dutch rightly saw the British as their principal competitors, so they fought and pushed them out of the archipelago. When a few local rulers continued to sell discreetly to representatives of the British East India Company, the Dutch either killed or deported them. They had no intention of tolerating a seller's market. They wanted a monopoly.

In 1610 the Dutch took control of the port of Jayakerta (Jakarta). They renamed the capital Batavia and made it their commercial command post. But their harsh treatment of Indonesian rulers had forged immediate animosities, and several of the local sultans rebelled. These regional rebellions continued on and off for the better part of a hundred years, culminating in the early 1700s with two bitter wars of succession, both of which the Indonesians lost. As a result the Dutch consolidated their power, gained complete control over the local rulers, and won the right to build forts wherever they wanted throughout the island of Java.

By about 1750 the Dutch had begun importing large colonies of Chinese, principally traders and craftsmen, to serve as a commercial buffer between themselves and the native Indonesians. The result was a doubling of hostility: Dutch against Chinese and Chinese against Indonesian. The Napoleonic Wars in the late eighteenth century tied up Dutch shipping for military purposes, and their spice trade dwindled. In 1808 the Netherlands was incorporated into the French Empire, and a year later the British occupied French-held Java. But by 1816, when the Napoleonic threat had passed, Dutch authority was reestablished in Indonesia and the Dutch reoccupied Batavia.

Around 1830 another rebellion, known as the Java War, broke out. This long and protracted war, during which nearly a quarter of a million Indonesians died, convinced the Dutch that they needed a system of shared power with the elite. So they created a triangular structure with the Dutch civil service at the top; an indigenous Indonesian contingent of talented bureaucrats, drawn from the aristocratic *priyayi* class, at the core; and Chinese entrepreneurs, who continued to dominate commerce and retail trade, at the base. The same triangular structure basically characterizes the Indonesian political economy today.

By the late 1800s one-third of Holland's total national revenues was generated from Indonesia. This wealth, stemming from an exploitive cultivation system, financed Dutch expansion in the outer islands (principally Sumatra, Kalimantan, and Sulawesi) and built the Dutch State Railroad. Peasants were directed by Dutch governors to cultivate a certain portion of village (*kampong*) land for cash crops, the most important and profitable of which were coffee, sugar, and indigo, all sold by the Dutch government monopoly in world markets.

Over time Java and portions of the outer islands were covered in a patchwork quilt of agricultural plots producing these valuable spices. Sugar quickly displaced rice as Java's most important cash crop, since the two used similar amounts of land but sugar was by far the more profitable; Indonesia, historically self-sufficient in rice, would be a net importer until the 1970s. Two-thirds of Indonesia's rural families were cultivating cash crops under this system, and half of them were growing coffee. While the cultivation system benefited the Dutch, the bureaucratic elite, and the Chinese entrepreneurs, it impoverished the Indonesian peasantry.

Throughout the early twentieth century the Dutch moved to take advantage of market forces unleashed by the new industrial age. World demand for rubber skyrocketed as automobile production took off, so the Dutch established huge plantations of new, high-yield rubber trees on Sumatra. Sumatran tin was also prized in world markets, and the Dutch imported still more Chinese labor to work the mines. When the Royal Dutch Company merged with Shell of Britain in 1907, crude oil production from newly discovered wells in Sumatra and Kalimantan soared. The outer islands now began to displace Java in importance; their exports of coffee, tobacco, tea, and sugar were multiples of those grown on the main island. Holland had a good thing going: in Amsterdam, Dutch leaders were saying that Indonesia would never be granted its independence from the Netherlands.

This situation might well have continued indefinitely had it not been for the Pacific War. Japan occupied the Indonesian archipelago (along with the rest of Southeast Asia except Thailand) for nearly four years from 1942 to 1945, and emerging nationalist forces under a young charismatic leader named Sukarno saw their opportunity. (Many Indonesians use only one name, their surname, as a form of address.) According to a twelfth-century legend, the prophet Jayabhaya had predicted that Indonesia would be occupied by "white men" for two hundred years, followed by three years of domination by "yellow men," who would then give way to freedom and independence.

Bung Karno (*bung* means comrade, or brother, in Bahasa Indonesian) welcomed the Japanese and used them strategically against the Dutch. For their part, too, the Japanese needed Sukarno to gain popular support for their own purposes. Born in 1901 to a lower *priyayi* official and his Balinese wife, Sukarno had studied engineering at the Technical College in Bandung, but his real love was politics. He teamed up with an Islamic leader, Mohammad Hatta, in cooperating with the Japanese, although other nationalist leaders (primarily Sutan Sjahrir) had no more love for Japanese fascism than they did for Dutch colonialism. But in 1943 the Japanese made Sukarno (with Hatta) head of a central advisory council, and although he opposed Tokyo's decision to make Indonesia part of Greater Japan, he traveled extensively throughout Java preparing the Indonesian people for ultimate independence. A charismatic speaker, he could bring huge crowds to the peak of frenzy with his nationalistic fervor.

By late 1944 the Japanese were being pushed back from their strongholds in Southeast Asia, and Tokyo made the decision to grant Indonesia its independence. The Investigating Committee for the Preparatory Work for Indonesian Independence, headed by Sukarno, was established in early 1945; it proposed a republican constitution, an elective People's Congress, which would elect the president and vice president every five years; and a broad territory for the republic that included not only all of the Dutch East Indies but also Portuguese Timor and the British possessions on Kalimantan and the Malay Peninsula.

On June 1, 1945, in a major national address, Bung Karno proclaimed five principles for the new Indonesian nation, called *Pançasila* (pronounced *pancha-sila*): belief in one God, humanitarianism, national unity, democracy, and social justice. As the ideology that frames the nation, *Pançasila* is celebrated as a unifying theme as frequently today as it was half a century ago.

But when Japan surrendered to the Allies on August 15, 1945, the Dutch had no intention of relinquishing control of their former colony. Sukarno had to move quickly; on August 17, 1945, he declared independence, and the infant Republic of Indonesia took its first steps. August 17 became Indonesia's national day, and its coat of arms featured a mythical golden eagle, the *garuda*, symbolizing both the date and the five principles of *Pançasila*: it had eight feathers in its tail, seventeen in its wide, outstretched wings, and forty-five in its muscular neck; on its chest, a broad shield displayed the five symbols for the national ideology; and in its tough talons below, it held a banner proclaiming the national slogan, Bhinneka Tunggal Ika, or "Unity in Diversity."

Sukarno was named provisional president of the new republic and Hatta his vice president. They stationed Japanese troops to protect valuable oil rigs from potential seizure by Holland, so when the Dutch returned to Java, armed confrontation erupted between Dutch and Indonesian troops, resulting in a bloody battle at Surabaya. Sukarno, distrusted by the Allies because of his collaboration with the Japanese and feared by other Indonesian nationalists, had to compromise to break a stalemate and yielded power to the socialist Sutan Sjahrir, who became prime minister in October 1945. After months of complicated negotiations the two sides created a federal system that resulted in Indonesian control over Java and Sumatra, with the remaining islands joining the Netherlands-Indonesian Union under the Dutch crown.

The system proved to be ungovernable from the beginning. The Dutch reverted to form by using force against republican troops, driving them out of Sumatra and most of Java in late 1947, confining them to a narrow enclave around Yogyakarta and cutting them off from their sources of supply in the coastal cities. But international pressure began to mount against the Dutch, coinciding with decolonization in the region and a fierce internal strategic conflict among the Indonesians. Pro-Communist units in the republican army called for the overthrow of the Indonesian republic, now headed by Hatta, but they were annihilated at Madiun by pro-Sukarno units headed by Sjahrir.

The Dutch then captured Sukarno and Hatta in Yogyakarta, which triggered an avalanche of international support for the new republic. In early 1949 the UN Security Council unanimously agreed that power be transferred back to the republican government, and Washington threatened to withhold Marshall Plan funds from the Netherlands if the Dutch did not accede. In May 1950 all the former possessions of the Dutch East Indies were formally absorbed into the Republic of Indonesia, Jakarta was designated the capital, and Bung Karno, as president, became the official head of state.

His problems, as it turned out, were just beginning. Although the nation was superficially united under *Pançasila*, and "Unity in Diversity" became its popular slogan, Indonesia remained seriously divided by ethnic splits, religious differences, and regional loyalties. Although the two major ethnic groups, Javanese and Sundanese, shared common norms of behavior, there was a natural rivalry between them. On the island of Sumatra three principal groups competed for dominance: the Achenese (fiercely Islamic), the Batak (nominally Protestant clans), and the Minangkabau (a matrilineal tribe). On Kalimantan the major groups were the Dayak and Buginese. In total more than 300 indigenous ethnic groups with nearly as many linguistic dialects formed the fragile beginnings of the new republic.

The Javanese prided themselves on a rich history of aristocratic folklore, highly artistic skills, and a strong mystical tradition based on the symbolism of shadow puppetry, called *wayang*, about which we will hear more later. On Java, with two-thirds of the country's population, Indonesians were set against the minority Chinese because of clear economic inequality, and Islam competed with Catholicism: where a church was built, a mosque soon appeared nearby. Within Islam the nominal *abangan* could be distinguished from the more devout *santri*, adding horizontal layers to a hierarchical society already vertically divided by class.

Reflecting these ethnic, regional, and religious splits, some thirteen political parties emerged in the early 1950s, the largest of which, Masyumi, had only forty-nine of 232 seats in the national legislature. Sukarno's party, the Nationalist Party of Indonesia (PNI), was the second-largest and predominantly Javanese. Sutan Sjahrir headed the Socialist Party of Indonesia (PSI), and a new generation of Communist leaders formed the Communist Party of Indonesia (PKI), which based its strategy on an appeal to the Javanese masses, organizing workers on the plantations and peasants in the poorer *kampong*. The PKI was smart; it supported Sukarno's all-important *Pançasila* ideology as well as his policy of anti-imperialism, which had broad popular appeal. Before long the PKI would become Indonesia's largest and richest political party.

Between 1950 and 1956 Sukarno formed six different cabinets. Political power was too diffuse, given the large number of parties and the imbalance among them. The first national election in 1955 simply served to draw regional and ethnic lines more clearly; the split between Java and the outer islands was especially stark. Sukarno was unable to form an effective political coalition, and the end result was chaos. Like quicksand, it submerged the parliamentary system.

Recognizing the futility of perpetuating an unworkable system, Sukarno proposed a new concept called "Guided Democracy" in late

1956. It was *Pançasila* all over again, but this time without the constraints of the legislative process: he and his military commander, General Nasution, emasculated the political parties (with the exception of the supportive PKI), reinstated the 1945 constitution, and dismantled the Parliament, creating a system of authoritarian rule. By early 1957, when he declared martial law, the parliamentary era had ended.

Sukarno's new era of Guided Democracy was characterized by his intense, flamboyant personality. He was a true political showman and played up his reputation as a revolutionary leader. He could hypnotize huge crowds with his rhetoric, and he created new political slogans around which the nation could rally—like *Nekolim*, which stood for opposition to neo-colonialism and imperialism, and *Nasakom*, an acronym for nationalism, communism, and Islam. He constructed enormous (and expensive) public monuments in Jakarta to symbolize his new era. Indonesia hosted the first conference of nonaligned nations at Bandung, in an attempt to establish Sukarno's credentials as a leader of the developing world. In 1964, when Malaysia, and not Indonesia, was made a nonpermanent member of the Security Council, Sukarno pulled Indonesia out of the UN.

In the early 1960s the PKI had become more aggressive, especially in the Javanese *kampong*. Under Sukarno's orders it implemented new land reform measures, displacing landlords and distributing land to poor peasants but exacerbating the schism between social classes. By 1962 the PKI had become the most powerful political party in Indonesia and the largest Communist party outside the Soviet Union and China. Foreign observers felt it was just a matter of time before the country fell to communism, putting a major dent in America's containment policy.

By 1965, with rising social tensions and economic instability the order of the day, Indonesia was a crucible of chaos and unrest. On September 30, assured of backing and arms from China, PKI supporters within the army attempted a coup, seizing the national radio station and assassinating six of the army's top generals. (General Nasution managed to escape, but his five-year-old daughter was murdered.) Sukarno refused to condemn the Communists, criticizing "imperialist, anti-Communist" elements instead, but the murders provoked such outrage that mob violence resulted. Javanese villagers ran amok (a uniquely appropriate Indonesian word) and waged a holy war against the Communists and their suspected sympathizers, killing nearly half a million people on Java alone.

Political order was restored by General Soeharto, head of the army's strategic reserve command and former commander of its elite Diponegoro division, which had courageously recaptured Yogyakarta from the Dutch back in 1949. He moved quickly to neutralize the pro-Communist faction in the army, and within a few days of the coup his troops had completely disarmed the rebels. On March 11, 1966, Bung Karno gave him supreme authority to restore order throughout the country, and in March 1967 the People's Consultative Assembly appointed Soeharto acting president. He became president of Indonesia in March 1968 and has been reelected every five years since, most recently in 1988.

The son of a lower *priyayi* official, Soeharto was born near Yogyakarta in 1921. His parents had separated when he was very young, so he spent his formative years living with an aunt in central Java to gain access to better schools. He entered the Indonesian army at an early age and rose quickly through the ranks in the years following independence. Like Sukarno, Soeharto was typically Javanese, but while Sukarno liked to compare himself to traditional Javanese warrior heroes, Soeharto identified with Semar, a clumsy but immensely powerful comical figure of the old *wayang* shadow plays. (The March 11, 1966, order giving Soeharto supreme power became known as Super Semar, an acronym formed from the date, in Indonesian, but a direct reference to Soeharto's favorite mystical hero.)

As president, Soeharto moved promptly to restore Indonesia's standing in the international community. By 1967 Indonesia had cut diplomatic relations with China (restored only in 1990), rejoined the UN, and participated as a founding member of ASEAN together with Singapore, Malaysia, Thailand, and the Philippines. More significantly, Soeharto created the concept of *dwi fungsi*, or dual function, whereby the army assumed a political function on top of its traditional military role: army officers took charge of government ministries and became directors of government agencies. Soeharto installed a powerful group of American-educated economists, nicknamed the Berkeley Mafia because most had been trained at the University of California at Berkeley, who began to replace revolutionary political ideology with modern economic theory.

Thanks to Soeharto, Indonesia had finally broken with its past, both colonial and revolutionary. The chaos of Sukarno's Guided Democracy was replaced by a more authoritarian New Order, ushering in an era of unprecedented political stability that created, over time, a firm foundation for economic growth.

THE ECONOMIC SYSTEM

When Soeharto assumed power in 1968, the Indonesian economy was in shambles. Inflation was out of control, interest rates were well into double digits, and export earnings were dwarfed by debt service on foreign borrowings. Indonesia had borrowed more than $2.3 billion from foreign lenders—nearly $1 billion from the Soviet Union alone—much of which was used to buy arms and to finance construction of Sukarno's symbolic monuments in Jakarta, like the enormous Senayan sports stadium, which seats 125,000, the Selamat Datang (welcome) statue near Menteng, and—proudest of all—the Monument Nasional, a towering white obelisk at Freedom Square that the Indonesians call *paku jagat*, the axis of the world.

Soeharto consolidated Indonesia's external debt by organizing an informal group of foreign lenders called the Inter-Governmental Group on Indonesia (IGGI), which over time came to exert a welcome influence on economic policy by working closely with the Berkeley Mafia. A series of creative five-year plans, called *repelita*, stressed higher food production and development of physical infrastructure, especially on Java. Unlike his predecessor, Soeharto welcomed foreign investment—Indonesia badly needed it—and he created new government agencies (such as Bappenas, the national planning council) and policy incentives (such as tax holidays for investors) to attract it.

But what really kicked the Indonesian economy into high gear was the war between Israel and Egypt in October 1972, which catapulted OPEC into power and quadrupled oil prices practically overnight. Indonesia's foreign exchange reserves soared, providing Soeharto with both revenues for new infrastructure development and collateral for new loans. By 1977 national income had more than doubled.

In other respects, too, the New Order had produced tangible

results. The percentage of people living below the poverty line dropped markedly, from 57 percent in 1970 to less than 40 percent in 1980. Rice output doubled between 1974 and 1987 as Indonesia became self-sufficient in its staff of life. Primary school enrollment reached 94 percent. Between 1968 and 1988 Indonesia implemented one of the most successful family planning programs in the world: nearly half of all eligible couples now use contraception, compared to less than 10 percent in 1970, and the crude birth rate today is twenty-eight per 1,000 compared to forty-three per 1,000 in 1970. Most significantly, again thanks to the tough fiscal discipline imposed by the Berkeley Mafia, Indonesia's federal budget deficit has been the lowest among all developing countries in the region, averaging less than 3 percent of GNP; compared to Bangladesh or India (at around 9 percent of GNP) or the Philippines (6 percent), Indonesia was golden.

The Indonesian political economy, as before, was characterized by a triangular partnership: the army, through *dwi fungsi*, controlled the political system; the technocrats in the bureaucracy, under strong army supervision, implemented policy; and the entrepreneurial class of Indonesian-Chinese businessmen, better assimilated now, managed the private sector. With Indonesia still under the all-embracing ideology of *Pançasila* but without the destructive interference of either communism or global politics, Soeharto could be a far more capable manager than Sukarno. He is affectionately referred to by all Indonesians as Pak Harto, *pak* being short for *bapak*, meaning father, a customary term of endearment for respected seniors.

Soeharto's accomplishments are indeed impressive. On a recent visit to Jakarta, I could not help noticing again how remarkably *clean* the city is. For a Third World capital its cleanliness is nothing short of remarkable. From the tiny taxi (an air-conditioned Ford Escort) that brought me into town from the French-inspired and -designed Sukarno-Hatta international airport, I watched as small armies of men and women swarmed throughout the city, sweeping the streets, cleaning the gutters, and carting away trash.

This was another stark contrast with its nearby neighbor, the Philippines; with raw garbage everywhere, Manila is filthy. Roxas Boulevard, Manila's main thoroughfare, passes through corrugated-tin-roofed squatter shacks and crumbling concrete office buildings, unfinished and vacant, whose cocoonlike shapes provide testimony to the Philippines' stillborn economy. And Jakarta has nothing to compare with Manila's Smokey Mountain, an enormous pile of steaming garbage that houses thousands of destitute scavengers.

As we neared the center of town, I could see the ubiquitous red sun-bleached rooftiles, a legacy of the Dutch, that seemed to make Jakarta glow. While its residential sections are undeniably poor, they are clean and extraordinarily well kept, an unmistakable sign of cultural pride. The Indonesian capital seems to reflect the brightness and color of the Javanese countryside rather than simply becoming a dirty blur of urban gray.

I noticed again a distinct sense of dynamism and drive in Jakarta, too. New shops and restaurant chains like Thai Garden and Bintang Seafood Barbecue were cropping up on downtown street corners like new saplings and seemed to attest to an energetic, emerging middle class of Indonesian entrepreneurs. The shops and stores appeared clean and neat and well tended, with friendly workers bedecked in colorful batik shirts or blouses, beckoning their potential customers out front with a warm wave.

In the central district, as I neared my hotel, the Borobudur, I recalled another distinct difference from the Philippines. Unlike in Manila, there are no armed guards at hotel entrances in Jakarta, no metal detectors, no body searches. Security is relatively relaxed here; no battalions of soldiers are goose-stepping stiffly on maneuvers through the streets of the capital as you might expect of another military government. There are no residential fortress compounds either, rimmed with high walls and topped with barbed wire or razor blades.

And no beggars at every intersection. In Manila blind beggars led by young, undernourished children emerge at stoplights and limp from car to car, arms extended. They are pursued by the skeletal bodies of young hawkers selling everything from plastic purses to rotting fruit. But in Jakarta teams of young, unemployed men aggressively hawk bottled water, newspapers, candy, fresh fruit, and gum, earning about $1 a day—the average industrial wage in Indonesia. They are poor, they are not well clothed, and most of them are barefoot. But they are *hustling*.

On that recent trip to Jakarta, I met with a former member of

the Berkeley Mafia, an economist-turned-technocrat named Mohammed Sadli who subsequently received advanced degrees from
MIT and Harvard and was minister of energy and mines in Soeharto's cabinet during the late 1970s. Well into his sixties, Sadli is
currently a director of the Indonesian Chamber of Commerce, where
we met to talk about the impressive accomplishments of Indonesia's
economy.

"How have we done it?" Pak Sadli asked rhetorically in flawless
English. "By building institutions under President Soeharto. And by
'institutions' I mean balanced budgets, low inflation, a more disciplined budget process. And by raising a crop of capable public
officials and competent bureaucrats who are arguably the best in
Southeast Asia outside of Singapore."

When asked about the role of the army in Indonesian politics,
its so-called dual function, he said, "One thing you must remember
is that Indonesia is *not* Latin America. I mean, this government is in
no way a military dictatorship. The process of policy formulation
and deliberation is more open and more results-driven. Plus there is
greater input into the policy process from the private sector. Young
pribumis—native Indonesians—are working better with the younger
Indonesian-Chinese now, so there's more interaction among them
than with the older generations."

In recent years Indonesia made commitments to expensive, often
questionable investments. About a decade ago President Soeharto
committed nearly $2 billion in foreign loans to develop a nationwide
satellite telecommunications system, called Palapa. It utilized two
orbiting satellites and fifty earth stations to connect twenty-six of the
nation's provincial capitals and fourteen other key points with Jakarta. By 1980 Indonesia could boast of fourteen television sets per
1,000 people, mostly in the urban areas, and nearly every village had
at least one set for public viewing. The total number of sets had
quadrupled since 1975. The government also spent large sums to
develop a floating fertilizer plant, an aluminum processing facility on
Sumatra, and a controversial, integrated steel complex at Krakatau,
on Java. I asked Pak Sadli about the quality of these investment
decisions.

"Sure, we may have our share of white elephants like Krakatau
Steel," he said, flashing a cherubic smile. "But it will eventually be

successful, as the fertilizer plant is now. And Palapa, despite what critics said at the time, was a brilliant political tactic by Pak Harto. He has done with technology what has never before been accomplished in our history: linked all the islands together to create a feeling of national belonging and pride. Even if not everyone has a TV—and many in the outlying *kampong* do not—they gather around the village headman's set and stay in the loop."

Some of these points were echoed by Anwar Nasution, another American-educated economist who studied at Harvard and Tufts and in the summer of 1989 was teaching at the University of Indonesia. In his early forties, he was soon to depart for Kyoto to teach economics and study Japanese.

"We have financed our growth mainly by debt," he was saying as we sat in his office downtown. "Completely different from the strategies of Japan and Taiwan but closer to the Korean model. In the past we were blessed by the oil boom, so we were late in developing incentives to increase tax revenues or to promote industrial development in the nonoil sectors. But when the oil revenues flowed, they were injected directly into the economy by the government, not siphoned off as in Nigeria."

Indonesia has traditionally earned two-thirds of its domestic revenues, and about 80 percent of its total export income, from oil. But in 1986 oil prices fell from nearly $35 a barrel to less than $12 before stabilizing at about $18. Then, too, since much of Indonesia's external debt is denominated in yen—Japan alone provides about one-fourth of Indonesia's total foreign borrowings—currency swings since the Plaza Accord in 1985 have increased the country's debt service requirements, in dollar terms, by about 50 percent. But the falloff in earnings from oil exports and the yen's rise, while shocks to the economy, have been blessings in disguise: they have forced the technocrats to bring even more discipline to economic planning.

"The Indonesian economy today is more broadly based, and there is more momentum, more spirit, more drive, as a result of these forced adjustments," Nasution went on, punctuating his comments with short jabs of his thin fingers. "Most importantly, manufactured goods as a percentage of our merchandise exports today are greater than oil and gas, a staggering accomplishment, when you think about it, for a country so abundantly endowed with natural resources. But the process of industrial restructuring now taking place in Japan and the Little Dragons leaves foreign investors really with just three options: China, India, and Indonesia. Well, China is politically unstable, as we are seeing; India is socially unstable, as everybody knows; so that leaves Indonesia as your best bet."

The numbers Nasution produced were indeed remarkable. In 1982 Indonesia's oil and natural gas exports totaled nearly $15 billion, against only $3.9 billion in nonoil exports—a catchall category that includes Indonesia's voluminous agricultural commodities and abundant minerals as well as manufactured goods. In fact less than $1 billion of the 1982 nonoil exports represented manufactured goods; commodities totaled $2.3 billion and minerals about $600 million.

But as a result of the structural adjustments made by the technocrats since 1985–86, the figures have almost completely reversed. In 1988 Indonesia exported $7.7 billion worth of oil and natural gas as against $12.1 billion in nonoil exports. Of those a remarkable $6.1 billion—more than half the total—represented manufactured goods, with agricultural exports at $4.6 billion and minerals at $1.4 billion. Moreover, the average real rates of growth in manufacturing were astounding: 33.8 percent a year between 1982 and 1986; 42.6 percent year-on-year from 1986 to 1987; and 27.1 percent from 1987 to 1988. And these were not merely processed fish or low-value-added jewelry, but textiles, plywood, iron and steel, footwear, glass, furniture—manufactured goods that represented significantly higher added value.

"The government took the initiative in developing incentives to stimulate the manufacturing sector," Nasution explained. His angular face was creased with a frown. "Beginning in the early 1980s, the process of deregulation began in earnest. Industrial policy reforms were designed to improve the international competitiveness of our private sector. Manufacturers who exported could import their product inputs free of tariffs and VAT. Many items were removed from restrictive import licensing procedures. Tariffs were cut. Customs clearance procedures were streamlined. Procedures for obtaining licenses to acquire land, build factories, store goods, control pollution, regulate safety, and operate a going concern were improved dramatically by adding better-trained staff and cutting red tape. A process that took thirty-five separate steps in 1977 could be completed in fewer than half as many by 1985. In 1983 we devalued the rupiah by 28 percent, to boost exports, and devalued it again by 31 percent in 1986. Our survival was on the line: we either did this or suffered the supreme embarrassment of restructuring and deferring a mountain of foreign debt."

Which was by no means inconsiderable. Indonesia's outstanding debt, including committed but undisbursed amounts, totaled about $15 billion in 1976 and rose in fairly predictable increments of around $2 billion a year through 1984. But the currency swings beginning in 1985 and the falloff in oil revenues starting in 1986 pushed these amounts far higher; the decline in the value of the dollar alone had pushed the debt level up by almost one-third, and debt service was taking more than a third of export earnings. By year-end 1985, total debt had soared to $42 billion; by the end of 1988 to $58 billion. At those levels, on a cumulative basis, Indonesia was borrowing more than 60 percent of GNP—a situation not entirely dissimilar to that of the United States, whose total public debt by 1990 was more than $3 trillion in a $5 trillion economy.

But Indonesia was surviving. As exports grew, payments of interest and principal were made on schedule, and while Japan had shown considerable flexibility in converting some soft loans (i.e., those with lower interest rates and longer payouts) into outright grants, Indonesia was succeeding where the Latin American borrowers (and the Philippines, which ultimately rescheduled its $30 billion of external debt) were not. There was no question that Indonesia would avoid rescheduling, out of national pride, and it remains a textbook case of structural adjustment and adaptation today, a successful story insufficiently recognized. Failure, it seems, brought more concessions than success.

"Inflation and economic mismanagement under Sukarno practically destroyed our social fabric," Nasution recalled. "In 1929 the rupiah bought more rice than in 1963. But look what Soeharto has done! I think we can continue this pace of development, and it will continue to be outward-looking, as it has in the past several years. We cannot emulate Japan or Taiwan, but we do have a substantial natural resource base and I am confident we will find a niche to take advantage of it."

In 1988 Indonesia's export markets were not only diverse—avoiding undue dependence on the United States, which took only 16 percent of the total, primarily oil and natural gas—but overwhelmingly in Asia. More than two-thirds of Indonesia's exports—69 percent—and over half of its imports, 55 percent, were to and from other nations in East Asia. Japan alone took 42 percent of Indonesian exports—again, primarily oil and gas—and accounted for about one-fourth of its total imports (goods and services not infrequently tied to foreign aid but also flowing to joint manufacturing ventures between Japanese and Indonesian firms). ASEAN countries bought 11 percent of Indonesia's exports and supplied about a similar percentage of imports; numbers for Europe were about the same.

These figures demonstrate that Indonesia's economy is not only externally oriented but externally oriented toward Asia. The World Bank estimates that nonoil exports will have to grow in real terms by around 10 percent a year over the next three years and by about 7 percent a year through the remainder of the 1990s. This will require both continued reforms—the banking and financial services sector is currently being targeted—and a competitive exchange rate. But savings and investment will have to grow faster in the future than both output and consumption.

The unavoidably high level of debt service as a percentage of exports—projected to decline by half over the next five years, assuming current export growth rates continue—has helped to create a sizable savings-investment gap in Indonesia of about 2.4 percent of GNP through 1988, which net new borrowings from external sources generally cover. (The private sector generates a net positive savings of around 0.7 percent of GNP, but the public sector a net dissavings of 3.1 percent.) Public and private savings, therefore, have to be increased, and the best way to raise public sector savings is to collect more taxes—what the World Bank calls "strengthening resource mobilization." The low rate of public savings also reflects the relatively low effective tax rates in Indonesia.

This point was raised when I met with Willem van der Wall Bake, a Dutchman with years of experience in Indonesia who manages Morgan Guaranty's Jakarta office. Unlike many of his countrymen, Willem was neither born nor reared in Indonesia.

"There was tremendous government savings during the oil

boom in the 1970s and early 1980s," he was telling me one evening over a traditional dinner of *saté lembat ayam*, a spiced grilled chicken served with hot chilies. "This resulted in a welcome period of underspending, but now there is a real problem as the reverse has occurred: Indonesia has expanding development needs but a shrinking revenue base."

Unfortunately Indonesia's tax collection rates are also among the lowest in East Asia, which contributes to its shrinking revenue base. Measured as a percentage of GNP, Indonesia's tax collection ratio in 1981 was only 7.2. By 1987 it had improved somewhat, to 9.4, but it was still far behind Korea at 15.3, Thailand at 14.9, and Malaysia at 13.1. In Asia only India and Bangladesh had lower rates.

But political support for greater tax collection has gained momentum, and President Soeharto said in a recent speech that the nation's tax effort should be an "all-out struggle." The number of civil servants in the Ministry of Finance has been increased, and the government has taken steps to conduct more tax audits. Computerization is also expected to help, and centralization of payment controls in Jakarta was scheduled to be completed by 1990.

Some progress has already been made. In 1983 Indonesia had only 325,000 registered individual taxpayers, but by 1987 they had more than doubled to nearly 700,000. (The number of registered corporate taxpayers had also about doubled over that time.) But even so, only 64 percent of individual taxpayers and 43.8 percent of corporations were filing returns. The government also has to be concerned about unemployment: the number of its civil servants has doubled in the past decade, too.

"Before we can expect to raise more taxes, we have to raise incomes," Minister of Industry Hartarto told me. "This is also true of our savings rate, because the ability to save is directly related to incomes. Since most of the Indonesian work force is rural and engaged in agriculture, raising incomes also means focusing on the value-added agribusiness sector."

Educated in Australia at the University of New South Wales, Minister Hartarto (like President Soeharto, he uses only his surname), worked initially in the pulp and paper industry and later in manufacturing, where he ultimately rose to become president of PT Cement Tomasa.

"I think we will succeed at both," he went on, chain-smoking

Djarum, a popular brand of Indonesian clove cigarettes called *kretek*, "because we're pushing agriculture up the value-added scale, too, like manufacturing. A decade ago we exported rubber; now we export tires and tennis shoes. We used to ship raw logs and rattan, but now we insist that wooden furniture be made in Indonesia first and then exported. We're now exporting ships, offshore drilling platforms, heat exchangers—a decade or two ahead we'll move into electronics—you can bet on it. And we have the advantage of an ample supply of low-cost labor."

Hartarto's optimism and confidence are fairly representative of the prevailing view in Indonesia today. Most foreign businesspeople in Jakarta tend to share his positive outlook, reflecting the kind of "can do" spirit that exists there.

Jim Castle is one of them. A young American who came to Indonesia more than a decade ago to complete work on his PhD, he is now a partner in Business Advisory Indonesia, a leading consulting firm in Jakarta.

"Without question, deregulation has had a profound effect on Indonesia's ability to export more competitive products," he said. "And now that the financial services sector is being deregulated, it will broaden the capital markets base significantly too, by bringing in more foreign banks and listing more domestic firms on the stock market. The government is basically concerned with infrastructure development—building roads, creating access to ports, making the bureaucracy more responsive. The driving force is now the private sector. Indonesia is developing a good class of entrepreneurs—very good in fact—and every year dozens of new companies are being incorporated. The pace is quite something."

But was the government pushing deregulation too fast? In classical capitalist development the starting point was light industry, and the process then moved on to the production of more capital-intensive goods. Heavy industries did not assume importance in the British economy until the end of the eighteenth century, with the invention of the lathe. But in Japan, where industrial development did not begin before the late nineteenth century, the order was reversed. The Japanese government played a leading role in guiding and coordinating that development for more than a century and is only now divesting itself of many of those earlier functions.

"In those states that were the first to industrialize," political economist Chalmers Johnson has written, "the state itself had little to do with the new forms of economic activity, [taking] on regulatory functions in the interest of maintaining competition. In nations late to industrialize, the state itself led the industrialization drive; that is, took on developmental functions. These two differing orientations toward private economic activity, the regulatory and the developmental, produced two different kinds of government-business relationships."

Even today the governments of Japan and the Little Dragons continue to exert more influence on the developmental *process* than their industrialized counterparts in the West. Streamlining the bureaucracy, eliminating thickets of red tape, and devaluing the currency are all welcome (if not necessary) steps to help the private sector compete more effectively. But to limit the government's role simply to infrastructure development, as many thoughtful Indonesians seem to be advocating—a kind of privatization process run amok—could well reduce Indonesia's future competitiveness by hindering government "intervention" in the very area it is most needed: establishing the kinds of disaggregated incentives that encourage growth in manufacturing and promote value-added exports.

Not all of Indonesia's bright young economists are sure that the Berkeley Mafia's high growth targets can be met. One who is not is a brilliant and articulate scholar named Dorodjatun Kuntjorojakti, himself educated at Berkeley in the late 1960s, who can rattle off a host of complicated economic data with ease. Jatun, as he is informally known, is vice dean of the Department of Economics at the University of Indonesia.

"To increase our savings rate sufficiently to finance the kind of growth we want, which we clearly need to do, exports will have to grow at 14 percent a year for the next five to seven years," Jatun was telling me one steamy Saturday afternoon in the spacious Borobudur lobby. "That is *twice* the annual rate of 7 percent we achieved from 1981 through 1988, when the world economy was growing at only 3 percent a year, more or less. But if we can't grow our exports that fast, we'll have to borrow more from IGGI, which means the government must increase taxes to generate additional revenues to service a higher level of foreign debt. That could bring about a real domestic battle for resources just when there ought to be growing consensus between the public and private sectors, not confrontation."

Early in his career Jatun had worked for Ali Wardhana, one of the original Berkeley Mafia and a former minister of finance in Soeharto's first, second, and third development cabinets (*repelitas* I, II, and III). An expert on industrial estates and tax-exempt export-processing zones, he makes no secret of his distaste for the study of neoclassical economics that is so common in the United States and believes a continued push toward industrialization in Indonesia is unavoidable.

"Indonesian young people *love* factories, no matter how dangerous or dirty or boring," he said as we sipped cup after cup of strong, aromatic java amid historical artifacts and stone sculptures that had been excavated from the famous monument at Borobudur. "Indonesia is only 18 percent urbanized today, which is low by developing country standards, and it will take a while to increase that rate. But in the rural areas kids have no lights and no entertainment, so they want to move into the cities, where they have both. These kids are one of the great things we have going for us: they're bright, and they're willing, and they want to be trained."

Professor Doktor Ingenieur Bacharuddin Jusuf Habibie poses another kind of problem for the Berkeley Mafia. Habibie is the minister of state for research and technology, a brilliant aerospace specialist who graduated summa cum laude from Aachen Technical University in Germany and then worked for the famed German aircraft manufacturer, Messerschmitt-Bölkow-Blohm, where he rose to become vice president for technology application.

Habibie today supervises the state-owned company known as Industri Pesawat Terbang Nusantara, or IPTN, headquartered in Bandung, that makes passenger aircraft and helicopters. He talks enthusiastically about his four-part dream for Indonesia: acquiring advanced technology by assembling foreign-designed aircraft under license, integrating this knowledge into high-tech joint ventures, developing indigenous technical skills through technical institutes, and finally providing competence in basic science on a par with the advanced industrial nations. In other words he applies a "trickle-down" theory to advanced technology and engineering.

Habibie is at odds with the Berkeley Mafia because he has to fight for his share of development funds from the government, and the technocrats frankly don't think his dreams can be realized, because they fly in the face of developmental economics—i.e., you must learn to walk before you try to run. They think he is like a child playing with expensive toys. But Habibie has the president's ear—they have known each other since boyhood—and Pak Harto has been supportive of his energetic efforts, up to now.

"Habibie's vision is long-term," his personal assistant, Wardiman, told me. "He has promised the people that it will take Indonesia fifty years to equal the advanced industrial nations, and he has just passed the first ten years."

To date Habibie, who also heads the agency responsible for all of Indonesia's technological needs, including nuclear power stations, has sold but a handful of IPTN's 250-odd aircraft to foreign buyers. Still, he argues that Fokker of Holland and America's Boeing, in addition to Messerschmitt, will over time become important joint venture partners with IPTN, which today makes some aircraft components for each of them. And his ideas do have a reasoned resonance to them, because of his focus on the development of human resources and his emphasis on manufacturing productivity as a priority.

Another brilliant Indonesian economist, Mohamed Hadi Soesastro, now heads the Center for Strategic and International Studies (CSIS) in Jakarta. CSIS, a private, nonprofit think tank, was founded in 1971 by two influential Indonesians who were former personal assistants to President Soeharto in his early cabinets: Lieutenant General Ali Moertopo, Soeharto's one-time principal assistant for political affairs, and Soedjono Hoemardani, the president's former personal assistant for economic affairs. From its inception CSIS played a key role as intermediary between the ruling elite and a group of Roman Catholic intellectuals and activists, primarily Indonesians of Chinese descent and Sumatran origin, such as Jusuf Wanandi, until recently executive director of CSIS and still a member of its board. Wanandi, whose given name is Liem Bian Kie, is one of Indonesia's most articulate spokesmen on international and strategic matters outside the foreign ministry. Another is Harry Tjan Silalahi (né Tjan Tjoen Hok), the son of a poor hospital worker, who earned his early political experience as a trade union organizer on Sumatra and today heads the Department of Political Affairs at CSIS. Hadi Soesastro, the current executive director, studied overseas at the Technische Hochschule in Aachen, Germany, and received his doctorate from the Rand Graduate Institute in Santa Monica.

Hadi Soesastro and I had first met in early 1989, when he was a visiting professor at Columbia. When we met at his CSIS office in central Jakarta later that year, I put back to him a question he had raised in a recent paper, "The Political Economy of Deregulation," presented at an annual meeting of the Association for Asian Studies in Washington: ". . . the aim of deregulation is improved economic performance. There is no doubt that the most immediate measure of success is the growth in non-oil exports. The past few years have seen encouraging results, both in terms of value and structure—manufacturing now contributes about 50 percent of the total. Would further improvements in non-oil exports support or put a brake on deregulation?"

Did Hadi think that the government's projections of 14–15 percent annual growth in nonoil exports over the next five years was realistic?

"On average, I'd say that's still within reach," he said in his typically soft-spoken manner. "Remember, that's a nominal rate, so it implies real growth of maybe 8–9 percent a year, which is not unrealistic at all, I'd say. But a lot depends on exchange rates, on continued smooth deregulation of the domestic economy, on our own economic growth, and on demand for Indonesian products in Japan, our major market."

Would Indonesia be able to generate the higher level of savings it would need to finance that growth? "We haven't done it yet," Hadi admitted, "but recent deregulation measures in the financial services sector are encouraging. Before deregulation in banking began in 1983, average annual growth in savings was only 7.5 percent in real terms, compared to 27.5 percent a year between 1983 and 1988. Between 1972 and 1983 inflation averaged around 12 percent a year, but for 1983–88 it has dropped to an average annual rate of about 7 percent. So I think the situation may not be so hopeless. It poses a neoclassical problem: prices are important, but they are not the only factor. Also important are institutions and markets—availability and access."

The banking reforms to which Hadi referred included a first round of regulatory changes beginning in 1983—when Indonesia removed lending and interest rate controls on all banks—and a more recent series of liberalization moves in 1988, called "Pakto," which have lifted restrictions on the opening of new branches by both domestic and foreign banks, cut reserve requirements, streamlined foreign exchange licensing procedures, imposed a 15 percent withholding tax on interest income, and improved access for foreign companies to Jakarta's emerging stock market, making it possible for foreign firms to buy up to 49 percent of any Indonesian company (except banks). The stock market has taken off in response, rising 50 percent within a year of the Pakto reforms, as foreign holdings increased from practically nothing to 30 percent of the market.

"The ratio of total bank assets to GNP has practically doubled, from 25 percent at the end of 1982 to 45 percent at year-end 1988," said Minister of Finance Johannes Sumarlin when I saw him at an Asia Society gathering in New York in late 1989. "Outstanding bank credits in the system have increased by nearly five times," continued the former minister of state for administration reforms and vice chairman of Bappenas, a trained economist and another member of the Berkeley Mafia. "And foreign banks have been coming into Jakarta aggressively under new joint venture provisions with Indonesian institutions—four from Japan alone in the past year. Our capital markets have a new life. In part this is due to recent regulatory changes, but more importantly, I think it reflects a growing awareness in world financial markets of the increasingly favorable prospects for Indonesia."

But deregulation does not mean *no* regulation—a crucial distinction that raises important questions about the nature of the country's government/business relationship. If the 2.5 million job-seeking youngsters entering the work force every year move to the cities, as Jatun predicted, there will be a major urban migration. Will the Indonesian government succeed in generating enough industrial growth to absorb them?

When I put that question to D. E. Setiyoso, a general manager of Bank Rakyat Indonesia, one of the largest state banks in Indonesia, his response was as measured as it was concise:

"It will be a close race," he said.

THE TRIANGULAR PARTNERSHIP
The Bureaucracy

By virtue of its stretching for some 3,000 miles along the equator, Indonesia does not experience much fluctuation in temperature—a few degrees up or down from its mean of eighty-five degrees is all one can expect. In Jakarta the longest day of the year exceeds the shortest only by about thirty minutes.

As they do in New York, London, and Tokyo, people complain about the traffic in Jakarta. Yet the traffic here moves relatively smoothly—*relatively*, because new roads and expressways always seem to be under construction, slowing things down, and the number of new cars (and drivers) is continually on the rise. Congestion in Jakarta actually is mild compared, for example, to Bangkok, where it can take fifteen minutes (or longer) just to turn one corner in front of the notorious Dusit Thani Hotel at the intersection of five broad, equally choked avenues.

So when traffic backs up in central Jakarta, either you can depart early and work on developing a more patient outlook on life as you sit in a Japanese subcompact taxi (hopefully air-conditioned, though many are not), trying to stay cool as the long line of cars inches slowly forward, or you can hop into a *bajaj* (a Sanskrit word, pronounced *ba-jai*).

The *bajaj*—the three-wheeled passenger scooter that has gradually replaced the old *beçak* (be-chak), the traditional pedicab—accommodate only two passengers under a tight-fitting canvas top, but they pop and sputter in and out of traffic with relative ease. They are all painted orange and blend in naturally with the sun-bleached roof tiles of Jakarta's tasteful houses. Their low-horsepower engines are imported from India, and the *bajaj* are assembled in Indonesia under strict local content regulations that prohibit the direct importation of finished transportation equipment.

On a recent visit I was scheduled to meet with the Deputy Minister for Trade, Soedradjat, whose office was a short distance from the Hotel Borobudur. Rather than take a chance of getting caught in early-morning rush-hour traffic, I hopped into a *bajaj*, slithered noisily through the long lines of idling buses and taxis, and arrived on time (though damp; they are not air-conditioned).

Soedradjat is a stout, strong-looking Indonesian who did undergraduate work at Wisconsin in the late 1960s and earned a Ph.D. in economics at Boston University. The silver streaks in his coal-black hair and the cumulative effect on his face of tightly packed six-day weeks belie his youth. It was a summer Saturday, and I was his first appointment. Despite his tired appearance, he voiced the quiet optimism that has become a trademark of Indonesia's competent, confident technocrats.

"There is some apprehension that we cannot repeat our past rapid growth," he acknowledged in response to my concern about projected exports, "but my optimism comes from this: regional developments in the Little Dragons and Thailand, where infrastructure problems have become endemic, mean a continuing shift in new investment to Indonesia. This makes me more comfortable in facing the future. We are the beneficiaries of political fallout from China, too, and Japan—our largest foreign market—is huge. I think our potential is enormous, because we are developing new manufactured products for export and new agribusiness commodities as well."

I asked him whether he thought Indonesia's overseas markets might not turn protectionist, thereby restraining Indonesia's new export opportunities.

"It's ironic, in a sense, that the Indonesian market is becoming more open through deregulation at precisely the time the world trading system seems to be suffering from contraction pains," he said. "We need the system to be kept open and free, but we are not dreaming that it will be. For our own protection we have to have a fallback position and are sending an ambassador to the Uruguay Round of GATT. Still, the new markets for us, and the fastest-growing ones, are Japan, China, ASEAN, the Pacific Rim, and of course countertrade. We have concluded several barter deals, for instance, whereby we buy refined petroleum products from the Middle East—more than $150 million a year now—and in turn require the sellers to use the proceeds to buy Indonesian products. If a student of neoclassical economics like me is practicing countertrade, that must really be something!"

Soedradjat is representative of a class of bright young Indonesian technocrats—and I have met many of them throughout the government—who are continuing the tradition set by Pak Sadli and

the Berkeley Mafia. They represent one side of the important triangular partnership among the army, the bureaucracy, and the Chinese
business class that guide and control the direction of the Indonesian
economy. He is dedicated, he is exceedingly well educated and well
trained, and above all he is proud—both of what his country has
accomplished in the recent past and of what he thinks it can achieve
in the future.

Sofjan Wanandi, younger brother of Jusuf, the former executive
director of CSIS, is typical of the younger generation of totally
assimilated Indonesian-Chinese businessmen who bring management
skills, leadership, and entrepreneurial spirit to this triangular partnership. Sofjan (pronounced *Sof-yan*) was born and reared in West
Sumatra but attended a Catholic high school in Jakarta and studied
at Pajajaran University in Bandung, on Java. He was active in the
Catholic student movement and, after the 1965 coup, became an
executive member of KAMI, a powerful anti-Communist students'
association, which catapulted him into politics. From 1967 to 1971
he was elected to the People's Representative Council (the Indonesian parliament) and appointed to the People's Consultative Assembly (Indonesia's highest state body, which convenes every five years
to elect the president). Sofjan also served as a personal assistant to
Soedjono Hoemardani in President Soeharto's initial cabinets and
acquired his early business experience running PT Garuda Mataram,
a firm belonging to the army's Strategic Reserve Command.

Today Sofjan Wanandi is president-director of the PT Gemala
Group—PT is short for *Perseroan Terbatas* which means "Inc." or
"Ltd.," and *gemala* is Indonesian for "precious stone"—and sits on
the executive board of CSIS. There are four key companies in this
small conglomerate of companies engaged in joint ventures with
Japanese firms that manufacture automotive parts. PT Gemala
Kempa Daya manufactures chassis frames and other press parts for
trucks, buses, and cars, while PT Inti Ganda Perdana makes rear
axles and transmissions. Both were partnered with Mitsubishi Motors, the automotive arm of Japan's Mitsubishi group. PT Tri
Dharma Wisesa, formed jointly with Akebono Brake, makes disc
and drum brakes; and PT Wahana Eka Paramitra, a joint venture
with Toyota, makes gearboxes and transmissions. Sofjan also manages a joint venture with Yuasa Battery of Japan. His principal

customers are domestic Indonesian auto assemblers that have links with the major Japanese automakers.

When I met with Sofjan at his modest corporate headquarters in central Jakarta—an old two-story Indonesian stucco house that had recently been remodeled into a series of small, interconnecting offices—I asked about Indonesia's growing competitiveness in manufacturing.

"We're not high-tech yet," he said, "but with basic technology and low labor costs we can produce low-cost products very cheaply here. That's why I think labor-intensive industries will thrive in Indonesia. The production of batteries, for example, has used the same technology for decades now. The government has played the biggest role in development, to push nonoil exports, but since the process of deregulation began, the impetus has shifted to the private sector as primary actor. Manufactured exports are now running at more than $1 billion a month. Basically we in the private sector want government to let us alone—give us the incentives to compete and remove the constraints. I'm very optimistic that we can compete effectively in the future."

I asked him about the country's strategic shift to manufacturing. "We have to fill more than 2 million new jobs a year," he said, "and there are still 12–15 million underemployed, most of them on Java. Up to now Sumatra has accounted for nearly two-thirds of Indonesia's total export earnings, and their focus is understandably on agribusiness products from the estates—principally palm oil, rubber, and tin, in addition to oil and gas. But Java will be Indonesia's *manufacturing* base for the future. We're sending more young people overseas for study and training now, and our top people are among the best in Southeast Asia. Middle-level managers are still a problem, I admit, but we're very competitive at the top. If we weren't, the foreign companies and banks wouldn't be pirating capable people away at twice the salary. No, I think we will solve these problems, and manufacturing is the way we'll do it."

The Chinese Business Class: Peranakan and Totok

Sofjan Wanandi is a *peranakan*, a native-born Indonesian of Chinese descent. He went to Indonesian schools, Indonesian is his native language, and he speaks Indonesian at home. His ancestors had come to Indonesia in the mid–nineteenth century during Dutch rule, when they were active as middlemen in retail trade. The Chinese had been coming to Indonesia since the early years of Dutch colonialization.

In 1619, there were only about 400 in Batavia, but by 1740 their numbers had increased to more than 10,000 (out of 100,000 Chinese on Java alone) and they owned half the houses in the capital. The increase was due not just to Dutch policy, but also to events in China: when the Manchus conquered the Central Kingdom in 1644, thousands of Chinese, especially from the south, in and around Fukien province, fled to the East Indies. Foreign-born Chinese who emigrated to Indonesia were called *totok*, an Indonesian word that means pure-blood foreigner. *Totoks* used Chinese as their native language, established Chinese schools for their children in Indonesia, and spoke only Chinese at home, managing enough Indonesian to conduct local business.

"By 1740 the economic position of the *totok* had grown so strong," the historian George McTurnan Kahin wrote, "that they were regarded as a dangerous threat to the Dutch." So the colonial rulers began to restrict Chinese activities in sectors they reserved for themselves, which threw a large number of immigrants out of work. These provocative policies precipitated an attack on Batavia by nearly 20,000 unemployed Chinese in West Java, as a result of which nearly 7,000 of the 10,000 Chinese inhabitants of the city were killed.

The Dutch regrouped and began leasing certain monopoly rights, called *pachtstelsel*, to the Chinese, who soon controlled the sale of salt and tobacco, road tolls, and, most importantly, bazaar leases, through which they acquired practically all of Indonesia's local market trade. In the regions they dominated it was only a matter of time before the Chinese monopolized the collection of taxes in kind, which they then sold, forcing native Indonesians, the *pribumi*, into a relationship of credit bondage and reinforcing a bitter social schism between *totok* and *pribumi*.

Though these feudal practices were eventually abolished by the beginning of the twentieth century, the forced class distinctions that they had produced over the preceding 200 years remained. By the 1970s, it was estimated that the Chinese ethnic minority, China-born *totok* and assimilated *peranakan* combined, was about 4 million in total—only about 3 percent of Indonesia's total population at the time—but they controlled more than a third of the Indonesian GNP and comprised 90 percent of the managerial class. They dominated industry, trade, and the processing of commodities such as rubber, palm oil, coffee, spices, and tin.

It was more likely for the average Chinese to live in a brick house, get a better education, own a car, and reside in urban areas than for the average *pribumi*. The Chinese did not control the modern Indonesian economy in the way the Dutch had before, but there was a wide enough gap to make the Chinese ethnic minority (and their foreignness) obvious targets of jealousy and hate. Over the years outbreaks of hostility toward the Chinese have punctuated the brittle relationship between *pribumi* and *totok* that had come to reflect a strong sense of economic nationalism.

In late 1959 the Sukarno government banned *totok*-owned retail stores in rural areas along with their use of non-Roman lettering on shop signs, a decision that alarmed the local Chinese, drove them closer to the Communists, and caused nearly 100,000 to leave the country. The ban took effect shortly after Sukarno's disastrous monetary purge, which decimated savings and liquid assets and threw all private businessmen, *pribumi* and *totok* alike, into despair. As part of the monetary reforms, private businessmen were now excluded from the lucrative import trade, which had been taken over by the state enterprise monopolies earlier that year. These actions escalated ethnic tension and resulted in violent clashes in Sukabumi, in central Java, with widespread property damage but no loss of life.

In May 1963 price inflation combined with product shortages stemming from Sukarno's backward economic policies generated an even higher level of resentment toward Chinese wealth in the midst of growing Indonesian poverty. Fighting erupted between Chinese and Indonesian students in West and North Java, followed by severe riots in Bandung, again resulting in destruction of property but little loss of life. In Bandung, long known as the Berkeley of Indonesia, a Chinese merchant begged rioters not to burn his Mercedes, offering them six million rupiah to spare it. The students accepted his money, stuffed it into the trunk, and torched both his cash and the car.

In 1966, following the violent September 1965 Communist

coup, Chinese newspapers were put out of business and Chinese-medium schools were closed; like the *pribumi*, the *totok* now had to send their children to Indonesian schools. Jakarta cut diplomatic ties with China, which were restored in mid-1990. Prior to 1966 Chinese were given the opportunity to choose between Indonesian and PRC citizenship at the age of eighteen, but after 1966, no more: you became an Indonesian citizen, or you left the country.

In August 1973, in the aftermath of a rice crisis that had created an inflationary spiral some months earlier, the Soeharto government introduced new legislation proposing a single marriage law for all Indonesians, which offended the polygamous Muslims and inflamed ethnic tensions. Severe riots broke out again in Bandung, triggered by an incident in which an Indonesian horsecart driver was beaten by a Chinese man whose Volkswagen had collided with the cart. Indonesian *beçak* drivers jumped into the fray and ganged up on the Chinese man, spreading the violence to Chinese (as well as to wealthy Indonesian) property nearby.

The Bandung riots soon spread to other urban centers, crystallizing in protests in Jakarta in late 1973 by university students, the press, and leading intellectuals, who jointly issued the "Petition of 24 October," which called on the military leaders, technocrats, and businessmen to review their development strategies in order to redress ethnic and economic inequality, eliminate corruption, and strengthen representative institutions. Months later, in January 1974, focusing their target more clearly on the *totok* businessmen, the intellectuals sharpened their demands by calling for abolition of the cadre of powerful personal assistants around Soeharto, reduction of consumer prices, and elimination of corruption.

The visit of Japan's prime minister, Kakuei Tanaka, on January 14 triggered the outbreak of the most severe rioting Jakarta had ever seen. Since Japan was Indonesia's most important foreign creditor and number-one overseas market for oil and gas, the Japanese were implicated by the petitioners because in their view a lot of foreign aid was being misdirected. Protesters met Tanaka on his arrival with posters calling Japan an "economic animal"; they filled the streets, demonstrated in the central business district, and proceeded to the Chinese commercial areas, where they attacked the headquarters of PT Astra, Indonesia's Chinese-owned Toyota agency, and began burning Japanese cars. Tanaka was forced to leave Jakarta the next day by helicopter from the roof of the Japanese embassy. In two days 800 cars had been burned, 150 buildings destroyed, and nearly 500 people arrested, although miraculously only eleven had been killed.

Yet aside from the more obvious aspects of class conflict between Indonesian and Chinese, there is a less visible but equally important factor involved in all of these ethnic clashes: the manipulation of anti-Chinese (or, as in 1974, anti-Japanese) sentiment as part of the struggle for power between the main factions in Indonesian national politics, a point that Dorodjatun Kuntjorojakti had made to me earlier. In fact, in the later outbreaks, not only Chinese property but that of wealthy Indonesians as well had been destroyed—government warehouses, for example, and oil depots. So while the ethnic conflict was real, the deteriorating economic conditions combined with the infighting among the powerful political factions around Soeharto were the main culprits.

Shortly after the Malari affair—Indonesian for "January 15 incident," as the early 1974 events became known—Soeharto moved decisively to alter the balance of power among the factions. The press had its wings clipped, with several newspapers either banned or temporarily restrained from publication; nearly fifty students and intellectuals were arrested or detained under protective custody without trial; the circle of presidential assistants was abolished; a new code of conduct that curtailed excessive displays of luxury by government officials was announced; and amendments to investment laws that stipulated higher shares of *pribumi* equity in domestic investments previously controlled by the Chinese were passed.

On a recent visit to Jakarta, I met with one of the detainees, a dissident intellectual high on the government's list of those who had signed the October petition and who had been held in protective custody for more than two years. He had not been permitted to leave the country, and his wife, though pregnant with their first child, was allowed to visit him only once a week. She smuggled notes to him from the Dutch and other foreign embassies, he said, so he was able to maintain some semblance of contact with the outside world.

"You must understand that the main issues behind the Malari affair had nothing to do with the Japanese," he told me. "Rather they dealt purely with domestic politics and the role of factions in the government. *Balancing* is the key to understanding Indonesian politics. When that delicate alignment of power among the factions becomes unbalanced, the political system wobbles until it can be realigned again. That's essentially what happened back in 1974."

In 1989 my informant was professionally active as a professor at one of Indonesia's leading universities. He could enter and leave Indonesia at will and even represented his country at various regional conferences in Asia, a role that has surprised representatives from other countries who knew of his prior detainment. Other informed observers told me that had he not been such an active and visible participant in the Malari affair, he would probably be a high-ranking technocrat today. Such is the price of dissent in an authoritarian system.

"The biggest regional rebellion that has occurred in our recent history was factional," he continued, "between officers in the revolutionary army, at Madiun, in 1948, when factions representing the ideological extremes of Islam and communism fought bitterly for leadership of the nationalist movement. That's why you have to look at policy formulation and changing political allegiances, not just at Chinese ethnic strife."

Among the Chinese, of course, the most ostentatiously successful businessmen were the *totok*. Among them Liem Sioe Liong, known also as Sudono Salim, had become one of the wealthiest and most powerful in Indonesia. Liem was born in Fukien in 1916 and emigrated to central Java at the age of twenty-two, illiterate and penniless, to join relatives there. He fought with republicans in their struggle against the Dutch, assisting them by smuggling cloves from Sulawesi to *kretek* factories in Java and by running guns and ammunition to the army through Singapore. During the 1950s he met Soeharto when he commanded the army's Diponegoro division and formed a cooperative arrangement by setting up light industries and marketing their products, the proceeds of which helped fund the division. He ingratiated himself with the circle of officers around Soeharto and made Sukarno's father-in-law, Hassan Din, the director of one of his companies.

After the 1965 coup Liem's fortunes soared. He controlled the clove trade he had known so well in his youth by sharing an import monopoly with Soeharto's younger brother. The Indonesian addiction to *kretek* cigarettes generated an incessant cash flow. In addition, he monopolized the flour-milling business on Java and Sumatra through PT Bogasari, a company whose shareholders included Soeharto's cousin and foster brother. Today Liem discretely controls about fifty separate companies with dominant interests in steel, textiles, car assembly operations, insurance, airlines, property development, timber, rubber processing, mining, retailing, massage parlors, and banking.

Two of his banks, Bank Windu Kencana and Bank Central Asia, whose board includes Soeharto's daughter, Siti, and his eldest son, Sigit, are among the largest and most profitable in Indonesia and have operations abroad (also in the United States). His wealth today is estimated to be nearly $3 billion, making him one of the richest men in the world. While not quite the Howard Hughes of Indonesia, Liem is notoriously reclusive and not only maintains tight security at his residence but also is constantly accompanied by armed bodyguards.

"Related to the feeling [of resentment between the haves and the have-nots]," the Australian historian J. A. C. Mackie has written, "is the widespread Indonesian belief in Chinese 'economic domination' of their country through a tight and allegedly impenetrable network of credit and personal ties, [giving] them enormous advantages over Indonesians in . . . access to capital, trading contacts, and market information."

Totok like Liem Sioe Liong are known pejoratively as *cukong*, foreign-born Chinese who became wealthy businessmen because of their collaboration with the power elite—especially with the military, the remaining third of Indonesia's ruling triangle and by far the strongest.

The Army: ABRI and *Dwi Fungsi*

The Indonesian armed forces are known officially as Angkatan Bersenjata Republik Indonesia—ABRI for short. ABRI officers (normally lieutenant generals and above) dominate the senior levels of the bureaucracy, hold key overseas ambassadorships, and run major government agencies such as Pertamina, the state-owned oil company. Power in the upper reaches of the Indonesian government is held by the 1945 generation, those military leaders of ABRI who, like President Soeharto, established their experience base, their loyalties, and their ambitions in the struggle for independence against the Dutch.

They were assisted in their struggle by the Japanese, who were regarded as temporary occupants during the Pacific War. Soeharto was one of many Indonesians who volunteered for security organizations set up by the Japanese, did well, was singled out for advancement, became a platoon commander in the new Volunteer Army of Defenders of the Homeland (known by its Indonesian acronym, PETA), and then attended the PETA military training school at Bogor, in the foothills not far from Jakarta. When he graduated, he spent the remaining months of the war training new commanders in the nearby countryside.

After the Japanese surrender PETA units regrouped to form a somewhat ragged republican army, seized weapons from the Japanese, and tried to consolidate their positions against the Dutch, who were attempting to regain control. Soeharto took command of a PETA unit near Yogyakarta in 1945, successfully attacked and defeated Japanese units near there, and soon became a battalion commander. The next four years were a time of intense struggle against the Dutch. When he was promoted to garrison commander in the republican stronghold of Yogyakarta, Soeharto worked closely with Sukarno and Hatta and got his first taste of both power and factional politics.

In 1948 Lieutenant Colonel Soeharto was dispatched to Madiun and played a significant role in bringing that internal rebellion under control. (Soeharto and his colleagues would later react to the 1965 Communist coup with the same decisiveness they had shown at Madiun.) In early 1949, within months of the Madiun affair, Dutch paratroopers had taken Yogyakarta, capturing Sukarno and Hatta. Soeharto moved his brigade back from Madiun and established his headquarters in a small hamlet nearby, living in caves that had been occupied a century earlier by the Javanese mystical hero Diponegoro. Through meditation in the caves Soeharto "acquired" Diponegoro's cosmic powers. He then executed one of the most daring exploits of the war when, in March 1949, he led his brigade in a surprise attack on the totally unprepared Dutch units in Yogyakarta, liberating the republican leaders, embarrassing the Dutch government, and setting the stage for negotiations that would make Indonesia independent by the end of that year.

Soeharto had established a solid reputation through his sound leadership capabilities and political caution. His background, education, and training were all Javanese. His colleagues were Javanese, too, including the brilliant young colonel, A. H. Nasution, who rose to head the West Java forces and later played a key supporting role in the aftermath of the 1965 coup. (It was General Nasution who in 1967 made a watershed speech called "the Middle Way" to ABRI forces, laying the groundwork for development of the army's concept of *dwi fungsi*.)

Soeharto's leadership was decisive but indirect, based on consensus and consultation, two very powerful Javanese cultural traditions. When the Sukarno era of Guided Democracy was swept away by the bloody coup of 1965, there was no question in Soeharto's mind that the succeeding political system would have to be much more authoritarian in nature. It would also have to be dominated by ABRI, the only unifying force capable of bringing stability and authority to chaos.

"[ABRI's] domination of political life was justified ultimately by the government's promise of economic development," the seasoned analyst Harold Crouch wrote in *The Army and Politics in Indonesia*. "The expansion of commercial opportunities was of vital importance for the army's role as a stabilizer. Inheriting a chaotic administration and a declining economy, the new government felt it had little prospect of raising adequate funds for [ABRI] by conventional means, [so] it permitted the continuation of practices established earlier, whereby the army resorted to raising its own funds to supplement what was available from the state budget, while many individual officers and men were permitted to engage in their own economic pursuits to supplement their salaries."

The government's budget allocation for defense funded only about half of total military expenditures. The balance was covered by ABRI's system of "unconventional" financing—joint business ventures with the *cukong*, state-controlled import and trading monopolies, and domination of the major state enterprises, such as the state-owned oil corporation, Pertamina. Fees, royalties, percentages of contracts, and margins on trading all flowed into ABRI's coffers to supplement an otherwise inadequate source of funding. ABRI's control of the political system stemmed directly from *dwi fungsi*, solidified under the ideological rubric of the five principles of *Pançasila*.

The most notorious example of joint political-military enterprise management was General Ibnu Sutowo, the autocratic head of Pertamina. It was he who sat atop the giant oil empire and overextended it between the two oil crises in the 1970s, creating a mountain of debt, taking personal corruption to new levels, and ultimately becoming such an embarrassment to the country that President Soeharto was left with no alternative but to remove his old army colleague from command.

Still, as Pak Sadli pointed out, Indonesia is not Latin America, and Jakarta is not the seat of a hard-nosed military dictatorship. What strikes a visitor to contemporary Indonesia is how *absent* the military is, quite unlike what one would expect of a country ruled by its armed forces. In Indonesia, military officers do not boss the technocrats, because they often *are* the technocrats.

"If ABRI officers can find their uniforms today, I'd be surprised," one longtime foreign resident of Jakarta told me. "And if the uniforms fit when they put them on, I'd be even *more* surprised."

Senior military officers and civilian technocrats alike dress in mufti, wearing either the colorful batik shirt or traditional lightweight safari suits. One popular story recently making the rounds in Jakarta concerned Benny Moerdani, the minister of defense. He drove to the Hotel Borobudur to attend a reception, intending to stay but a short while, and asked the doorman if he could just park near the entrance. "No," the doorman was overheard to have said, "these are VIP spaces, you must park in the garage." Moerdani, who as usual was without bodyguards or security personnel and was dressed casually in a safari suit, simply got back in his car and drove around to the garage. When the doorman later learned the VIP's identity, he was dumbstruck.

Part of the reason for ABRI's mystique is that its officers need not display their power to communicate that they have it. According to the Javanese concept, power radiates outward like energy from a light bulb rather than being wielded visibly like a gun.

"Power is that intangible, mysterious, and divine energy which animates the universe," Benedict Anderson, a highly respected Indonesian specialist at Cornell University, once wrote. "It is manifested in every aspect of the natural world, but is expressed quintessentially in the central mystery of life, the process of generation and regeneration. When I say that the Javanese have a radically different idea of power from that which obtains in the contemporary West, properly speaking this statement is meaningless, since the Javanese have no equivalent word or concept."

The Western concept of power is more abstract and flows from other abstract concepts, such as authority or legitimacy. Its sources are heterogeneous and may include wealth, social status, formal office, or military strength. Because it is abstract, it has no limits, and it is also morally ambiguous.

Javanese power, on the other hand, is concrete; it exists independent of its users. It is homogeneous, always traceable back to the same universal source. It has limits, since the quantum of power in the universe is constant. And it does not even raise the question of moral legitimacy; it is inherently neither good nor evil, neither legitimate nor illegitimate. Power simply *is*.

Soeharto is the best example of Javanese power incarnate. He is said to have a quiet charisma, but Javanese charisma is less a quality of the person than a quality attributed to him by his followers, who see him as "someone extraordinary, someone with a historic mission," someone who has power in much the same sense that traditional rulers of Java had it. Soeharto is regarded as the center from which power radiates, and followers attach themselves to this power, rather than submitting to it as one might in the West. His power is revealed rather than demonstrated. And as the ruler of the New Order "dynasty," Soeharto is thought to have received the *wahyu*, the divine radiance that was passed from the ebbing power of one ruler (Sukarno) to the next.

This divine radiance is part of a strong Javanese mystical tradition called *kebatinan*, which derives from the realm of the hidden and the mysterious. In *kebatinan* mysticism, man is considered to possess a spark from the cosmic essence, and by cultivating this mystic element he achieves unity with a higher reality. The Javanese mystical tradition has been handed down over the centuries through the *wayang*, mythological stories and shadow plays that, not unlike our Greek myths, dramatize universal themes through popular puppet characters who symbolize the elements of comedy, tragedy, loyalty, love, and war.

It was said that legendary Javanese sword makers could forge the sharp, iron blades with the strength of their thumbs alone, and in the intense concentration of the puppeteer's meditation the ocean in the backdrop to the *wayang* would always "boil and bubble." Soeharto identified most strongly with Semar, the modest clown-god of comedy. In turn, since Soeharto's power radiates outward, it infuses those people and institutions closest to him, like ABRI, with unquestioned authority.

The other interesting aspect of ABRI's power is that it is also understated. ABRI has fewer than 300,000 men under arms, and its annual defense budget is less than 3 percent of GNP *and declining*. This is because Indonesia's primary threat is internal—domestic political instability—and not external, such as attack or invasion from hostile foreign powers. In fact Indonesia's defense spending, as a percentage of GNP, as a percentage of the national budget, and in terms of armed forces per 1,000 of population, is the *lowest* in Southeast Asia, which is all the more remarkable considering the country's immense size and the fact that it is governed by a military regime.

"If we had to defend the Indonesian archipelago with conventional forces," Brigadier General Bantu Hardjijo, the energetic but soft-spoken director of strategic intelligence for ABRI, told me, "we would need to spend an amount greater than the entire Indonesian national budget. And if we put just one man on each island, we would need 13,700 marines."

During the 1980s the most experienced military officers of the 1945 generation have gradually retired from active service, and their places have been taken by younger officers, members of a new generation of leaders who are graduates of either the military academy established in Magelang in 1957 or ABRI's own engineering academy. Some critics have suggested that the younger generation of officers might be less likely to continue the tradition of military control over the political economy set by the generation of 1945 and would gradually hand over power to non-ABRI civilians.

But recent developments tend to indicate otherwise. Magelang has steeped the young officers in the twin concepts of *dwi fungsi* and *Pançasila*, and it was at Magelang, on the occasion of its tenth anniversary, that General Nasution gave his famous "Middle Way" speech in which he spelled out a continued political role for the military. The young Magelang officers have already spent the past two decades in important administrative positions within the bureaucratic hierarchy, many of them being high-ranking technocrats themselves. They appear to be much less inclined than their predecessors to participate in excessive commercial ventures and less blatantly involved in winning personal or financial favors for their enterprises (all the more so as those enterprises have become commercially successful and now generate their own flow of funds). If anything, ABRI has lost some of its *military* capability over the past twenty years, a fact that became apparent when Indonesian forces took control of Portuguese Timor (Irian Jaya) in the late 1970s.

The first class of younger officers received appointment as regional commanders in 1979, and by 1986 they held all the ABRI regional commands. One of them, Lieutenant General Try Sutrisno, was chief of staff until selected by Soeharto in 1988 as the new commander in chief of the armed forces, replacing one of the last members of the 1945 generation, General Benny Moerdani, who became minister of defense and retired from active service.

Like the traditional Javanese sultans, Soeharto manages the military elite by keeping rival groups of officers off balance, making sure no single group can challenge his power and no clear-out candidate will emerge to succeed him as president. The rank of commander in chief is critical—Soeharto had himself succeeded Sukarno from that position—and until he appointed Sutrisno in 1988 he had always selected officers for that position who were not Javanese, to minimize their threat as potential successors or pretenders to his power.

Soeharto's inner circle of presidential assistants rivaled his senior military officers for power, but that group grew less influential after the deaths of Ali Moertopo and Soedjono Hoemardani, clearly the most prominent among them, in the early 1980s. In their place the influence of another member of the inner circle, Lieutenant General Soedharmono, expanded as he rose to become state secretary, then general secretary of Golkar (short for Golongan Karya, a political federation that represents a majority of the nation's youth, women, workers, and farmers and functions as Indonesia's major party), and then vice president, a position he holds today. Soedhar-mono, Sutrisno, and Minister of Defense Moerdani are the three most frequently mentioned successors to Soeharto.

"I fully understand how bad an army would be without leadership," Benny Moerdani said at a bilateral conference organized by CSIS in late 1989. "Such is the picture I have of the world economy today. What we are facing seems to be chaos rather than mere uncertainty. We have to do our best to prevent it from being plagued by irremediable anarchy, because a mistake in the political field is in my view less difficult to rectify than one in economic policy."

Moerdani's remarks had been cleared for publication, but listening between the lines, I wondered if he wasn't offering a more subtle message for his listeners, a message that used the backdrop of global politics as a metaphor for Indonesia's own political setting. He was dressed in mufti, of course, and his face looked tired and drawn. But he seemed to be suggesting the necessity of avoiding chaos by extending ABRI's concept of *dwi fungsi* into the future and preventing civilian politicians from assuming control.

That point was later reinforced by Brigadier General Hardjijo when he said that ABRI could support more openness or liberalization in the domestic political system *provided* it was in the spirit of *Pançasila*.

"ABRI is like the armed forces of Yugoslavia," one thoughtful Indonesian suggested to me. "It is very intellectual and has kept us from turning guerrillas into gorillas. It became unified because of the Dutch, but they created the *mystique* of unity through *Pançasila*, which is really an anti-ideology ideology. Change creates imbalance, uncertainty, fear. But since Indonesia is democratic, you cannot force your way in doing things, so ABRI uses a very *restrained* show of force and tolerates neither the extreme right nor the extreme left. The key to understanding power in Indonesia is realizing that the New Order government is essentially a coalition among ABRI, the bureaucracy, and the Chinese. These are the most powerful factions in a political economy dominated by factional allegiances."

How this triangular partnership benefits these factions raises the specter of *korupsi* (corruption) in Indonesian politics.

THE "C" WORD

What differentiates Asian forms of corruption from the more familiar Western strains is the distinction between perquisites and bribery. In the West "fees" are paid or "payments" made to "grease the skids" of an otherwise inefficient and unresponsive bureaucratic system or to curry personal or political favor. Indeed, if you consider recent as well as historical political behavior in New York or New Jersey or Washington, D.C., this comes as no surprise; when it is discovered and revealed, it is generally punished. In the West you *leave* politics and government—and go into private business, like real estate or investment banking—to get rich.

In the East, on the other hand, there are certain "benefits of office" that are expected to accrue to the officeholder, and when these perks are received in the course of conducting official business, they are not considered illegal or immoral. They are simply an accepted form of behavior, provided they are not excessive. So in Asian societies corruption becomes a question of what is too much, and the subject of corruption in Indonesia revolves around this very theme of excessiveness. As one friend in Jakarta thoughtfully phrased it, "You can put your finger in, but not your whole hand." In Asia, then, in contrast with America or Europe, you *enter* politics and government to get rich.

Specialists tell us this is so because of the nature of Asian society. A distinct pattern develops in stages: first, political ties are determined largely by traditional patterns of deference. When the deference patterns begin to weaken in a period of rapid socioeconomic change, vertical ties can be maintained only through relationships based on material reciprocity: the greater the competitive pressures, the wider the distribution of inducements. Finally in the course of economic growth new loyalties emerge that stress increasing horizontal, functional, or occupational ties, and the nature of inducements is more likely to emphasize policy or ideology.

Other considerations, too, may influence the level of corruption in an Asian country. In developing nations, where rates of private savings and capital formation are low and government lacks an efficient tax collection mechanism, those in power can, through corruption, accumulate income that will—if reinvested in the local economy—produce a higher rate of capital formation than would otherwise be possible. This may occur, however, at the expense of social or political equality. And there is always the risk that that income may not be reinvested locally at all but simply transferred out of the country to bank accounts in Switzerland or elsewhere, in which case it becomes flight capital. As we have already seen in Indonesia's case, the ratio of taxes collected to GNP is fairly low compared to other industrializing nations in the region, so this process of accumulating "personal income" does tend to occur, yet *most* (though by no means all) of it tends to stay in the country and get reinvested.

Indonesia's political economy reflects the vertical structure of its society. Tradition, especially in Javanese culture, holds that a local ruler bestows certain benefits on those who surround him and assist in the execution of his office. As Cornell political scientist Benedict Anderson put it so well, "The central government is essentially an extension of the ruler's personal household and staff. Officials are granted their positions and the perquisites that go with them as personal favors of the ruler, and they may be dismissed or degraded at his personal whim. No feudal caste exists as such. Payment of officials is essentially in the form of specified benefits allotted by the ruler for the tenure of each particular office."

Problems occur when these "specified benefits" become excessive, and there is perhaps no greater or more dramatic symbol of excessiveness in recent Indonesian political history than General Ibnu Sutowo, a man of "electric brilliance" who moved in a world of sheikh-like luxury and credit-card extravagance, proving to Indonesians and the outside world alike that the tables could be turned on the dreaded colonialists and foreigners—but at a very high price.

Sutowo was known as the Black Diamond, an intensely loyal man who could cut through Jakarta's bureaucratic red tape with seeming ease and get things done. He was outside the realm of constitutional accountability, responsible only to President Soeharto, and set an example of personal conduct that was repeated in hundreds of smaller ways throughout the burgeoning empire of "specified benefits" that slowly came to dominate Indonesian politics.

Sutowo was born into a wealthy Javanese family and went to medical school in Surabaya, but he came into his own in the Indonesian army when he moved to Sumatra to fight the Dutch for control of Indonesia's oil fields. To arm the insurrection against the Japanese, Sutowo smuggled Indonesian rubber, tin, and palm oil from Sumatra to Singapore and sold them to buy weapons. After the war he was appointed commander of ABRI's Srivijaya division in South Sumatra and quickly gave it a reputation as the army's number one revenue-producing division (it occupied many of Indonesia's richest export-producing areas).

In 1960 OPEC was formed and began to extract more beneficial financial terms from the major oil companies; Indonesia joined OPEC in 1962, and Sutowo was Jakarta's official representative. He quickly applied OPEC's terms to the three companies active in Indonesia (Caltex, Mobil, and Shell), under which revenues from production-sharing contracts would be shared sixty-forty between the Indonesian government and the private firms. In 1968 Indonesia's three state oil companies were merged into Pertamina. Sutowo headed it and reported directly to President Soeharto, not to the minister for energy and mines.

The origins of Sutowo's relationship with Soeharto are unclear, but intelligence sources suggest that Sutowo started funneling money from Sumatra into ABRI's Diponegoro division on Java as far back as the mid-1950s, when Soeharto was its commander. Sutowo's willingness to back Soeharto financially was crucial to Soeharto's decision to exercise power against Sukarno in 1965 in the aftermath of the Communist coup. From then on they had the closest of relationships, defined by the president himself as *tepo seliru*, a Javanese phrase signifying a deep, intuitive bond.

Soeharto needed Pertamina as a symbol to show the outside world that Indonesia was capable of standing on its own two feet. The fact that it was managed by a native Indonesian and not by a *peranakan* was also important, and Sutowo enjoyed supreme protection from Soeharto. He could do no wrong.

With his growing power Sutowo began escalating the terms of his production-sharing contracts with the oil companies. He demanded management control over the oil fields for Pertamina and got a higher percentage of revenues for the government. All exploration and production equipment now had to become Indonesian property when it entered the country. Rivers of cash started flowing through Pertamina, and it built hospitals, mosques, schools, and roads all over Java and Sumatra. Its famous emblem, a five-pointed star flanked by two sea horses, became a symbol of pride and status throughout the country.

After the first oil crisis in 1972, what had been a river of cash for Pertamina turned into a tidal wave, as oil prices quadrupled overnight. The oil firms began pouring $1 billion a year into Indonesia, whose oil was, in industry terms, "sweet"—it had a very low sulfur content. Indonesia's oil revenues skyrocketed from $900 million in 1972 to $5.5 billion in 1975. Foreign banks fell all over themselves to lend Pertamina (and the Indonesian government) more money; they were now viewed as prime international borrowers. Pertamina diversified into liquefied natural gas, fertilizer production, petrochemicals, and steel—some of the white elephants Pak Sadli referred to—and built up a controversial fleet of tankers totaling 3 million tons at a time when the shipping industry was cutting back. Its own airline, Pelita, had Asia's largest fleet of helicopters, and it branched out into passenger transport, even though that was the preserve of Indonesia's national airline, Garuda.

Sutowo and his senior officers affected lifestyles that emulated those of private industry executives in New York or Houston. One celebrated his birthday in Geneva. Another took a safari vacation in Africa. Others had their pick of Jakarta's most beautiful fashion models as mistresses. Sutowo branched out into profitable personal investments, including car imports and cattle ranching. As icing on the cake he ordered a Boeing 727 tailor-made for Pertamina's executive class, outfitted with the latest in computer-era gadgetry and the most luxurious appointments, including a king-size bed and a Jacuzzi.

That, needless to say, represented a degree of excessiveness never before seen in Indonesia. When the bills started coming due, Sutowo had to juggle Pertamina's debt, since foreign banks had put cross-default clauses into their loan agreements: if Sutowo defaulted on any of his payments, Indonesia's entire debt could be called. In 1975, on the heels of the OPEC-induced recession in the West, Pertamina fell behind on repayments to two banks. Now it was not just the technocrats who were worried. President Soeharto was afraid the future of the New Order might be on the line, too.

In early 1976 President Soeharto made reference to the Pertamina crisis in his budget speech, and Pak Sadli was given the task of going before Parliament to announce publicly that the crisis would be resolved. Sutowo was sacked and "dismissed with honor." His replacement, Major General Haryono, who had worked for many years with the Berkeley Mafia on budget matters in the finance ministry, quickly purged Sutowo's executives, calling them "cannibals" in a public address. The era of the Black Diamond was over.

Yet it wasn't just the threat to the New Order's economic and political future that had driven Soeharto to act. It was Sutowo's unwillingness to show even the slightest repentance. And that, in the context of Javanese society, where modesty and understatement are acknowledged norms of behavior, was not only wrong; it was unforgivable.

"You have to know how the perks of office work under normal circumstances to understand how really screwed up the system got under Sutowo," a ranking foreign official in Jakarta recently told me. "First of all, civil service salaries in Indonesia are pitifully low, maybe $60 a month for entry-level positions. Can *anybody* make a respectable living on $2 a day?"

He then proceeded to explain a typical case involving the payment of "fees" to Indonesian officials.

"Let's say a foreign government wants to demonstrate a new helicopter for the Indonesian army," my informant went on. "First the officer in charge will collect a 'demonstration fee' of $1,000 from the foreigners, put a few dollars in his own pocket, and give some to his superiors, to his subordinates, and to his peers. Then he'll set aside an amount for the 'Widows and Orphans' fund, which is used to help pay for births, weddings, and funerals in the department. Then the equipment gets demonstrated. If the Indonesians decide to buy it, a procurement contract is negotiated, and 10 percent is paid to the local agent who arranged the deal in the first place. There is always an agent, maybe a retired army officer, perhaps an influential businessman. The agent then makes the appropriate distributions throughout *his* hierarchy. When you have a contract worth $500 million or $1 billion, 10 percent is no small change."

Journalist Ray Bonner gave a similar account of this process in a recent *New Yorker* article. He told the story of a prominent businessman whose daughter's car had been stolen. When the car was found some ten months later, the man was handed a list of the names of seven police officers and the amount that each expected to be paid. At the top was the assistant to the deputy chief of the department, who received the rupiah equivalent of about $400. Then the captain, who was paid about $250. Another officer received $150. Finally, four cops on the beat each got $30. Altogether the businessman paid less than $1,000 to get his daughter's car back, by no means an extortionate amount, given the time and effort spent retrieving it.

Again unlike the West, Indonesia has no conflict-of-interest laws. Excessiveness aside, as in the Sutowo example, there is some understandable confusion between what constitutes corruption and what doesn't.

"To us corruption is when you steal money from your department and put it in your own pocket," Sarwono Kusuma-atmadja, Indonesia's youthful minister for administrative reform and former general secretary of Golkar, told me. "When you accept a 'fee' for certain projects, you can argue about whether that's corruption. To me it is, but as the older generation sees it, when you're in power you have the right to receive these benefits so long as they don't run counter to the public interest.

"My job is to reform the bureaucracy before it reforms me," continued Sarwono, who is bright, articulate, and scrupulously honest, a model of the new generation of Indonesian leaders who are rising in the government. "People now see a need for bureaucratic reforms because we no longer enjoy a windfall from oil revenues, and while we have to increase tax revenues, we can't do that without also providing better public services. As we eliminate overemployment in the civil service—and we have already cut recruitment by half—we can offer higher salaries, which will help reduce the need for outside income."

"It's okay with me if they take 25,000 rupiah [about $15] and give 75,000 to the people," an Indonesian cabdriver recently remarked. "But when they put 95,000 in their pocket and give only 5,000 to the people, the people get angry."

In other words, you can put your finger in, but not your whole hand.

During the entire period of the New Order up through 1976 only two officials were tried for corruption. One was Brigadier

General Sudarman, who managed the national tin mines and had apparently failed to establish close ties with the dominant military circle surrounding Soeharto. He was convicted and sentenced to two and one-half years in prison. The other was Major General Hartono, a deputy commander of the army for administration and finance, who had used his position in a way that brought considerable international criticism and embarrassment to the Indonesian government: he facilitated the smuggling of arms to Biafra during the Nigerian civil war and also reportedly to Israel. He, too, was convicted, and served two years.

Other arrests and convictions seem rather petty by comparison, but they are served up as examples of enforcement. The head of the Jakarta Metropolitan School District, Rukanda, recently announced the suspension of several principals for collecting registration fees in excess of those set by the government. They were supposed to collect $1, but they were apparently asking (and getting) $20 and pocketing the difference.

As another measure of the government's perception of what constitutes corruption and what doesn't, nine minor officials of the state electricity corporation were charged with embezzling the corporation's funds. Four of them were accused of taking about $90 each, while the remaining five were said to have taken amounts less than $5 each.

As a result of these and other incidents, the Indonesian government has passed a new law enabling Indonesian citizens to sue government officials who inflict losses on them. When he announced the new law, Sarwono Kusuma-atmadja said that many officials still maintain an attitude of "expecting to be served rather than to serve." He reminded the public that Indonesia is a state based on law, not power, and asked government officials to perform their duties with a higher sense of discipline.

One prominent Indonesian industrialist put it to me like this: "As businessmen, we have lots of contacts with 'dominant factors.' Dominant factors are politicians, senior ministers, and army generals. That is why, when the students and the critical press complain about abuses of power, the government persists in viewing corruption simply as dishonesty on the part of minor officials. Their argument, not entirely invalid, is that when the pace of economic development advances, it will lead to higher salaries in the civil service and higher living standards, and bureaucrats will no longer need to depend on outside income. But in the upper strata, where the economic benefits for these 'dominant factors' are appreciably larger and where the practices are more culturally accepted, I doubt things will change very much."

Another prominent businessman, an American whose extensive experience in Indonesia goes back two decades, told me, "At least corruption here is *relatively* better, compared to Africa or even the Philippines, where the ruling oligarchy just dips into the national treasury and takes pretty much what they want. Here the barometer of acceptability levels off at about 20 percent of income that needs to be supplemented in cash, regardless of where the individual is in the hierarchy. There are instances of people getting first-class air tickets for travel outside the country, then cashing them in for coach fare and pocketing the difference. That sort of thing goes on in the United States too, but if anybody working for me tried it, I'd fire 'em."

His contrast with the Philippines was an appropriate one and is often cited by thoughtful Indonesians as an example of how *korupsi* differs from "the benefits of office." When I asked various senior officials how much capital they thought had been remitted—however surreptitiously—out of the country during the more than twenty years of Soeharto's New Order, the most frequently cited figure came in at around $2 billion. Now this sounds like a lot of money, and it is, but put into perspective over two decades, it is positively *minuscule* when compared to the amounts squirreled out of Manila by the Philippine oligarchy. (Several years ago, when an Australian journalist who should have known better wrote that Soeharto was the Indonesian equivalent of then–Philippine president Ferdinand Marcos, Pak Harto was so infuriated that he ordered a planeload of Australian tourists about to land in Bali to turn back *while it was still in the air.*)

"These 'perks' are still a national asset," one skilled observer pointed out to me, "because most of this so-called leakage stays in the country. It goes to finance the opening of new restaurants, beauty parlors, shops, and stores. Entrepreneurialism is the real strength of the Indonesian economy, and we are more like Taiwan in this regard than South Korea. So what Soeharto has done is to slow down the process compared to before. I'm relatively relaxed about *korupsi* in a national sense, but very much opposed to the attitude of self-righteousness in so many top people, which causes feelings of injustice, discouragement, and antagonism among the common people."

By some accounts senior Indonesian officials will often decline offers of study grants or project aid from foreign governments or institutions if the amounts are small, because the appropriate "fees" on those amounts are not really worth the time or effort. Yet some organizations operate in Indonesia without paying the freight, though they may suffer market-share losses as a result. IBM, which does not pay bribes in Indonesia (or anywhere else in the world), is said to have only a 50 percent share of the mainframe computer market in Indonesia rather than the 80 percent share it might otherwise have. And unlike their Japanese or European counterparts, who are free of domestic reporting constraints, American businessmen are obligated to account for and report any such payments under the Foreign Corrupt Practices Act, passed by Congress in the aftermath of the 1974 Lockheed scandal.

Attempts have been made to calculate the loss to the Indonesian economy caused by these "perquisites" and "benefits of office." Some estimate as much as one-quarter to one-third of Indonesia's GNP—perhaps upward of $30 billion—disappears this way every year. (Reportedly the World Bank itself automatically calculates a "leakage" factor of about 15 percent on loan and grant-in-aid projects for Indonesia, which has the effect of making everything from legitimate consulting fees to materials purchases more expensive.) Yet the situation is considerably better than in the Philippines, where an estimated 45 percent of GNP is lost to embezzlement, theft, tax evasion, bribery, smuggling, and capital flight.

"If government spending is a hundred," one confidential informant suggested, "what is the real government spending level here? 120? 135? 200? In any case, it's all off–balance sheet, and some ABRI-controlled companies are so profitable they get no budget support whatever from the government. But how will they get all this back on budget after the process of deregulation and privatization works its way through the economy and it is no longer necessary to make so many regulatory stops along the way in the bureaucracy?

That's why financial sector reforms are so important, because they will strengthen Indonesia's financial institutions and make its capital market stronger."

There *is*, in any case, relative progress. Recently, in a major speech in Jakarta, a senior government official had the courage to mention the "C" word, and he was not criticized afterward for doing so. As early as 1985, fed up with the long delays involved in clearing imports through customs and growing international criticism of import procedures that necessitated as many as twenty separate payments, President Soeharto sacked the entire customs service and hired a private Swiss company, Société Générale de Surveillance (SGS), to take over the customs department, which it runs (at a small profit) today. A decade or so ago it cost an individual traveler about ten bucks just to clear immigration formalities at the airport; today you pass through as you would anywhere else in the developed world—not without delays, but for free.

Despite the impressive list of accomplishments in deregulating and liberalizing the economy, several industries—such as steel, tin, plastics, and food products—remain state monopolies and subject to the cumbersome licensing procedures of the past. This is not by oversight. These monopolies are controlled by Soeharto's family members, who have replaced Ibnu Sutowo as contemporary symbols of excessiveness in the art of maximizing the perks and benefits of office.

The Family Business

This is the euphemism Indonesians use when they refer to the excessive privileges stemming from the business interests of President Soeharto's family. While their activities were pretty much ignored until about five years ago, today they are the topic of intense conversation. Their wealth has become, in the words of one sympathetic American observer, a public secret. "President Soeharto is the undisputed ruler of 190 million loyal Indonesians," he said to me rather wistfully one day. "Minus five." Those five are his four oldest children and his wife.

"Today, when Indonesians talk about Toshiba," journalist Ray Bonner recently wrote, "they aren't talking about the Japanese electronics firm. They are using an acronym for four of the president's most economically active children." They are Hutomo (Tommy) Mandala Putra, twenty-seven; Sigit Harjojudanto, thirty-nine; and Bambang Trihatmodjo, thirty-six—Soeharto's three sons—and Siti Hardijanti, his daughter, forty-one. A fifth cohort is Sudwikatmono, the president's cousin. The feeling is widespread that they have gone too far, transgressing the culturally permissible line between toler-ance and resentment. It would probably be easier, in fact—and quicker—to list the parts of the economy they do not control, than to detail those they do. Their business interests dominate nearly a dozen critical sectors.

Plastics: PT Mega Eltra, a state-owned company, holds an import monopoly on virtually all essential raw materials, including polyethylene and polypropylene, which are imported through its designated agent, Panca Holding, a Hong Kong–based firm. Sigit (through his own holding company, called Humpuss) and Bambang are two of Panca's directors, along with Sudwikatmono.

Steel: Since 1984 PT Giwang Selogam has had a monopoly on imports of cold-rolled sheet steel, a basic necessity for automobile assembly operations. Its executive director is Sudwikatmono, who owns 6.7 percent of the company; *totok* billionaire Liem Sioe Liong is chairman of the supervisory board and owns 20 percent of the firm. Giwang Selogam monopolized imports until PT Cold Rolling Mill Indonesia Utama, formed in the early 1980s as a partnership between Liem and the government (which took a 40 percent share), came on stream. By mid-1989 Utama had accumulated losses of $150 million and debts of nearly $500 million, and was on the verge of being rescued by the state.

Tin Plate: All imports of tin plate, essential in the manufacture of canned goods, must be imported through PT Pelat Timah Nusan-tara (Latinusa), which is controlled by the state tin company, PT Tamgang Timah, but 24 percent is owned by Nusamba, one of whose shareholders is Sigit. (Another is Mohamed [Bob] Hasan, a close business associate of Liem.)

Foodstuffs: PT Bimantara Citra, a holding company owned by Bambang and his brother-in-law, Indra Rukmana Kowara (Siti's husband), controls a group of fifty companies that monopolizes the import of many food products into Indonesia. Bimantara is Nestlé's local joint venture partner, one of just three entities permitted to produce milk powder. The Liem Group and Sigit own 55 percent of PT Sinar Mas Inti Perkasa, another holding company that dominates the palm oil and cooking oil sectors; Sudwikatmono is its president. Indonesian sugar imports are restricted, and two family companies on Sumatra dominate the local business: PT Gunung Madu and PT Gula Putih Mataram. Sigit is a director of Gunung Madu, and Indra is its president; Bambang is executive director of Gula Putih, and Hutomo and Indra are directors. (When McDonald's announced plans to franchise in Jakarta, Bambang, Sigit, and Siti all visited Big Mac headquarters near Chicago to solicit the business. McDonald's declined their offers, and it reportedly took them three years or longer to get the necessary licenses.)

Oil and Gas Trading: PT Samudra Petrindo Asia, a company owned equally by Bambang and Indra, receives quarterly allocations of Indonesian oil from Pertamina. Permindo Oil Trading, a joint venture with Pertamina, is 65 percent owned by another Hong Kong company in which Bambang, Indra, and Sudwikatmono are the largest shareholders. Bambang is part owner of one of the two Indonesian tankers that handle all shipment of liquefied natural gas to Korea under a twenty-year contract.

Cement: Roughly half of Indonesia's cement-making capacity is owned by PT Indocement Tunggal Prakarsa, a company in the Liem group. Sudwikatmono is president-director of Indocement and owns about 10 percent of the shares. In 1985 the Indonesian government acquired 35 percent of Indocement for about $350 million, despite the fact that the industry, which is protected from imports, suffers from severe overcapacity.

Property Development: On one of Jakarta's prime downtown avenues the ten-lane Jalan Thamrin, Bambang's Bimantara group is busy building Plaza Indonesia, which will house a new Grand Hyatt hotel and office towers. Local businessmen suggest that no new permits for office construction will be issued until Plaza Indonesia is full (though at present rates of economic expansion, that may not take long at all). Bimantara also owns 40 percent of the company that handles all the passengers and aircraft at Jakarta's new Sukarno-Hatta International Airport; Hutomo has a monopoly on the airport's advertising space.

Insurance: Sigit and his associates own about 35 percent of PT Tugu Pratama Indonesia, another joint venture with Pertamina. Tugu Pratama is not only Pertamina's sole insurer but also the only firm that is allowed to insure the thirty-five foreign oil companies that operate in Indonesia.

Telecommunications: Nusamba, one of Sigit's companies active in the tin plate business, has been appointed by the government as the sole local partner in the next expansion of Indonesia's telephone network. The contract, on which NEC and AT&T were bidding, was worth about $1 billion. (AT&T won the bid in early 1991.)

The president's wife, Tien—known locally as "Madame Tien Percent" for her share in various deals over the years—is also culpable, but in recent years she has been less visible, as the children now dominate the family's economic interests and thus incur the public's wrath. Tien has displayed a taste for a wide variety of luxury goods, including diamonds, orchids, and Paris fashions. Years ago she jointly established a local philanthropic foundation, Yayasan Harapan Kita (Our Hope Foundation), with Ibnu Sutowo's wife, and a similar venture with ABRI wives. In 1971 she announced plans to build a national cultural exposition called Indonesia in Miniature, which was subsequently built near Jakarta at an estimated cost of $24 million. Several years later her foundation financed the construction of a spanking-new hospital for Pertamina, also in Jakarta.

What is the difference between the lavishness of Ibnu Sutowo and that of Soeharto's family? The answer is as complex as the fabric of Javanese society is tightly woven. Sutowo was a senior officer in ABRI, acting on official duty, running Indonesia's largest and most powerful state enterprise, Indonesians would say, but the Soeharto children, well, they're *family.* Sutowo almost buried Indonesia under a mountain of official Pertamina debt and embarrassed the country internationally in the process; the activities of the children, while rapacious and irksome, are more private and entrepreneurial in nature. Still, that neither explains nor justifies the excesses, which are made all the more intolerable by some of the kids' personal habits. Hutomo races Porsches, and Sigit is addicted to gambling; he recently ran up a $2 million casino debt in Las Vegas and was reportedly held hostage until he could be bailed out by Liem

In 1986 the Indonesian government abolished 165 state monopolies affecting imports valued at nearly $500 million a year and replaced them with competitive tariffs, a move the Berkeley Mafia had struggled for years to achieve. But the New Order left the children's monopolies in place, and *they* affected imports worth nearly three times as much—an estimated $1.5 billion. As a result the monopoly on plastics adds about 20 percent to the country's final cost for raw materials, and tin plate winds up costing Indonesian consumers over 50 percent more than the cost of importing tin cans. This is what bothers Indonesians the most—the inflated costs of doing business.

As for the financial excesses themselves, ordinary Indonesians I have spoken with, from taxidrivers to bellhops to hotel clerks, seem predictably tolerant. "Pak Harto is a good father," one told me. "He looks after his children." "For sure, the president is not corrupt," said another, "but he is very weak toward his family." Another shrugged his shoulders philosophically and said, "What his children are doing is not wrong. It's Pak Harto's right to share his *sawab* [good fortune] with his children. If any of us were in his position, we would do exactly the same."

Yet resentment, especially among the influential business class, is articulate and outspoken.

"The president's children may well be one of the best things that has ever happened to the Chinese," one prominent Indonesian businessman told me. "All this pent-up hostility may be directed against the family instead, and they will take the heat next time, not the Chinese."

"The Soeharto kids want to be known as the Rockefellers of Indonesia," a senior expatriate with many years of experience in Jakarta said. "They would like to be the senators and governors of the future." That view, shared by many, may not be far off the mark. The original Rockefeller, of course, was one of America's most famous robber barons.

"Once Soeharto dies, the kids will simply disappear and vanish into the woodwork," a longtime Jakarta resident reasoned. "Another leader will come along with his own kids, and the process will repeat itself. But make no mistake: the president is an impressive man, and honest; he has really made this country what it is today."

Another perceptive observer, a Westerner with contacts in high places, disagreed. "Up until several years ago," he said, "President Soeharto was not involved in the kids' affairs. But now all indications seem to be that he is actively involved, opening doors and advancing their own interests. It is a serious issue, and generating a lot of discomfort and distress. No, I think when he disappears, the kids may just be lined up by his successor and shot."

"The president gets very angry when people criticize his children," one senior government official told me. "Have pity on him; is he not like all good fathers in that he loves those the most who are closest to him?"

Those sentiments seemed to cut to the quick of a very emotional issue for Pak Harto. Himself the product of an insecure childhood, having lived much of his young life apart from his parents, by all acounts he seems bound and determined *not* to have his own children suffer the pains of emotional insecurity. That is why all the rational arguments simply miss the point; the logic of reason does not address the strong, underlying emotions at play.

Soeharto himself has been outspoken in defense of his family because he knows there are ulterior motives behind the criticism. As with the past ethnic attacks against the Chinese, they reflect the factional strains of domestic politics.

In an impassioned speech a few years ago Soeharto asked aloud what the critics' real goal was. Not the children, he suggested. "Their real goal, in the short term, is to discredit the government, and the person responsible, myself, as president. And in the long run, they want to kick the armed forces out of the executive branch and eliminate *dwi fungsi*. . . . I have been criticized for doing things too cautiously, abused as a Javanese who is like a walking snail, whose shell is too heavy for its body. Never mind. The main reason was to safeguard the nation. For that reason, if there are now people trying to defy the Constitution, I will go back to the attitude I had on October 1, 1965: quite frankly, I will smash them, whoever they are, and I will certainly have the full support of the armed forces."

Still, when all is said and done, the millions of dollars that may be siphoned out of the domestic economy by the commercial activities of Soeharto's children every year *stay in Indonesia*. The economy pays a price, to be sure, and perhaps time will judge that price to have been too high. Yet unlike in neighboring Malaysia and the Philippines, Soeharto stops far short of collusion to profit from corruption; prior to the September 1986 devaluation of the rupiah he pointedly did not inform Liem Sioe Liong in advance. So while Westerners may recoil at the degree of the first family's rapaciousness, it must be put into Javanese perspective and considered in the context of domestic Indonesian politics.

INDONESIAN POLITICS:
CONSENSUS AND COERCION

In March 1988, when Soeharto was elected to an unprecedented fifth five-year term by the People's Consultative Assembly, the political system of the New Order was entering only its third decade. But Pak Harto had satisfied a compelling need for political stability by forging national unity under the secular state ideology of Pançasila, which had replaced all the frenetic "isms" of Sukarno—nationalism, socialism, Communism.

The armed forces of ABRI, under the mandate of dwi fungsi, continued to be the politically dominant institution, providing not only loyal support for the president but also a cadre of bureaucrats, politicians, and businessmen to manage the political economy. And Golkar thus emerged as Indonesia's dominant political organization.

One of Soeharto's first priorities upon becoming president in 1968 was to reorganize the many political parties that had become so splintered and fractious in the Guided Democracy years. In addition to Sukarno's Nationalist Party of Indonesia, a dozen others—including the Communists and those representing Muslims, socialists, and communalists—were all competing for power but in the end perpetuating instability.

Soeharto wanted to create a two-party, dominant-submissive political structure, but his ABRI advisers persuaded him to establish a three-party system. Prior to the 1971 elections all nine parties existing at the time were "urged" to run on the basis of a three-way realignment: one group was affiliated with the secularist Golkar, created to "engage in politics to suppress politics"; a second was encouraged to consolidate the Muslim parties, along religious lines; and a third, identified broadly as nationalist in scope, represented all the others.

Golkar's landslide victory surprised practically everybody. By 1973, weakened by both internal squabbling and government pressure, the remaining parties were "obliged" to form two new opposition parties, to be officially recognized by the New Order as the only two formal political parties beyond Golkar. The four Muslim parties combined to form the Development Unity Party (PPP), and five former nationalist parties organized the Indonesian Democratic Party (PDI). They both agreed to uphold the validity of *Pançasila* and the 1945 Constitution. In 1975 a national law was passed recognizing these three parties as Indonesia's only legitimate political organizations.

But while the PPP and the PDI are called "parties," Golkar is popularly referred to as "functional groups"—partly because political parties had a negative image in the past and partly because Soeharto believes the political system should refrain from even using the word *opposition*. He prefers instead what he calls a "true family spirit" of consultation, consensus, and national unity—Javanese beliefs that are widely shared among Indonesians. There may be legitimate differences of opinion, Pak Harto says, but they do not constitute opposition.

Golkar itself was created in 1964 by ABRI technocrats who saw a need to counter the growing power of the Communists. By 1969 it had been brought under quasi-government control as a political machine that could co-opt various social groups in the country and provide a necessary political base for the New Order. Golkar claimed to speak for nearly 300 different groups composed of Indonesian students, farmers, workers, civil servants, fishermen, businessmen and professionals, intellectuals, and workers, in addition to uniformed members of the armed forces. After the 1971 elections Golkar unified its leadership under a central executive board, chaired by President Soeharto, and tightened its internal discipline and organization.

Throughout the past two decades Golkar has steadily strengthened its power and control, consistently winning two-thirds of the popular vote for both the Parliament and the People's Consultative Assembly. (In the March 1988 elections, Golkar swept 70.1 percent of the vote.) It campaigns on a platform that reinforces both the five principles of *Pançasila* and the government's development-centered policies. While the political leadership of the New Order points to

Golkar's overwhelming electoral victories as proof of Soeharto's popularity, critics say that, with the unwavering support of the triangular partnership that runs the country, what else would you expect?

"In the past we've been called a 'vote-getting machine,' but in truth we're more like a Rube Goldberg contraption," Rachmat Witoelar, the fortyish secretary-general of Golkar, told me with a characteristically quick and easy smile. "Obviously the party has to represent its various groups, and in the past we were very dependent on the bureaucracy, but much less so today. We cooperate with ABRI, naturally, even though some of its own factions take more extreme positions in the Parliament than we think are warranted. But Golkar also serves as a conduit for grievances, giving the people channels for complaint and feedback—little streams and rivulets, if you will, that prevent a tidal wave. If there is only one party in Indonesia, how then are we different from the Kremlin?"

Rachmat, who is sometimes called Rocky by his foreign friends, is another example of bright young *pribumi* on their way up. He is articulate; he is thoughtful; and he is unquestionably future ministerial material.

When I asked him whether he thought ABRI would retain its dual function, he said, "Civilians will be taking more positions in what I call a process of dynamic equilibrium. You don't change a winning strategy, but ABRI is willing to change if a civilian comes along and shows he can be just as effective a leader."

When Rachmat contrasted Golkar with the Kremlin, he was of course making the point that Indonesia's system, like Japan's, is authoritarian but not totalitarian. That is a distinction foreign observers often miss, and it is an important one since authoritarianism is one of the basic building blocks used by the Little Dragons in developing their political economies. When I suggested that, in fact, Golkar could be viewed as Indonesia's Liberal Democratic Party, which has dominated Japan's authoritarian political system for nearly forty years, Rachmat said, "Well, maybe the LDP is a good example, and maybe PRI—the Partido Revolucionario Institucional in Mexico—is too. We have studied them both. But we don't use the same platform for discussion as these parties do, because of the importance of *Pançasila* as our dominant ideology. Westerners have a hard time understanding our political system, because Indonesia is not

Latin America or Greece. By the time of our next presidential elections, in 1993, though, I think we'll show that our format really works. You're beginning to see real debate on policies and issues now. We're that close, I think."

Witoelar's mention of 1993 raised two issues that are currently the hottest political topics in Jakarta today: succession and openness.

Succession

Everybody is talking about who may succeed Soeharto these days, both because Soeharto has been in power so long and because of the excesses of his children. Though he still had three years left in power, foreigners at least seemed to feel there was reason for concern even in early 1990. Indonesia's only other transition period—between Sukarno and Soeharto—was fraught with chaos, instability, and bloodshed. As one man put it, how can you have a lot of faith in a future transition when the country has had only *one* in its entire history?

"There are two schools of thought here," a seasoned observer of Indonesian politics told me. "One says Soeharto will retire gracefully, the other that he'll run for another term. The problem with the former is, when has a sitting ruler *ever* voluntarily stepped down from office? And the problem with the latter is, the longer he stays in power, the more others will feel they are being denied their chance."

"I don't see any evidence to indicate that Soeharto will step down now, or in 1993, or anytime after that," a veteran American journalist told me. "I don't buy the 'voluntary retirement' argument as 'statesmanship' for one second. Javanese society—its political culture—is outrageously feudalistic: if the heat gets turned up, it'll be Soeharto himself controlling the thermostat. I see him leaving this world as president."

A senior Indonesian official, now retired, said: "Speculation on Soeharto's successor is highly premature. The president strikes a good balance between the technocrats and the economic nationalists, and there is certainly no one else around right now who can do that. But if the succession doesn't take place smoothly, it will be a real setback for this country."

In any discussion of who might succeed Soeharto the same three or four names keep cropping up. But as one American businessman and longtime Jakarta resident observed, they all have their drawbacks.

For starters, there is Try Sutrisno, the ABRI commander in chief. He's Javanese, too, but a lightweight compared to the president. Then there's the vice president, Soedharmono, though the rumor mill continues to raise questions about his murky past—he's suspected of being a former Communist, which of course he strongly denies. Then there is the interior minister, Rudini, and the minister of defense, Benny Moerdani, but Rudini is not that close to Soeharto and Moerdani is no longer in the inner circle. So the field is limited.

In a mid-1989 poll conducted by the respected weekly magazine *Tempo*, 80 percent of those questioned wanted more than one candidate, but 77 percent of the respondents said they definitely wanted someone from ABRI to succeed the president. Similar results came from a poll conducted by *Editor*, another Jakarta newsweekly: 47 percent wanted an ABRI man for vice president too, and only 20 percent even wanted the outcome put to a vote. Seventy percent stated the president should be chosen through "deliberations," and 8 percent said he should be picked by "consensus." "Deliberation" (aka coercion) and "consensus" are the two political pillars of the New Order.

In early 1989 the president published his in-office memoirs, *Soeharto: Pikiran Ucapan dan Tindakan Saya* (*Soeharto: My Thoughts, Words, and Deeds*), which fueled speculation about his intentions. Soeharto appeared to have contravened the basic Javanese cultural trait of modesty by taking full credit for *all* of the New Order's economic and political accomplishments and including no close colleagues—not his fellow generals in ABRI, not the technocrats of the Berkeley Mafia, and definitely not the Indonesian-Chinese entrepreneurs.

In the final analysis the succession issue may be a convenient topic for idle cocktail conversation at the Borobudur but is hardly a subject of serious political discourse—at least not until 1993 looms closer. Indonesians seem much more relaxed about it than foreigners and are inclined to take a more fatalistic view, and I tend to agree with the Javanese who say it is a little early to begin worrying about it. I also agree that Soeharto is unlikely to step down and will opt for a sixth term, both out of justifiable concern for the safety of his family and because Javanese rulers cannot withdraw to a hillside villa. Retiring would mean a total loss of power and would be a very un-Javanese thing to do.

Openness

The issue of openness—the process of greater political liberalization that most foreign (and many Indonesian) observers would like to see occur—is something else again. It calls into question the very authoritarian nature of the Indonesian political system, the roles of Golkar and ABRI, and the government's debatable tolerance of disagreement and dissent.

President Soeharto has a wide latitude of power (and authority) in his economic policy-making because he enjoys the strong support of ABRI, the civilian bureaucracy, and many other groups in society, such as landowning farmers, workers, and urban businesspeople. It is entirely conceivable, based on the results of the Soekarno era, that a political structure more open to participation by various groups could prove less stable and produce a much lower rate of economic growth than that achieved by the New Order technocrats. Indeed the potential for political instability and economic uncertainty, rather than the possible threat to his power, may be one reason Soeharto appears cautious about liberalizing the political process too fast.

Indonesia's leaders have only to look around their own region to find reason for concern over experiments in democracy. In South Korea labor strikes and student riots have put a serious crimp in the country's economic growth rate. In the Philippines, the Aquino administration is grappling with chaos and instability again, not to mention a serious homegrown insurgency that produces frequent coups. And in China, where the most violent incidents have occurred of late, the brutal repression of students in Tiananmen Square in June 1989 was a reminder of how little the students could realistically expect to achieve in a totalitarian state.

But in Taiwan, another island nation similar to Indonesia in both its economic structure (consisting of a large number of small entrepreneurial enterprises) and its political makeup (an authoritarian regime dominated by one party, the Kuomintang), the transition to a more participatory democratic system is being made more smoothly, at a slow pace controlled by the government and set by its leaders. If Indonesia's ruling elite control the pace at which domestic liberalization occurs, then the chances of a smoother transition may be enhanced. My sense is that many are following the Taiwan case with understandably strong interest.

Unfortunately most American (and practically all Western) observers of the Indonesian political economy fall short of fully understanding the issue because they view the process of change solely through Western eyes and in accordance with preconceived Western ideas. Most foreigners fail to see that "openness" is the flip side of the "opposition" coin. We have already seen that Soeharto subsumes opposition under the Javanese philosophical rubric of consultation and consensus. So demands for more openness, in the form of petitions, protests, and demonstrations, must inevitably be seen by him as opposition to his policies. This is by no means a contemporary development, either; it has characterized New Order politics practically since inception.

In late 1973 opposition to the New Order's economic policies that were resulting in greater economic inequality coupled with growing concern about blatant corruption—Sutowo's excessiveness at Pertamina was becoming a major problem about this time—led first to the October petition and then to student protests and demonstrations, which in turn evolved into the ugly Malari affair in Jakarta in early 1974.

In 1978, just prior to the presidential election that March, students at the Bandung Institute of Technology in West Java took to the streets again to protest corruption. They published a pamphlet listing companies thought to be owned by members of the president's family, issued a rather unrealistic demand that Soeharto step down, and carried large banners with the slogan "We don't trust president-candidate Soeharto anymore." The government reacted by dismissing the institute's rector and sending in ABRI troops to occupy the campus.

In 1980 fifty prominent Indonesians signed a petition protesting the military's continued dominance of government, calling for broader democratic participation in the political process. Signers of the famous Petition of Fifty, as it became known, included Soeharto's old friend General Nasution and Slamet Bratanata, a cabinet minister during the early New Order years, in addition to other former high-level government officials, business leaders, and intellectuals who spoke out for a more pluralistic society. The government silenced the critics by revoking their passports, ordering the press not to quote them, and asking foreign embassies to exclude them from social events.

In 1984, when a law on social organizations was being debated in Parliament, Muslim demonstrators and ABRI troops clashed in the Jakarta port district of Tanjungpriok. When a group of angry young Muslims marched through the streets brandishing antigovernment slogans, soldiers blocked their way. Retreating, they attacked police posts and Chinese businesses; more than thirty protesters were killed.

More recently, in late 1987, demonstrating in the port city of Ujung Pandang on the island of Sulawesi, students protested a new motorcycle helmet law. Motor scooters are a major mode of personal transport in Indonesia, and the use of helmets by both drivers and passengers is typically lax. The demonstrations were triggered when the police began enforcing the law overzealously. But the helmet law was not the real focus of the students' anger; it was a combination of difficult employment conditions and political corruption.

The student demonstrations spread from four university campuses into the streets, where students collected helmets and burned them. ABRI reacted promptly, occupying Ujung Pandang in armored vehicles and snuffing out the protests. Several people were shot, and three died. The Jakarta press was ordered by the Ministry of Information not to report on the demonstrations, with the exception of the government's views.

The Press

The New Order government expects the press to refrain from publishing accounts that might exacerbate racial, religious, or ethnic strains. Newspapers are not supposed to mention the signers of the Petition of Fifty, for example, or to quote them on political matters. Also taboo are references to the economic interests of the Soeharto family. And the government exercises control not just through censorship but also through the granting or withholding of licenses to publish.

As a consequence Indonesian writers are forced to be more "creative" when they report on events that relate to current policy, and "reading between the lines" becomes a necessary skill. Some years ago Nono Anwar Makarim, one of Indonesia's veteran newspapermen, wrote an insightful monograph called *The Indonesian Press: An Editor's Perspective*. In it he talked about the imperfect relationship among the ruling elite, the press, and society at large—imperfect, Makarim felt, because reporters found themselves part of both the elite and the reading public. The editor's difficult task was to strike a delicate balance between the two.

"There was the time when a startled editorial writer received a personal telephone call from a very highly placed official," Makarim wrote, "pleading with him not to write on a specific issue the editor had already pledged to do in a previous editorial. When the editor very politely explained why he could not accept the 'advice,' the official very sadly informed him that he would be forced to take drastic action, but that he wanted the editor to know the measure was not intended to hurt, it was to be merely a 'face-saving' device. The next day the newspaper was closed down for two days, after which there was a marked increase in its circulation."

Sinar Harapan, one of Jakarta's most popular dailies, had its license yanked when it published, in advance, the tentative list of import monopolies the government intended to abolish in 1986. When *Kompas*, Indonesia's largest daily newspaper, got hold of the list, its editor made a few discreet inquiries and was asked not to publish it, since the final decision had not been made by Soeharto, and the technocrats felt he would react negatively if the news appeared prior to his decision. (In Washington this would be a "leak.") *Kompas* complied.

But *Sinar Harapan* did run the list, although it avoided any direct mention of the first family. When President Soeharto saw the article, his reaction was swift and predictable. He accused his economic advisers of using the press to pressure him into a decision and subsequently revoked the paper's publishing permit, charging that its story had "spread confusion, unrest, anxiety, apprehension, and pessimism."

Within a week of its closing *Sinar Harapan*'s editors got a call from Soeharto's cousin, Sudwikatmono, proposing to issue the paper a new license if Minister of Information Harmoko, Vice President Soedharmono, and Minister of Defense Moerdani were given a say in management. The editors wanted to keep the paper's name, which meant "Ray of Hope," but the government insisted it be changed; both sides finally agreed on *Suara Pembaruan*, which means "Force of Renewal." Despite the new name and new managers on the masthead, the editors (with one exception) were the same, the reporters were the same, the office was the same, and everybody's job was the same. The government knew this but used the closing as a warning to other newspapers.

When I asked an Indonesian friend about the incident, his response was indicative of the way Asian elites view the press.

"Opposition has to be informal," he said. "Though it exists in some intellectual circles and at the universities, it's a little like Tom Wicker's op-ed pieces in the *New York Times*: he's good for breakfast, but so what?"

Westerners are openly critical of the Indonesian press, but the kinds of control exercised by the Indonesian government are not unusual in Asia. Outside criticism has relatively little effect on the system; to the contrary, in fact, it tends more often to outrage Asian governments than to change them.

Over the years President Soeharto and his colleagues have grown more tolerant of Western criticism, for two principal reasons. One is a natural outgrowth of the self-assurance and self-confidence that Indonesia's ruling elite feel as a result of their demonstrably successful economic policies.

As one of President Soeharto's senior advisers, a Sumatran, said to me, "The people that really count praise us for our accomplishments. In 1988, the UN singled out Pak Harto as 'Father of Development' and gave him its highest award for his efforts in slowing population growth. The World Bank is constantly telling our technocrats what a good job they are doing managing the economy and amortizing our foreign debt without missing a single payment of principal or interest, virtually unheard of in the developing world. Japan—by far our most important lender and overseas market—is equally lavish in its praise. So why should we worry so much about what others may think?"

The other is a gradual recognition of what political leaders in the advanced industrial economies have also learned: today's sensation is tomorrow's dead fish. This may in part explain Soeharto's tolerance of the three-part *Asian Wall Street Journal* series in late 1986 that detailed the businesses and interlocking directorships of his children. To react, and react forcefully, makes Western reporters (and Western readers) pay more attention. Not to react means the story just dies.

Islam and Authoritarianism

Authoritarianism in the New Order has been a problem not only for university students and the press but also for many Muslims, particularly the fundamentalist Islamic groups. In 1978 the Soeharto government launched an intensive campaign to reinforce the *Pançasila* ideology. The bureaucracy prepares educational materials and conducts courses. All government employees (and teachers) are required to attend once a year, attendance records are kept, and diplomas are granted. A civil servant must have his or her *Pançasila* diploma before being granted an exit visa to travel abroad. The courses vary in length from a few days for unskilled workers to a week or ten days for university students and Chinese businessmen.

Then, in 1985, the New Order government passed a law requiring social organizations to adopt *Pançasila* as their underlying principle. Under the law all organizations, whether social, functional, or religious, are required to register with the Ministry of Interior Affairs, and their officers reportedly must be approved by the ministry. Accordingly the government also has control over any funds that an organization may receive from foreign sources, such as foundations or development agencies of other governments, and must issue the organization a permit before it can apply for, or receive, the funds.

While the *Pançasila* ideology is readily accepted by most Indonesians, it is not accepted by many Muslims. One of the five fundamental principles of *Pançasila* is a belief in one god. Secular Indonesians contend, therefore, that *Pançasila* is all-embracing, and recognizes every religion. Islamic fundamentalists, on the other hand, say that it contravenes a basic tenet of the Muslim faith, that there is no god but Allah.

Most Indonesians, the overwhelming majority in fact, belong to the Sunni branch of Islam (the devout followers of the late ayatollah of Iran are Shiites, the other major branch). The more important division, however, is between the devout (*santri* in Indonesian) and nominal (*abángan*). Nominal Muslims are dominant throughout society, including ABRI, the government, and business. Islam in Indonesia is basically much more relaxed than it is in the more militant Middle East or even in neighboring Malaysia, which has become for all intents and purposes an Islamic state. But even so, there are many in the devout Islamic community in Indonesia who have trouble with the New Order's insistence on keeping Islam and politics separate.

"Muslims say they need a more effective political structure, but what is that structure likely to be?" asked Abdurrahman Wahid, the leader of Nahdlatul Ulama (NU), the most conservative and traditional of the country's Muslim organizations. "I don't think this country wants to be like Malaysia [where Islam is stricter and more pervasive in daily life, closer to custom in Iran] at all; in fact, quite the reverse. But if the demand for social and economic equality is not met, then there could be more unrest. Mudslinging between Catholics and Muslims may lead to more conflict and misunderstanding if it is not checked.

"The fundamental conflict we have is economic, not religious," he continued. "The growth of the middle class brings growing conflict with the lower classes. The dropout rate in our secondary schools is getting to be so big now that the potential for social instability is growing, too."

Wahid's Nahdlatul Ulama became a nongovernmental organization (NGO) to have more flexibility on domestic political issues, but NGOs like NU prefer to call themselves self-reliant community development organizations, because NGO connotes an *antigovernment* flavor.

The Penalties for Opposition

The Soeharto government, not unlike powerful regimes elsewhere, has derived much of its power from the resourceful distribution of patronage. This has given the president and his inner circle the ability not only to reward obedience but also to punish disloyalty. New

Order leaders have at times taken an almost Nixonian attitude toward victimizing their political opponents. Retired army officers, who could easily make $1-2 million from commissions on government contracts (and thereby start up a small business or live comfortably on the interest income), would find themselves out of the reward loop if they chose not to support the president and his policies—paying some rather hefty penalties for their "sour grapes."

And if they chose to oppose the president more vociferously, they suffered more direct forms of punishment. Besides the forms of punishment meted out to the signers of the Petition of Fifty in 1980, they often found their work permits and business licenses were allowed to lapse, or they had trouble getting them renewed. Their credit lines in state banks were cut or eliminated, and they could no longer bid on government contracts. Opposition in any authoritarian political system is a very risky business, especially when the opponents are supposed to know the rules under which policy debate is permitted.

Still, Soeharto's political opponents were not systematically executed or tortured, as they might have been under a totalitarian regime, nor were they exiled, although their passports were often canceled so they could not leave the country. Indonesians are a gentle people, and Javanese culture has little tolerance for public displays of overt hostility. This gentleness also extends to Indonesian prisons, which are not torture chambers.

Indonesians do not live in fear that ABRI troops will come in the middle of the night to haul dissidents off to jail, as happens frequently in some so-called democracies in Latin America, for example. Several years ago, however, there was an outbreak of what people called "mysterious killings" in Jakarta and East Java, when an estimated 4,000 people were shot and killed as a result of the New Order's crackdown on crime. (Sections of Jakarta had been taken over by local crime syndicates.) Most Indonesians seemed to welcome the government's action, even though the killings were bloody and unlawful.

One lesson to be drawn from all these demonstrations of opposition to Soeharto is that, as children of the elite, the university students *know* what the limits of tolerance are. Consequently they also know what the punishment for exceeding those limits will be.

Indonesia is not alone in this regard; societies the world over have had trouble containing the exuberance of their young—witness Berkeley in 1968, Seoul in 1987, and Beijing's Tiananmen Square in 1989.

One is sympathetic to these students, to be sure. They are idealistic and energetic. But they are also young and impatient, and they lack the hard seasoning of experience that will come later, experience that adult leaders have acquired over years of often difficult and painful adjustment.

Social Unrest: The Javanese Crocodile

In scrutinizing social unrest in Indonesia, it is also important to understand that student demonstrations are more than just symbols of a generation gap or an ideological conflict between factions. They are also vents for letting off social steam in a society that shuns public displays of anger. *Amok* is, after all, an Indonesian word; run amok is what Indonesians did en masse in the aftermath of the 1965 coup, and that is what Indonesians do on a smaller scale when public opposition erupts.

Indonesian newspapers are filled with stories of *beçak* drivers who run amok when their pedicabs collide with larger cars. They simply lose their cool and beat other drivers furiously, often joined by other *beçak* operators in the process. One day when my own driver, a tall, stout Sumatran from the Islamic fundamentalist stronghold of Aceh, brought me back to Jakarta from nearby Bogor, he told the story of a foreign woman who drove into a motorized *bajaj*, injuring its young occupant. A swarm of *bajaj* drivers surrounded her car and pelted it with rocks, holding her hostage until the police arrived to break it up.

Indonesian social unrest is often compared to the Javanese crocodile, which spends most of its time lumbering somnolently beneath the murky surface of the water. When it is periodically disturbed, however, it explodes quickly above the surface, thrashing about violently until it disappears again. Perhaps the most interesting thing about Indonesian demonstrations is that, while much property is destroyed, very few people are killed. During the period of confrontation between Indonesia and Malaysia in the mid-1960s the students, encouraged by an ideological Sukarno, attacked British property rather blatantly in Jakarta. But before they did, they contacted the ambassador, told him when and where the attacks would take place, and asked him to empty the buildings so no one would be hurt. The same has typically been true of ethnic attacks on the Chinese; while much property is destroyed, relatively few homocides result.

"Indonesians are very emotional," one Javanese friend admitted. "They have an agrarian temperament, and they're very artistic, but their anger is quite powerful and short-lived."

Indonesians are quick to point out that their politics cannot be modeled after the more pluralistic American system. In America politicians vote to settle an argument. In Indonesia, when politicians vote they *start* an argument, which is why the Javanese traditions of consultation and consensus prevail. There is also greater income inequality in America, they will say, a gap between rich and poor that would never be acceptable in Indonesia. Therefore the model that is becoming most attractive to many is the one pioneered by Japan and the Little Dragons, which grafts a very strong system of political authoritarianism onto a rather high-octane mix of turbocharged capitalism.

"The New Order is one of Indonesia's great successes," a thoughtful American who has resided in Jakarta for many years told me. "Looking at the ethnic disputes, the economic roller coaster, Islamic fundamentalism, and official corruption, the one thing that impresses me is that Soeharto really does have things nailed down. I mean, Islam is nailed down, the press is nailed down, the courts, population growth, economic development, infrastructure plans, measured political progress, they're all under control. In this sense Indonesia is a genuine success story."

INDONESIAN FOREIGN POLICY: LOOKING OUTWARD

"The Javanese concept of power also has implications for ideas of sovereignty, territorial integrity, and foreign relations," the Cornell scholar Benedict Anderson wrote in a brilliant essay, "The Idea of Power in Javanese Culture." "The state is typically defined, not by its perimeter, but by its center. [Historically,] there were no political frontiers at all, the power of one ruler gradually fading into the distance and merging imperceptibly with the ascending power of a neighboring sovereign."

After nearly twenty-five years of New Order rule, Indonesia has achieved an image of competence, self-confidence, and optimism. It is the recognized leader of maritime Southeast Asia and the largest member nation of ASEAN, and its most important bilateral relationship, by far, is with Japan.

Japan and the Flying Geese Formation

"ASEAN sees Japan only as a money bag, which they think they should use for their own purposes," Mochtar Kusuma-atmadja, Indonesia's charismatic former foreign minister, told me. "But Indonesia knows the opportunities that are there for capital injection in industry, for technology transfer, and so on. Japan is a natural partner for Indonesia; we ought to be able to marry our considerable strengths in both manpower and natural resources with Japan's formidable financial power. But we need more entrepreneurs, skilled managers, and talented executives, or Japanese capital will flow increasingly to other nations in the region whose people's skills exceed ours."

Indonesia is Japan's single most important overseas market for direct investment in Asia. As of mid-1989 Japanese firms had invested nearly $10 billion there and ranked number one on Indonesia's list of foreign investors, representing nearly half of the $21.5 billion total invested there. (Of Japan's $10 billion total, $7 billion alone was in manufacturing; Hong Kong was in second place with more than $2 billion invested and the United States third with just under $2 billion, mostly in oil and gas.) For all of 1988 Japanese firms alone accounted for twenty-four of the 145 new investments recorded by Indonesia's investment coordinating board, BKPM (Badan Koordinasi Penanaman Modal)—investments in the strategic manufacturing sectors and in value-added industries like textiles and automotive parts.

Of the $4.3 billion in foreign credits provided to Indonesia by IGGI in 1989, Japan had the lead share of $1.5 billion, or about one-third. And Japan is Indonesia's number-one foreign lender as well, accounting for $12.2 billion of Indonesia's total of $19.4 billion in bilateral loans outstanding as of year-end 1988. Japan accounts for virtually all of Indonesia's external supplier credits, too, and is by far the largest aid donor, giving Indonesia nearly $1 billion in official development assistance (ODA) in 1988. When all is said and done, Indonesia depends on Japan for about a third of its nearly $60 billion in total disbursed and outstanding debt and ranks number one on Japan's list of client states in Asia, well ahead of China.

That overwhelming degree of dependence created some problems in the past—as with the violent outbursts in Jakarta in 1974 (the Malari affair)—but the Japanese are managing their relationship with Indonesia much more skillfully today. Their presence is less visible—surprisingly low-profile, in fact, given the degree of economic dominance—and handled in very responsible and impressive ways. When Japanese nationals are dispatched to Indonesia, for example, by either the government or the private sector, they are likely to be returning on their second or third assignments and tend to speak fluent Indonesian.

That was clearly the case with most of the Japanese I met recently while I was there, including Shizuo Okabe, who had spent several years previously in Johore, Malaysia, learning Bahasa and running operations for Unitika, a leading Japanese textile firm. After returning for an interim assignment to Osaka, where the company is headquartered, he came to Indonesia in 1985, fluent in the language, to serve as president-director of PT Unitex, a joint manufacturing venture in Ciawi, near the foothills of Punçak, not far from Jakarta. PT Unitex is a spinning and weaving company created by Unitika and Marubeni, one of Japan's largest trading companies, together with private Indonesian business interests, including a 20 percent stake held by the public. It is one of twenty-five firms listed on Jakarta's small but exploding stock exchange, itself one of Asia's fastest-growing.

Ciawi is the proud host of two foreign factories (Goodyear is the other) but is otherwise a typical rural Javanese setting. Row upon row of diminutive, neatly planted cassava and pepper trees dot the landscape. Soft green rice paddies, stitched together far into the distance like a giant quilt, shimmer in the hot sun, with ubiquitous carabao plodding slowly through the mud. Bent-backed men hack away at weeds with *ani-ani*, the small scythes they have used for centuries, while women nearby slap their family wash against low stone walls or thresh rice by hand.

Just past Ciawi is Bogor, one of the old provincial capitals; Sukarno maintained his primary residence in the Dutch governor's mansion there, which borders the botanical gardens, arguably one of the world's most impressive. And beyond Bogor, ascending through the neatly terraced rice paddies and impeccably manicured tea plantations into the foothills of central Java, is Bandung. Throughout all this eye-pleasing Indonesian landscape is the unmistakable stamp of cultural pride.

"There's not much anti-Japanese feeling anymore," Okabe said, in Japanese, as we walked through his large, noisy factory. "But there may be anti*foreign* feelings in Indonesia, because Westerners aren't so friendly—they don't shake hands with the Indonesians. We do shake hands with them. We share the same skin color, we have the same island-based, wet-rice agriculture, and we're neighbors in the same region."

PT Unitex has annual sales of some 30 billion rupiah, equivalent to about $18 million, of which half represents exports. It produces a high-quality 65/35 blend of polyester and cotton fabric used in making shirts and blouses for both the Indonesian and overseas markets. About half the company's exports go to Australia and New Zealand, the balance to garment manufacturers in Europe and Asia, including Japan. PT Unitex has about 25,000 spindles and 500 looms in place; as of mid-1989 there were some 3 million spindles and about 100,000 looms in all of Indonesia. The polyester yarn used to make the fabric is spun in Indonesia, and the cotton is imported from China, Australia, and the United States.

"We use Indonesian cotton, too, and want to use more," Okabe said, "but the local villagers on Lombok, where we buy it, keep the new burlap bales to wear as clothing and bale their cotton in the old burlap, which tends to add impurities."

As we toured the factory, covering our ears to muffle the noise, I glanced at the equipment PT Unitex had in place. Nitto Unicard machines pulled impurities from the cotton, making uniform slivers of yarn; Hara Shokki machines mixed and blended the cotton with polyester; Toyoda looms made bobbins with the blended yarn; and Yamada Dobby weaving machines wove the cloth. There were Murata winding machines, sectional warpers made by Okui, and Toyoda woof yarn bobbins, which shot back and forth at high speed like tiny rockets. The only machines *not* made in Japan were warpers imported from Schlafhorst, in Germany; there wasn't a "Made in USA" label to be seen.

This pattern of exclusively using Japanese equipment was typical and has been cited over the years, by Indonesians and foreigners alike, as evidence of Japan's using financial aid and technical assistance in its own narrow national interest. While Japanese foreign aid is high (Japan is presently the world's number-one aid donor in dollar terms), critics say that most of that aid is "tied" to Japanese exports and cycles back in Japan's favor: Japanese machinery overwhelmingly dominates local manufacturing ventures, as with PT Unitex; it is shipped to Indonesia on Japanese bottoms; Japanese engineering and construction firms design and build the factories for the joint ventures; and the underlying technological know-how mostly comes from Japan, too. For their part, Japanese officials say their hands are tied by laws and regulations that include "buy Japanese" provisions, and their managers will tell you quite frankly that their equipment is by far the best anyway.

PT Unitex pays its 1,200 factory workers an average wage of 100,000 rupiah (about $60) per month, or just under $3 a day, which incidentally is what entry-level bureaucrats earn in Indonesia's civil service. Okabe's starting workers make 45,000 rupiah ($25) a month, assuming they have completed middle school, and university graduates make 240,000 rupiah a month, about $150 at current exchange rates. Unitex provides generous benefits including full medical insurance, interest-free housing loans, maternity leave for women, and a local transportation allowance.

"Malaysian and Indonesian workers are about the same in quality," Unitex's Okabe told me, "and in their productivity. The difference is, there are more Chinese engineers and technical staff in Malaysia. But the morale of our employees is higher, and we have a very close relationship with the Ciawi villagers. Every year on National Day, about 3,000 of them come here to use our mosque for prayers."

Just how closely Indonesian and Japanese officials work together was impressed on me by Shuji Kita, a young MITI bureaucrat dispatched to Jakarta from Tokyo to represent JETRO, the Japan External Trade Organization, which comes under MITI's purview. Kita had been in Indonesia for about two years when I saw him in mid-1989, and he said he planned to stay longer.

"BKPM is now putting on seminars all over Japan," Kita told me, "to attract more investment in Indonesia. I recently took part in one of them, in Osaka. We expected 150 Japanese managers, but more than 400 showed up. Bangkok is so congested, and the political situation in China so unpredictable, that Japanese manufacturers are coming increasingly to Indonesia. And recent deregulation efforts here have definitely encouraged investment from Japan."

Kita gave me a copy of JETRO's recent statistical review of Japanese investment in Indonesia, a thick document that ran nearly 250 pages, together with a 350-page MITI analysis of Japanese manufacturing investment in ASEAN and a report from the Jakarta Japan Club, all, of course, written in Japanese. This was evidence again of the thoroughness with which the Japanese painstakingly dissect, analyze, and study their most important markets.

Kita's report showed a total of 247 Japanese joint ventures operating in Indonesia, out of about 1,000 in all. Japanese investment is predominantly in manufacturing: 177 of the ventures comprising 95 percent of total value were engaged in food processing, textiles, pulp and paper, chemicals, basic metals, or metal fabrication. The manufacturing sector is Indonesia's fastest-growing and the one where growth is all value-added.

PT Surya Toto Indonesia, another Japanese joint manufacturing venture, adds value to clay by making vitreous china and producing most of Indonesia's urinals and toilets. Toto Ltd. is literally a household name in Japan, where it dominates the domestic market for sanitary ware, selling more than $2 billion worth last year, which ranked it number 348 on the *Fortune* 500 list of international companies. Jakarta alone represents half the sanitary ware market in Indonesia, and PT Surya Toto controls more than half of that, including 90 *percent* of all of Jakarta's modern office buildings.

"This is a smiling market for us," Toto's technical vice president, Sakae Ogo, told me. "We started out by exporting here in

1968, established a joint venture in 1977, and have been expanding rapidly ever since."

Ogo had only recently transferred to Jakarta from Japan, but he introduced me to his president-director, Mardjoeki Atmadiredja, a young, handsome *peranakan* with a pencil-thin moustache who had been Toto's original agent twenty years ago and now spoke fluent Japanese.

Surya Toto's Japanese parent recently achieved a distinction of sorts when it jointly introduced a new high-tech toilet into the Japanese market with two of Japan's leading electronics firms, Omron Tateishi and NTT. Its state-of-the-art john comes equipped with a seat warmer, a combination water-pulse and air-dry cleaning device, and an automatic flushing mechanism. It automatically analyzes urine and stool samples and relays the results to a hospital or laboratory via a digital modem that comes included as standard equipment.

"Our sanitary ware is certainly not high-tech," Mardjoeki said with a smile as we sat in his office in central Jakarta, "but it does add value to the manufacturing process. We have competitors, of course. American Standard and one other local firm are here, but the market is growing so fast all three of us can survive. We have just increased our production capacity to 800,000 units a year, and we employ 1,000 workers at our plant in Tangerang. Our reputation for quality is so strong that it exceeds Toto's own inspection standard, which is stricter than Japanese industrial standard specifications for sanitary ware."

PT Surya Toto is a 65/35 venture between Mardjoeki's company, CV Surya, and Toto Ltd. It pays its workers on average about what PT Unitex does, including the standard corporate benefits. The labor supply is more than adequate; if Toto needs a hundred workers, 3,000 will apply for jobs, a common refrain I heard from most factory managers I met. About half of the company's output is exported, primarily to western Europe and the rest of Asia, including Japan.

Japan's dynamic manufacturing investments throughout Asia—from high-tech factories in the NICs, such as Singapore and Taiwan, to more basic industrial production in the NIEs, like Indonesia—suggest to many observers that a "yen bloc" may be forming, because Japan is beating ever stronger as the region's commercial and economic pulse. Unlike the United States, which typically views its national security interests in traditional political-military terms, Japan bases its security interests on economic strength, a fundamental premise of Japanese foreign policy.

The shift to more overseas investment by Japan has been accelerated by the rapid rise in the value of the yen since 1985 (an appreciation of more than 50 percent against the U.S. dollar), by the broader role of the yen in financing Japan's trade (fully a third of Japan's exports today are denominated in yen, compared to less than 29 percent as of 1980), and by greater use of the yen as a reserve currency (averaging about 30 percent of reserves held by Asian nations).

It was the Japanese economist Kaname Akamatsu who, more than half a century ago, coined the concept of the flying geese formation mentioned in Chapter 1. His concept, and the Greater East Asia Co-Prosperity Sphere of the 1930s along with it, were rejected by Asia then, but the idea has recently resurfaced in the guise of a new theory of regional economic development called "the multi-layered chase," promoted by Tokyo University's Toshio Watanabe. Watanabe sees Japan as a "first tier" economy leading "second tier" economies like South Korea and Taiwan, followed by the "third tier" of Indonesia, Thailand, and Malaysia.

The Japanese government has gotten into the act through a 1988 MITI study called "Promoting Comprehensive Economic Cooperation in an International Economic Environment Undergoing Upheaval: Toward the Construction of an Asian Network," which suggests integrating all the NICs and NIEs of Asia into a regional grouping that would greatly resemble a regional Japan, Inc. Its core would be Japan. Industrial and macroeconomic policy would be coordinated from Tokyo. And all overseas aid and industrial investment would be coordinated in the region by a body dubbed "the Asian Brain," the core of which is Japan's elite civil service, notably MITI itself.

But a yen bloc, while perhaps not only welcomed but eagerly anticipated by many of Japan's bureaucratic elite, is not necessarily embraced with wholehearted enthusiasm by the rest of Asia, including Indonesia. The older generation still has memories of Japan's aggressive exploits during the war, although most younger leaders take a much more realistic (and objective) view of Japan's new role.

Still, as one friend in Jakarta said, "The Japanese are now trying to do to us with their technology what they failed to do with their bayonets."

And Japanese investments in the region are not all in the higher value-added, strategic manufacturing industries. Japan imports nearly 20 million cubic meters of logs and timber every year from Southeast Asia, about 20 percent of its total needs. Japanese banks supply the capital, Japanese bulldozers carve out the logging roads, Japanese ships transport the logs to mills in Japan, Japanese insurance companies provide cover, and Japanese trading firms facilitate the whole process. Most of the timber is milled for two principal products: disposable chopsticks and low-value plywood for construction scaffolding and billboards. Indonesia has now banned the export of raw logs, insisting that the value-added manufacturing, as for wooden furniture, be done in-country.

America: Missing in Action

Thoughtful Indonesians also wonder what has happened to America in Asia, especially since its strategic withdrawal from Vietnam in 1975. Other than its historic presence in Indonesia's oil and gas sector, the United States has virtually ignored manufacturing investments in the archipelago by focusing on the extractive sector, in effect forfeiting the game to Japan.

"I can't tell you why more U.S. companies don't come out here," one American expatriate said as we sat in his Jakarta office high above the city, overlooking one of Sukarno's monuments below. "Our Indonesian workers are first-rate. Their IQs are high, their loyalty is unquestionable, and from a technical standpoint, they make excellent engineers and computer people. I'd put them up against any in Southeast Asia."

"I don't think there is any chance of America withdrawing entirely from this part of the world," Indonesia's foreign minister, Ali Alatas, told me when I saw him in Jakarta. "But since the U.S. clearly has a reduced capacity to carry the full strategic burden, there must be more multilateral sharing of this responsiblity now. It is counterproductive to divide the role functions too narrowly, with the U.S. responsible solely for defense and Japan responsible for economic and financial matters. You also have to consider the threats posed by the Soviet Union and China."

Alatas, known to friends as Alex, is one of Indonesia's finest career bureaucrats, a graduate of the diplomat school and a former Indonesian ambassador to the UN. "Japan is without question our largest market and the dominant commercial and financial power in the region," he continued, "as well as the source of most of our technology. A country with such overwhelming economic power may one day want to play an equivalent role politically and militarily. How does that affect us? Can we be ambivalent? And how can we possibly offset Japan's strength? Well, one way is by the process of multilateralization, by encouraging the U.S. to invest more here."

When I repeated this comment to Hasnan Habib, Indonesia's former ambassador to the United States, he said, "When I was in Washington, I tried to encourage American investors to come here, but they always thought we were too protectionist. Now the government is in a precarious position because of the steep drop in oil prices, so the technocrats are deregulating the economy to stimulate manufacturing industries and encourage the private sector. Japanese investment is pouring in as a result, but where are the Americans?"

"In oil and gas, mostly," one knowledgeable American expatriate in Jakarta told me. "Ninety percent of U.S. investment in Indonesia is underground, and if it's not in oil and gas, it's in mining, in tin or copper. American risk assessment has always tended to get Indonesia wrong, while the Japanese have slowly, steadily built up their position here. And in services American firms have been pulling out. Chemical Bank and Morgan Guaranty have both withdrawn from their joint ventures in the past couple of years. That amazes me, quite frankly, because this place is brimming with self-confidence and optimism now. America's relationship with Indonesia is driven by politics, not by economics."

While Tokyo and Jakarta discuss technology-sharing agreements, capital flows, and foreign aid, Washington focuses on the far more sensitive Western issues of political openness, corruption, and human rights. But this American political rhetoric tends to be viewed as somewhat of a mismatch in terms of economic reality.

"If the U.S. were to withdraw completely from its bases in the Philippines," John Monjo, the American ambassador to Indonesia and a veteran of Southeast Asia, told me, "then whom does the region want to see fill that vacuum? Japan? China? India? The Soviet Union? And hasn't our presence contributed to the stability and rapid economic growth in the region? Of course it has. The region is robust and strong now, but will it remain so, or is the potential there for even greater intraregional conflict in the future? As these Asian nations grow economically, their de facto positions change vis-à-vis the U.S. and they give the impression that American power is declining. But I can assure you that our commitment to the region is *not* declining."

"America has to command respect, not demand it," Professor Kernial Sandhu said to me somewhat wistfully when we met over lunch one hazy summer day, looking across Singapore Harbor toward some of the smaller islands of Indonesia on the far horizon. "And you have to face reality: all the blustering and table-pounding by Washington is losing your country an immense amount of friendship and goodwill. Americans spend far too much time cultivating ideology, whereas the Japanese cultivate people. Look at how they have done it. They ask themselves, 'What do we need to study first in order to understand Indonesian culture?' The answer: rice. So they start their official relationships by sending out scientists—agronomists or horticulturists who work on improving rice yields. Then they may dispatch some traditional economists and industrial policy specialists to join them, but only as a last resort do they send out any political scientists. Americans *start* by sending political scientists, and they are the *least* accepting of institutions in place—they always want to change them, make them more like their own."

Professor Sandhu, executive director of the Institute of Southeast Asian Studies in Singapore and a longtime friend, was born in Malaysia and educated in the UK and Canada. Both articulate and engaging, he has the kind of historical perspective most American observers lack.

When I asked him whether the contrasting Japanese and American styles reflected differences in their attempts to develop Southeast Asia, he said, "The Third World is supposed to be negative, closed, unstable, repressive, and volatile. But Westerners spend too much time and emphasis concerning themselves with institutions and politics. American officials in Indonesia reflect this institutional bias and work from the top down: they concern themselves with Parliament, with government agencies, with legal systems, with the courts. The Japanese approach is based instead on people and is structured from the bottom up."

In Indonesia, Americans have focused their attention on trying to make the political system more open, on the human rights abuses inevitable in any authoritarian regime, on perceived instances of protectionism, and on corruption. From America's perspective these are understandable and even reasonable foreign policy goals. But the zeal with which they are pursued, often infected by a strong dose of American morality, can irritate if not infuriate foreign friends. (This also tends to be true of our dealings with Japan.) And then we sit back and wonder why we lose competitive position in their markets or why the bilateral political relationships grow cold.

"Indonesia views America as the only multidimensional global power," former ambassador Habib told me. "But the problem for Indonesia and other small developing nations is that America has been so preoccupied with its containment strategy in the past that it hasn't cared much about their interests. Because of its preoccupation with the Soviet threat, America has tended to misunderstand the aspirations of the Third World nonaligned countries, and its attitude toward other countries has historically been conditioned by their relations with Moscow. But now that superpower confrontation is giving way to a more benign relationship between capitalism and communism, the U.S. may adopt a less obsessive posture toward the Soviets, which could enable it to give more attention to the problems and hopes of the developing world."

Former foreign minister Mochtar Kusuma-atmadja expressed a similar sentiment with a slightly different twist.

"Indonesia has traditionally been low on America's priority list," he told me. "In 1989 President Bush went to Tokyo, Seoul, and Beijing, and Dan Quayle came to Jakarta. Not only that, but he arrived several hours late for his appointment with President Soeharto. The U.S. has put everything in its 'China card' strategy and does not pay enough attention to the other East Asian nations where it has strategic interests."

I asked Pak Mochtar why the United States has not recognized more of Indonesia's positive accomplishments and why the American press seems to hold Indonesia in relative disregard.

"There are three primary reasons," he said. "One, Indonesia is led by the military, so most Americans think it is just another Latin America–type dictatorship. Two, Washington cannot accept the fact that a country not tied to its apron strings has done well, that Indonesia has built its development and its political system pretty much on its own design. And three, the U.S cannot admit that another Asian country built in its own image—the Philippines—is an abject failure."

Another senior Indonesian official put it this way: "Henry Kissinger was a disaster for U.S. foreign policy," he said. "His China policy, his Vietnam policy, his Middle East policy, his disrespectful, condescending attitude toward Japan have *all* turned out wrong. Kissinger created the China card as a means of leveraging power against the Soviets, but in doing so he relegated Japan to second-class status, which irritated the Japanese no end; no wonder they are always edgy and critical toward you. Kissinger thought he was being very clever in all this, but the moral of that story is, you can get *too* clever."

Indonesia's relations with the other two superpowers—the Soviet Union and China—are distant. Jakarta has not had much to do with Moscow since Sukarno's fall from power in 1965, and it reestablished diplomatic relations with China only in 1990. Otherwise Indonesia's primary foreign policy concerns are regional, within ASEAN.

ASEAN

ASEAN's secretariat is headquartered in Jakarta, which is fitting for the capital city of a nation that is the hub of maritime Southeast Asia. Its intramural relations are governed by a Treaty of Amity and Friendship among member states, and its principal contribution to regional stability is a concept called the Zone of Peace, Freedom, and Neutrality, better known by its popular acronym, ZOPFAN, a kind of diplomatic radar formulated in 1971 to keep the superpowers from meddling. There was considerable apprehension, therefore, when Vietnam invaded Cambodia in 1979 to roust out the homicidal, Chinese-backed Khmer Rouge; more than 300,000 refugees fled the country, most of them settling in temporary camps across the Thai border.

With the relative calm and stability that prevails in ASEAN today, it is difficult to recall just how precarious the strategic balance in the region was at ASEAN's inception a short two decades ago. The United States and the Soviet Union had escalated the war in Vietnam to a peak of hostility; suspected North Vietnamese troop sanctuaries in Laos and Cambodia were regular bombing targets; Malaysia had just subdued a Communist insurgency; Thailand was coping with its own Communist insurgents, giving rise to the fear of the "domino theory" so popular at the time; the Philippines had (and still has) a menacing New People's Army that was (and still is) destabilizing the rural areas; Singapore had just become an independent republic, having been unceremoniously booted out of Malaysia; and Indonesia was incubating the New Order, reeling from the bloody aftereffects of the 1965 coup.

Indonesia's most impressive foreign policy accomplishment in recent years was to bring the feuding factions in Cambodia together for diplomatic negotiations in Jakarta, a process that lasted several years in the late 1980s and became known as the Jakarta Informal Meetings (JIM, for short), culminating in the international peace conference held in Paris in late 1989. The Paris talks cratered, and the Cambodian factions are still feuding. Premier Hun Sen, the Vietnamese puppet, still holds titular power. Prince Sihanouk and his son head the neutralist faction, China continues to support the Khmer Rouge, and for a long while America backed a fourth group under Son Sann called the Khmer People's National Liberation Front. ASEAN agrees Vietnamese troops should go; they began withdrawing in the fall of 1989.

By mid-1990, though, Washington had shifted its policy. Fearing a Khmer Rouge military victory, the U.S. government formally withdrew its diplomatic support of the Son Sann coalition, leading to direct negotiations with Vietnam that by the end of August had enabled the five permanent members of the UN Security Council to agree unanimously on UN–supervised elections for Cambodia, thus resolving this long-festering problem.

Indonesia's foreign minister, Ali Alatas, played a key role in the Paris talks, as did the late Husni Thamrin Pane, secretary general of ASEAN during those years. I asked Alatas whether the recent thaw in superpower relations might lead to more intra-ASEAN hostility, since the glue that has kept the original five together could be now viewed as coming unstuck.

"There is the fear expressed that centrifugal forces might pull us apart," he told me, "but I think that is a misreading of what brought us together in the first place. That may also be an unrealistic reading of conflict as a response to current trends."

Husni Pane studied at Harvard in the 1950s. He was in Kuala Lumpur in the 1960s during the period of confrontation with Malaysia, was in Washington when Nixon resigned, in New Delhi when Nehru died, and ambassador to Mexico from 1981 to 1984. I saw him in Jakarta just weeks before his death due to an untimely heart attack in the fall of 1989. Boasting an agile mind and a quick sense of humor, he was scheduled to be Indonesia's next ambassador to Canada. I asked him about the prospects for bringing Southeast Asia's two renegade powers—Vietnam and Burma—into ASEAN.

"Burma declined to join ASEAN at its inception in 1967," he told me, "preferring to maintain what they called 'rigid equidistance' from the major power blocs. And Vietnam is still further down the road, depending on what finally happens in Cambodia. The first step for either would be to sign the Treaty of Amity and Friendship, which we hold open for all Southeast Asian nations, whether they are members of ASEAN or not. Papua New Guinea has signed it, and Vietnam, Laos, and Cambodia have all indicated they will sign as a first step toward achieving resolution of conflict by peaceful means."

Still, even when the Cambodian conflict has been completely resolved, other differences might further divide ASEAN. Thailand is pushing its "Souvannaphoum" concept, under which the Thais want to turn plowshares into market shares by creating a mini-bloc with Indochina. Jakarta views this somewhat jealously as Bangkok's attempt to reestablish its dominance as the hub of mainland Southeast Asia. Tiny Singapore, surrounded by much larger neighbors, offered to expand U.S. military facilities there if Washington withdraws its bases from the Philippines, as it is being pressured to do. Malaysia recently concluded a multibillion-dollar purchase of Tornado aircraft from Britain, the better to defend its claim to the Spratly Islands (which it contests with China, Vietnam, and the Philippines). And Malaysia and the Philippines still bitterly contest a common claim to Sabah, the easternmost province of Malaysia that was once the British possession of North Borneo.

"ASEAN needs to have a better strategic vision of its role in the future," Indonesia's former foreign minister Mochtar Kusuma-atmadja told me. "Or at least a better strategic concept for economic cooperation and mutual defense. Thailand appears to be siding with China on Cambodia; the Philippines is allied with the U.S.; and Malaysia, Singapore, and Brunei have developed a five-power defense concept with Australia and New Zealand. As the superpower relations thaw, potential conflict within ASEAN could well increase, both economically and politically."

The cultural mix of the ASEAN six might also be difficult to maintain without a strong external threat to hold them together. Thai Buddhism is tolerant, but Malaysian Islam is not. Indonesia has *Pançasila*, which is nonthreatening to outsiders, but Singapore is dominated by the Chinese, who are nothing if not aggressive. The Philippines has to contend with both a quicksand economy and its own Communist insurgency. So this could all portend some fairly tough times ahead for the region, and might well test ASEAN's ability to hang together. Japan could be the new glue to help the six nations do that, for despite two decades of political togetherness there has not yet been a *single* cross-border commercial project created by ASEAN to test its ability to cooperate economically.

"I see three or four key issues affecting ASEAN in the years ahead," a Singapore government official confided to me. "One is political succession in each country. Second, satisfactory resolution of the conflict in Cambodia. Third, the external threat—both economic and strategic—to the group. And fourth, the overarching security question surrounding U.S. withdrawal from the Philippines, which has to make up its mind whether or not it wants to be America's fifty-first state. Compared to Gorbachev's 'smiling diplomacy' and China's brutal suppression of dissent in Tiananmen Square, I would say that the U.S. presence is still the key to stability in this region. A more isolationist America or a remilitarized Japan would also bear significantly on ASEAN."

In contrast to the Cambodian talks, Indonesia's *least* impressive foreign policy accomplishment in recent years was East Timor. During three decades of New Order rule Indonesia has been spared the foreign policy crises it had seen as a regular diet under Sukarno. The sole exception was East Timor, geographically a part of the Indonesian archipelago but colonized by the Portuguese, not by the

Dutch. When Portugal began to decolonize in the mid-1970s, three local political factions in East Timor started fighting for local control. One group, known by its acronym APODETI, wanted immediate integration into Indonesia; a second, UDT, preferred integration with Portugal and eventual independence; a third, FRETILIN, demanded instant independence. Following a brief but bloody civil war, FRETILIN declared independence on November 28, 1975, and about a week later Indonesian troops invaded.

ABRI expected to mop up rather handily but instead met fierce resistance from more than 20,000 FRETILIN troops. The Indonesians waged what by all accounts was a brutal, aggressive war. They bombed villages and conducted mass executions of FRETILIN sympathizers. An estimated 60,000 people died—fully 10 percent of East Timor's population. Famine and starvation added to the Timorese misery, and before long East Timor was being equated with Biafra. This issue united liberals and conservatives alike; Bill Buckley's *National Review* called the Indonesian action "one of the grislier stories of human-rights violations, mass starvation, and wholesale slaughter."

Portugal was never one of the world's beneficent colonial powers. In East Timor it left behind a legacy of illiteracy (90 percent of the Timorese were illiterate), no secondary schools, few miles of paved roads, and a subsistence coffee economy. For the past decade the New Order government has spent more per capita in East Timor than in any other province. President Soeharto has opened more than 500 schools, established 350 health clinics in local *kampong*, and constructed a hospital in Dili, the capital, reported to be among the best in the country. Today diplomats and journalists who have visited there say that the Timorese are better off as a part of Indonesia than they were under Portuguese rule. But the nagging question remains, at what price?

America's official response to the East Timor crisis was muted by its own hamstrung withdrawal from Vietnam and the persistent handwringing in Washington over the future U.S. role in Southeast Asia. But in the words of one senior Indonesian official, East Timor was "like a bone in our throat."

One can't help being sympathetic to the question of national integration; consider, for example, Washington's predictable response to a hypothetical case of Puerto Rico declaring independence from the United States. Given Cuba's truculent relationship with the United States, President Reagan's invasion of Grenada, the Bush administration's intervention in Panama, and the perennial problems with Marxist strongholds in Central America, there is no question that the United States would act, and act decisively, to keep Puerto Rico strategically American (without, one assumes, killing 10 percent of Puerto Rico's population in the process).

This is by no means intended to justify Indonesia's cruel attack on East Timor, but the redrawing of artificial national boundaries, colonial or otherwise, is always done from the perspective of the invader's national interest. Still, Alaska and Hawaii survived as possessions for more than half a century before they became states, and one could reasonably fault Soeharto, particularly since tolerance and consultation are such strong Javanese traits; more patience by Jakarta would probably have saved thousands of lives and produced the same end result.

"Despite this major setback," the Australian scholar Michael Leifer wrote in *Indonesia's Foreign Policy*, "Indonesia has retained its regional vision based on an exclusive pattern of relations among resident states, [and] the longstanding suspicion of all external powers has been sustained but tempered with an evident pragmatism. But it is still some distance from assuming the position of a regional power center able to shape that pattern. . . . The gap between aspiration and achievement remains, sustained because quantitative assets such as population and territorial scale remain liabilities. President Soeharto's comment in 1969 that 'we shall only be able to play an effective role if we ourselves are possessed of a great national vitality' is likely to remain valid for the rest of this century."

INDONESIA'S FUTURE:
BALANCING THE EQUATION

Where does Indonesia go from here? Can it sustain the recent high rates of growth and the steady progress it has consistently achieved? Is the *Pançasila* state really a serious candidate for Little Dragonhood? Most signs seem to be positive, not least the government's creative economic policies that have achieved such dramatic growth in value-added manufacturing and nonoil exports in recent years.

Politically, on the other hand, Indonesia is in a quandary, not unlike South Korea and Taiwan before it. Authoritarianism is its political cornerstone, and the New Order has built the foundation for economic takeoff. But the nation must now come to grips with the issue of openness, of greater and more meaningful participation in the political process by those who have heretofore been either dissidents or seen as threats to the system—university students, intellectuals, the Muslims, the press.

Economically Indonesia lags behind both Korea and Taiwan by far more than a decade, and yet it is being pressured to make substantive political changes—both quietly, from the outside, by friends such as the United States, and not so quietly, from the inside, by those who oppose ABRI's continued dominance of domestic politics. But the New Order could easily use another decade of sustained growth, with all that implies for rising living standards, a broader middle class, and higher educational attainment, before having to let go of the reins.

It may well be able to use that time if there is a sixth term for President Soeharto after 1993, but again, the question remains, at what price? Will the domestic pressures then become so uncontrollable that they may erupt volcanically, and the country run amok, as happened in 1974 with the Malari affair? Or can some safety valves be built into the system in the meantime to handle the transition from the harder variety of New Order authoritarianism to a softer style of authoritarian rule, perhaps along the lines of a dominant one-party system as practiced in Singapore, in Japan, or more recently in Korea?

The overriding question is whether change will come gradually, as in Korea and Taiwan, or suddenly, as in the case of the Philippines, where Marcos was thrown out of power in 1986 by Cory Aquino's so-called Yellow Revolution. Indonesians are a gentle, patient people, with a preference for compromise over revolution. But there is a limit even to Javanese tolerance, as the dramatic events of 1965 showed, events that are very much in the minds of most thoughtful Indonesians.

Such as General T. B. Simatupang, an ABRI officer who now heads the Indonesian Council of Churches and is an advocate of a "softer" style of authoritarianism. He unequivocally accepts the role of ABRI in providing the stability necessary for economic growth, but he also argues that change is inevitable.

"I am convinced we can go the right way," he said in a recent interview, referring to the transition to a more liberal and open political economy. "We can't just impose a Western system, but we want to strive for the same principles: respect for the ordinary human being and the law, the control of power, and the recognition that authority is subject to criticism."

The consensus tends toward optimism, but the process will not be automatic.

"The struggle will be between a greater pluralism and a turning inward," Gordon Hein, representative for the Asia Foundation in Jakarta, told me. "What is the future focus of *dwi fungsi*, and can ABRI adjust to an even greater political role? No one knows what the actual mechanisms will be."

Culturally Indonesians prefer strong, centralized leadership, which has been the key to their stability. Greater openness can and will emerge only if the transition process is endorsed at the top. Indonesians know it has to be addressed, but at their pace, not ours. As one senior technocrat put it, it may be better to have a future mediocre ruler and a smooth transition than to have another strong ruler who comes to power through bloodshed.

"I think there is great progress toward democratization, Indonesian style," Rachmat Witoelar told me. "New values for political interaction are being established. But Indonesia cannot change overnight. Young people are pushing for new standards of conduct, and these will come, gradually, in time."

If Indonesia has an Achilles' heel, it may well be education. Human resources development remains a core problem for all the NIEs, and they are in a race against time.

"The level of idleness in Indonesia is stunning," one longtime American observer told me, "and education is a real problem area here. Outside the oil industry, which has been training people here for more than two decades, the overall skill base is still extremely low."

Yet Indonesia's accomplishments in education during the New Order are impressive considering the country's late start. Total schools more than doubled in number between 1971 and 1985, and secondary schools alone doubled *again* between 1985 and 1988, with nearly half the school-age population enrolled. For a diverse nation whose citizens are so widely scattered across so many islands, that is a truly remarkable achievement. But now the focus has to shift even higher, to training more engineers and technical specialists as well as to keeping the pipeline open for bright young technocrats in the public sector.

"This will be a difficult area for us to tackle," admitted Sarwono Kusuma-atmadja, "especially if we try to be somebody we're not. Indonesians are artisans, not precision workers. Therefore, the economic model for us may be Italy or Spain, not Japan or Germany."

Fortunately Indonesia seems to have the built-in advantage of a "reverse brain drain," unlike its neighbors, whose bright young students go overseas, primarily to the United States, for their university and graduate educations and simply stay. Indonesia's students invariably come back; in 1988, 96 percent of them did.

"We have more than 10,000 students studying now at American institutions," said Dorodjatun Kuntjorojakti, "and an equivalent number in Europe and in Australia as well. But the demand for well-trained people is high, because we have another 'reverse brain drain' to worry about. Since government salaries are so low, we are losing too many good people to the private sector."

"There is an awful lot of raiding and pirating going on," confessed Soedradjat. "This is a strong signal that we are lacking in the advanced skills necessary to take us where we want to go—engineers, production specialists, accountants, data processors—the numbers are still too small. We have maybe half a dozen good institutions providing training programs, but I admit it's a real constraint for our expansion in the future."

As these concerns for human resources development indicate, the real threats to Indonesia's stability may be domestic—economic, social, and political—not external in nature.

Consequently, the country has some important challenges to face in the coming years. It must reset education as a top priority— not just the formal, institutional system of public education but also the ways in which knowledge is transmitted to large segments of its society, such as by publishing, which must become freer and less politically constrained.

Demands for social justice, too, must be given serious attention, as the old era of top-down Javanese control gives way to a more liberal, autonomous age and brings with it greater pressure to democratize the political system more fully. Participatory politics is in many ways incompatible with Javanese values that underscore harmony and consensus. But once Indonesia's targeted economic goals have been met and higher growth rates achieved, its social and political institutions also need to modernize to keep pace with growing aspirations, as developments elsewhere in the region (such as Korea and Taiwan) have shown.

Similarly, Indonesia's economic strategy must adhere to its new value-added orientation and not become distracted by temporarily rising commodities prices. Surely the Persian Gulf crisis of 1990, which doubled crude oil prices for OPEC producers, will serve as a temptation to countries like Indonesia to abandon their hard-won gains in manufacturing and manufactured goods exports and fall back on the "easy" days of high margins in low-cost natural resources. Indonesia saw a windfall of $2 billion in oil profits in 1990, and at current production levels every $1-per-barrel increase in world prices would generate about $500 million in additional revenues for the country. To create the employment necessary for 2 million people coming into the work force every year, however, Indonesia must keep its sights set on the manufacturing sector.

By all accounts Indonesia possesses tremendous potential. Its present economic momentum, coupled with the cautious steps toward greater openness, suggest a possible future on the Japanese model, with a single-party authoritarian political system underpinning a turbocharged capitalist economy. Not the high-tech, leading-edge Japan of the 1990s, to be sure, but the fastgrowing, income-doubling Japan of the 1950s and 1960s, moving rung by rung up the value-added ladder of production in the strategic manufacturing sectors. Ultimately it may emerge, like a butterfly from its cocoon, as an Italy or a Spain, as Sarwono said, rather than as a heavy industrial powerhouse like Germany or Japan.

Indonesia's next generation of leaders, many of whom have been interviewed in these pages, give the nation its dynamism and sustain

its drive, positioning the country effectively for the daunting challenges that lie ahead.

The role model for Indonesia's new mystical hero may no longer
be the legendary clown-god of Javanese *wayang*, the traditional
puppet theater, but rather the successful *pribumi* entrepreneur—
young indigenous businesspeople and technocrats who are creating
such a strong desire to win in the hearts of the new generation. The
days of rioting and running amok may be past now, because those
are their own cars they risk setting on fire.

"In human history, 'final' pictures are final until they change,"
Clifford Geertz wrote in his classic work, *Agricultural Involution*.
"But despite the sloganeering about 'winds of change,' 'the awaken-
ing East,' or 'the revolution of rising expectations,' and despite, too,
the real possibility of a totalitarian triumph in Jakarta, there is no
evidence that the major outlines of the Indonesian pattern of adaptation, of the plurality of diverse cultural cores which compose it, are
likely to alter in the foreseeable future. For all the proclaimed, if only
half-believed, optimism at its apex, Indonesia at its base is an anthology of missed opportunities, a conservatory of squandered possibil-
ities."

Geertz wrote those words in the final, chaotic moments of the
Sukarno era, at the end of the disjointed period of Guided Democracy and well before Soeharto had imposed an authoritarian mark on
his New Order that was to follow. Twenty-five years later, following
the obvious successes and clear accomplishments of the Berkeley
Mafia technocrats under ABRI's congealing rule, one wonders
whether, or how, Geertz might be inclined to change that view. In the
past, it is true, optimism may have been only half believed at its
apex, but today that optimism infuses Indonesia's base, giving it an
anthology of bountiful opportunities and a conservatory of incredible potential.

For the more one probes this magnificent archipelago, with its
uncompromising beauty, its rich storehouse of natural resources, and
its incomparable depth of human talent, the more one comes away
with the sense that, for Indonesia, the best is yet to come. As
skeptics greeted the emergence of Meiji Japan more than a century
ago, and nonbelievers relegated a postwar Japan prematurely to the
dustbin of history, so does the conventional wisdom shortchange

Indonesia's prospects. Above all its people, who are warm, open, friendly, and hospitable—traits Americans so often use when describing themselves. As has been said many times before, there is perhaps no country as important or as exciting—or about which Americans know so little.

The rest of the developing world, especially in Africa and Latin America, should be paying closer attention to Indonesia now, both to its impressive recent accomplishments and to the successful policy mix of its present political economy, as it adjusts and adapts to the uncertainties of the future. That is what Little Dragonhood is all about, and it is coming soon for Indonesia, as surely as the sun sets beyond the lush, neatly terraced rice paddies of central Java.

3
THAILAND
The Bangkok Connection

Compared with the traditional system of Siamese governance, democratic institutions [in Thailand] are a new phenomenon. Western constitutional norms have not been internalized, even though military leaders after each coup proclaim "democracy" as their own ideology. Form dominates over substance. In modern Thailand, the most stable institutions have been the monarchy, the military (which dominates the civil bureaucracy), and the Sangha [the Buddhist monastic order]. Side by side with the outcry for freedom, liberty, equality, and social justice is the affirmative statement of "Nation, Religion, and Monarchy."

[But] Western-style constitutional government in Thailand has been highly unstable and ineffectual. While the democratic pattern remains formalistic, traditional autocratic traits have remained pervasive. The legacies of the traditional pattern of authority have worked against effective institutionalization of [a] democratic system of government, and autocratic tendencies still dominate in the attitudes and behavior of both the new Thai elites and the masses.

—Somsakdi Xuto (Ed.), Government and Politics of Thailand

SOUTHEAST ASIA'S LONE STAR

Imagine, for a moment, a direct parallel between the largest country in mainland Southeast Asia and the largest state in the continental United States.

Thailand, like Texas, managed for years to avoid domination by foreign powers, despite the fact that most of its neighbors had been easily colonized. Also like Texas, Thailand shares borders with five

135

other states, now independent but formerly colonies: Burma to the west, once a colony of Britain; Laos to the north, a former French possession; Cambodia and, beyond it, Vietnam to the east, both former fiefdoms of France; and Malaysia, also colonized by the British, to the south.

For centuries Thailand existed in relative isolation from the rest of the world, secure in the benevolent monarchy that was its political cocoon and, again like Texas, strongly independent and priding itself on its uniqueness. The king was all-powerful and Thai society highly feudalistic, based on a strong tradition of loyalty to the crown. Thailand assimilated nomadic migrants from neighboring states with relative ease, much as Texas commonly absorbed newcomers from well beyond its borders.

Thoroughly Buddhist, Thailand's predominantly rural society centered on the local village temple. Thais had the reputation of being a kind, gentle, happy people, long-suffering and tolerant. But when their patience was stretched to the breaking point, it snapped. It was often said of Thais that they were always the last to go to war but the first to kill.

The monarchic kingdom of Thailand managed to survive well into the twentieth century without undergoing systemic change. But in 1932 a handful of Thai generals engineered a coup and ushered in an era of democratic government under a new constitution, dominated by a military elite. In the subsequent half-century Thailand would experience no fewer than two dozen military coups and a dozen different constitutional revisions.

The economy of Thailand was a one-product affair: it depended on rice much as Texas based its wealth on oil. For years it was the only self-sufficient country in Southeast Asia, and producing a consistent rice surplus for export. Thailand was overwhelmingly rural too, with mile after undulating mile of paddy stretching across an endless alluvial plain. Life was simple and uncomplicated, punctuated by the dreary regularity of annual summer monsoons.

Except for Bangkok. The capital was the locus of Thailand's central government bureaucracy, its business elite, its foreign trade, its only deep-water port, its major universities, the Parliament, the military, every foreign legation, all of its industrial factories, which were either wholly or partly foreign-owned, and its only international airport. Bangkok was, above all, the sex and vice capital of Thailand: three-quarters of all foreign visitors were unaccompanied men who came from all over the world to work or to play there.

Today Bangkok *defines* Thailand. The rest of the kingdom is practically a ghost town by comparison.

CULTURAL AND HISTORICAL ROOTS

Thailand, the hub of mainland Southeast Asia, sits like a reverse comma between the Indian Ocean and the South China Sea. It is the site of numerous ancient kingdoms known for their wealth and advanced culture, the first of which was created in the thirteenth century at Sukhothai in the dense hardwood forests bordering the Mae Nam Chao Phraya river, near Burma.

As early as the ninth century B.C. nomadic Mon, Tai, and Khmer tribes from southern China roved across what is now central Thailand, carrying on maritime and commercial trade with India. By the sixth century A.D. the Mon occupied Burma, the Tai populated what is now central Thailand, and the Khmer settled in Cambodia (later to become the great kingdom of Angkor). By the tenth century A.D. the strongest of these tribes had coalesced to become part of Indonesia's dominant Srivijaya Empire, which controlled regional trade.

The Mon, Tai, and Khmer tribes were receptive to the art and literature of India, which brought Hindu concepts to Southeast Asia along with the Sanskrit alphabet. Buddhist missionaries from the Sangha in Ceylon, the formal Buddhist monastic order, introduced Theravada Buddhism to the Tai, and the two religions coexisted, Hindu values dominating the formal culture and Buddhism forming the core of Tai ethical beliefs. Though tolerant, the Tai were repeatedly subdued by the aggressive Burmese and by their nearby Khmer neighbors in Cambodia.

Dialects of the Tai family of languages have been traced to the mountainous plateaus of Yunnan province in southwestern China. The Tai shared an agricultural heritage with the Chinese based on wet-rice cultivation and apportioned land to each family based on rank, as was the custom in Yunnan. In 1238 the Tai successfully defended their rich rice fields from attack by the Khmer and established the first formal kingdom, called Sukhothai.

Thais generally consider the founding of Sukhothai as marking their emergence as a distinct nation; it was at that time that they adopted the Thai name to distinguish themselves from their more aggressive Mon and Khmer neighbors. They established formal diplomatic relations with China, whose emperor was acknowledged to be the nominal overlord of the Thai kingdom. The Sukhothai dynasty also formally developed the Thai written language, based on a Khmer script that was itself derived from Sanskrit.

But this kingdom was short-lived, plagued by weak leaders and subject to domestic rivalries that resulted in the ascension of the combative king of Ayutthaya, located farther south on the Chao Phraya river, about sixty miles north of Bangkok. (The rivalries among these various vassal states of early Thai kingdoms are the precursors of contemporary Thai coups, perhaps the best paradigm for the factional struggles that characterize Thai politics today.)

By the end of the fourteenth century Ayutthaya was considered the strongest power in mainland Southeast Asia. It secured Thailand's eastern frontier by subduing the Khmer, and it pushed westward to stake out a more advantageous border claim with Burma. Ayutthaya was not a unified kingdom but a federation of self-governing vassal states and tributary provinces that maintained allegiance to the king. The states were ruled by members of the royal family who had their own armies and fought constantly among themselves, forming both domestic and occasionally foreign alliances as a means of consolidating power. Ayutthaya existed in much this fashion until the mid–eighteenth century.

During the four centuries of Ayutthaya dominance the Thai king became an absolute monarch whose royalty was derived from divine right. He was the moral model for the Thai people, personifying virtue, revered as a noble father, and considered divine. He stood at the apex of a political and social hierarchy that was highly feudal. The basic social unit was the *muang*, an autonomous communal grouping of extended-family households. Ordinary people registered with the local lord as servants of the king and were pressed into service to till the land, for military duty, or as corvée labor for public works. If a man found the forced labor excessive, he could sell himself into slavery to a more beneficial lord, who then paid a fee to the king as compensation; vestiges of this practice still exist.

Wealth, status, and influence were thus organically interrelated. The degree of control by the elite reflected their elevated status in the hierarchy and was a barometer by which wealth was measured. The king was the largest landholder, allotting rice fields to governors, military commanders, and court officials as payment for their services. Chinese immigrants operated outside this social structure and were not obliged to register for corvée duty, provided they wore their hair in the requisite pigtail. By the sixteenth century the Chinese dominated domestic Ayutthaya commerce and had considerable influence in the civil service as well.

In 1569 Ayutthaya was overrun by armies of attacking Burmese and their hordes of elephants, which decimated the native Thai, destroying both their architectural monuments and their artistic and literary archives. But in a generation Ayutthaya recovered, unified its central authority, and threw the Burmese out. The king now had a monopoly on all manpower and land; ministerial positions, civil service functions, and provincial governorships became inherited positions dominated by a few families connected to the royal family by marriage. But in 1767 Ayutthaya again was invaded by the Burmese, its city destroyed, its greatest art treasures obliterated. Ayutthaya was reduced to ruins, and the country was in chaos. (To this day, in public opinion polls, Thais cite the Burmese as a greater threat to their security than any other foreign power.)

But the Thais were nothing if not resourceful. A young military officer named Taksin organized a quick and successful resistance to the Burmese, pushing them back after a long and bitter war. Taksin abandoned Ayutthaya and moved downstream on the Chao Phraya to establish a new capital in the delta at Thon Buri, part of what is now Bangkok. Having reunited the Thai kingdom, he was given a royal title, but success went to his head: he suffered delusions of divinity and was executed. His successor was Chakkri, another general who became Rama I, the first of three Chakkri kings who gave the Thai kingdom an era of unprecedented political stability that would last until the constitutional era was proclaimed in 1932.

King Mongkut (Rama IV) is the Thai king perhaps best known in the West. In the mid–nineteenth century he engaged the services of a Welshwoman, Anna Leonowens, as tutor in the royal household, an encounter she would popularize in *The English Governess at the Siamese Court* (which Rodgers and Hammerstein rewrote almost a century later as *The King and I*). It was Mongkut who adopted the name Siam for Thailand, derived from a Tai word meaning "dark-skinned." It was Mongkut, too, whose knowledge of Western ways convinced him that Siam must interact as an equal with the European powers to avoid the fate that had befallen China.

In 1855 Mongkut signed Siam's first treaty of friendship and commerce, the Bowring Treaty, with Britain, followed shortly thereafter by similar treaties with the United States and France. These treaties spurred trade with the West, connected the Thai economy to the world monetary system, and brought in Western specialists who helped modernize Siam's legal and administrative systems.

Thailand's first contacts with the West had been Portuguese traders from Malacca in 1511, followed by numerous contacts with the Dutch in Indonesia about a century later. Holland's aggressiveness had encouraged both France and Britain, which eventually sent warships steaming up the Chao Phraya around 1700 as a show of strength. But these incursions sparked a spontaneous outburst against the pushy Europeans, and Thailand closed itself off from the outside world for the next 150 years.

When Mongkut died, his son, Chulalongkorn (Rama V) succeeded him, reigning from 1868 to 1910, and became the first Thai king ever to travel abroad. He continued his father's administrative reforms and broadened them in the 1890s, establishing schools modeled along European lines, abolishing slavery and the old system of corvée labor, and reorganizing the government into specific ministries along functional lines—reforms that were carefully calculated to increase the king's power.

It was during his reign that France moved into Indochina and Britain colonized Burma; Chulalongkorn negotiated separate treaties with each of them that guaranteed Anglo-French recognition of Siam as a neutral and independent buffer between Indochina and Burma. He also passed laws requiring the adoption of Thai surnames, a universal practice in the West but one that would encourage faster and smoother assimilation of the Chinese minority. (Previously the Thais had used only one name; surnames were not necessary since everyone was considered a member of one immense family headed by the king.)

Chulalongkorn's son, Vajiravudh (Rama VI), had only one claim to fame, and that was Siam's decision to declare war on Germany in World War I. His successor, King Prajadhipok (Rama VII), presided over a momentous occasion, however. On June 24, 1932, faced with severe economic problems stemming from the global depression, a group of young military officers engineered a coup d'état against the conservative royal government (but, importantly, not against the king).

A constitution was drafted, and subsequently approved by the king, that provided for a quasi-parliamentary system with executive power resting in the monarch and legislative power vested in a unicameral legislature, half of whose members would be elected by limited suffrage, the other half appointed by the king. Prajadhipok later abdicated without naming a successor. His ten-year-old nephew, Ananda Mahidol, was named to succeed him, reigning as Rama VIII from 1935 to 1946, when the present king, Bhumibol Adulyadej (Rama IX), acceded the throne.

In 1939 the government of Siam officially changed the country's name to Thailand (literally Muang Thai, Land of the Free.) During the Pacific War, Thailand again escaped colonization, this time by Japan, when the government agreed to remain neutral but allowed Japanese forces overland access to Burma and Malaya. Under pressure from Tokyo, Thailand reluctantly declared war against the United States, but the Thai ambassador in Washington refused to deliver the declaration. In 1954 Thailand became a founding member of the Southeast Asia Treaty Organization (SEATO) and was one of the five countries that formed ASEAN in 1967.

Thailand's rapid economic growth in the 1960s was attributable primarily to the massive U.S. military expenditures for the war in Vietnam—there were large American airfields at Udon Thani and U Thapao from which bombing raids against North Vietnamese targets were launched. This was when the popular "domino theory" prevailed—suggesting that first Thailand and then the other states in mainland Southeast Asia would fall to Communist subversion. While that theory subsequently became discredited, Thailand had problems with its own insurgent movement, primarily in the Northeast, but it was ironically brought under control after the United States withdrew from Vietnam in 1975.

Between 1932, when the constitutional monarchy was created, and 1988, when the civilian government of prime minister Chatichai Choonhavan was elected, Thailand experienced a total of twenty-six coups and countercoups and more than a dozen constitutional revisions. Most were peaceful and bloodless, with the notable exception of October 1973, when a quarter of a million people rallied at the Democracy Memorial in Bangkok to express their opposition to a Thai government that had become rigid and inflexible. Troops opened fire on the demonstrators, killing seventy-five and bringing down Prime Minister Thanom.

During the past half-century these coups have occurred in Thailand with almost the same relative frequency and about as peaceably as public elections in functioning democracies like the United States or Great Britain. They reflect the constantly shifting factional alliances in the Thai elite and the military; they have run the full range of political temperament from repressive military dictatorships, including periods of martial law, to more relaxed civilian regimes as with the current Chatichai government. There were even some coups in which the sitting government threw *itself* out of power in order to restore its leadership through stronger factional alliances.

The king is the invisible power behind it all, however, symbolizing both continuity and stability in the Thai state. King Bhumibol has established a record as the longest-reigning monarch. His is a unifying presence, a kind of political glue that prevents the jigsawlike factions from otherwise disintegrating into total chaos. Widely revered by his subjects, the king regularly visits rural Thai villages and is a sponsor of popular environmental projects throughout the country. The overwhelming sense in Thailand today is that regardless of the form of government, as long as the substance of the monarchy prevails, the people will be happy.

That and a booming economy go a long way toward mending domestic political fences. It is ironic that Japan dominates the hyperactive Thai economy today far more than it might have as a would-be colonizer half a century ago. One cannot understand how Thailand has come as far as it has without also understanding how the Japanese helped it get there. Most Thais never tire of reiterating their pride in never having been colonized, yet Thailand's present dependence on Japan has virtually turned that historical fact on its head.

THE THAI ECONOMY

A Japanese Colony by Any Other Name

It doesn't take long for a visitor to Bangkok to realize that Japan is to Thailand much as the United States is to Puerto Rico. This realization begins on the long drive into town from Don Muang International Airport (recently expanded with Japanese money, equipment, and engineering skills). Billboards boosting Japanese products line both sides of the six-lane highway, as prevalent as broadleaf weeds in summer. NEC, Sony, Toshiba, Toyota, JVC, Nikon—companies that have become household words in America are household names in Thailand too.

Honda, Mazda, National (the brand name for Matsushita's Panasonic products in Asia), Mitsubishi, Kawasaki, Canon, Yamaha—you don't have to read *kanji* to distinguish the familiar vertical Japanese ideographs from the native spaghettilike Thai script. The list is endless, the number of billboards virtually uncountable. Except for Esso and Caltex gasoline stations, signs touting American products can literally be counted on the fingers of one hand: 3M, Xerox, 7-Eleven, McDonald's, and 7-Up. There, in a nutshell, is the story of Japanese dominance writ large: the world's highest quality manufactured products competing against the world's most popular fast foods in one of Southeast Asia's dynamic industrializing economies.

Even without the ubiquitous billboards, you might wonder if you were in Tokyo rather than Bangkok: on the streets there is neither a passenger car nor a commercial van that is not Japanese. (My driver, Thongpool, drives a white 1970 Toyota Corona that, judging from its odometer, has been around the world several times now, but he cares for it so lovingly it looks almost brand new.) In 1988 Toyota alone had a 29 percent share of the Thai automobile market, while Mitsubishi and Honda had about 14 percent each. The top six Japanese automakers together controlled 75 percent of the market. (The shares of GM and Ford combined were less than 1 percent.)

In commercial vehicles, too, Japanese dominance is overwhelming. Isuzu had a 29 percent share of all trucks and vans sold in 1988, followed by Toyota with 27 percent and Nissan with 22 percent; together Japanese makers controlled 98.5 percent of the market. Six other foreign truck makers made up the remaining 1.5 percent, of which Ford was the largest with a stunning 0.5 percent share of the Thai market. Four Japanese companies—Honda, Yamaha, Suzuki, and Kawasaki—control the entire Thai market for motorbikes. (All foreign vehicles are assembled locally from either imported or domestically produced components; they contain about 60 percent local content today.) No recent phenomenon, Japan's market-share dominance in transportation equipment is structural and goes back decades, to the time when nearly all manufactured goods were imported.

You have ample time to read the billboards carefully and study the traffic closely, too, because the trip into town, which should take no more than thirty minutes on a reasonably open road, now takes an hour and a half. Traffic has exploded in Bangkok in recent years, and the urban infrastructure has become clogged to the point of gridlock. On average, more than 100,000 new cars and trucks and 350,000 motorbikes have been added to Bangkok's crowded streets every year since 1981. Today an estimated 2 million cars in Bangkok move at an average speed of eight miles per hour. In the city center there are ten major railroad crossings, and an average of 129 trains a day pass over them, each taking ten minutes in passing.

In truth traffic does not move; it *creeps*—four and five lanes wide on the major thoroughfares, as if the entire city were going to the Super Bowl every day, 365 days a year, Sundays included. Frustration levels rise with the thermometer in this tropical version of Manhattan madness: drivers make no effort to seek shortcuts through the back alleys because they, too, are all now bumper-to-bumper. Traffic is so bad it foiled at least one recent coup attempt, in late 1985, by delaying the armed vehicles from capturing their intended targets before government troops could respond. Some city planners devised a unique solution: put loudspeakers at strategic intersections to blare at vehicles that block the crossings. But they found that drivers of air-conditioned cars can't hear behind closed windows, and diesel trucks idle so noisily their drivers can't either: their engines burn up an estimated $1 million in wasted fuel every day.

Bangkok was traditionally known as the Venice of Asia, but you would never guess it today. Many of the capital city's narrower roads were once functioning *klong*, canals that carried waste and debris out of the crowded metropolis to the muddy waters of the Chao Phraya and on into the Gulf of Thailand. The Chao Phraya is Bangkok's swimming hole, bathtub, and toilet combined: two-thirds of the effluent discharged into the river or the canals is untreated sewage. "Lomotil," a Thai friend reminded me. "Don't leave home without it."

Most of the canals have been paved over and now carry small vans, motorbikes, and *tuk-tuks*, Thailand's raucous three-wheeled, motorized pedicabs, adding to the congestion that has become the new symbol of Bangkok today. The city was built on a sandy delta that could comfortably accommodate perhaps 10 percent of the 8 million people that now cram its narrow confines. The population is expected to exceed 9 million by 1991, making Bangkok one of the world's ten largest cities. Bursting at every seam, it has become an urban cul-de-sac, a city that has no place to go. It is sinking into the sand at the rate of two inches a year.

Japanese investment in Thailand is overwhelmingly concentrated in the manufacturing sector and, like everything else, situated predominantly in Bangkok. For several years Japan has been Thailand's number-one foreign investor. In 1987 Japanese firms invested in 200 approved ventures totaling $1 billion; in 1988 nearly 300 investments totaling almost $3 billion were registered. The second most active foreign investor is Taiwan, at $1 billion in 1988; the United States, with a hundred approved projects in 1988 valued at about $700 million, is in distant third place.

In 1985 Japan accounted for 26.7 percent of all foreign investment in Thailand, but by 1988 it was more than half. (America's share slipped from 16.6 percent of the total to less than 10 percent over the same period.) So it is not just on the streets that Japan's presence is felt; in the department stores, like Daimaru and Tokyu, which are also Japanese, all the home appliances and electronic equipment—TVs, VCRs, rice cookers, stereo sets, telephones, and personal computers—are made in Thailand with Japanese management, capital, and technology. As one Thai friend casually remarked, "About the only thing not Japanese in this country is my wife."

There being no better source on Japan's direct investments than the Japanese themselves, I made my way (slowly) across town to the

Japanese embassy to talk about these rising investment levels with Shoichi Ikuta, MITI's representative in Bangkok.

"Japanese investment in Thailand is overwhelmingly in production," Ikuta told me, "with nearly 90 percent of it in the manufacturing sector. Those figures are high, I guess, when compared to the United States, because more than half of your investments here are in energy-related areas, like petroleum refining and chemicals, or in import-marketing services or hotel construction. But they are consistent with our concentration on manufacturing as a priority in all overseas markets."

MITI regularly sends its people to Japanese embassy and consular staffs abroad to work closely with private businessmen, to monitor economic data, and above all to collect vital intelligence and statistics on the market, which are regularly fed back to Tokyo. In 1989 Ikuta was a young MITI bureaucrat on his first overseas assignment, having been in Bangkok for about two years. Like most Japanese who represent their country abroad, he was neatly attired and well groomed, his skin darkened from prolonged exposure to the hot Thai sun. His knowledge of the market was, as one would expect, detailed and thorough. We discussed recent trends, and I asked him about Bangkok's overtaxed infrastructure being a barrier to further investment.

"No question about it," he said matter-of-factly. "It now takes container trucks nearly half a day to make an hour-long trip from the industrial estates north of the city fifty kilometers down to Klong Toey, the port area south of Bangkok, where ships line up six deep in the harbor waiting to off-load or take on new cargo. They have to wait four or five days now to get an open berth. This is one reason the Board of Investment has put such a high priority on developing new estates outside Bangkok, but that will take time. Meanwhile we're beginning to see a lot of new investment flowing to Indonesia and Malaysia, where the infrastructure is still adequate."

True to form, Ikuta provided me with what was by far the most comprehensive supply of statistical data on the Thai political economy—all in Japanese, of course, but detailed, precise, and very up to date. In addition to his own 150-page report for Tokyo, which covered social, cultural, and political trends as well as the requisite sections on the economy and foreign investment, he managed to procure for me the two most recent annual publications of the Japanese Chamber of Commerce in Thailand, which went into even more detail: the 1988 edition ran 637 pages, the 1989 edition 483, and both contained as much information about each industry sector as they did about the government agencies and bureaucrats who supervised them.

The U.S. embassy has not quite made it into the information age: its reports are considerably shorter and much less thorough than those prepared by the Japanese. The staff gave me a twelve-page document published regularly by the Department of Commerce called "Thailand: Foreign Economic Trends," which contains data about a year out of date, and a more current twenty-nine-page memo titled "Thailand: Investment Climate Statement." The American Chamber of Commerce annual directory contains lots of nice portrait photos of its members together with a typically legalistic description of the procedures American investors should follow when coming to Thailand, including how and where to get a visa, but it is otherwise also short on substance. Tom Seale, a former army officer who is the AmCham's executive director in Bangkok, is well aware of Japan's competitive surge. The way he put it to me was, "We're being left behind in a cloud of dust."

All these publications, the U.S. pamphlets included, depend on two Thai institutions for their hard statistical data. One is the National Economic and Social Development Board (NESDB), which is attached to the prime minister's office and regularly cranks out the government's white papers. The other is the Board of Investment.

The Board of Investment (BOI) is also an adjunct of the prime minister's office and was created some years ago to facilitate the complicated licensing procedures and red tape necessary to clear inward foreign investments. Among foreigners it is known as the government's "Bus Lane," a not inappropriate nickname that conveys the image of investment applications scooting rather quickly through a congested bureaucratic maze, much as Thai buses (try to) navigate unimpeded through Bangkok traffic. BOI also formulates Thailand's industrial policies. In 1986 BOI approved 431 foreign investment projects worth $2.4 billion; in 1987, 1,058 projects valued at $8.4 billion; and in 1988, 2,083 ventures worth $13.3 billion, more than half of which were Japanese.

Ikuta had agreed to accompany me on a visit to several Japanese factories just north of Bangkok in the Nava Nakorn industrial estate, an immense compound of some 12,500 acres acquired by BOI to help foreign manufacturers by providing incentives such as access to a stable source of electric power, waste-water treatment, up-to-date telecommunications facilities, and a supply of reliable Thai workers. Nava Nakorn, which means "new town" in Thai, has more than ninety factories in operation and is Thailand's largest industrial park.

We crawled through the early-morning traffic at a turtle's pace, leaving the city in a stream of cars and trucks that seemed as long as the line coming in. As I glanced out the window at the urban landscape, I noticed that Bangkok is not unlike Tokyo in other respects as well. It is by and large a concrete city, with row after row of squat gray buildings totally lacking in character and charm. Absent are the undulating waves of red sun-bleached roof tiles that give Jakarta such distinctive charm. And despite the steamy climate, few trees provide shade or add a touch of softness to the paved hardness. During the wet season the tropical rains often turn the city into a torrent of flooded streets; this was the dry season, though, and the thoroughfares were hot and dusty. Here and there I could see the familiar rooflines of the famous Buddhist *wat*, golden temples that glisten magically in the bright sunshine. Once out of Bangkok, however, the rest of Thailand becomes flat and stays flat, as one Thai friend remarked, "forever."

We drove through the main gate at Nava Nakorn, and familiar Japanese names appeared in rapid succession as we passed by factory after factory in the huge industrial park. Mitsuboshi Belting (industrial belts). Nisshin Denki (electric cables). Mizuki Denki (ditto). Musashi Auto Parts (components). Musashi Denki (electrical systems). Sanyo (home appliances). Fujikura (more electric cables). Takachiho Chemicals. Tomy (toys). One nagging question was unavoidable: *where were the Americans?*

Noboru Isowa, on his first overseas assignment, is director of the international division for Tomy (Thailand), Ltd., one of Japan's largest toy makers, which has had a manufacturing facility in Nava Nakorn since early 1988. Appearing relatively cool in the ubiquitous open-necked, short-sleeved safari suit, he gave us a tour of Tomy's automated assembly lines as he explained the factory's operations.

"Ninety-four percent of our output is for export," he said proudly, "about a third direct to Japan and two-thirds via our distribution center in Hong Kong to other overseas markets. We employ about 600 people in this plant; they work an eight-hour shift, although we keep our plastic injection molding machines operating twenty-four hours a day."

The majority of the workers busy on the assembly line were young women, Isowa told us, teenagers mostly, who commuted to work each day on a bus provided by Tomy. They were paid seventy-eight baht a day, which was about $3, the standard industrial wage in Thailand (and about three times Indonesia's average of $1 a day). They also received a minimum bonus of one month's salary every year, he said, and more as their output and experience increased.

"Thais are very good quality workers," Isowa explained. "They learn quickly and well and do exactly as they are taught."

I watched a pair of nimble-fingered girls assemble small battery operated police cars as we walked by. They concentrated intently as they inserted miniature plastic steering wheels, windshields, and colorful roof lights onto a preassembled chassis. One of them looked up and smiled as she placed the finished toy in its box. I said a word or two in Thai (the only greeting I knew), and her smile broadened into a wide grin.

The production area was air-conditioned—a necessity in Thailand's relentless tropical heat—and brightly lit, a pleasant working environment under any conditions. Each young worker wore sneakers, slacks, and a light blue Tomy blouse, the company's standard uniform. Across the hall, where the injection molding process took place, long lines of Toshiba equipment automatically stamped out parts and components that would later be assembled by hand and exported overseas—exports that were technically Thai but for all intents and purposes Japanese.

Not far from Nava Nakorn, near the ancient capital of Ayutthaya, Citizen Watch Co., Ltd., had just opened a new plant, so Ikuta and I drove out to have a look. The managing director of Royal Thai Citi Co., Ltd., was Yutaka Kuroda, an older man with considerable overseas experience, who met us at the entrance and escorted us through his factory.

As I listened to Kuroda's description of how Citizen had built its investment in Thailand, it became clear that his company was typical of Japanese corporate investments overseas. It had formed a partnership with a prominent Thai businessman, Dilok Mahadumrongkul, who served as an appointed senator in the upper house of Parliament and thus had the requisite political connections (he also owned 20 percent of the company). Of an $8 million initial investment about $2 million represented Citizen's paid-in capital, the balance a combination of fixed assets, equipment, and working capital.

When the BOI approvals came through, Citizen purchased several acres of land and contracted with a Japanese engineering company, Shimizu Construction, to build the plant. Production equipment was imported from Japan through Japanese trading companies in Japanese containers on Japanese ships, financed by the Bangkok branch of Citizen's Japanese bank, insured by a Japanese fire and marine company, off-loaded at the Klong Toey dock with Japanese cranes and forklift trucks, and transported to the plant site by local affiliates in Japanese commercial vehicles. Very thorough and very smart.

"We received our BOI approval in August 1988," Kuroda was telling us, "started construction that September, and by February 1989 we were up and running. We employ 140 people in our first stage of operations, all of whom have at least a middle school education. Because we are in Ayutthaya and not in Bangkok, we have a different compensation schedule and can pay our workers ten baht less—they make about $2.60 a day compared to the $3 standard. Otherwise the benefits are roughly the same: transportation, health and medical insurance, and subsidized lunches that cost employees only five baht, or about 20¢."

Like the Tomy facility we had just seen, Citizen's factory was clean, neat, well-lit, and air-conditioned. The workers assembling some rather basic wristwatch models were clad identically in Citizen jackets, as, needless to say, was Kuroda.

Glancing at the production lines, I could see that the major equipment was Japanese: Yamazaki machine tools, Oki Denki milling machines, Sakaguchi Electric testing equipment, Eifuku Sangyo wrapping and sealing machines, Citizen's own make of quartz accuracy testers, and Vibrograf manual testers from Osaka. The few pieces of equipment that were *not* Japanese came from elsewhere in

Asia: small West Lake drill presses from mainland China, Chit Hong presses from Taiwan, and simple watch case milling machines made in Hong Kong. There wasn't a single piece of American equipment in the place.

"We have one line fully operational now," Kuroda told us, "and will probably expand to three lines next year. We are assembling only wristwatches for the time being, which we air-freight to our distribution center in Hong Kong for reexport to third markets. The precision works we import preassembled from Japan and just mill the watch cases here. Our next expansion phase will include wall clocks, and the final phase will produce the more sophisticated timepieces."

Kuroda escorted us back to his office, a small, spartan space toward the front of the factory. Citizen's inspirational "5-S" slogan—*seiketsu, seito, seiri, seiso, shitsuke*—was prominently displayed on the wall behind his desk. Roughly translated, they stand for neatness, proper behavior, order, cleanliness, and discipline—not at all inappropriate for a manufacturer of precision products.

When I excused myself briefly and stepped into the men's room adjoining his office, I suddenly discovered the answer to that nagging question of where all the American equipment was now going. As my precious bodily fluids flowed into a brand-new bright-blue vitreous porcelain bowl, my eyes riveted on the unmistakable logo of the premier manufacturer of bathroom fixtures in the United States: American Standard. That anecdotal evidence was confirmed on subsequent visits to most factories in Thailand and practically everywhere else: Japanese equipment dominated the production rooms, American equipment the bathrooms.

After Ikuta and I bade Kuroda farewell, we decided to visit the ancient ruins of Ayutthaya nearby on our way back into Bangkok. "Rush hour" is a modern-day oxymoron in most major cities, no less so even on the outskirts of Bangkok, regardless of the time of day, so we took our time as we crept through the shapeless Thai countryside. The dusty brown rice paddies, parched and dry now, stretched to the horizon in all directions, bringing back memories of the formless desolation I had seen so much of while growing up in Texas.

The bell-shaped stone towers and conical spires of Ayutthaya's monuments were in a state of cared-for disrepair that reminded me of similar ruins at the Parthenon in Athens or the buried city at

Ephesus, where Paul once preached. Vestiges of history, to be sure, but proud ones, evidence of a different kind of achievement, centuries ago, in an age when accomplishment was measured not by the quality of its technological competence but by the grandeur of its architectural icons. The same stray dogs seemed to be there, too, roving about in search of scraps tossed away by passing tourists. Small armies of peddlers massed at the entrance and hawked typical trinkets; most of them were young women who would clearly be better off working in one of the Japanese factories.

Japan dominates not only Thailand's domestic economy but its foreign trade as well, as we shall see. The two countries have long had a close commercial relationship, but it became practically incestuous after 1985. That was the year the United States decided to part with one ineffective macroeconomic policy—benign neglect of the dollar—and replace it with another: dollar devaluation. Following the Plaza Accord in September of that year, which depreciated the dollar against major OECD currencies, the Japanese yen began a process of appreciation that virtually doubled its value in eighteen months.

Washington's public policy makers undoubtedly figured the strong yen would put a crimp in Japan's overseas competitiveness and help shrink America's trade deficit, which was running about $50 billion a year with Japan and comprising fully *half* of its global deficit. But instead of wimping out, which the Japanese (in peace or at war) rarely do, major Japanese corporations began a massive shift of their lower-value-added manufacturing processes from Japan to lower-wage, weaker-currency countries like Thailand, Indonesia, and Malaysia, creating new overseas production centers like those at Tomy and Citizen.

The strategy has helped Japan retain its price competitiveness in manufactured exports; protect market share in its key industrial markets, America and Europe; preserve, if not actually increase, corporate profit and operating margins; strengthen bilateral relations with its important Asian markets; reinforce its need to stay lean and mean in foreign trade; restructure its own economy from export-led to domestic-led growth; keep the higher-valued-added manufacturing processes at home; and spur capital spending on new plant and equipment to historic highs.

The results, three and four years later, have been spectacular. By the second quarter of 1986 Japan's domestic economy was expanding at the highest rate among OECD countries. Capacity utilization rates in its manufacturing sector rose from less than 90 percent to more than 100 percent between 1986 and 1989. Average profit margins for manufacturers jumped from just over 4 percent in 1984 to nearly 6 percent in 1989. R&D as a percentage of sales rose from 6 percent to 7 percent. Corporate debt was slashed and stockholders' equity radically increased: during 1988 Japanese corporations raised more than $100 billion in new equity, compared to only $20 billion for all U.S. firms (reflecting the continuing influence of LBOs). And for the same twelve-month period Japanese companies outspent their American rivals on new plant and equipment investment as well—$521.4 billion to $494.8 billion, a two-to-one per capita advantage.

Meanwhile, as a further result of this restructuring process, direct exports from Japan dropped from an average 34 percent of sales to 27 percent between 1986 and 1989, while average overseas production rose from about 4 percent of consolidated sales to nearly 6 percent. In three years overseas production as a percentage of sales for the league leaders had jumped even higher: Hitachi from 20 percent to 35 percent, Toshiba from 23 to 40 percent, Matsushita from 26 to 43 percent, Sony from 30 to 35 percent, Honda from 29 to 38 percent, Toyota from 12 to 20 percent. When it came to overseas production, Thailand was one of the chosen few: the baht was weak, BOI incentives were strong, and industrial wages were but a fraction of the level prevailing in Japan.

The effects of Japan's supercharged growth in overseas production were clearly felt in the domestic Thai economy. Thailand's GNP, which was growing at an average annual rate of about 4 percent in 1985 and 1986, took off in 1987 with a jump start from all this Japanese investment. It grew at 8.4 percent in 1987, 11 percent in 1988, and 8 percent again in 1989, giving Thailand a total GNP of some $60 billion and a per-capita income of just over $1,000 by 1989. But averages mask the figures for Bangkok: average population density overall in the kingdom is about a hundred people per square kilometer; in Bangkok there are 4,000 inhabitants per square kilometer, and its per-capita income is closer to $3,000. So while Thailand may not have achieved the status of a newly industrializing *country*,

Bangkok could well be considered a newly industrializing *city*.

GNP macroeconomic growth rates also mask sectoral changes taking place at the micro level. Agricultural production, which accounted for nearly 25 percent of GNP in 1980, had dropped to less than 17 percent by 1988, and manufacturing output had risen from 21 percent to 24 percent of GNP in the same period. But two-thirds of the Thai work force were still employed in agricultural production as of 1988, reflecting a high degree of mechanization in the manufacturing sector, again partially due to the strong levels of Japanese investment.

Thailand's principal agricultural products are rice (it produced some 20 million tons in 1988, a good year), sugarcane (32 million tons), tapioca (22 million tons), and maize (about 5 million tons). One-half of the kingdom's agricultural commodities are consumed domestically; half are exported. In 1988 Thailand earned $1 billion each from exports of rice and tapioca (cassava) and another $1 billion from overseas sales of rubber.

As mentioned in Chapter 1, Thailand includes under manufactured goods anything that is processed. Of Thailand's top twenty export products only a handful can reasonably be called *manufactured*, in the sense that Japan and the Little Dragons use the term.

In 1988, for example, Thailand exported nearly $2.3 billion worth of textiles and garments, about $500 million worth of integrated circuits, some $400 million worth of footwear, around $200 million worth of steel pipes and ball bearings, and about $200 million worth of wooden furniture, out of $16 billion in total exports. Almost all of its other major exports were processed commodities.

Still, Thailand's year-to-year export growth rate has been impressive: 21 percent in 1986, 29 percent in 1987, 36 percent in 1988, 33 percent in 1989. Unfortunately, so has the annual growth rate for imports: 30 percent in 1987, 47 percent in 1988, 37 percent in 1989. As a result Thailand has been running a chronic balance of payments deficit in its merchandise trade account averaging close to $3 billion a year. And nowhere is that deficit more apparent than in its bilateral relationship with Japan. In fact, were it not for Japan, Thailand's overall trade account would practically be in balance.

Three countries account for nearly half of Thailand's total

exports: the United States takes about 20 percent (mostly textiles and garments), Japan 16 percent, and Singapore nearly 9 percent (virtually all of Singapore's food is imported from Thailand). The balance is roughly split between Europe and Asia. But Japan alone accounts for nearly one-third of Thailand's total imports; the United States furnishes about 14 percent and Singapore 7 percent. A whopping 75 percent of Thailand's imports are higher-value-added capital goods, intermediate products, and manufactured components, most of which are supplied by Japan. It comes as no surprise, then, that in 1985 Thailand's bilateral trade deficit with Japan was $1.6 billion; in 1986, $1.2 billion; in 1987, $1.7 billion; and in 1988, $3.2 billion.

The textile sector is Thailand's leading export industry, with some $2.3 billion in 1988 exports, about 15 percent of the country's total (and more than half of all its manufactured exports). Garments accounted for about half the sectoral total, yarns and fabrics the balance. By the early 1980s, after more than two decades of rapid though uneven growth, the industry slumped. Small, local companies tended to specialize in a single product line, such as polyester fabric or cotton cloth, while the large, foreign-affiliated, vertically integrated firms dominated production and, above all, exports. These included several Japanese textile giants such as Teijin and Toray (along with their huge trading company partners), half of whose total production was outside Japan.

The Ministry of Industry was responsible for supervising textiles, but BOI held all the incentive cards. In the late 1970s, for example, as one incentive, it stipulated that all Thai firms had to export four times the value of their imported machinery within five years. When many companies failed to meet those targets, BOI simply adjusted its requirements, preferring instead to control output, and the industry became saddled with excess capacity. Complete bans on the establishment of new factories were implemented in 1978, 1980, 1981, and 1984; control over capacity was BOI's industrial policy tactic of choice.

In 1984, though, for the first time, machinery imports also became subject to Ministry of Industry approval. Two things happened: new machinery was smuggled illegally into the country, and some factory expansion projects proceeded without the necessary approvals. Illegal plants soon made up about *one-fifth* of total industry capacity, but rather than cracking down, the ministry simply granted amnesties during which the illegal plants could be registered. (This process, typically Thai, was exacerbated by two social phenomena, as we shall see: conflict avoidance, otherwise known as saving face, and corruption.)

In the 1960s Japan's favored foreign investment sites for textile production were Korea, Taiwan, Thailand, and Hong Kong; prior to 1973 about *four-fifths* of total capital and employment in the Thai textile industry was being provided by Japanese joint ventures. In the 1970s, because of perceived political instability (as a consequence of the many coups), Japan bypassed Thailand and focused instead on Korea, Taiwan, and Indonesia. But after the yen began appreciating rapidly in late 1985, Japanese investment in textiles returned to Thailand in a big way. In the first half of 1987 alone BOI approved nine new Japanese textile investments; by the end of that year Thai textile and garment exports to Japan had jumped by 50 percent over 1986, and about half of Thailand's total textile exports were being generated by Japanese joint ventures.

The dominance of Japanese over American firms in the higher-productivity, higher-value-added manufacturing sectors in Thailand (as in most markets) has become a matter of some concern to former Prime Minister Chatichai Choonhavan.

"America doesn't compete enough with Japan," he said rather wistfully in a recent interview. "I don't want my children to speak Japanese; I want them to speak English."

It was also an important issue to Banharn Silpa-archa, who was Thailand's minister of industry when I spoke to him in mid-1989.

"The U.S. looks at Thailand as if it were a small country and underdeveloped," Banharn said in his raspy voice as we sat in his spacious office at the ministry in central Bangkok. "Americans also tend to be risk-averse and very political, whereas the Japanese are risk takers, more action-oriented, less ideological. The Japanese come to Thailand, load up on information, study the market, analyze it in detail, and then bring in their capital and their technology, set up their factories, and make things. We would like to see more American investment in Thailand, to avoid an overdependence on Japan, but after we create the incentives it's up to you to come in."

Now minister of the interior and a member of the lower house, representing Suphanburi province, Banharn also had served as minister of agriculture and minister of communication and received the Knight Grand Cordon (Special Class) of the Most Exalted Order of the White Elephant for his long years of public service. When I asked him whether illegal textile machinery was still a problem for the industry, he refused even to acknowledge that the problem existed.

"Totally wrong information," he said, wagging a finger at me from his large, overstuffed, antimacassared chair. "Before any equipment can come into the country, it has to be cross-checked between BOI and customs, and before it can be installed my ministry has to approve the license. Market mechanisms drive the textile business. The industry is self-policing."

While in Bangkok, I decided to test the product quality of these supposedly smuggled looms by purchasing two shirts in a typical Thai store. Within a week the buttons had popped off the sleeve of one and the collar had come unstitched on the other. It may be a while before Thailand garners even South Korea's hard-earned accolade as the Land of the Almost Perfect. (I also bought a $9.95 Rolex knockoff, which worked fine until I left for Singapore some weeks later, when the minute hand began to dangle limply at the bottom of the watch face, hovering permanently between twenty-five and thirty-five minutes past the hour. Then, when I tried to adjust it by winding the stem, the crystal popped out. Rolex has little to fear, it seems to me, from Thai abuses of intellectual property rights.)

Subin Pinkayan, now Thailand's foreign minister but minister of commerce when I saw him, had a somewhat different perspective on the U.S.–Japan imbalance.

"Statistically, one country alone accounts for virtually all of Thailand's global trade deficit," admitted the former deputy minister of finance and minister of university affairs, "and we would certainly like Japan to buy more from us. But we run a small trade surplus with the United States, and yet America has such negative feelings toward us. When Washington eliminated the GSP, the Thai public felt strongly that this was unfair. It is true that we have a number of unresolved issues—tobacco, to be sure, and intellectual property rights—but when the Thai government is seen by the public as caving in to foreign pressure, it reacts very strongly. That's part of our heritage in never having been colonized."

Lean and trim, Pinkayan is from the Northwest, a native of

Chiang Mai, the largest city outside Bangkok, and a graduate of Thailand's elite Chulalongkorn University. He earned his master's degree at the Asian Institute of Technology in Bangkok, which is supported by Japanese capital, management, and technical training, and obtained his Ph.D. in civil engineering from the University of Colorado. He looked younger than his fifty-five years. In mentioning the GSP he was referring to an early 1989 decision by Washington to revoke special trading privileges for about $165 million worth of Thai products—artificial flowers, ceramic floor tiles, and wooden furniture—in retaliation against Thailand's refusal to grant copyright protection for American pharmaceuticals and software.

Thailand also bans the import of cigarettes. A state monopoly controls the domestic Thai market for tobacco products and officially permits only the sale of locally made goods, but there is widespread (though officially unacknowledged) smuggling of foreign cigarettes, which can be purchased readily at just about any street-corner tobacconist in Bangkok, at market prices.

I suggested that American firms' moving more aggressively into the Thai market might help restore the balance, and Pinkayan responded, "I don't know why U.S. firms are slower to react than the Japanese, but the Japanese are *very* aggressive here, investing nonstop in new plant and equipment. We would like to see the Americans invest here the same way the Japanese are doing: actively, in manufacturing, and with large amounts of capital. The few American manufacturers already here seem to be very happy."

Seagate, the largest manufacturer of disk drives in America, if not the world, is one of those happy firms. When I met with its senior management, they told me that nearly two-thirds of their assembly line technicians—mostly women—had the equivalent of a high school education and that their yields in Thailand were 15 percent higher than those of their flagship operations in Singapore. Seagate is the largest foreign employer in Thailand, too, with about 13,000 people. Labor, including overhead, accounts for less than 5 percent of the cost of producing a disk drive, they said; important factors are data communications, operator skills, and materials sourcing. The company had recently moved another full-drive line into its Thai plant, which was now operating at capacity. And they would gladly expand further, but the company's policy on global diversification militated against it; Spain would likely be the next target.

But Seagate is just one American firm—an exception—and the Japanese are coming to Thailand *in droves*.

"The Thais love learning, as most Asians do," said Michael Parrott, the general manager of Glaxo (Thailand) Ltd., as we had lunch in the British Club overlooking two finely manicured lawn tennis courts, arguably the only wide expanse of green in central Bangkok. "Marketing is our biggest problem, but in sales, administration, data processing, and production, the Thais are extremely capable, and fast learners."

Glaxo is one of the United Kingdom's giant pharmaceutical companies, with operations all over the world. Parrott, a senior executive with extensive overseas experience in Africa and the Middle East as well as in Asia, had been in Thailand for about four years when we met. He is sensitive to the problem of intellectual property rights but appears considerably more relaxed about it than his American counterparts.

"There must be nearly 200 local manufacturers of drug products in Thailand," he said with a shrug of his shoulders, "and of these, only three or four do any copying to any great degree. There are also about 250 registered importers, and since communication with government departments is not easy, as with bureaucracies all over the world, you have to spend a lot of time walking your products through the regulatory process. We have about 220 people working for us here, and someone goes over to the ministries *every day* to follow up on our applications for drug approvals."

All the foreign capital flowing into Thailand cancels out the trade deficit and enables Thailand to generate a small balance of payments surplus of about $1 billion each year. As a result the kingdom's international reserves have risen from about $1.7 billion in 1984 to just over $8 billion in 1989, and the Bank of Thailand's accommodative monetary policies (which include the tactic of keeping the baht relatively stable against the dollar, despite the yen's rise) have been successful, too, holding the average annual rate of inflation under 4 percent since 1981.

But the backlog of pressing infrastructure projects—new highways, roads, bridges, overpasses, and port facilities—has pushed the government to commit about $15 billion between 1989 and 1992 (with an equivalent amount from the private sector) and caused its foreign borrowing to soar. Thailand's total external debt had already doubled from $10.8 billion in 1981 to nearly $20 billion in 1988. It is constrained by an official ceiling that limits new borrowings to a maximum of $1 billion a year, but it is a limit that many argue should be doubled.

Bolstering the Infrastructure

One man is responsible for overseeing the coordination of new infrastructure projects in Bangkok, and he is its extremely popular governor, General Chamlong Srimuang. Retired from active service now, "Uncle Chamlong," as he is called, was a career military officer educated at the Chulachomklao Royal Military Academy; he rose to prominence as a signal company commander in the army, helping to quell the Communist insurgency years ago, and later obtained an advanced degree in management from the U.S. Navy's graduate school in Monterey.

"Lots of people, lots of problems," he said with a tight, no-nonsense smile in response to my query about the city's daunting physical needs. "It's the same with big cities everywhere. Our problems are not so large that we cannot solve them, but we need money, and the BMA [Bangkok Metropolitan Administration] prevents Bangkok from borrowing, so we have to use available tax revenues only. Three-quarters of all taxes collected in Thailand come from Bangkok. And tax evasion is a big problem here, as it is in any Third World capital. But not all of the streets in Bangkok come under our authority. Some are supervised by the government's Mass Transit Authority, others by the National Highway Department, so coordination of policy is also part of the problem. Theoretically, we Thais are not supposed to have conflict because we are all related, but we do. I have sole responsibility for all the dirty stuff: street cleaning, garbage collection, sewage."

When I met him at his spartan office in the BMA building, Chamlong was sporting a burr haircut and had a lean, hard look about him, the result of allowing himself just one meal a day, a disciplined Buddhist diet of vegetables and rice. I asked him about

Skytrain, the elevated monorail project that has been in gestation for some time, and about a possible subway to ease congestion.

"The Canadians made a successful bid for the Skytrain project," he told me, "but the unsuccessful bidders have appealed in protest, so I don't know when that will move forward. And a subway is technically feasible but extremely costly. The Japanese tell us it would have to be built over the canals, so financially that is probably too expensive for us to undertake. We're trying our best to improve things, but it will take time."

Could regular contacts with Singapore, its nearest major counterpart and long a model for city planning, help? "Singapore is very strict," replied Chamlong. "It has only 2.5 million people, and when Lee Kuan Yew says jump, people obey. From a man who never forgives, orders are seldom ignored. But Bangkok has more than 8 million people, 15 percent of our total population. We can't replicate Singapore's example. We don't have an authoritarian form of government here."

So long as policy coordination remains difficult, Bangkok's streets will remain clogged. No one I spoke to could suggest the name of the city planner who laid them all out, but he deserves honorable mention in the *Guinness Book of Records*: on most major thoroughfares, like Rama IV Road and Ploenchit Road and New Petchburi, all six lanes wide, automobile traffic flows in one direction in five lanes, leaving one lane dedicated for buses traveling in the opposite direction. This has given rise to a recent (and tragic) anecdote in the form of a query: What were the famous last words of an American tourist in Thailand? Answer: What's a bus lane? (The well-known and highly respected American scholar Walter Vella was killed by a bus on a visit to Bangkok because he was watching only the flow of cars to his right before he stepped into the street.)

Bangkok's considerable physical infrastructure deficiencies, along with Thailand's mushrooming merchandise trade deficit, fears of growing protectionism by the United States, inadequate technical manpower, and the overconcentration of industry in the Bangkok area could all be major constraints on Thailand's continued economic growth. Demand for steel and cement have skyrocketed in recent years due to three unrelated factors: new hotel construction to accommodate a constantly rising influx of foreign tourists; new factory construction, mostly Japanese, as we have seen; and a nation-wide ban on logging, which the prime minister put into effect in 1988 following severe mud slides that had occurred in areas severely deforested by loggers. (Twenty years ago more than half of Thailand's land area was forested, but today less than 20 percent is.)

In an attempt to shift new industrial investment away from Bangkok, BOI has adjusted its incentive schemes to favor the more distant provinces. Beginning in 1989, new investments in Bangkok and its five contiguous provinces no longer qualified for tax exemption on machinery, equipment, or corporate profits, but investments farther out—to the southeast, for example, in Chachoengsao or Chonburi, straddling the Gulf of Thailand some hundred miles away—could claim a 50 percent tax reduction on machinery and a complete exemption on all corporate taxes for a period of three years.

BOI was also pushing ahead with the massive, multibillion-dollar Eastern Seaboard Development Project at Map Ta Phut in Chonburi province, about eighty-five miles southeast of Bangkok. A government-controlled agency, the National Petrochemical Corporation, has been created to provide feedstock from the world's longest undersea gas pipeline in the Gulf of Thailand to connect gas and condensate deposits with what will be Thailand's largest petrochemical project. When Map Ta Phut goes on-line in 1992, it will produce a complete line of petrochemicals and derivatives for both domestic consumption and export.

"The easy phase of our economic development is over," Staporn Kavitanon, deputy secretary general of BOI, told me. "Now we have to lure more investment in those sectors that are primarily export-oriented, substantially increase employment, are willing to locate in the distant provinces, promote constructive technology transfer, and help upgrade Thai product quality."

It was now becoming apparent that no two Thais had either the same first or last name, a throwback to Rama V and his adoption of surnames for the Thai people. (In several weeks of traveling about the country I never once met two Thais with the same surname.) Staporn—or, more correctly, khun Staporn, khun meaning "Mr."—was a large, heavyset man with a very can-do attitude.

"Thailand has a resilient and dynamic economy with a well-diversified product structure, abundant natural resources, a large and productive labor force, a growing domestic market, a wide range of services, and a population whose average age is less than thirty," he said when asked whether he felt the constraints might outweigh Thailand's considerable strengths. "True, we have infrastructure problems today, but it is just a question of time. *Mai pen rai.*"

Mai pen rai: "No problem."

If ever there were an expression that captured the essence of a culture, this was it. The Thais have an uncommonly optimistic and upbeat attitude that is at once refreshing and yet disconcerting. It is a manner that gives the Thai society such remarkable resilience, but it also suggests a hint of unreality, like the inability to cope with Bangkok's daunting infrastructure problems or the continued economic dominance by Japan. Chatichai Choonhavan has become known as the *mai pen rai* prime minister because of his frequent use of the term.

Boosting Manpower

"No problem" is also the attitude many Thais have toward manpower development in the face of their rapid economic growth. For a country fewer than half of whose primary school graduates go on to high school, meeting the demands of an increasingly sophisticated economy is indeed a daunting task. The numbers simply aren't there, in terms of either the eligible students or the technical institutes necessary for training them in advanced skills like production management, data processing, basic science, and engineering. And that has some rather serious implications for immigration, too; with insufficient Thais available to manage the economy, foreigners (Japanese, mainly) will have to do it for them.

"The number of potential scientists and engineers in Thailand . . . is lower than that of Indonesia, the Philippines, Singapore, and Korea," the Thailand Development Research Institute concluded in a recent report, "while the number of potential technicians is much lower than that of Indonesia and Korea. In fact the ratio of total science and technology manpower per 10,000 population in Thailand is the lowest among [all] Asian countries."

Japan, Asia's front-runner, has a total of 49.6 scientists and engineers per 10,000 population, compared to 24.4 for Korea, 7.3

for Indonesia, and 4.8 for Thailand. The technical manpower potential, defined as the ability to train suitable personnel for the future, based on available institutions and students coming out of the pipeline, is even lower: Korea has 524.8 potential scientists and technicians per 10,000 population, Singapore 256.7, Indonesia 78.6, and Thailand only 13.8. The *total* number of Thai scientists and engineers engaged in R&D in the entire country is only about 2,700; Japan boasts some 330,000, while Korea, with two-thirds of Thailand's population, has 30,000, and Singapore, with a population of only 2.5 million, has as many as Thailand. And Thailand produces a total of only 2,500 science and technology graduates each year, most of them Thai students of Chinese descent.

"Prominent scientists and policy makers in Thailand frequently assert that the lack of qualified manpower at all levels is a major constraint on development," the report concluded. "The heavy reliance on imported technology has led to low R&D activities in the private sector, [and] a higher proportion of university students are in non-science and technology fields than in Korea, mainly due to low job prospects, remuneration, and prestige."

The Thailand Development Research Institute, or TDRI, was created in 1984 by NESDB as a private, nonprofit organization to conduct more detailed policy research in areas related to Thailand's economic development. TDRI is funded by a number of private and semipublic institutions, including the Association of Thai Industries, the Asia Foundation, and the World Bank. Its specific research projects have individual sponsors, many of which are Japanese, such as the Economic Planning Agency, the National Institute for Research Advancement, and the Asian Productivity Center, all in Tokyo, as well as the Asian Development Bank, which is headquartered in Manila and whose principal shareholder is Japan.

Narongchai Akrasanee is executive vice president of TDRI. Educated in Australia and the United States (he received his master's and Ph.D. degrees in economics from Johns Hopkins University), Narongchai is a former dean of the faculty of economics at Thammasat University in Bangkok and a consultant to the Federation of Thai Industries. He was at the time of the interview a member of prime minister Chatichai's council of advisers. A handsome man in his mid-forties who sports a Rolex knockoff that works, Narongchai views Thailand's manpower problems with anything but the typical *mai pen rai* attitude.

"Everybody complains about the inadequacy of our physical infrastructure, but these critical manpower needs are evidence of our inadequate *human* infrastructure," he told me as we sat in his office high atop the Raja Park building overlooking central Bangkok. "Fewer than 50 percent of our primary school children continue on to secondary school, and we have only a very few scientists and engineers doing R&D in the whole country. With this recent economic boom, even though we have abundant labor and good young entrepreneurs, we have had to import skilled labor from India and the Philippines."

The shortage of skilled labor was so severe that the English editions of Thai newspapers, such as the *Nation* and the *Bangkok Post*, were running huge want ads every day for accountants, production specialists, computer programmers, software consultants, and electrical engineers. I asked Narongchai, who represents his country frequently in economic conferences overseas, whether government planners were sufficiently aware of the magnitude of the problem.

"There's more than just awareness," he said. "We have dramatically increased public funds available for engineering and science students to study overseas, and grants for more intensive technical education have also been increased. Yet the effects of these measures will take time; we obviously can't double the number of our engineers overnight. In the meantime, Japan and the Little Dragons will continue to have an advantage in the higher-value-added industries. But the problem is not just assisting young people to get more education; we also need to support their parents by helping them earn money, since most dropouts leave school to work in the family business. So poverty is a contributory factor. Also, there is the related problem of spiritual growth and satisfaction in a Buddhist country that has seen such dramatic accumulation of material wealth, especially in Bangkok. It's not as easy as it sounds."

A more typical "no problem" attitude was expressed by Phisit Pakkasem, secretary general of NESDB. Phisit is a career technocrat who completed his higher education in the United States. He earned a master's degree in economics at Harvard and got his Ph.D. from Pitt.

"Don't worry about that," he said when I asked him about the social implications of more schooling for Thai students. "Thai parents sacrifice for their children's education, and in Bangkok children also sacrifice to give their parents money. We have the best private hospitals in this part of the world, and we'll give our schools that reputation, too."

NESDB recently proposed that the government increase compulsory education from the present six years to nine years, which is standard throughout the rest of Asia, certainly in the NICs. At the end of NESDB's sixth national economic and social development plan, in 1990, Thailand had secondary schools in every school district in the kingdom, even though only 44 percent of the school-age population (the current ratio) were enrolled in them. Thailand today awards only 50,000 bachelor's degrees (most of them nontechnical) and a mere 3,000 master's degrees from its public institutions.

I asked Phisit whether the prevailing attitude of optimism, of which his was characteristic, might be a little unrealistic.

"I agree this will all take time," he said, shaking his head, "and we obviously need more teachers and laboratory equipment. But there is more the private sector can do too, by creating joint ventures with American universities and giving scholarships for our students to study abroad. We will make a clearer link between education and industry—no question about it. Also, Japan is giving us a lot of money to train teachers and buy more advanced laboratory equipment. *Mai pen rai*."

Thailand's considerable education problems, both in the normal curricula and in the technical institutes so widely acknowledged to be inadequate, coupled with Japan's overwhelming dominance of the local economy, prompt an interesting comparison between the two countries at similar stages in their development. More than a century ago, in the late Tokugawa era, Japan already had a more advanced educational base and a higher level of scientific knowledge than was the case in pre-Chulalongkorn Siam, so Japan was clearly better prepared for modernization than its Thai counterpart at that time was or, for that matter, is today. So while Japan forged ahead as an industrial power, Siam lagged far behind. Thailand has thus become known as a case of modernization without industrialization.

Bridging the Savings-Investment Gap

Another problem that the Thais have been slow to recognize, let alone solve, is an inadequate savings rate. While gross capital formation averaged just over 20 percent of GNP throughout the 1980s, that rate was insufficient to remedy either the physical infrastructure problems, which require massive funding, or education, as we have seen. (Japan and the Little Dragons have capital formation rates well in excess of 30 percent of GNP.) NESDB calculates that a savings rate equivalent to 27–30 percent of GNP will be necessary to fund the country's physical plant and equipment investments in the future if the economy keeps chugging along at a healthy annual rate of 9 percent. (Economists reckon that GNPs double every seven years at rates of expansion of 10 percent a year, assuming simple mathematical compounding.)

Without a higher rate of domestic savings, both public and private, Thailand will have no option but to increase its dependence on foreign (mainly Japanese) investment and external borrowings. While Thailand's rate of tax collection has been in the moderate range for developing countries at about 14 percent of GNP (compared to Indonesia, which is under 10 percent), it lags behind the Little Dragons like Korea and Singapore, whose rates are much higher, around 17–20 percent of GNP.

Given the many investment needs of Thailand's booming economy and the inadequate savings available to fund them, Banyong Lamsam, president of the Thai Farmer's Bank, the third-largest commercial bank in Thailand, has calculated that the country will have about a 700-billion-baht savings-investment gap between 1990 and 1995 (about $30 billion at current exchange rates), based on requirements of some 3.2 trillion baht for new roads, bridges, the Skytrain project, port expansion, and added electrical generating capacity (frequent brownouts occur because there is only a 5 percent margin between capacity and usage)—projects that have been planned and are now under way. But, he says, even assuming the savings rate is increased marginally to 24 percent of GNP for the next five years, the country will be able to generate a total of only 2.5 trillion baht. (Thailand's savings-investment gap has averaged about

5 percent of GNP since 1980, and its public sector deficit is around 4 percent.)

Since reducing interest rates alone is an insufficient tactical tool of monetary policy, he figures Thailand will have to push ahead aggressively in developing new incentives to save, devising new sources of tax revenue, strengthening its tax collection ability, expanding its capital markets, and creating a more effective system of retirement funds—all of which will take much longer than the three- to five-year time frame required for the planned investments. The obvious alternatives seem to be few, none of them very propitious: expanding foreign debt, increasing foreign (Japanese) investment, or simply printing more money.

Chinese Dominance

One major component of Thailand's domestic capital formation has been the ethnic Chinese, who historically remitted much of their income back to families in China. The private sector in Thailand, as in Indonesia, has traditionally been dominated by the Chinese, though without the attendant economic friction and social strife more characteristic of Indonesia in years past. This is true for a number of reasons, not least because of Thailand's closer proximity to China, its better record of cultural assimilation of the Chinese ethnic minority, and its decision early on to require resident Chinese to attend Thai schools, learn the Thai language, and take Thai names. Generally speaking, indigenous Thais tended to dominate the agricultural sector, the Thai elite prevailed in the government bureaucracy, and the Chinese controlled retail commerce. Up to half of Bangkok's population today is ethnically Chinese, but third- and fourth-generation Sino-Thais retain none of their ethnicity and neither read nor write Chinese. They do, however, tend to dominate the specialized science and engineering schools.

The largest business groups in Thailand today reflect this Chinese dominance, and many of them have substantial alliances with the Japanese. A quick look at some of them shows why. Bodhiratanangkura, headed by Sukri Bodhiratanangkura, is the biggest textile group in Thailand. The Boonsoong family, which made its original fortune in tin mining, today has a number of Japanese joint ventures: Isuzu Motor (Thailand), which assembles vans and trucks; Nippondenso Thailand, which manufactures automotive parts; and Thai Bridgestone, a major producer of tires. The biggest agribusiness group in Thailand was established by two Teochew brothers, Chia Ek Chaw and Chia Seow Whooy, whose Charoen Pokphand Feed Mill today dominates the production of broiler chicks and eggs. Thai Farmer's Bank was established years ago by the Lamsam family and has substantial investments in real estate and trading as well as in other financial fields. The Sophonpanich family controls the Bangkok Bank, Ltd., the largest commercial bank not only in Thailand but in all of Southeast Asia.

Another sizable Chinese interest is the Siam Cement Group, a Thai conglomerate that probably has more joint ventures with the Japanese than any other Thai group. Established in 1913, today it has six divisions that manufacture more than 8,000 products, from cement and construction materials to industrial machinery and equipment, with total annual revenues of about $1 billion. Siam Toyota makes car engines using Toyota technology; Thai-CRT manufactures TV tubes based on Mitsubishi Electric technology; Siam-NEC makes color TVs and home appliances in a joint venture with Nippon Electric Corporation; Siam Sanitary Fittings is an alliance with Toto, Ltd.; Siam Kubota Diesel makes engines, tractors, power tillers, and farm machinery; Thai Polyethylene Co. Ltd. uses machinery provided by Mitsui Shipbuilding and Engineering. It controls 48 percent of Pacific Plastics (Thailand), the country's largest polystyrene maker (America's Dow Chemical owns the rest), and it owns Michelin Siam, which produces tires for both the domestic and export markets. About 37 percent of Siam Cement's shares are held by the royal family's Crown Property Bureau.

The Bottom Line

"There is an old Thai saying," Amaret Sila-On, senior vice president of the Siam Cement Group, told me, "that ten merchants are not as well off as their civil service ministers. In the old days, prior to these periods of rapid economic growth, the Thai economy was characterized simply by survival. It favored strong, centralized control by government; management employed simple supervision as a rule; staffs were generally small; and nepotism was the general rule if your sole objective was to survive."

Amaret was a founder of the Thai Management Association. Educated in Britain, at Manchester University, where he received both his B.A. and Ph.D. in economics, he later studied in the advanced management program at Harvard. He started his business career with the Shell group in 1958 and joined Siam Cement in 1974.

I asked him how he viewed Thailand's manpower problems in the competitive years ahead.

"In the 1980s," he said, "after the slowdown resulting from the end of the Vietnam War, foreign investment, primarily from Japan, has fueled double-digit rates of growth in our economy. Computerized information is now key, and it is clear that we need more professional, better-educated workers as we begin to compete more earnestly in the international markets. It is rather obvious, I think, that in order to compete more effectively, we will have to build a competitive edge based on productivity and technology. Unless we can mobilize all the relevant forces in our society to make this happen, Thailand's future progress is likely to be stunted."

Just as America's political involvement in Thailand, with the Vietnam War as a backdrop in the 1960s and 1970s, led to rapid economic growth, so has Japan's strategic investment in Thailand in the 1980s led to a comparable burst of growth. Unlike the earlier American model, however, Japan's presence today is much broader, much deeper, and much more likely to last.

In the meantime Thailand must deal with its savings rate, infrastructure development, and technical manpower problems, but these are not just economic questions; they are political questions too. So we also need to take a look at Thailand's politics. As Uncle Chamlong, the popular governor of Bangkok remarked, Thailand is not Singapore; it does not have an authoritarian form of government. And in that gem of unconventional wisdom is a kernel of truth that raises some doubts about Thailand's longer-term potential as one of Asia's emerging Little Dragons.

THAI POLITICS:
EQUILIBRIUM WITHOUT CONSENSUS

With twenty-six separate governments and thirteen constitutions over the past half-century, Thailand at first glance seems to have a rather unstable political system. It does not. Shifts in Thai political power that have resulted in wholesale changes in government tend to reflect differences among the ruling elite rather than any underlying systemic weakness or instability. Yet it is the very *process* of resolving those factional differences that leads to so much confusion when outsiders try to understand how the political system works.

Thai politics has about as many descriptions as it does participants. Some call it a "prism," through which many different political views are refracted. Others call it a "triangular partnership," which includes the king, the military, and the political parties. Or a "rectangular partnership," which includes those three plus the competent Thai bureaucracy (also frequently referred to as the "four pillars of Thai politics"). Or a "pentagonal partnership," which includes those four plus the Buddhist Sangha, Thailand's powerful monastic order.

None of these paradigms is inaccurate, but the last is perhaps the most comprehensive and the one that will serve as our default model. Those five powerful constituencies together—the king, the military, the politicians, the bureaucracy, and the monks—make up an elite minority that governs the country. And as their power relative to each other ebbs and flows, a process of equilibrium is achieved. It is that equilibrium that most accurately characterizes the Thai political system.

Visualize one of those popular hand games with a pentagon etched on the surface, five small holes—one at each corner—and five steel balls rolling around under a glass cover. The trick is to manipulate the game delicately so that one ball ultimately nestles into each corner hole. When that has been achieved, the game is over—equilibrium has been achieved. But it is by no means a simple process: as you tilt it ever so slightly to capture one ball, another ball may pop out of its corner and throw the game into disequilibrium again.

Devilishly frustrating. Just like Thai politics.

"The Thai system is a moving equilibrium," the veteran observer William Overholt once wrote. "It is a unique system for managing change and achieving goals. The Thai system is not an inferior form of Western democracy or a peculiarly unstable form of Asian dictatorship; it is utterly different from Asian dictatorships and Western democracies. The moving equilibrium maintains itself in part through frequent coups, irregular elections, and personnel reshuffles, which create an appearance of instability but are mechanisms for attaining a deeper stability."

Thai Coups: A Mechanism for Stability

A book of this length cannot go back sixty years and analyze each of the twenty-six coups since 1932. But a look at the last two or three will convey a sense of how this cycle of coups and countercoups defines Thai politics and characterizes the process of equilibrium.

In November 1971 Prime Minister Thanom Kittikachorn, who was also field marshal and supreme commander of the Thai armed forces, felt Parliament was becoming too unruly, so he staged a coup against his own government, dissolved Parliament, reshuffled his cabinet, and promised a new constitution within three years. Prapass Charusathiara, the deputy prime minister and deputy supreme commander, was put in charge of drafting the new constitution, but he purposely dragged his feet.

By October 1973, with no new constitution in sight, a coalition of students and intellectuals emerged to goad the Thanom-Prapass dictatorship into action. Thirteen were arrested for causing unrest (disequilibrium), denied bail, and accused of being Communist (Hanoi had taken the upper hand in Indochina, and Thailand was widely considered to be the next so-called domino). Nearly half a million Thais took to the streets to protest the arrests, terrifying the dictatorship. The students were released, and prompt production of the new constitution was promised, but riot police clashed with the demonstrators. Violence escalated when heavily armed troops of the 11th Infantry, commanded by Colonel Narong Kittikachorn, Thanom's son, were dispatched to quell the unrest. More than a hundred demonstrators were killed, and Bangkok came unglued.

When the smoke lifted, Thanom, Prapass, and Narong all resigned their government and military positions and fled the country in exile. The king appointed as interim prime minister Professor Sanya Dhammasakdi of Thammasat University, who promptly froze some 400 million baht worth of the departed troika's assets and proclaimed a new democratic era.

The students had also expressed considerable anti-Japanese sentiment, reflecting widespread concern about Thailand's growing external trade deficit with Japan, and this anti-Japanese tactic was used for political purposes to end the military regime. Once the Thanom government had been dissolved, however, everybody promptly forgot about the deficits, which in fact became much worse. As in Indonesia with the Malari affair, antiforeign sentiment in Thailand can also be used to mask fractious disputes within the ruling elite.

The emerging period of participatory democracy expressed the ideals of the intelligentsia, the business class, and labor, but it was extremely threatening to the established elite, for whom the concept of popular sovereignty might go too far. The government had run budget and trade surpluses under the Thanom-Prapass dictatorship and had a strong currency because it had neglected social development projects. After 1973, however, the government began to generate deficits as development spending picked up. For three years, even though the democratic governments were headed by elected representatives of the old elite (such as Prime Minister Kukrit Pramoj, a banker and cousin of the king), disequilibrium reemerged. Students and intellectuals fought among themselves, and the political parties, of which there were more than a dozen, fell into disarray. By 1976 security was an even graver problem, too, because Vietnam had then fallen to the Communists.

So in October 1976 factional disputes within the student movement erupted in riots at Thammasat University, precipitating the declaration of martial law and the appointment by the king of former supreme court justice Thanin Kraivichien as prime minister. Thanin restored equilibrium but overreacted in doing so, again planting the seeds of disequilibrium: ideologically rigid and inflexibly anti-Communist, his regime was as repressive as the democratic period had been pluralistic. Ironically, Thanin, a civilian and a lawyer, was more authoritarian than his military predecessors. He proved too extreme for most Thais and drove hundreds of intellectuals into sympathy with the Thai insurgents when he imposed press censorship, dissolved the labor unions, and purged the bureaucracy of dissidents.

His regime was short-lived. In October 1977 General Kriangsak Chomanand staged a coup, promised a new constitution within two years, stemmed the right-wing repression, and encouraged exiles to return from the countryside. Kriangsak lifted the press sanctions and pardoned the purged dissidents. Equilibrium was once again restored. But by the time elections were held again in 1979, Kriangsak's position had weakened, not least because Vietnam had invaded Cambodia and he was perceived now to be excessively elitist and weak. In early 1980 he resigned, and General Prem Tinsulanond formed a new cabinet by forging a more powerful coalition between his Democratic Party and Kukrit's Social Action Party.

Prem had the strong backing of the Thai armed forces, and his government lasted for eight years—practically unheard of in Thai politics—until he retired after the 1988 elections. General Chatichai Choonhavan emerged as the new prime minister in another coalition government, this time between his Chat Thai party and five others, in the first popularly elected government in more than a decade. Toward the end of Prem's stay in power, when he was toying with the idea of continuing as PM, ninety-nine ranking Thai academicians submitted a signed petition asking that he *not* consider remaining longer. And during the eight years of Prem's rule he suffered *nine* coups, all of them unsuccessful.

Two were near successes. In April 1981 a group of lower-ranking officers calling themselves the Young Turks declared a coup, announcing a program of greater discipline, a broader role for the military, and nationalization of the banking system. (They were also ambitious and feared they might not get their spoils if Prem stayed in power for too long.) Prem narrowly missed being captured, fled Bangkok with the king, established a provisional government in Khorat, and drafted a message supporting his government that was read by the queen over national radio. When the Young Turks heard that and saw subsequent pictures of Prem lounging around with the king in his pajamas, they surrendered. But they then traveled to Khorat and presented Prem and the king with joss sticks in penitence. When Prem asked if they had had their breakfast, they knew they had been forgiven.

The other close call occurred in 1985, when Prime Minister Prem and Commander in Chief Arthit were overseas on an official trip. Remnants of the 1981 Young Turks tried again, backed by retired officers and some senior politicians, but they, too, failed because they could not win the support of either the monarchy or the armed forces as a whole.

Earlier that year, opposed to devaluation of the baht (because it would make his weapons procurement program prohibitively expensive), General Arthit had told the Pentagon that the Thai currency would not be devalued. But Prem depreciated the baht anyway, embarrassing Arthit, who then delivered a scathing speech in public, lambasting the devaluation and the Prem regime. But in showing such an open display of anger he had gone too far, offending Thai cultural sensibilities and causing loss of face. The king and queen refused to attend Arthit's official ceremonies, and the general was publicly disgraced.

Prem subsequently reappointed Arthit as commander in chief of the army *anyway*, making sure the position traditionally most threatening to a prime minister in Thailand was in the hands of a bona fide political cripple. Then, in 1986, when he orchestrated another coup, Prem simply dismissed him, dissolved the government, and called new elections. Today, retired from the army, Arthit heads the fourth-largest opposition group, the Thai People's Party, with seventeen seats in the lower house.

Equilibrium. Disequilibrium. Restoration of balance. As Fred Riggs wrote in *Thailand: The Modernization of a Bureaucratic Polity*, "Successive coups d'état by which Thai ruling circles are modified and then replaced have become as much a constitutional formula for changing elites as the periodic electoral battles which take place in the United States, or the cabinet crises of France during the Third and Fourth Republics."

Riggs might also have added the cabinet crises of Italy in the postwar era. The point is that these changes of government not only are *not* dysfunctional, as many believe, but are inherently stable. They reflect shifts in factional alliances among the ruling elite. The question they raise, however, compared to the more authoritarian systems of government prevalent in Japan and the Little Dragons, is whether they drain too much energy and effort from development in the process of maintaining political equilibrium.

"There is a flexible tolerance here, a natural self-assurance," M. R. Sukhumband Paribatra told me. "It's not just Buddhism, al-

though that may account for part of it, and it's not just due to the
fact that we've never been colonized, but there's an indefinable
quality about us. We cope with good humor and a high level of self-
confidence. We have also assimilated the Chinese well, much better
than other nations in the region, but in my mind the most important
factor is the monarchy—the king. He has a very strong grass-roots
foundation, not the kind of detached anonymity historically found in
China, for example. Our king is divine, too, of course, but he is also
rooted to the people. Here the polity and the monarchy reinforce
each other."

Sukhumband is associate professor of political science at Chulalongkorn University in Bangkok, Thailand's most prestigious university, and concurrently director of its Institute for Strategic and
International Studies. He is a direct descendant of King Chulalongkorn; hence his title, M. R., which stands for Mom Rajawang, or
member of royalty. Sukhumband personally reflects the Thai trait of
soft-spoken, self-effacing gentleness, despite his reputation as one of
Thailand's most brilliant and outspoken foreign policy analysts. Just
thirty-eight, he was until 1989 a member of the prime minister's
policy advisory council, a small group of young intellectuals serving
the PM as an independent think tank on policy issues.

"I'm just a myopic academician trying to keep my head above
water in a sea of politicians and bureaucrats," he said modestly. "But
the days of countless coups are gone, I think. The king plays a more
harmonizing role now, and the public is so much more sophisticated.
They could tolerate endless successions of coups in the past perhaps,
but democracy and the parliamentary system are here to stay, although the armed forces remains a powerful, united entity."

King Bhumibol Adulyadej ascended the throne in 1946 at the
age of eighteen and was crowned Rama IX in 1950. He is currently
the longest-serving monarch in Thailand's 209-year-old Chakkri
dynasty. He rejects the stiff, detached style of Japan's imperial family,
on the one hand, and the casual manner of England's royal family, on
the other. As the grandson of King Chulalongkorn, he is intimately
involved with the common people, as Sukhumband noted, and
serves as a thread of continuity in Thailand's frequently changing
governments.

The king travels constantly to monitor more than 1,000 development projects that have been established around the country

under his patronage—projects such as milk-pasteurizing plants, rural dams, and synfuel plants that use sugarcane stalks as feedstock. His name means "Strength of the Land, Incomparable Power," and he was born the third and youngest child of Prince Mahidol, a Harvard medical student who later became known as the father of modern medicine in Thailand.

King Bhumibol and his wife, Queen Sirikit, have four children—three daughters and a son. The crown prince, Maha Vajiralongkorn, is the self-admitted "black sheep" of the royal family. He is willful, temperamental, and sometimes violent, in addition to being a crack jet pilot and a major general in command of his own regiment. In 1977 the king bestowed on his middle daughter, Princess Sirindhorn, the title Somdet Phra Debaratana Rajasuda Chao Fa Maha Chakri Sirindhorn, or "Beloved Daughter and Great Princess of the Chakkri Dynasty Who Possesses Glory and Goodness," simultaneously amending the succession law to allow women to succeed to the Thai throne. She is now the crown princess and her father's favored successor.

When the king intervenes in the political process to restore equilibrium, he serves as a focal point for restraining excesses. He legitimizes the political leadership of the elites *so long as* they exercise power within tolerable though vaguely defined limits, and he is also considered the system's last resort, accessible by individual petitioner and public opinion alike. He is literally the father of his country, imbued with both the mythical presence and embodiment of tradition Americans normally ascribe to George Washington.

King Bhumibol's power is moral and social as well as political, so when the monarchy is abused, however innocently, a severe price is paid. In 1987 Veera Musikapong, a former minister, committed lèse-majesté by publicly suggesting in an informal, offhand way that if he could choose he would be born a prince in the heart of the Grand Palace. He was arrested and acquitted in a lower court because he had not referred to the king directly, but a higher court reversed that decision and sentenced him to six years in jail for slander.

The royal family has financial power, too, since by tradition all land in Thailand originally belonged to the king. In 1906 King Chulalongkorn (Rama V) created the first Thai bank (Siam Commercial), and several years later his successor, King Vajiravudh (Rama VI), established the Siam Cement Company. Today the

Crown Property Bureau, which manages the royal wealth, owns 31.75 percent of the bank and 37.4 percent of Siam Cement, in addition to 13,000 acres of prime real estate in central Bangkok. Altogether the royal family has shareholdings in some forty Thai companies, including 10 percent of Honda (Thailand), 10 percent of YKK Zipper (Thailand), and 7.5 percent of Minebea Electronics, all major Japanese affiliates.

One inherent weakness in this system of flexible equilibrium is that the decision-making process is slow, cumbersome, and more often than not ambiguous. In part this is attributable to Thai culture (loss of face is to be avoided at all costs) and to the Thai personality: when more than two people get together, it takes forever to reach agreement. Thais say that loud chatter and hurried movements are associated with the behavior of monkeys, not people, so they tend to speak in gentle tones and take their time. But the government is four years behind schedule in building new roads to ease Bangkok's congestion, primarily because of the bureaucracy's inability to achieve consensus, despite the obvious priority.

"When a policy is required," William Overholt observed in "Thailand: A Moving Equilibrium," "senior officials are afraid to decide because they have little job security in the face of a negative reaction from any sector. Each fears to act. Each waits for someone else to broach the issue. [One] ministry passes responsibility to another. The government forms a committee, dissolves it, then forms another one. While temporising behavior occurs in all governments, it is extreme in Thailand."

While the armed forces may have had a monopoly on political power in the past, conventional wisdom today holds that power is now held more diffusely.

"The army and the politicians tend to share power now," one Western diplomat with years of experience in Bangkok told me. "In truth there are four real factions within the elite today: the army, civilian politicians, the businessmen, and the technocrats. I agree with the sentiment that there will probably be no more coups, not only because the people are more sophisticated and will no longer tolerate them but because the armed forces themselves have come to accept a more limited role. The economy today is so complex, it takes more than just a traditional military mind to run it. And the military budget comes under the general budget now, so it's harder to carve out a separate financial fiefdom. Sure, there are occasionally vague, anticapitalist views expressed within the military, but they're in the minority and lack a broad power base. The coalition of Thai political parties in power today functions much like factions within Japan's dominant Liberal Democratic Party: they may have different names, but they all subscribe to the same basic ideology. And Thailand's semidemocracy takes them all into account."

For a country with such a high level of political tension on its borders, especially with the nations of Laos and Cambodia, which buffer it from Vietnam, Thailand spends rather modestly for its national defense. Since 1973 defense spending has averaged only slightly more than 3 percent of GNP, and it is slightly less than that today, about $1.8 billion a year in absolute terms. Thailand has averaged a steady 20 percent of central government expenditures for the past two decades, including the difficult Vietnam War years. Its armed forces total just under 300,000 men, about the same level as Indonesia's but three times that of neighboring Malaysia.

"When the military orders 250 single-band radios from Hewlett-Packard," another experienced Westerner observed wryly, "word gets around that a coup is in the making. The last two were blowouts: in 1981 the Young Turks chose to move on April Fool's Day, and in 1985 they got stuck in Bangkok's infernal traffic and couldn't reach their destinations. But to ask how to prevent the Thai military from getting involved in politics is to start with the wrong premise, because you can't separate the military from the political process to begin with."

One senior Western diplomat, reflecting on past coups, said, "A coup is now no longer possible, though we said that in 1985, too, just before the Young Turks made their move in September. But while it's definitely a thing of the past, perhaps it's safer to say that it's simply *less* likely to happen since one could unpredictably recur at any time. Businessmen and technocrats now drive the government, and their relationship is not unlike that between the LDP and the Keidanren in Japan."

Succession and the Military

The greater complexity of Thai political power today inevitably means the prime minister and his potential successors are scrutinized much more carefully now than they might have been in the recent past.

Former Prime Minister Chatichai Choonhavan brought years of political experience and a strong bureaucratic background to the job, in addition to having been the youngest major general in the army in Thai history. (His father, Marshal Phin Choonhavan, participated in the 1947 coup and became commander in chief of the army in 1948 and then minister of defense, a position Chatichai held concurrently until early 1990.) Born in 1922, he graduated from the Chulachom-klao Royal Military Academy, spent more than a decade in the armed services; he was a military attaché in Washington, ambassador to Argentina from 1960 to 1963, and then ambassador to Austria for five years, after which he became Thailand's permanent representative to the UN. He returned to Bangkok in 1973 as deputy minister of foreign affairs, entered Parliament as an MP, and later became minister of industry in Prem's first cabinet, rising to deputy prime minister by the time Prem retired.

"Chatichai is without question a highly capable politician," one Western diplomat acknowledged to me, "and has produced some bold policy initiatives. But he also has a dangerous tendency to shoot from the lip."

Chatichai's reputation as Thailand's "no problem" prime minister, mentioned earlier, has gotten him into serious trouble at times. In late 1989, after a powerful typhoon devastated coastal areas in the southern province of Chumphon, Chatichai made the *mai pen rai* comment when he visited a village that had suffered comparatively minor damage. But his staff had informed him poorly about the severity of damage in other villages, so there was widespread outrage at his insensitivity, by the local villagers as well as by the political opposition. The opposition's largest party, Solidarity, threatened a no-confidence motion against his government and caused him to cancel a strategic visit to the United States, including a long-planned meeting with President Bush, forcing him to stay at home and mend his political fences.

When Chatichai suffers the consequences of his glibness, he tries to shuffle around them by saying that at age sixty-nine he finds his twelve-hour days as prime minister rough going and intends to retire midway through his first term anyway. Few take him seriously, but if he persists in this dangerous tendency to shoot from the lip, someday he may have to eat his words.

Recently the highly respected Chulalongkorn academician Chai-Anan Samudavanija, himself an appointed senator in the upper house and arguably Thailand's most renowned political scientist, observed that while local political parties have done a fine job of representing the elite in Bangkok, they have done less well at establishing grass-roots ties to the rural electorate. There is a distinct need to decentralize power to the rural areas, he has said, and to change Thai tax and administrative law to help bring that about. While Bangkok has been the historical and traditional source of political power in Thailand, going back more than 200 years to the establishment of the Chakkri dynasty, the Thai political system risks alienating its huge rural population by concentrating power so visibly in the capital. In each of the last two elections, the political parties spent more than $120 million buying votes in the countryside.

Many of these parties are quite new. Chamlong Srimuang, the popular governor of Bangkok, established his Palang Dharma (Force of Spiritual Righteousness) party in 1985; it won no seats in the 1986 lower house elections but took fourteen in 1988. Similarly, the Prachachon (People's) Party won no seats in 1986 but grabbed nineteen in 1988. These two, along with seven others, including General Arthit's Puangchon Chao Thai (Thai People's) Party, make up the nine opposition parties that together control 137 of the 357 seats in the lower house.

Prime Minister Chatichai's Chat Thai (Thai Nation) Party is the largest, controlling eighty-seven seats in Parliament; the next-largest is the Social Action Party, until recently headed by the former foreign minister, Air Chief Marshal Siddhi Savetsila, with fifty-four. These two, together with four others, comprise the six coalition parties that formed the present Thai government after the 1988 elections; they control 220 seats in the lower house.

By mid-1990 cracks had begun to appear in the coalition, however, forcing Chatichai to reshuffle his cabinet. Allegations of corruption were hanging over two junior ministers in the government, both members of the Social Action Party, prompting Siddhi to resign when the officials were dismissed. Minister of Commerce Subin Pinkayan replaced Siddhi as foreign minister, and former prime minister Kukrit Pramoj took his position as party head. Nearly eighty, Kukrit is the elder statesman of Thai politics. As a longtime defender and allay of Chatichai, he was able to calm the rough political waters, keep the Social Action Party in the coalition, and restore equilibrium.

If one weakness of flexible equilibrium in Thai politics is a slow decision-making process, the problem of succession is another. If Prime Minister Chatichai were to decide to retire before his current term expires in 1992 or (in the vernacular) is hit by a bus tomorrow, there is no automatic successor. The six-party governing coalition would have to agree on one or dissolve itself and call elections if it can't. Most thoughtful Thais say that a prime minister must be at least sixty years old to command respect; they complain that Chatichai is not grooming a successor. Most also admit that whoever his successor may be he will have to be a military man, which suggests "Uncle Chamlong" might be in the running. Chamlong is popularly known as Mr. Clean among Thai politicians, not only because of his ascetic behavior and Buddhist beliefs but also because he lives entirely on his army pension and gives both his government salary and allowances back to the city as contributions. When I asked him, during our long interview, why the people of Bangkok loved him so, he told me simply, "I work hard, and I am honest." Chamlong had been a secretary general during one of the latter Prem administrations, despite his rumored participation in the Young Turks' coup of 1981. His personal assistant in the Bangkok Metropolitan Administration, Boonyakit Tansakul, who spent ten years in boarding school in England and has a degree from Liverpool University, told me that "all the generals know each other quite well. They are the knights of the Thai round table." Nonetheless, at age fifty-five Chamlong is still considered too young, and his asceticism is thought by many to be too extreme.

Considerable attention therefore focuses on Chatichai's former commander in chief, General Chaovalit Yongchaiyuth, who until June 1990 was deputy prime minister and the minister of defense. A career soldier who rose to prominence in the Prem government, his star began to shine in 1986, when he was named Arthit's successor. Prior to the 1988 general elections General Chaovalit made a few spines shiver by saying that he would in fact be glad to stage a coup if he received the go-ahead from the people, though he later back-tracked and pledged not to do so when many senior politicians and politically influential technocrats spoke out against him as a potentially destabilizing force. A member of the influential Class 5 of the Chulachomklao Royal Military Academy, Chaovalit also came under fire in early 1988 for the Thai army's reportedly poor showing in border fighting with Laos and Cambodia and for his insistence that the Constitution be amended to prevent members of Parliament from concurrently serving as ministers.

Chaovalit's political philosophy is based on *sapa patiwat*, his concept of a "peaceful revolution" that will turn Thailand into an agricultural superpower and bring greater power to the country's rural areas. This concept has considerable appeal to the military, which not only has responsibility for development projects in the countryside but is also concerned about the undue concentration of wealth in Bangkok. Yet *sapa patiwat* makes many Thais uncomfortable because they ask how Thailand can possibly have a revolution without another coup.

Nearly sixty, Chaovalit made a difficult decision in March 1990 when he resigned as commander in chief to join Chatichai's cabinet as minister of defense and deputy PM. He had been feeling lots of pressure from his younger generals, who were eager to move up. They were getting impatient for him to retire so they could be promoted. Otherwise, as one foreign observer put it to me, they wouldn't have had the opportunity even to sniff the bar rag of political power. But then, when he resigned abruptly from Chatichai's cabinet in June 1990, only ten weeks after retiring as supreme commander and being appointed deputy PM, rumors of another coup circulated in Bangkok like freshly printed bank notes and caused the Thai stock exchange to drop 4 percent overnight. The former cabinet minister behaved himself, however; rather than starting a coup, he began laying the groundwork for yet another political party and decided to bide his time.

Chaovalit had been embarrassed previously when supporters of his "peaceful revolution" distributed seditious leaflets in mid-1989 to dissolve Parliament and make him their prime minister of choice. He had had to disavow the group and order their arrest to preserve his political future. Former prime minister Kukrit said he thought the *sapa patiwat* group was "crazy" and agreed that if Chaovalit really wanted to be prime minister he would never have sanctioned their support. And the fact that he moved directly into the cabinet prompted much press criticism about the connections, still strong, between the Thai military and political power.

"Chaovalit clearly has political ambitions," one seasoned expatriate in Bangkok told me, "but the question is whether the *sapa patiwat* incident will set him back. Two years ago, when his followers pushed him for PM, he sank like a stone. I think people may want Chaovalit to stay where he is. He's now more dependent on Chatichai than the other way around."

That sentiment held true until early 1991, when the Thai military, under the leadership of Commander in Chief Sunthorn Kongsompong, staged a bloodless coup that successfully deposed Prime Minister Chatichai. In late February, the military placed Chatichai under house arrest, suspended the Constitution, and imposed martial law but promised national elections and a new Constitution by the end of the year. General Sunthorn assumed the interim position of caretaker prime minister, and a half-dozen other top military officers followed him into the new government as the Thai stock market plunged 7 percent overnight.

Despite the pronouncements of many Western observers who felt Thailand had made coups a thing of the political past, the army takeover represented nothing more than the restoration of equilibrium between the nation's powerful military and its elected politicians after long-festering claims and counterclaims of corruption on both sides. The coup was triggered by Chatichai's appointment of former commander in chief Arthit as deputy defense minister, on top of accusations by the army that the Chatichai government had attempted to "distort" a recently opened investigation into a 1982 assassination plot against Thai leaders, including former prime minister Prem.

Since Arthit was so unpopular among the current generation of Class 5 military leaders, they had no alternative but to topple the Chatichai regime. It was widely rumored that former supreme commander Chaovalit would use the coup as a stepping-stone to power and emerge as a leading candidate for prime minister in the next elections. While Chaovalit has spoken contemptuously of politicians and denounced their corrupt behavior, little is expected to change should he head the next elected government. No stranger to corruption himself, as we shall see, his wife is known as a "walking jewelry box."

Privatization: A Political Problem

A third weakness of the Thai political system is its inability to privatize many of the inefficient state enterprises, essentially an economic problem in most countries except in Thailand, where, given the constraints on consensus that the system of flexible equilibrium imposes, it is primarily political.

According to estimates of NESDB, two-thirds of Thailand's total public sector foreign debt is held by these state enterprises—entities like the Telephone Authority of Thailand (TAT), Thai International Airways, and the Electrical Generating Authority of Thailand (EGAT)—most of which are managed inefficiently and generate sizable operating losses. NESDB also discovered that state firms increased employment—a political function—at more than 10 percent a year, even in recession years, and that their chauffeurs often earned more than mid-ranking technocrats in government ministries. When it recently issued a white paper recommending the government speed up the privatization process, the state unions balked and senior politicians told NESDB to mind its own business.

"It is true," Amnuay Viravan told me, "that our state firms are characterized by operating deficits, overstaffing, heavy indebtedness, low labor productivity, and poor-quality services. For more than two decades enthusiasm for privatization has waxed and waned. Though we have reduced the total number of state enterprises from 150 to about sixty, most of that reduction occurred in the late 1960s, when we abolished seventy provincial trading companies—one in each province—whose combined assets were only a few million dollars. But we had to go against vested interests, which is the same everywhere."

Amnuay is executive board chairman of the Bangkok Bank, Ltd. American-educated, with advanced degrees in economics and business administration from the University of Michigan, he was a leading technocrat prior to retirement from government service—a former secretary general of BOI and minister of finance in Prem's first cabinet. An elegant man with a keen mind, he is a frequent speaker at international gatherings.

"The need to expand our economic infrastructure is painfully obvious," he continued as we sat in his top-floor office in the bank's headquarters building, far above Bangkok's clogged streets, "And it is complicated by a severe savings-investment gap in this country. There is no way we can finance these requirements through government expenditures alone, and our foreign debt ceiling restricts external borrowing. So we have to proceed with privatization if for no other reason than to keep the economy going. The problem is, both workers and managers in the state firms perceive privatization as a threat to their incomes, to their autonomy, and to their security."

Thai International Airways, the state-owned national airline, has a high standard of service and low labor costs, averaging 15 percent of overhead compared to about 30 percent for European airlines. It also has twenty-five consecutive years of profitable operations—a record in Thailand. Its senior staff (and NESDB too, for that matter) believe it could be even more competitive if some of its shares were sold to the public, giving it greater managerial autonomy and helping to reduce the government's high budget deficit. But by tradition the chief executive is always a retired Thai air force general, so political considerations become paramount: the military does not want its influence diluted.

Privatizing Thailand's state enterprises would benefit the stock exchange as well as both local and foreign investors. Maruey Phadoongsidhi, chairman of the Securities Exchange of Thailand, told me that as of 1988 the SET had 144 listed companies with a total market capitalization of $4 billion and that they had targeted 200 listings by year-end 1990, on the assumption that more state firms would sell minority shareholdings to the public to raise capital, following the recent example of Singapore Airlines. Selling 20 or 30 percent of a firm still gives the state control, he reasoned, so the politicians should not be unduly concerned about losing either autonomy or security.

"Privatization is absolutely necessary for development of Thailand's capital markets," Akira Ogino, board director of Nomura Securities and head of its Asia division, told me. "This is only natural as companies shift from debt to equity for funding. The key issue is how to turn political opponents into supporters, because in the past they have been bureaucrats comfortable with so many perks from state ownership. In Korea government has shown a strong commitment to privatization by keeping senior officers of public corporations as senior advisers. In our own case the Japanese government turned to public employees for support, which sped the privatization of NTT, the national railway corporation, and the tobacco monopoly."

The government's foot dragging on privatization, coupled with NESDB's efforts to spur faster action, resulted in some rather uncustomary political meddling in NESDB's affairs. Chaloem Yubamrung, one of eight ministers attached to the prime minister's office with direct oversight responsibility for NESDB, began calling the agency's senior officials to task for overstepping their bounds and ultimately caused the resignation of Snoh Unakul, NESDB's secretary general and Thailand's most widely respected planner, in mid-1989, replacing him with a *mai pen rai* technocrat, Phisit Pakkasem. (Phisit's attitude toward future political interference was as nonchalant as his view on Thailand's education problem, mentioned earlier: "No problem. We all have extended friendships and know each other well.") Snoh, meanwhile, now devotes his attention full time to TDRI, where he is chairman of the board.

Political meddling seems to have taken on a life all its own under Chatichai, who created a policy advisory council shortly after he was elected PM, to leapfrog the often stubborn bureaucracy. Heading his kitchen cabinet, as it has come to be called, is London University–educated Pansak Vinyaratn, who at forty-seven is the oldest of the group; the average age is thirty-eight.

"Our role is to collect data, analyze it, and make recommendations to the prime minister," Pansak said in a recent interview. "The PM orders us to carry out policy analysis on a wide range of issues."

The seven (now six) advisers created a buzz in the hallowed halls of the foreign ministry in early 1989 when they persuaded Chatichai to hand President Bush an aide-mémoire in Tokyo on the occasion of the emperor's funeral, asking that all subsequent bilateral negotiations between the two countries be handled by their executive staffs, who could resolve the issues on a more comprehensive basis. Neither

Bush nor his secretary of state, James Baker, nor Chatichai's foreign minister, Siddhi Savetsila, had any idea of what the group was up to. Other, similar cases have surfaced in which the young advisers have either ignored the bureaucracy or kept them out of the loop, and the technocrats are not amused.

Critics have said openly that the think tank's approach to problem resolution is arrogant at worst and naive at best. Chatichai's deputy prime minister, Pong Sarasin, calls the advisers overzealous kids who are bent on showing off and who exceed their brief by "meddling" in affairs of state. "They're all sons of millionaires," one friend admitted. "Chatichai wants to control the technocrats, and he may be getting his way."

The prime minister's son, Kraisak Choonhavan, known affectionately as Tong but less affectionately as a playboy, is a member of his father's policy advisory council. Two of the more respected members of the group are Narongchai Akrasanee, the executive vice president at TDRI, and, until recently, M. R. Sukhumband Paribatra, the Chulalongkorn political scientist. Sukhumband's departure from the group was precipitated in mid-1989 by General Chaovalit, who publicly told the PM that he ought to do something about corruption in government, saying that Thailand had recently been ranked by a foreign magazine as ninth on a list of the world's most corrupt countries. In a speech the next day Sukhumband suggested that any military leader who comments on corruption in a civilian government ought to put his own house in order first. The armed forces were furious and demanded Sukhumband's resignation; he voluntarily and happily complied. (He had told me personally that, tiring of petty politics, he longed to return to his academic work full-time.)

The Role of Buddhism

All these active political ingredients are mixed together in a crucible with one more or less inert but potentially very powerful chemical element: the Sangha, Thailand's Buddhist monastic order. Theravada Buddhism, the professed religion of 95 percent of the population, exerts a considerable influence on Thai behavior. It permeates society through the *wat*, Buddhist temples that serve as community centers in every village, as well as through the saffron-robed monks who are a visible part of everyday life in Thailand.

Thai Buddhism places a high premium on the avoidance of personal conflict—Thais seldom express emotion, for example—and on the accumulation of merit in this life in anticipation of the next. Buddhist concepts of time—not just spiritually but in more practical ways as well—are prevalent in Thailand. Government publications, daily newspapers, and magazines all reflect the religious calendar: because Thais count from the birth of Buddha and not Christ, 1991 appears on mastheads and in statistical tables as the year 2534.

"While the interaction of Buddhism with politics is recognized," the Thai scholar Somboon Suksamran recently wrote in *Buddhism and Politics in Thailand*, "it is seldom acknowledged and frequently denied. This paradox derives from two deeply rooted notions: that politics is the dirtiest business and the most distasteful manipulation of power in human affairs, and that only a pure Buddhism and a sound Sangha can ensure the moral welfare of the nation. Studying the interaction of Buddhism and politics therefore probes areas which are sensitive for both the government and the Sangha authorities, and they discourage it."

Any scholarly proposal to study the interaction of Buddhism and politics in Thailand has to go through a close scrutiny by the government's Department of Religious Affairs and through the Sangha authorities before being approved. In the last twenty years perhaps half a dozen studies have been officially sanctioned; many more were undertaken without authorization.

In Thai thinking, their society is built on three strong pillars: the nation, the monarchy, and the Sangha, which preserves and disseminates the teachings of Buddha. It is therefore a traditional function of the political elite to promote, support, and protect Buddhism and the Sangha; Thai politicians believe that if they do not perform this function successfully, the people will lose faith in the Sangha and eventually in society's moral foundation. For their part the monks believe they play an integrative role in the social and cultural life of Thais and provide a set of basic Buddhist values for the regulation of that life.

This concept is hard to convey to most Westerners. Thai Buddhism fits somewhere between the role of the Anglican Church in England and the power of the Vatican in Catholicism, though it is probably conceptually closer to the former. It is estimated that there are close to 300,000 monks in Thailand—about 5 percent of the population—who are ordained by the Sangha and must adhere to its behavioral precepts. At some point most Thai men shave their heads, don saffron robes, and spend a brief portion of their lives living in a *wat*, alternately meditating and walking the streets begging for alms.

"I guess you could say we believe in moderation in all things," one Thai friend confessed to me. "The *mai pen rai* attitude pertains to Buddhism as well."

But Thailand's reputation for tolerance and for its self-proclaimed separation of political and religious affairs was somewhat tarnished in 1989 when Phra Bodhirak, the founder of a controversial Buddhist sect called Santi Asoke, was arrested for violating the Sangha's religious laws. Prior to entering the monkhood in 1970, Bodhirak was Rak Rakpong, a prime-time television entertainer who had become disillusioned by rampant materialism in Thai society. After he was ordained (Phra is Thai for "monk"), Bodhirak wrote that his mission was to revitalize Buddhism in Thailand, and he criticized the mainstream sects for supporting, through their traditional tolerance, the increasingly materialistic behavior of Thai society.

His outspokenness attracted immediate attention, and his superiors kept him under close watch. But his asceticism attracted many followers, not least General Chamlong Srimuang, whose party received some $250,000 in unsolicited contributions from Santi Asoke believers. Bodhirak's sect now has seventy-nine monks and more than 100,000 adherents who subscribe to his simple doctrine of self-discipline, antimaterialism, and individual enlightenment. (It is the last that has gotten him into hot water with the authorities; the Sangha's laws, not individual monks, prescribe the process of enlightenment, which can be attained only by a bodhisattva.)

Bodhirak has been described by the Bangkok politician and former minister of industry Samak Sundaravej, whose Prachakorn Thai Party competes with Uncle Chamlong's Palang Dharma for influence, as a "termite which could destroy the country," and he has suggested that Chamlong himself may be the Ayatollah Khomeini of Thai politics. After his arrest in June 1989, Bodhirak was released on token bail ($800). He changed his robe from saffron to white but refused to defrock himself as the Sangha demanded, or to reject the monkhood, maintaining he had the right to interpret the Lord Buddha's teachings in his own way.

Reporting on this issue has been a delicate test for the Thai press. The interior ministry issued a warning to Bangkok media to refrain from even commenting on it, which in turn prompted an editorial in the *Bangkok Post* criticizing the government for limiting the freedom of the press. The Reporters Association of Thailand used the incident to ask the government to scrap a 1976 law that gives it unlimited power to close a newspaper for publishing articles that it considers a threat to religion, national security, or "good morals."

In a summary article in the August 21, 1989, issue of the *Asian Wall Street Journal*, entitled "A Sectarian Dispute Roils Thai Buddhism," John Berthelsen wrote, "Early one recent morning, the Supreme Patriarch of Thailand's 54 million Buddhists blessed an Airbus A-300, sprinkling holy water and daubing sandalwood paste and gold flake onto the nose of the aircraft. When the service was over, he was driven away in a cream-colored Mercedes-Benz."

The interior ministry said Berthelsen's article offended the Thai notion of national dignity by suggesting that Buddhist practices can sometimes be less than pure, and the government temporarily banned the newspaper's circulation. Then when the August cover of a popular Thai monthly, *Bangkok 30*, showed a man in a bright saffron robe listening to a Sony Walkman and reading a copy of *Playboy* magazine, the ministry confiscated that issue from all newsstands.

But there was more than irony in that cover photo. Phra Bodhirak had brought to light certain practices of mainstream monks that would shock the Lord Buddha today, such as drinking liquor, selling divine tips on the state lottery, and practicing mumbo-jumbo fortune-telling trades. "There are thirty-two items named in the Buddhist scriptures that monks shouldn't do," one former monk observed, "and thirty-one of them are popular in Thailand." Phra Bodhirak has sucessfully attracted a wide following of middle-class Thais, he says, because they too are revulsed by such behavior. Bodhirak maintains the Sangha's charges are motivated by politics, but its leaders counter that, if the wayward monk is not punished, trouble will reign in Sangha society.

Political repression, peasant misery, social injustice, and rapid economic growth are just a few of the factors that may turn mainstream monks into political monks like Phra Bodhirak. (In the early 1970s Phra Kitthiwuttho Bhikku declared a holy war on communism and maintained that, because Communists were less than human, killing them did not contradict the Sangha law against murder.) But the question remains whether patronized and co-opted members of the Sangha will continue to cooperate with the political elite in resisting adjustment to Thailand's rapidly changing socioeconomic structure or may eventually act as a brake on further high-speed economic growth. In this sense Buddhism, like the ideology of privatization, is very much a political factor.

Summing Up

Flexible equilibrium? Flexible tolerance? The traditional Thai virtues of balance and moderation may give the country's political system some advantages over other Third World governments that lack those traits, but in the absence of an overriding authority to neutralize factional conflict within the elite the possibility of future political coups can never be discounted. Despite what the conventional wisdom *says*, I am more persuaded by what recent history *shows*, that over the past half-century coups (successful or not) have been a regular staple of Thai politics. Prior to 1932 Thai politics was authoritarian, under an absolute monarchy. But after 1932, under a constitutional monarchy, the Thai political system did not simply transform itself, like a beautiful butterfly emerging from its cocoon, into a new and complete creature. It remains fundamentally flawed.

"Politics and government [in Thailand] during the long period of absolute monarchy were generally stable, secure, and orderly," Somsakdi Xuto wrote in *Government and Politics of Thailand*, "despite occasional changes of dynasty as well as conflicts and wars with her neighbors. On the other hand, the track record under constitutional monarchy has generally been, to say the least, much less favorable. One unfortunate characteristic has been the frequent changes in government. The usual pattern has been change in existing government through the use of military force . . . [creating] a vicious cycle of Thai politics. In the final analysis, the most decisive factor shaping Thai politics, whether short-term or long-term, will continue to be the armed forces."

Precisely that faction with the most power to knock more than a few of those five balls out of their corner sockets.

CORRUPTION, THAI STYLE

When General Chaovalit recently remarked that the government ought to clean house because a foreign magazine had named Thailand the ninth-most-corrupt country in the world, he was not being moralistic. He was making a political statement carefully calculated to boost his future fortunes.

"It costs a billion baht to become a general," one Thai friend told me. "But it's worth it."

In Thailand, as in most other Asian countries (Singapore again being the notable exception), corruption is an obvious fact of life. Because their pay is so low, lower-level civil servants collect small bribes to supplement their incomes. Higher-ranking officials are paid through "fees" related to projects their ministries ultimately approve. And the generals profit through sizable rake-offs on military procurement contracts.

"Every bureaucrat has his price," another Thai informant with considerable experience told me. "It costs about 500 baht to facilitate paperwork at the lower levels and around 10,000 baht for the same purpose higher up. The prime minister's salary is 30,000 baht a month, not including allowances, which total another 10,000 baht. How can he maintain a weekend home, buy golf club memberships, take overseas vacations, and entertain so lavishly on that income? The answer is, he can't, and neither can cabinet ministers or senators or representatives, so they have to supplement their incomes somehow."

Not unlike in Indonesia, when Thai generals get their "fees" from lucrative weapons procurement contracts, they pass part of that income down the chain of command to their younger loyalists. This helps seal their support and is used by them to build a new barracks or a soccer field that might otherwise go begging for lack of funds under defense budgets that have, on average, been declining. In 1987 the budget for the armed forces was 18 percent of total government expenditures, or 3.23 percent of GNP; in 1988, its share was 17.7 and 2.98 percent respectively and declining.

Taxes—or, more accurately, tax avoidance—are another way to supplement income in Thailand. Some revenue department officials actually help large companies prepare their annual income tax returns so they don't have to pay taxes at all—in exchange for an appropriate fee. Most big firms report losses every year, and their accounts are "certified" by licensed Thai accountants, many of whom are also on the take and will sign off on just about anything. Again, as in most Asian countries, Thai companies keep several sets of books: one for the tax authorities, one for the shareholders, one for their banks, and one for the family members (also called "the real thing").

"Indirect taxes, like sales taxes and tariffs, are the preferred means of revenue collection," another Thai source suggested, "even though they are regressive. We need to lower tax *rates* to increase tax *revenues*; at 20 percent of gross income people might be more willing to be honest, but at 35 percent the rate is too high, so people avoid paying. If taxes are forced savings for the public sector, then tax avoidance is forced savings for the private sector. Our tax laws allow lavish deductions for expenses, too, which is one reason you see so many Mercedes sedans and BMWs running around Bangkok."

In the opinion of the *Far Eastern Economic Review*, oppressive practices by corrupt civil servants and unscrupulous entrepreneurs are the prime culprits behind these lucrative supplemental fee income payments. Cabinet ministers are most frequently singled out for blame. When Prime Minister Chatichai formed his new cabinet following the 1988 elections, his Chat Thai party secretary (and then-minister of industry), Banharn Silpa-archa, immediately canceled three major government contracts that his predecessor, Samak Sundaravej, had initiated in the previous Prem administration.

Item: A contract for $130 million worth of new buses from Van Hool of Belgium for the Bangkok Mass Transit Authority, signed in 1986, was terminated abruptly by Banharn, prompting a diplomatic protest from Brussels to the Thai foreign ministry.

Item: Banharn canceled plans by a French consortium to undertake the first private construction and operation of toll roads in Thailand, rejecting a previously accepted $300 million Bouyges bid to build two major highways in the central plains.

Item: Banharn derailed the proposed purchase of nine Royal Express trains from Commonwealth Engineering of Australia, previously contracted for and timed to coincide with King Bhumibol's sixtieth birthday that December.

Foreigners were left asking whether Thai government policies—and its procurement programs—would change every time a minister left office, the clear implication being that all-important up-front "fees" would have to be renegotiated with each new cabinet. When he was still minister of communications in the previous Prem cabinet, Banharn created a stir when he decided to grant a lucrative crane monopoly to a company partly owned by Chat Thai party members. (He fought bitterly with former NESDB secretary general Snoh Unakul, who opposed the transaction on the grounds that it was not in the best interests of the economy, and Snoh was later proven correct when the company went bankrupt.)

In an unrelated incident several months later the Korean construction giant Hyundai, clearly no stranger to the ways of Asian governments, was disqualified on a "technical fault" when it bid on a major Klong Toey port expansion project (its bank guarantee was reportedly not acceptable). Thai sources suggested that the Siam Cement group wanted the deal so badly it was willing to go to any lengths to get Hyundai out.

"In Thailand, if a business family wants to prosper," another Thai acquaintance told me, "it is essential to have patrons in the government. Good relationships with senior officials are necessary if a company wants to become large: only the government has the authority to approve certain projects, it is an important source of funds, and it can use taxing powers at its discretion."

Wives of Thai cabinet ministers are the beneficiaries of choice for these up-front "fees," so that their minister husbands are never seen actually receiving them. Payments are reportedly made in any number of ways, including cash, jewelry, shares of stock, titles to land, and deposits into foreign bank accounts. Like everything else about Thai life, corruption is understated, because ostentatiousness is frowned on. People who get it don't talk, and people who give it don't either.

Following persistent criticism of corruption at high levels of his government in mid-1990, Prime Minister Chatichai sacked the suspects (both junior ministers) and shuffled his cabinet in an attempt to silence his critics. Chatichai asked the leader of the Social Action Party (and Thailand's foreign minister for the past ten years), Siddhi Savetsila, to step down, because the prime corruption suspects had been members of his party. The results were typical of Thai behavior; when faced with accusation of corruption in high places, the most honest man often winds up resigning. The junior ministers who were dismissed had been accused of accepting bribes to ease government regulations.

According to a Thai government committee on local administration, about $2 million in UN refugee resettlement funds disappears each year through embezzlement and skimming practices by the interior ministry, a relatively small sum in the world of Thai corruption. But the Golden Triangle at the common borders of Thailand, Laos, and Burma has for years been the source of most of the world's supply of heroin and involves huge sums.

"A harvest worth one trillion baht" was how the *Bangkok Post* began one recent editorial when it described the 170-million-ton bumper crop of opium harvested in 1988. And *that* was 20 percent higher than the previous year's production, generating nearly $50 billion in revenues for the Asian criminals who grow it. Drugs are big-time business in Thailand, the *Post* said, implying that without the connivance of local law enforcement officials drug-trafficking syndicates could never succeed.

When it comes to law enforcement, there is arguably no sector of the service economy more lucrative for the beneficiaries of corruption than prostitution: with Beirut now in shambles as a result of a festering war, and Manila exporting so many barmaids and hostesses to Japan and elsewhere, Bangkok has today become the undisputed sex capital of the world. And the cash it generates—$3 billion a year, or about 5 percent of a booming GNP—just happens to be Thailand's number-one source of export earnings, corrupting not just the Thai polity but Thai values as well.

THE THAI LUST FOR LIFE . . . AND DEATH

In 1988 4.3 million tourists visited Thailand, fully three-quarters of them unaccompanied men from all over the world who came to enjoy not just the pristine white beaches at Phuket but Bangkok's coffeehouses, bars, and ubiquitous massage parlors that help make sex one of the most valuable subsectors of the Thai economy. At $3 billion in invisible receipts, tourism alone accounts for a third of all services in Thailand. By comparison, textiles, the leading Thai export, generated only $2.3 billion in 1988.

But sex is more than just a subsector of the Thai economy; it plays an important and traditional role in Thai society. Prostitutes serviced immigrant men in Ayutthaya times, and after the Bowring Treaty of 1855 brought waves of immigrant labor, young women from China serviced the corvée. Thai women were also legally sold into prostitution until that practice was abolished under King Chulalongkorn's reforms in 1868.

Beginning in the 1960s the American military buildup provided a supercharged demand for prostitution as an industry, launching its worldwide reputation among *farang* (foreigners). Even now, when the Pacific Fleet visits Thai ports, the reaction is enthusiastic. "We need the U.S. Navy," one small hotelier said recently when 8,000 American sailors landed in Pattaya, a small resort town south of Bangkok. "July is a slow month, and the American navy plays a major role in supporting the local economy." The sailors spent $3 million in five days.

Although it officially disavows the industry, which in fact is illegal in Thailand today, the Thai government has from time to time indirectly encouraged it. In 1980 the former deputy prime minister, Boonchu Rojanasathian, advised provincial governors to "encourage certain entertainment activities which some may find disgusting or embarrassing because they are related to sexual pleasures, [but] we must do this because we have to consider the jobs that will be created for the people."

And quite some number of jobs. Official estimates indicate that about 500,000 Thai women are employed as prostitutes today—nearly 1 percent of the population—and even that number may be low; private estimates are closer to 1 million. On a per-capita basis fully twice as many women are prostitutes as men are monks. The higher level of sexual activity for men than for women is generally related to Thai tolerance of both prostitution and polygamy, neither of which is legal.

Rural poverty is cited as the principal reason for the popularity of prostitution as a career. There are countless case studies of Thai teenagers being sold by their debt-burdened parents or simply escaping from their dead-end lives as tenant farmers. The rationale invariably given is economic, and yet the major portion of the young prostitutes' earnings is remitted back to their villages, to help their parents buy a house, acquire land, or purchase needed equipment. In Bangkok, where the average industrial wage is $3 a day, prostitutes can net as much as $40 an hour in upscale bars and coffeehouses.

Good prostitutes make good money, Thais say, and lots of it. They earn high wages from foreign clients and send it home, thus preserving the cultural tradition of being good daughters: they take care of their parents, they return home regularly for the New Year celebrations, and they fulfill the Buddhist expectations by donating to the local *wat*. Importantly, they are not stigmatized by society. What's more, they stay in the business only long enough to put away a comfortable nest egg for themselves and their families and then get out.

"The way of the prostitute is also a way to cope with Thai culture and social reality," the venerable Dutch scholar Niels Mulder once wrote. "She cashes in on the ambiguous cultural equation of prestige, power, and money. There is nothing wrong in prostituting oneself as long as it results in money or powerful protection. And as long as she cares for her relatives in terms of gifts and money, she can still present herself as a good person. [Then] when she has accumulated enough, or when her fortunes turn, she may resettle in her village of origin, marry, and be accepted."

One young girl who does just that calls herself Thoo. She comes from the poorest section of the country in the Northeast, near Udon Thani, and works at the Crown Royale, a bar in Patpong, Bangkok's central nightclub district. She bore a striking resemblance to Audrey Hepburn, I thought, with dark, shiny hair that created a soft halo around her smooth face. We sat and nursed a beer one hot, dry summer afternoon as we talked about her job.

"I get paid 2,500 baht a month appearance money," she was telling me in workable English, "and I can earn another 2,500 baht in tips. My rent costs 1,500 a month, food 2,000, and personal things another 1,500, so the straight money covers living expenses. But I can make much more than that on dates, and I send it all home to my mother."

Thoo said the "market" for "dates" is anywhere from 800 baht to 2,000 baht, depending on the "service" and how long she is engaged—even more if she can negotiate it. At four o'clock in the afternoon the Crown Royale was painfully quiet. Cleopatra's was next door, followed by Blue Jeans, Thigh Girls, Night Wings, Love Boat, Crazy Horse, and Mike's Place, on down the short, neon-lit Patpong strip, which is also the curbside market of choice for night-time vendors of Thailand's Rolex knockoffs. Thaniya, a section of Patpong just a few blocks away, is popular with the Japanese; the Thais now call it Little Ginza.

Patpong is also the stuff of fiction. Thailand's famed novelist, Pira Sudham, who was nominated for a 1989 Nobel Prize in literature, captured the flavor of this floating world in his novel *Monsoon Country*.

"I longed to know her life story, the road that took her to that crowded, noisy, smoky bar full of *farang* in Patpong," Pira wrote. "When we arrived in her village, she acted like a splendid well-off lady and treated me just like any taxi driver who drove her all the way home, . . . It was a game of life. I was so ashamed of myself, I never went back to that Patpong bar again, even though I am still quite curious to know whether the girl from Udorn is still dancing there."

At night practically everything imaginable occurs onstage in Patpong's countless bars, from live sex acts to striptease to game shows: young women will smoke cigarettes, paint *sumi*-ink calligraphy, and pick up coins with their lips—using just their vaginal muscles. Rock music deadens the ears in one popular place where a shiny chrome motorbike hangs from the ceiling as two young Thais, balanced precariously, copulate.

Sex so predominates the *farang* image of Thailand as a tourist haven that Red Wing, a UK tour operator partly owned by British Airways, recently published travel brochures containing rather lurid accounts of this entertainment. "Many of the girly bars and sex shows have that flavour of the first encounter behind the bike shed at school," the brochure read. "Technically speaking, they're all whores, but in truth they're just little girls showing you their knickers." The Thai government has sought to ban the company from bringing tours to Thailand.

"I came to Bangkok to get away from my aunt," another young Thai girl named Noi told me over coffee. "She was very strict to me and made me work in her hotel doing boring jobs. This was in Phuket. There is nothing in Phuket. Everything is in Bangkok. *Everything*. That is why we all come here."

According to some recent estimates, Bangkok has more than 800 "coffeehouses" (massage parlors), 400 nightclubs, and fifty-five gay bars, many of which are reputed to be partially owned by Thai politicians, their staffs, and even the police. Of a recent sampling of 1,000 prostitutes, 44 percent were found to be HIV-positive, and although the official government "count" of prostitutes with AIDS is only 3,000, more reasonable estimates are ten times that figure. Add to them the number of HIV-positive among Thailand's immense drug population, and you have what one public health official has called "a ticking time bomb."

To counter the AIDS threat the public health ministry has begun promoting the use of condoms through educational shows sponsored by the World Health Organization, among others. At the Superlex, one of Patpong's most popular bars, some 200 barboys from seven local gay bars recently watched just such a show put on by the Purple String, a gay dance troupe founded by the well-known gay activist Natee Teerarojjanapong. Most of Bangkok's upscale "coffeehouses" now insist that their girls provide customers with condoms.

The Thai word for condom is *mechai*, from Mechai Viravaidya, Thailand's charismatic, Australian-educated economist who for many years was responsible for the country's population control program. He halved the birthrate from 3.2 percent a year in 1970 to less than 1.8 percent in 1986 and today heads the Population and Community Development Association in Bangkok. It has become Thailand's largest nonprofit organization.

"We have to treat AIDS like we did family planning," Mechai told me as we sat in his modestly appointed office at the PDA. "The next three years are crucial, and for a developing country like Thailand prevention is the only cure. Not the best cure, the *only* one. We need a massive program of education and information, working with the police, the *wat*, the economic development funds, and the media—*all* media, not just the press, but taxidrivers, gas station operators, primary school teachers—we have more than 300,000 of them—urban employers, salesclerks, shoeshine boys, and curbside vendors."

Mechai's definition of media expanded geometrically when he ran the nation's population control program, and the popularity of his methods, built on the Thai concept of *sanuk*, or fun, helped achieve such stunning results. He devised rhyming games and balloon-blowing contests with condoms for kids, invented a game he called "cops and rubbers," painted posters on water buffalo hides (the rural version of billboards), made tape recordings that he distributed to taxidrivers for their sound systems, and practically inundated the country with condoms.

"I wanted to take the taboo out of birth control," he said, "to remove it from the realm of the secretive and make it fun. I found that if you could make people laugh, they were more inclined to be on your side. So my helpers—usually pretty girls—went around offering the villagers condoms in baskets, and I would say, 'People with dirty minds are not allowed to have any.' Everyone took them."

His most famous device was a key ring with a clear plastic holder; a sample condom was placed on one side and an educational message on the other, such as "Stop AIDS," or "Now I'm Safe," or "In Case of Emergency, Break Glass." For the *farang*, he made key rings with Japanese or American or various European flags on one side, and a message that said "Don't Leave Home Without It," on the other. He also thought up a T-shirt showing Winston Churchill with his famous V for victory sign, below which was the inscription "Stop at Two."

Mechai's charisma is contagious. He has a staff of 600 at the PDA supervising sixteen branch offices and has recruited a staff of 12,000 volunteers—what he calls his "grass-roots motivators"—covering 16,000 villages. As a result of these successful community development efforts, Mechai was tapped as a deputy minister of industry in the last Prem cabinet and subsequently appointed senator in the upper house by the king, a position he still holds. He had just returned from a year's leave of absence at Harvard when I saw him in Bangkok.

"We obviously have to cover the massage parlors and the coffeehouses and the bars," he went on, "to inform the undereducated prostitutes. And we have to keep working with the police too. The highest risk here, as elsewhere, is the intravenous drug users, so we have to isolate them and try to segregate them from normal society, to keep women and children from being infected. As with family

planning and population control, we simply have to broadcast the
message every way we can."

Mechai is plainly worried, and for good reason. Thailand has the
world's fastest rate of increase for AIDS. In most countries AIDS is
regarded as serious if it is doubling every year. It quadrupled in
Northern Thailand during the 12-month period from July 1988 to
June 1989, and in Bangkok alone the level of HIV infection recorded
in donated blood registered an *eight-fold* increase that year among
blood donors. Based on these rates, Mechai suspects widespread
underreporting has occurred.

In a recent survey conducted at Klong Toey port, 84 percent of
male intravenous drug users tested positive for the HIV virus. Assuming a more conservative average rate of infection of, say, two-
thirds or 67 percent, that would imply some 67,000 men have the
virus in Bangkok, based on police records of 100,000 confirmed IV
drug users in the city. Thai men have a *minimum*—not an average—
of two sex partners each; if just one of them becomes infected, those
numbers then double.

"We can't wait for the government to take action," Mechai told
me soberly, "and we can't wait for the doctors. We've got to take
action ourselves. Avon and AIA have already begun to spread the
word through their own advertising and marketing campaigns. We
can't just sit back and watch a disaster."

Mechai has substantiated evidence of AIDS in every province in
Thailand. In one prison the highest infection rate was 51 percent, and
high levels of infection have been found in Thai fishermen (Thailand
has the seventh-largest fishing fleet in the world). Fishermen have
access to heroin and thus to shared needles. And when they dock,
they go straight to the brothels. Mechai thinks about 1 percent of
Thailand's population has the virus today. Conservatively estimated,
that's 600,000 people.

"Nowhere in the world but Thailand can you find more prostitutes than teachers or more brothels than schools," Mechai went on.
"Once people get AIDS, they stop working. Their contribution to
society is finished, they have no salary, and they begin withdrawing
money from the bank. Once bank deposits start to come down, the
banks will fail. You think foreign companies are going to stay or
invest in Thailand under those conditions?"

A survey recently conducted in the Northwest by Chiengmai University's school of medicine and corroborated by the Ministry of Health showed 44 percent of all prostitutes in that quadrant of the country had the virus. But an analysis of the results by price range was even more stunning. Those prostitutes with the lowest prices for their services—thirty baht to fifty baht, or no more than $2—had an infection rate of 72 percent. Prostitution is so pervasive that at water buffalo auctions *mobile* brothels often tag along—cheap prostitutes taken by enterprising young men on motorbikes to service poor farmers who attend to buy or sell a new carabao.

"The implications for our society are simply staggering," Mechai said, shaking his head. "I have a daughter who is thirteen, and I wonder about my chances of becoming a grandfather. I assume ten years from now she'll get married, but how many Thai males will there be without AIDS then?"

The tolerance of Thai Buddhism is often cited as a factor behind prostitution as a thriving trade, despite the fact that it is illegal. (Polygamy, too, while against the law, is practiced openly, which is one reason the Thai divorce rate is so low—0.69 per 1,000 of population except in Bangkok, where it is three times that high.) Women are the hindlegs of the elephant, Thais say, meaning society stands or falls by them. The problem is that while there are families in Thailand, there is no family system as in Japan or Korea.

Violence is a another aspect of Thai society that belies its Buddhist reputation for gentleness and tolerance. In 1987 more than 20,000 violent crimes were reported, of which at least 6,000 were murders. On a per-capita basis the murder rate in Thailand is twice that of America, which is already ten times as high as that of Japan, making the official Thai murder rate one of the highest in the world. Nor are *farang* exempt. In early 1989 a honeymooning Japanese tourist and his young wife were murdered by a Thai taxidriver and his accomplice on their arrival in Bangkok. Shortly thereafter a young Toyo Engineering employee was killed by Thai thugs near Pattaya. In Bangkok the police mounted a massive manhunt and announced a ten-day crackdown on violent crime, which resulted in the arrest of more than 6,000 suspects and the confiscation of thirty guns.

In Thailand people have been killed simply for staring at a

stranger, without smiling, in which case the offended person may pick up his symbol of masculinity and riddle the staring person with bullets because he fears an intrusion on his ego by the other, an intrusion that is also dangerous and therefore insulting and therefore commands revenge. Social scientists suggest that in Thai interpersonal relationships the attributes of power dominate interaction. Power is necessary, and one deals with it pragmatically, the same way one deals with money. In a society where one finds it difficult to cope with the competition of threatening power, one may opt for radical solutions. Like murder.

"Violence lurks beneath a veneer of smiles and pleasantry" was the way one Thai friend explained it to me. On rural highways "Caution" and "Dangerous Curve" signs are frequently removed from the roadside to "encourage accidents," as one friend told me, so villagers can loot the dead bodies. If three people die in an automobile crash, Thais will simply shrug their shoulders; in Thailand it's considered no big deal unless hundreds are killed when a bus veers off the road.

Perhaps in a Buddhist spirit of denial, incidents such as these are seldom publicly revealed. We have already seen what happened to former minister Veera Musikapong for his indiscretion and to the *Asian Wall Street Journal* and England's Red Wing tours. In early 1988, when an Australian archaeologist determined that the kilns he had unearthed at Ban Ko Noi may have predated the Sukhothai era, he was expelled from the country.

Another Problem, the Same Solution: Education

Societal flaws point to the crucial importance of strengthening Thai education. While Thailand has the highest literacy rate in Southeast Asia, it has the lowest matriculation rate into secondary school: fewer than half of its children move on from grade school to high school. Although the government has advocated extending compulsory education to nine years, as with so many other things in Thailand, form is valued more than substance.

"When I say compulsory, I don't actually mean students should be required to go on to lower secondary school," a senior government official confided to me, "but rather that they should be *encour-*

aged to do so." This attitude represents a fundamental philosophical difference between Thailand and Japan, Korea, or Taiwan, where commitment to public education is such a strong national priority— the Asian moral equivalent of the *jihad*.

In that sense Bangkok's Chulalongkorn High School may be the exception to the rule. With 1,300 students, it serves as a combination experimental teaching laboratory and a feeder school for Chulalongkorn University, one of Thailand's elite institutions, which receives about half of its graduates (some 85 percent go on to university). Its motto is "Knowledge with Morality." Still, it seemed to lack those competitive qualities so prevalent in public schools throughout Northeast Asia.

"The students know about competition, sure," Nopphong Bunyajitradulya, Chula's American-educated principal, admitted to me. "But I honestly don't know whether they can face the facts. The level of homework required here is not very high, even by American standards. And because of our *mai pen rai* mentality, it's not the parents so much as the cultural environment that influences Thai students. So I find it hard to be optimistic about the future, because the future is going to be even more competitive than anything these kids have yet experienced, especially considering what high school students in Japan and Korea and Singapore are achieving. I don't think we've even begun to see the implications of this yet."

The only other school in Bangkok that even remotely reflects the quality of public education so widely available in the Little Dragons is Vajiravudh, the elite prep school established in 1910 by King Vajiravudh (Rama VI) and modeled after Eton, in England, where the king himself once studied. Enrollment is limited to only 900 students, and the tone of the school is highly competitive; all of its graduates go on to university, half of whom then proceed to the private sector, the other half to government service. Of the many Thai leaders interviewed for this book, M. R. Sukhumband Paribatra of Chulalongkorn; Narongchai Akrasanee at TDRI; Amnuay Viravan, the former minister of finance; and Mechai Viravaidya, Thailand's charismatic family planner, are all Vajiravudh graduates.

Having spent considerable time visiting public schools in Japan and all the Little Dragons, I am impressed not only with the rigor of their curricula but also with the discipline, the seriousness, and the élan of their students. These Northeast Asian countries and Singapore, all poor in natural resources, have accurately assessed the challenge of the emerging information age and are developing the skilled human resources necessary to confront it. So far Thailand's response has been mere lip service, though it desperately needs more trained scientists and engineers. Otherwise, as Charoen Kanthawongs, the deputy minister of agriculture, admitted to me, value-added jobs for Thais will never materialize, and Thailand will not be able to persuade its best students overseas to come home in the kind of reverse brain drain that Korea and Taiwan have been benefiting from for years.

"Thai society has been characterized by loose structure, Buddhism, and individualism," the Dutch scholar Niels Mulder wrote in *Everyday Life in Thailand*. "Thais are individualists because they are Buddhists, and [individualism and Buddhism] make for a loosely structured social system where rules are flaunted. . . . At the high point, Thai society always travels on the brink of social chaos. The ethos of Thailand is still an ethos of a highly autocratic society that breeds conformity more than initiative and value-avoidance more than involvement."

THAI FOREIGN POLICY:
A PRECARIOUS EQUILIBRIUM

The value triumvirate of nation, religion, and king dominates the thinking of most Thais. According to a recent poll of several hundred local village leaders throughout Thailand—whose religious beliefs (95 percent were Buddhist), sex (97 percent were male), educational background (70 percent had completed only the first four years of primary school), and occupation (75 percent were rice farmers) represent the nation's homogeneous rural population outside Bangkok—the feelings of Thai nationalism are quite strong.

Two-thirds of the poll respondents indicated in response to one question that the sole components of Thai national pride were nation, religion, and king. Only 2.4 percent suggested democracy played a role, just 1 percent thought prosperity was somehow related, and the remaining 30 percent had no answer. Two out of three also said that Thailand was "a great nation," 95 percent wanted to be born Thai again in the next life, and 93 percent had absolutely no desire whatever to emigrate. Among the *farang* only Westerners and Japanese "could be strongly trusted" (though only after fellow Thais); Vietnamese, Cambodian, Lao, and Burmese neighbors were all to be strongly distrusted.

ASEAN, Souvannaphoum, and the Struggle for a Regional Niche

Centuries of hostility and outright war between Thailand and its immediate neighbors have fueled these strongly nationalistic feelings. In Southeast Asia there is the sense that Thailand is the traditional hub of the mainland, a sense that Thais themselves share (and, needless to say, help maintain). Since the U.S. withdrawal from Vietnam in 1975 and Vietnam's subsequent invasion of Cambodia in 1978, tension between Thailand and its neighbors has escalated, shifting the balance of power to Vietnam and disrupting this hub concept.

In the decade up to the withdrawal of Vietnamese forces from Cambodia in late 1989, more than 300,000 Cambodian refugees had to be resettled in neighboring Thai provinces, creating new border conflicts and heavy burdens for relief agencies. An old Khmer proverb says when two Cambodians get into bed they will fight over who gets to sleep in the middle. Attempts to resolve the Cambodian question still drag on, even though diplomatic sessions in both Jakarta and Paris have brought the four domestic Cambodian factions together to compromise on power-sharing arrangements through UN-supervised elections in early 1991.

"People tend to forget that Vietnam and Siam fought four wars in the nineteenth century," Sukhumband Paribatra reminded me as we sat in his office at the Institute for Strategic and International Studies. "The present conflict with Cambodia stems directly from Vietnam's reunification in 1975. Now that Vietnamese troops have begun to leave Cambodia, however, there is greater dialogue between Thai and Vietnamese foreign ministers, who met six times in 1988 and 1989 alone—an unprecedented series of meetings. Since Vietnam's economy is so anemic, like all the central command systems, there is a growing realization in Hanoi that Thailand should be the primary conduit for trade and investment in Indochina. Indochinese markets can never replace our external markets, but they are necessary for stable political relationships, especially now that economic considerations are replacing geopolitical factors in the world of superpower relations."

These geo-economic considerations were apparently important enough for Prime Minister Chatichai to proclaim, in mid-1989, his Souvannaphoum concept for mainland Southeast Asia. Souvannaphoum is a Thai word meaning "Golden Peninsula," which prompted criticism from both the Vietnamese, who saw in it a veiled attempt on Thailand's part to reestablish hegemonic power on the mainland, and Sukhumband, who felt Thailand's ASEAN allies might misinterpret it as a military ploy. It also rekindled Chatichai's reputation as a politician who "shoots from the lip"—he said without much prior reflection that he wanted to "convert plowshares into market shares"—which prompted one Thai friend to suggest that the prime minister was doing it simply for publicity value since he was known to be hungry for a Nobel Peace Prize. Given Thailand's historically volatile relationship with Indonesia, it was a statement that lacked sensitivity.

"Chatichai's Souvannaphoum proclamation was poorly timed, coming *before* any Cambodian settlement had been reached," a senior Singapore government official told me. "The Thais want to be the center of Southeast Asia, but they probably can't capitalize on that until they get their infrastructure mess straightened out, for starters. But if civil war continues in Cambodia, then the Thais will be unavoidably distracted and possibly suffer from a potential misallocation of resources."

Thailand's external relations with the various members of ASEAN are, on the whole, good. Authoritarian Singapore almost created a serious split with Thailand in 1989, though, when it threatened to cane a Thai worker who had overstayed his visa in violation of a controversial retroactive immigration law. (Caning is customary punishment for a variety of offenses in Singapore.) Mindful of the bitter resentment its execution of several Indonesian sailors for spying had generated a decade earlier, the Singapore foreign ministry ultimately reached a compromise that spared the Thai worker from the bamboo cane.

With Thailand looking at Indonesia as its new frontier, some fear that it may be jettisoning ASEAN. "There are two schools of thought here," one senior official in the Thai foreign ministry explained to me. "One sees us as the hub of this so-called Golden Peninsula, which could grow in strength and eventually weaken ASEAN. A second sees us keeping ASEAN intact and eventually trying to draw Burma, Vietnam, Laos, and Cambodia in. But Souvannaphoum averts the external world and focuses solely on our peninsular self-sufficiency, perhaps even challenging Singapore. That would run the risk of bringing ASEAN to an end."

Thailand's relations with Burma, Southeast Asia's hermit kingdom, are for the most part stable and quiet. Much goes on, however, that is not reported, such as collusion on illicit drug trade in the Golden Triangle and illegal logging operations that thrive near the invisible Burmese border. In mid-1989, when Burmese troops chased armed insurgents of the Karen National Union into Thailand, apparently undetected, and seized the Thai border villages of Huay Hai and Wang Kaew, isolated clashes occurred between the Burmese and Thai border police, but the incident escalated no further despite intense questioning in Bangkok by Chatichai's political opponents.

Pro-democracy demonstrations in Rangoon in September 1988 were about the same size as those occurring in Beijing in June 1989—about a million people took part in each—but twice as many Burmese demonstrators were shot and killed by the troops of Burma's brutal and xenophobic military dictatorship. Isolated and completely ostracized, Burma today is less a nation than a patchwork quilt of ethnic, religious, and regional conflicts that have hardened its political leadership, derailed its economy, and created a crucible of intense pressure for change. Few recall that Burma was the region's wealthiest country a generation ago—Southeast Asia's greatest rice exporter and a major trading power in silk and gems, commodities markets now dominated by its traditional nemesis, Thailand.

The Superpower Game: Japan vs. the United States

As with Indonesia, Thailand's most important bilateral relationship is with Japan, overwhelmingly and unarguably its largest foreign investor, aid donor, and trading partner. Thailand ranks fourth on

Japan's list of major recipients of overseas development assistance (ODA), with nearly $400 million in 1988 (following Indonesia, China, and the Philippines), accounting for nearly 5 percent of Japan's total foreign aid. While that assistance has brought Thailand much-needed infrastructure development—roads, bridges, and airport improvements are just a few of the projects Japan has financed—not a little resentment has been created because so much of Japan's foreign aid is irrevocably tied to the sale of Japanese goods, services, and technology.

Some of the biggest construction contracts ever awarded in Thailand have gone to Japanese firms because of their connections to Japan's ODA, including the 1984 Dao Khanong–Bangkok expressway project, valued at nearly $300 million; the Thailand Cultural Center in Ayutthaya, $50 million; and a recent $40 million expansion of Bangkok's international airport. Engineering specifications for these Japanese projects tend to be too narrowly written, Thai experts claim, making it impossible for Thai firms to compete. In many instances the machinery and equipment necessary are available only in Japan, and building design often does not take Thai climatic or cultural factors into account, factors disregarded so frequently and consistently that they prompted the Association of Siamese Architects to lodge a formal complaint with the Japanese government in 1987.

"We called that cultural center at Ayutthaya 'the elephant house' because it was so clumsy-looking," Prasert Chittiwatanapong, a political economist at Thammasat University and a leading Thai expert on Japan, told me. "Thai architects were really offended by that project, believe me, because it was built to commemorate the king's sixtieth birthday. Bidding for the design work was open only to Japanese architectural firms, who drew the plans in such a way that no Thai features were incorporated into the design, either outside or inside the buildings. And they had the gall to put a small Japanese garden inside that bore no relation whatsoever to the whole concept!"

Japanese foreign aid is administered principally by two agencies, the Overseas Economic Cooperation Fund (OECF), which makes yen loans, and the Japanese International Cooperation Agency (JICA), which is responsible for technical supervision. For their part, despite the closed bidding process and equipment procurement restrictions—which simply reflect the way they do business in their own domestic market—the Japanese don't understand why the Thais react so negatively since Japan views foreign aid primarily as a gift. "You don't comment on a present someone gives you," one high-ranking official in Japan's Ministry of Foreign Affairs recently commented. "The Thai people should appreciate our efforts."

Overall they do, certainly much more today than two decades ago, when anti-Japanese sentiment was rife. In 1972 the National Students Center of Thailand staged a week-long boycott of Japanese goods to protest Japan's dominance of the economy, and in January 1974, on an overseas trip during which he was greeted with violence in every Southeast Asian capital he visited, Prime Minister Tanaka met the same hostility in Bangkok that he did in Jakarta. Still, those demonstrations primarily masked domestic political discontent, and more recent attempts by the students to organize opposition to the flood of Japanese goods into Thailand have not met with the public's approval and have not succeeded. A recent hit tune by a popular singing group, the Carabao (water buffalo), reflected the mood of Thailand's strong ethnocentric nationalism. It was called, simply, "Made in Thailand" and avoided any anti-Japanese lyrics.

Prasert agrees that Japan's presence in Thailand today is much more effective than it was years ago. "The Japanese have incredible access to sources of information here," he said, "to technocrats, to politicians, and even to the king, based on their overwhelming economic strength. This access has given rise to a low-key, subtle, quiet, understated political role, which suits the Japanese just fine."

Sukhumband Paribatra concurred. "Japan's influence in the region is definitely on the rise, though it will not increase in a straight-line fashion. Japan has a dilemma both domestically and internationally with regard to military spending and deployment of armed forces. Given its economic and financial strengths, I think Japan will increase its political influence even though it says it may not want to. Thailand's experience during the Japanese occupation fifty years ago was not that bad, certainly not in comparison to other countries in the region, so I think we can accommodate a stronger Japanese role, though other countries may not because they don't have the same self-confidence we do."

A senior official in the Thai foreign ministry put it a little less delicately when he said, "The Japanese still want to win the Second World War, and I think you have to realize that Tokyo wants to do you in. You can't get them to tone down their economic power, and you have to accept that. There are no other options for us but to work together with the U.S. on political and strategic issues. The way to get around cutthroat economic competition is through regional cooperation, but Japanese-style economic dominance is a basic fact and here to stay."

The days are gone when U.S. security interests could dominate Thai foreign policy considerations; America's sole political role now seems to revolve around resolution of the Cambodian conflict, but its contributions are hampered by the bitter aftertaste of the Vietnam war, which constrains Washington's policy options. Until mid-1990 the United States favored a coalition government in Cambodia headed by its former head of state, Prince Sihanouk, and functional leader Son Sann, saying it would never recognize a regime headed by an illegitimate Vietnamese puppet. But a Washington policy shift cleared the way for UN–supervised elections scheduled for early 1991.

"The Americans are amicable and friendly, but they're not really 'into' things here," a European expatriate with more than two decades of experience in Bangkok admitted to me. "They enjoy their two- or three-year assignment, and that's about it. But they never seem to make the effort, and I'm never quite sure what they do. The embassy has its annual barbecue and raffle every July 4th, and American companies invite us to their Christmas parties and river cruises on the *Oriental Queen*, but they have nowhere near the depth and thoroughness of the Japanese."

Part of this ambiguity can be explained by the fact that the Thai–U.S. relationship is very much in transition today, being reshaped by both economic and political factors in light of Japan's overwhelming dominance. The United States does not see the strategic significance of East Asia in economic terms, as Japan does, which makes it more difficult for Washington to respond to Thailand's concern that Japan is becoming so strong that it totally dominates Thailand's external relations. (One recent case illustrates the peripheral position of the United States: Washington recently gave

NESDB a $450,000 grant for a feasibility study to convert the U Tapao air base—from which major bombing runs in Vietnam were launched years ago—into a commercial airport for Bangkok, despite the fact that it is located nearly a hundred miles away and is virtually inaccessible.)

"Thailand was effectively a client-state of the U.S. for forty years, but now the Thais are asking what they are getting from the relationship," Kernial Sandhu, the congenial executive director of the Institute of Southeast Asian Studies in Singapore, told me. "They perceive the U.S. to be in decline economically relative to Japan, and America's influence is felt to be on the wane. But they need America to counterbalance Japan—as do all other nations in the region—so the U.S. ought to refine its economic policies and stop lumping Thailand in with the rest of Northeast Asia when it criticizes them all for violating intellectual property rights or for having closed markets."

I asked Sandhu whether it was realistic to think the United States capable of doing this, given America's predisposition toward superpower politics, and he said, "Washington is playing the game with about five strikes against it. President Bush feels somehow personally involved with China; China experts outnumber Japanese specialists in the U.S. government at least ten to one; the Americans still focus on geopolitical rather than economic issues; they don't take advantage of using other strategic alliances in Asia to compete more effectively with Japan; and their trade policies seem increasingly strident and moralistic in tone. It's hard to be optimistic."

When I raised that question with Siddhi Savetsila, his response was characteristically diplomatic.

"We have very close cooperation with the U.S. on narcotics control and on the Cambodian refugee problem," he told me. "But economically there have been some big changes for the U.S. in the last ten years—the budget deficit, the trade deficit, and its very low rate of capital formation—which have forced it to take a tougher posture on trade. Still, in view of our past relationship, the U.S. ought to treat us as a friend, not as a pawn. Patience, education, and understanding are required on both sides, because these issues need time and because we can't be seen as giving in to a foreign power."

Siddhi was until August 1990 the leader of the coalition government's second-largest political group, the Social Action Party, and had been Thailand's foreign minister continuously since 1980, when he retired from a career in the air force with the rank of air chief marshal, a title he still holds. He stepped down as foreign minister in mid-1990, a casualty of some domestic mudslinging in a political corruption case that involved other members of his party but not him. Now in his early seventies, Siddhi is the son of an English father and a Thai mother (his father's surname was Alibaster); he was educated at Chulalongkorn University and at MIT. An outspoken supporter of ASEAN, he stresses interdependence over Thai nationalism in articulating his country's foreign policy.

"The Thai–U.S. relationship is evolving from a state of dependency to one of reciprocity," he went on. "But American economic pressure on Thailand, such as countervailing duties on Thai manufactured exports and Section 301 threats to brand us as an unfair trader if we do not amend our intellectual property rights law are viewed by the Thai public, rightly or wrongly, as evidence of U.S. hostility against Thailand and are poisoning the relationship. If this condition is allowed to fester, it will become increasingly difficult for any Thai government to cooperate with the U.S. in other fields, such as narcotics suppression or national security."

This is a pattern repeated with all-too-familiar frequency throughout Asia. A small trade surplus with the United States emerges and then grows larger. Responding to domestic political pressure from strong special interest groups, American trade negotiators begin by demanding open markets and greater access for American goods, like beef and tobacco—which are generally either under quota or closely controlled—and gradually become confrontational as Asians dig in their heels. Fearful of losing face, the local governments can't afford to give in and have no alternative but to hang tough.

"Japan, with its own closed domestic market, is now giving in to us, little by little, in quiet negotiations, so we are seeing our exports to Japan grow," Narongchai Akrasanee of TDRI explained. "But America, with such a huge, open market, is now tightening up, little by little, using negotiating tactics that are harsh and adversarial. I find this very strange."

"The U.S. gets frustrated with Japan, and that frustration spills over onto us smaller Asian countries," a senior trade official in the Ministry of Commerce told me. "The Americans are straightforward to the point of being blunt, almost rude. I mean, who do they think we are?"

America's frustration with Thailand, as with most Asian nations, revolves around the issues of intellectual property rights—pharmaceuticals and computer software, as we saw earlier—and market access. Virasak Futrakul, one of Thailand's bright young technocrats who is now the deputy director general for political affairs at the Thai foreign ministry, put these issues into perspective in flawless English.

"There's a little hypocrisy at work here," he suggested, "because the U.S. was the last nation in the nineteenth century to join the international copyright convention and sign the treaties covering patents and royalties. We tried to push through an amendment to our copyright law in 1987, but the process became very contentious because there was immense opposition to the image of a big bully shoving a smaller ally around. The computer software issue is still outstanding, mostly because there is no international consensus on it yet, and as for pharmaceuticals, we are willing to amend our laws to protect process, but the U.S. wants product protection as well. Our basic position is that we cannot be seen amending our laws under pressure from *any* foreign government, yet we somehow have to show compliance with standards accepted by the international community. Therefore we think this ought to be resolved in a multilateral forum like the General Agreement on Tariffs and Trade."

I asked Sukhumband Paribatra how he saw this superpower game being played out with Thailand.

"In a way the U.S. is a victim of its own success," he said, "because its past policies have strengthened the political process in Thailand and helped give us great self-confidence and strength. In this part of the world the Soviet Union is a peripheral power, and the most predictable thing about China is its unpredictability. The Chinese have always taken a hard line in foreign policy following domestic turmoil in the past and will likely do so again. But as Washington becomes increasingly frustrated with Japan, and the U.S. takes a harder position toward the smaller nations, it is tempting for us to take a hard line too. Politically that would be very popular here and would play to the home crowd very well. You could very easily see anti-American demonstrations taking place right in front of the U.S. embassy. There are lots of problems for political scientists to solve, and I think we've got our work cut out for us."

THAILAND'S FUTURE:
THE MULTILAYERED CHASE

From late 1985, when the yen began to rise and Japanese investment poured into the country, the Thai economy has experienced unprecedented double-digit rates of growth. As a result, Thailand has now become the darling of international economists, who have increasingly singled it out as the world's next NIC, the next Little Dragon, and the most dynamic among Asia's newly industrializing economies, close on the heels of the conventional pick, Malaysia.

Thailand's strengths are indeed many. They include unparalleled cultural tolerance, which has helped it assimilate so smoothly both the ethnic Chinese minority and the high levels of Japanese investment; personal friendliness and gentility, which make the Thais such pleasant people to work with; an innate love of learning, so prevalent throughout Asia; a highly educated and disciplined elite, who as technocrats and business leaders have guided its political economy so capably; and a political system of "flexible equilibrium" that has generated considerable self-confidence.

But self-confidence often becomes a way of masking a subtle arrogance, of disguising faults and flaws. Against its extraordinary strengths Thailand has a veritable abundance of shortcomings—a long list of liabilities that could eventually cause the Thai economy to stagnate and fall behind its regional competitors. I see ten obstacles to Thailand's becoming a full-fledged Little Dragon:

1. The level of Japanese economic dominance: Now that Tokyo is shifting more of its new investment to Indonesia, can Thailand keep the momentum moving from other foreign investors?

2. Bangkok's gridlocked infrastructure: Can it diversify domestically to avoid further urban overconcentration?

3. Public education: With only six years of compulsory education and an acknowledged shortage of scientists and engineers, can Thailand reasonably expect to keep pace?

4. "Flexible equilibrium" and the coup mentality: Thailand has had a tradition of military intervention in politics for more than fifty years, and elections are next scheduled to occur in 1992. Will we see yet another successful military takeover then, if not before, that may destroy the political stability necessary for further growth?

5. Inadequate savings and capital formation: Thailand has an acknowledged savings-investment gap for at least the next five years. Can its technocrats devise—and implement—the kinds of financial incentives the Little Dragons have used so successfully to close that gap?

6. Monarchical succession: With the law now changed to permit women to succeed to the throne, what will it mean to a male-dominant Thai society if Princess Sirindhorn replaces her father when King Bhumibol, who by all accounts provides the authoritarian underpinning to Thai politics, leaves the scene? Though a remote probability, it is nonetheless legally possible.

7. U.S. intransigence: If American budget and trade deficits persist, will Washington take an even tougher stance with Bangkok on market access, intellectual property rights, and other politically motivated issues, forcing Thailand into even greater dependence on Japan?

8. A Buddhist backlash: As the Thai economy grows and its many tangible benefits are shared by an increasingly wealthy urban middle class, could the Phra Bodhiraks of Bangkok spark a cultural revolt against materialism—or possibly against the rising specter of AIDS—and successfully turn back the clock?

9. Souvannaphoum: Will the prime minister's grandiose scheme for a Golden Peninsula result in political and economic rapprochement with Indochina, or will his ambitious plan drive a wedge through ASEAN, weakening Asia's only regional grouping?

10. Unbalanced income distribution: Unlike in Korea or Taiwan, where the richest 20 percent of the population controls about 40 percent of the wealth, in Thailand the richest 20 percent controls two-thirds of the nation's wealth. Nearly 90 percent of Thailand's population is rural and poor, with an estimated 10 million (20 percent) at the poverty level. Will these conditions be ameliorated or create new political strains?

These considerations far outweigh simple mathematical mea-

surements of performance based on per-capita income or manufactured goods as a percent of total exports. Thailand's future seems to
lie squarely on Japan's path to global dominance in the higher-value-
added, high-productivity industries that appear destined to control
the emerging information age.

Japan needs Thailand as a vital cog in its growing overseas
manufacturing machine. But Thailand needs Japan even more; given
its own considerable shortcomings, Thailand ought not to fear Japanese dominance but embrace it. For Tokyo can engineer industrial
policies for Bangkok that Thai technocrats themselves may be incapable of devising. That may be Thailand's best guarantee that it will
develop the disciplined human resources, the indigenous technologies, and the better-educated, stronger middle class it needs to compete successfully in a global market.

As much as Japan needs Thailand to manufacture its lower-
value-added componentry (and as a controlled market for some of its
goods), Thailand desperately needs Japan for its capital, for its
market, and for its technology. It can thus achieve Little Dragon
status by staying in the slipstream of Japan's flying geese formation,
or, in more current parlance, by sticking to its assigned flight plan in
the multilayered chase.

All this fits right into Japan's strategy of creating an "Asian
Brain" in Tokyo, led by the brilliant technocrats of MITI, the Ministry of Finance, and the Ministry of Foreign Affairs. These experienced economic architects may guide Japanese industrial investment
throughout the Little Dragons and Southeast Asia, coordinating
necessary policy support from the governments of each of those
countries. The end result of this economic and industrial policy
integration might be a regional Japan, Inc., that could gradually
assume the trappings of a more closely knit community, perhaps—
who can say?—evolving into a United States of Asia. Eventually
Japan may need a stronger military presence in the region to fill the
void created by a vacating America; then again, it may simply rely on
its overwhelming economic leverage to control regional political
conflict in the future as it creates a kinder, gentler co-prosperity
sphere.

Some critics maintain that Japanese foreign policy is like bamboo, attractive in appearance and resilient in turbulent weather but

lacking in substance and crowding out everything reached by its roots. But the nine Asian markets outside Japan *together* account for some 20 percent of Japan's GNP now, which is why the prospects for growing intraregional trade are so strong and why complementary patterns of interdependence are emerging. All of the world's fastest-growing economies, its highest rates of savings and capital formation, and its greatest share of manufactured goods exports are now in the industrializing economies of East Asia. This is no longer a prediction. It is a fact.

There are other considerations that could lend support to a growing Thai-Japanese interdependence. They relate to the demise of communism and growing economic interdependence among the superpowers. Japan could thus enhance its political standing by playing a mediating role in any regional conflicts.

And there could be potentially more, not less, conflict between Thailand and Vietnam over traditional issues of regional hegemony; between Malaysia and Singapore over traditional ethnic rivalries; between Singapore and Thailand over the vagaries of high-tech competition; between the Philippines and Malaysia over territorial disputes (Sabah); *within* the Philippines, between a corrupt central government and a stubborn rural insurgency over land reform and more equitable economic growth; and possibly between Malaysia and Indonesia over dominance in global markets for the products of their common agro-industries.

Though the conventional wisdom on Indonesia says it will continue to lag, my sense is it will eventually move to the front of the pack, for all the reasons cited in Chapter 2, not least because its economic stability is predicated on a politically authoritarian culture. And while it is not entirely certain that Thailand will succeed as a newly industrializing *country*, there is no question that Bangkok is becoming a newly industrializing *city*, so one way or another the Thais can proudly say they are achieving NIC status.

4
MALAYSIA
Quintessential Affirmative Action

Bumis *are* bumiputras, *literally the sons of the soil, the Malays and the tribes of Sarawak and Sabah, who altogether make up a little over half the population of Malaysia. As sons of the soil, they regard the Chinese and Indians as immigrants. Since independence from the British in 1957, they have tried to shape the country in their own image: Islam is the official religion, Malay the official language. It is government policy to favor Malays, in education, in business, in the arts, indeed in every sphere of public life. It is the Malays who receive the government grants, scholarships, special loans, and plum government jobs. Malays run the country.*

Yet it is the Malays who look dispossessed in Kuala Lumpur, many of them huddled together in shabby estates on the city's outskirts, their children skulking in shopping arcades with nothing to do, taking to drugs or religion, dressed like punks or in the pseudo-Arab gear of Muslim fundamentalists. Mrs. Lim, the wife of a dapper Chinese entrepreneur in his early forties, deals with bumis, a few shopkeepers here and there, the odd business contact of her husband's, a taxi driver on occasion; otherwise, they might as well not exist.

Not a word of Malay is spoken in her house. The maid is Chinese. Her friends are Chinese. She speaks English to her husband. She watches American sit-coms on TV and Cantonese soap operas from Hong Kong on her video machine. It all points to the basic fact of Malaysia: the Village is Malay, but the City still belongs to the immigrants.

—Ian Buruma
God's Dust: A Modern Asian Journey

THE PENINSULAR STATE

Consider, if you will, a direct parallel between the peninsular state of Malaysia in Southeast Asia and the peninsular state of Florida in the United States.

Like Florida, whose panhandle shares a common border with two other states (Alabama and Georgia), the peninsula of Malaysia has two common borders: one with Thailand, to the north, the other with Singapore, to the south.

Unlike Florida, though, which is self-contained within its peninsular boundaries, two other Malaysian states, Sabah and Sarawak, are separated from the peninsula across several hundred miles of ocean to the east, much as Cuba and Puerto Rico lie well offshore in the Atlantic.

Just as Spain settled Florida, England colonized Malaysia, and where Spanish or Moorish influence (in place names, language, and cuisine) can be felt from Miami to St. Petersburg, the effects of British influence (from flush toilets to road signs to left-side driving) are still seen in Kuala Lumpur, Johore, and Penang.

And just as Florida has three dominant racial groups today—Caucasian, Hispanic, and African-American—Malaysia is populated by descendants of three distinct ethnic groups: indigenous Malaysian (the numerical majority), immigrant Chinese (with dominant commercial and economic power), and the migratory Indian. The principal difference is that Florida, as a microcosm of the United States, represents a serious attempt at social integration. In Malaysia, on the other hand, public policies have produced the arguably intended effect of ethnic separation.

Florida's economy is well known, of course, for its abundant citrus fruit—oranges, lemons, grapefruit—while Miami has become a financial services hub for Latin America. Malaysia's economy is also a tale of many commodities—principally palm oil, rubber, and tin, for which it is either the world's number-one producer or its largest exporter. And Kuala Lumpur and the nearby offshore island of Penang have become microelectronic production hubs for both Japanese and American manufacturers.

At the end of World War II, after a century and a half of British colonial rule, Malaysia pressed Britain for independence. Political rule then accrued to the dominant Malaysian majority, which coopted both Chinese and Indian complicity in a cozy but increasingly corrupt relationship. Racial tension was unavoidable, and resentment festered. Violence became prevalent. Economic growth lagged well behind its neighbors.

Malaysia's uptight political system, the spoils of which over the years have disproportionately favored indigenous Malaysians, generated the region's most serious race riots, in 1969, in Kuala Lumpur. Since 1970 Malay has replaced English as the national language, Islam has become the state religion, and the press has become a mouthpiece of the country's controlling elite.

But because it is a small, peninsular state, with a population totaling barely 17 million, neither Malaysia nor its many problems show up on the world's radar screen. Today, unlike Florida, Malaysia hovers on the brink of political bankruptcy with a regime that has become inexorably totalitarian.

CULTURAL AND HISTORICAL ROOTS

Malaysia juts down like a long thumb at the southern tip of Thailand, a peninsula bordered by the Strait of Malacca on the west and the South China Sea to the east. More accurately, the eleven states that comprise peninsular Malaysia are so situated, with a population of 10 million in an area the size of the state of Florida. Two distant states, Sabah and Sarawak, share nearly 7 million tribal inhabitants and occupy a narrow strip along the northern edge of the Indonesian island of Kalimantan, 400 miles farther east across the South China Sea. The city-state of Singapore, with 2.5 million people, lies at the southern end of the peninsula; it was once an integral part of Malaysia but has been a sovereign nation since 1965.

Historical references to the Malay Peninsula much before the sixteenth century are rare. It was settled by indigenous people of Malay stock, the *bumiputras*, a combination of seagoing traders and wet-rice cultivators who were later joined by Minangkabau and Batak immigrants from the nearby Indonesian island of Sumatra to the west. The Strait of Malacca was strategic—all trade between China and the West passed through it—giving rise to the Indonesian entrepôt states of Srivijaya, in the seventh century, and Majapahit several hundred years after that.

Malacca, located on the western edge of the Malay Peninsula and bordering the strait that bears its name, flourished during the fifteenth century, when Malay became the principal language and Islam the dominant religion throughout maritime Southeast Asia. (Descendants of the Malaccan royal family established sultanates on the peninsula that ultimately grew into Malaysia's states.) In the sixteenth century the Portuguese occupied Malacca, and during the next 300 years the Malay world became hopelessly fragmented as the major European powers—England, Holland, Portugal, and Spain— fought for control of the region's valuable commodities.

In 1786 the British East India Company established a strategic and commercial port on the island of Penang, situated in the Strait of Malacca directly across from the Malay state of Kedah. While the Dutch carved out their sphere of influence in Indonesia to the south, the British concentrated on India, Burma, Malaysia, and Singapore. Singapore, claimed for Britain by Sir Thomas Stamford Raffles in 1819, took control of the entrepôt trade between East and West; Malaysia became the world's largest exporter of rubber and tin for the British empire. The British cultivated vast rubber tree plantations and imported Tamil immigrants from southern India to work them; Chinese laborers were brought to Malaysia from their poverty-stricken coastal provinces to mine the tin. The Chinese settled in Malaya's urban centers, which they later came to dominate, and their entrepreneurial skills, though resented by the Malays and the cause of much hostility, basically created the local Malaysian economy.

By 1900 the Chinese made up nearly a third of Malaysia's total population (the Tamil about 10 percent), and the Malay Peninsula had become a patchwork quilt of British possessions and local sultanates. It included the Straits Settlements (Singapore, Malacca, and Penang, all British colonies administered from India); the Federated Malay States (where local residents ruled); and the unfederated Malay states (which were governed autonomously by sultans but subject to British influence). Across the South China Sea, on Borneo, England's "White Raja," Sir James Brooke, controlled the state of Sarawak, and the British North Borneo Company governed the state of Sabah, both of which were prime producers of rubber and logs.

The occupation of British Malaya by Japan between 1942 and

1945 shattered any illusions that Winston Churchill may have had of retaining Malaya as part of the British Empire after the war. Out of loyalty and patriotism Malayan Chinese had supported China's war of resistance against Japan; consequently the Japanese executed thousands of them during the occupation, while elevating native Malays to privileged administrative positions vacated by the departing British. In response the Chinese formed the only effective resistance group to fight the Japanese, the core of which was the Communist party of Malaya, headquartered in densely forested sections of the peninsula and covertly armed by the British. When the Japanese ordered Malayan police to attack Chinese insurgents, the Chinese retaliated by assassinating Malays as pro-Japanese collaborators, and the *bumis* then escalated the violence by killing Chinese civilians—all a harbinger of the ethnic hatred that would eventually come to characterize postwar Malaysia.

In 1946 the British established what was called the Malayan Union, a constitutional amalgamation of the federated and unfederated Malay states, together with Penang and Malacca, into a single crown colony. (Singapore had become a separate crown colony in 1867 and was now Britain's principal military base east of the Suez.) All residents of peninsular Malaysia were made Malaysian citizens, regardless of ethnicity; English became the national language; and the sultans relinquished their sovereignty. Sensing punishment by the British for their wartime collaboration with the Japanese, Malay leaders formed the United Malay National Organization (UMNO), Malaysia's first postwar political party. UMNO argued for an independent federation of Malaya that would supplant the Malayan Union and give Malays effective political control.

But the Communist party had been busy forming trade unions and controlled the largest organized body of workers, the Pan-Malayan Federation of Labor, which in 1947 called more than 300 strikes. Throughout 1948, under directives from Peking, the Communists attempted to cripple the Malaysian economy by attacking rubber plantations and tin mines, leaving the British with no alternative but to declare an emergency that lasted nearly a decade until the insurgents were finally brought under control.

By 1957, when the independent Federation of Malaya was proclaimed, UMNO had become Malaysia's dominant political organization, open only to native Malays. The Chinese, just a small minority of whom had supported the Communists, had earlier created their own political party, the Malaysian Chinese Association (MCA), and ethnic Tamils formed the Malaysian Indian Congress (MIC). Dato' Onn bin Ja'afar, UMNO's first president, had tried to make UMNO a multiethnic party, but when he failed he resigned from UMNO and established the Independence of Malaya Party (IMP). It went nowhere; Dato' Onn was succeeded by Tengku Abdul Rahman as UMNO's president and Malaysia's first prime minister.

With British encouragement UMNO formed a working coalition with the two ethnic minority parties, MCA and MIC, and its efforts paid off in subsequent national elections. The three parties, known as the Alliance, have dominated Malaysian politics ever since. With the coming of independence in 1957 Malay became the national language, Islam was made the state religion, and a constitutional monarchy was created to solve the problem of what to do with the local sultans. The "king" of Malaysia, or *yang di-pertuan agong*, is "elected" by the nine provincial rulers from among themselves and serves a five-year term on a rotating basis.

Singapore remained a separate crown colony, however, and for the next several years Lee Kuan Yew pushed for merger of the city-state into a new federation of Malaysia. Malay leaders, however, including Tengku Abdul Rahman, were opposed, which was not surprising since Singapore's ethnic mix was the reverse of Malaya's: among Singaporeans 70 percent were Chinese, 20 percent Malay, and 10 percent Tamil. Malayans feared that by including Singapore the Chinese would emerge as dominant, despite the fact that Lee Kuan Yew had achieved the kind of multiracial integration that would remain empty rhetoric in Malaysia. In late 1962 the pro-merger referendum finally won, and in 1963 Singapore, Sabah, and Sarawak became members of the federation.

As a condition of the merger Singapore had to accept substantial underrepresentation in the Malaysian parliament in exchange for retaining autonomy in education (English was the national language in Singapore, as one means of encouraging ethnic integration) and its own state revenues. Lee Kuan Yew, a brilliant politician who has governed Singapore capably under a "soft" authoritarian system for more than thirty years, retiring only in late 1990, saw the Chinese

MCA party as a roadblock to further political and ethnic integration in Malaysia.

Singapore's own People's Action Party had become the major opposition group on the peninsula, through its counterpart, the Democratic Action Party (DAP), and argued for a "Malaysian Malaysia" in which no single ethnic group would be singled out for special privileges; Malays themselves interpreted this proposal as a direct threat to the UMNO/MCA/MIC Alliance. Nervous about the growing strength of Lee Kuan Yew's multiracial following, Tengku Abdul Rahman knew that keeping Singapore as part of the federation would never work, so in 1965 he insisted (and Lee Kuan Yew reluctantly agreed) that Singapore must withdraw from Malaysia to become an independent and sovereign nation.

After 1965, with the tripartite coalition in power but with Malays the covertly favored race, Malaysia became a case study in ethnic chauvinism. Political campaigns grew nasty. Ethnic violence escalated. Racial taunts became commonplace. By the time national elections took place again, in 1969, Kuala Lumpur, the capital city, had become disoriented and rudderless. New political parties had emerged on both the left and the right; joining the DAP in competing for multiethnic votes were the Gerakan Rakyat Malaysia (or the People's Movement, known simply as Gerakan), headquartered in Penang, and the People's Progressive Party, while a right-wing Pan-Malaysia Islamic Party called PAS (for Parti Islam Si-Malaysia) campaigned on a platform of religious fundamentalism.

The results of the May 1969 election stunned the Alliance. Its total share of the national vote declined from nearly 60 percent to less than 50 percent, and it lost twenty-three seats in Parliament, winning only sixty-six, not enough for a majority. The MCA lost fourteen seats to the DAP, and UMNO lost three to PAS, while the opposition parties won twenty-five of the 154 seats in the lower house. The Alliance collapsed when the MCA withdrew its support.

When the mostly Chinese opposition parties held victory rallies in Kuala Lumpur to celebrate their gains, Malays felt they were rubbing it in. Racial taunts intensified, fistfights broke out, and then communal riots erupted. Several hundred Chinese were killed in the worst violence since independence. A state of emergency was declared, Parliament was suspended, and Malaysia was governed for two years by the National Operations Council (NOC) under the leadership of Deputy Prime Minister Tun Abdul Razak.

The NOC amended the Sedition Act of 1948 and prohibited public questioning of the special status of Malays, the status of Malay as a national language, and the citizenship laws. It promulgated a state ideology and then passed a constitutional amendment to prohibit any public discussion of these sensitive subjects. "We are swiftly reaching a stage where the practice of racism is a virtue," said the fiery opposition leader Lim Kit Siang, "and the criticism of racism a crime."

By 1974 UMNO had brought the MCA back into the Alliance with the MIC and formed a new coalition called the National Front (Barisan Nasional, or BN). In the 1974 elections BN won overwhelmingly, taking 130 of the 154 parliamentary seats, and the old UMNO/MCA/MIC Alliance alone captured a total of eighty-five seats, enough for control.

But the real victim of the 1969 race riots in Kuala Lumpur was not the old Alliance; it was the potential for multiethnic integration in Malaysian society. (BN controlled the government, and the cozy UMNO/MCA/MIC Alliance controlled the BN, dictated by Malay privilege; each of the three owned a major Malaysian newspaper, and they all benefited from corrupt pork barrel legislation.) The New Economic Policy (NEP) was adopted in an attempt to bring economic equality to the Malays, who languished in the rural kampong (villages)—which lagged behind the urban areas economically—while the Chinese continued to create most of Malaysia's national wealth through their entrepreneurial skills, managerial talent, and innate aggressiveness. Malaysia had become the world's leading exporter of rubber, tin, and palm oil, but the sons of the soil weren't sharing in the spoils.

The NEP set a goal of 30 percent Malay (bumi) ownership in the commercial and industrial sectors by 1990; non-Malays (i.e., Chinese and Indian) would control just 40 percent; and foreign control would be reduced to 30 percent. Special schools and institutes were created for bumis only; they got the best government jobs; only they could qualify for certain commercial licenses (which they would often turn around and sell back to the Chinese); special government scholarships were granted exclusively to Malays; and new national enterprises like the Malaysian Industrial Development Authority were set up to fund purchases of stock reserved solely for *bumiputra*, to increase their ownership stake.

In short Malaysia tried through the NEP to legislate a system of social and economic affirmative action, but without success. The twin goals of the NEP—to eradicate Malay poverty and to restructure society—had failed. By 1989 *bumiputra* equity in public companies was up to only 13 percent of the total; government trust funds for *bumis* held 6 percent; non-Malays still controlled nearly 60 percent; and foreigners owned 23 percent. Malaysia's recent transition from commodities to high tech could be attributed to one dominant (and not unfamiliar) factor: Japan.

In 1981 Mohamad Mahathir, a forceful advocate of even greater privilege for Malays, was elected president of UMNO and became prime minister, succeeding Tun Hussein Onn. In the past decade Mahathir has stepped up control of Malaysian politics by UMNO, invoked the Internal Security Act (ISA) to detain, without trial, his strongest political opponents, emasculated Malaysia's formerly independent judiciary, and put himself in position to remain prime minister, as he proudly boasts, "for as long as I shall live." Having suffered a major heart attack in late 1988 but still in power today, his prediction is not without irony.

For the *bumis*, wealth creation remains an elusive goal; for the Indians, theirs is a precarious position of political impotence; and for many embittered Chinese, emigration now appears to be an inescapable conclusion. Unabashedly racist, Malaysia seems on the verge of creating a new and unpredictable Islamic state, a dangerous trend that may have serious implications for the peninsula's rather dubious claim to NIC status, based solely on the one-dimensional indicator of per-capita income.

Far from restructuring society, or even striving to make it a multiethnic melting pot, Malay leadership has done everything it can to make sure that a system of racial segregation and strict ethnic quotas remains. In this sense socially tripartite Malaysia more nearly resembles a house of kindling wood and paper, with UMNO little more than a lighted match in the hands of unsupervised children.

THE MALAYSIAN ECONOMY:
A TALE OF TWO COMMODITIES

Anyone who visits Malaysia and spends much time there, as I recently did, cannot help coming away with the feeling that Malaysia's political economy is overwhelmingly *political*. Expatriates who have lived in Kuala Lumpur for many years told me that prior to coming to Malaysia they had heard how pervasive Malaysian politics was and were determined not to get caught up in it.

But in the same breath they admitted that, after they arrived, they could do nothing but follow politics because it was the only game in town. They may be right, but beneath the clamor and virulence of Malaysia's political strife lies a struggle for economic survival that is going badly.

Many Malaysians will be quick to tell you that, with manufacturing at 25 percent of GNP, a per-capita income of nearly $2,000, and manufactured goods representing almost half of its total exports, Malaysia is, by definition, a newly industrializing country. But as with Thailand, there is more to its claim than meets the eye.

Malaysia's traditional claim to fame (and wealth) can be laid to two primary products, rubber and tin. The world's largest producer of rubber, Malaysia produced 1.6 million tons in 1989 (about a third of the world total), exporting virtually all of it—nearly $2.5 billion worth—making rubber Malaysia's number-three export after electrical products and crude oil. Rubber trees cover nearly 5 million acres of land, mostly in large estates that have been carved out of dense forest. Malaysia is a founding member of the Association of Natural Rubber Producing Countries and host of the International Natural Rubber Council, which manages market prices through a large buffer stock.

Tin today is not the valuable commodity it once was, but in 1989 Malaysia mined 52,000 tons of it, worth $1 billion in exports, enough to make it the world's leading producer with nearly 25 percent of total production. In 1983 the country founded the Association of Tin Producing Countries, based in Kuala Lumpur, whose six member countries account for 95 percent of total world output. Two years earlier, under one of Mahathir's bizarre schemes, Malaysia tried illegally to corner the world tin market by organizing a massive buying campaign through London, but output today is cartelized by the producers, including strict export controls and a buffer stock of 50,000 tons.

Palm oil has replaced tin as Malaysia's second-most-valuable natural resource after rubber. In 1988 Malaysia exported 5 million tons, worth nearly $2 billion, and was the world's leading producer with a 60 percent market share, a position it has held for more than twenty years. (In 1989 Malaysian palm oil producers incurred the wrath of American soybean oil makers by claiming their product was lower in saturated fat, a dispute of Liechtensteinian proportions that nonetheless threatened to become an international tempest until it was settled with an agreement covering the labeling of cooking oils.)

Overall, agriculture is the economy's second-largest sector after manufacturing, accounting for 21 percent of GNP and nearly 30 percent of total employment. Malaysia is the world's leading exporter of raw hardwood logs and cut timber (21 million tons in 1988, worth $1.5 billion) and the third-largest exporter of cocoa (250,000 tons, worth nearly $500 million, in 1988). Though a modest producer of oil by world standards, its production of 20 million tons (more than 100 million barrels) in 1988 generated some $2.5 billion in export revenues. These six commodities alone made up about 45 percent of Malaysia's total merchandise trade exports in 1988.

And you are never very far from any of them. The Malay Peninsula is like a bony spine covered with dense blue-green forests and lush plants. Its steamy climate is conducive to thick undergrowth, and the roads that splay out from the capital like the spokes of a wheel have more hairpin turns than a bowl of spaghetti. In the countryside, past the eerily quiet Malay *kampong* with their simple wooden houses, one sees acre after acre of palm oil plantations and rubber estates whose neatly planted trees blanket the landscape. The lushness of Malaysia speaks less of lassitude than of luxury, or as V. S. Naipaul once wrote, "of rich things growing fast, of money."

By now it should come as no surprise that Japan, as for Indonesia and Thailand, is Malaysia's number-one trading partner, accounting for about a fifth of Malaysia's total trade (23 percent of all its imports and over 20 percent of exports). More specifically, Japan buys a third of Malaysia's oil, 30 percent of its tin, two-thirds of its raw logs and cut timber, and virtually all of its natural gas. In return Japanese capital goods, technology, and manufactured components make up more than 80 percent of Malaysia's imports from Japan. (Singapore is in second place, accounting for almost 17 percent of Malaysia's total trade and three-quarters of its entire trade with ASEAN.)

Japan has given Malaysia another contemporary claim to fame, and that is its position as the world's third-largest producer of semiconductors (the United States is still number one, Japan number two), though it is the leading exporter of chips because they are virtually all shipped out. More than twenty-five Japanese semiconductor companies—with familiar names such as Hitachi, Toshiba, and NEC—have direct investments in Malaysia, primarily in the country's industrial estates of Penang and Shah Alam, near the capital of Kuala Lumpur, or K.L., as it is called.

K.L. is without a doubt the least Asian capital in all of East Asia. It lacks a distinctive touch, like the golden spires of Bangkok's Buddhist *wat*, or the waves of red roof tiles that are so characteristic of Jakarta, or even the high-tech "smart" buildings that dominate Tokyo and Singapore. Instead it combines a very Islamic, almost Arabian flavor with the most pedestrian of Chinese commercial architecture and tasteless British style, including zebra stripes on the curbstones and flashing amber lamps at pedestrian crossings. Large, colorless minarets and oversized onion domes dominate the city's many mosques, which sit, cheek by jowl, among office buildings and row after row of squat, retail shophouses. Arabic script fights for attention with Chinese ideographs, Bahasa Malay, and the ubiquitous English in a confusing linguistic jumble. (The Malay language is virtually identical to Bahasa Indonesian.)

Malaysia's electronics sector is in effect a spillover from Singapore, which has a total land area of only some 200 square miles. In an industry in which labor accounts for less than 10 percent of total production costs, automation and engineering talent become major factors. Kuala Lumpur and Penang are only a half hour from Singapore by air, and management of foreign electronics investments in the industrial estates is mainly in the hands of Chinese entrepreneurs, so it is somewhat misleading to call this sector Malaysian.

"Malaysia has a huge base of natural resources at the bottom and a big influx of foreign capital to fund its manufacturing sector at the top," Sadahiro Sugita, MITI's representative at the Japanese embassy in Kuala Lumpur, told me, "but very little in between. There is no solid middle core of indigenous entrepreneurial talent like you have in either Indonesia or Thailand, just a mass of what we would call entry-level factory workers."

Sugita is another inveterate foot soldier in Japan's vast commercial army that has invaded Southeast Asia with such success. In addition to his own detailed report, he procured for me a copy of the voluminous 500-page analysis on the Malaysian political economy put out by the Japanese Chamber of Trade and Industry of Malaysia (JACTIM), both of course in Japanese.

"The only real market in Malaysia is the Chinese market," he said as we talked over tea in his spartan office. "The real commercial engine of this economy is the Chinese community. Malaysia's primary economic interests seem to be dictated primarily by domestic politics."

In ASEAN's deck of economic playing cards, Malaysia is what I would call the two of clubs; in other words, the runt of the ASEAN litter. It has the region's smallest population and, at $30 billion, its smallest GNP. The land areas of Japan and Malaysia are about the same—roughly 130,000 square miles—but Japan's population density is seven times that of Malaysia and its GNP is a hundred times larger.

After Japan, Singapore is Malaysia's second-largest foreign investor, followed by Taiwan and then the United States. Two-thirds of the American investment is in oil and gas, and most of that is accounted for by one company, an offshore production subsidiary of Exxon. By comparison, Japanese investment is overwhelmingly in manufacturing. In 1989, of 442 Japanese companies doing business in Malaysia, 295 were manufacturers, assemblers, or exporters, and Japan had a cumulative direct investment there of nearly $2 billion, representing about 1 percent of its total foreign investment worldwide. U.S. manufacturing totals less than $1 billion, about 25 percent of its total investment there, but it includes some familiar names, like Texas Instruments, Motorola, and National Semiconductor.

One result of all this foreign investment in Malaysia has been a significant drain on balance of payments. Its balance of trade generates a moderate surplus, but after remitting investment income (dividends and interest) due foreign investors, its overall balance has been in deficit since about 1981. This, in turn, has caused a mushrooming of Malaysia's foreign debt, from just over $5 billion in 1981 to nearly $20 billion in 1987, and a corresponding deterioration in its debt service ratio from 3.5 to 14.3 during that seven-year period, leading Moody's to consider downgrading the country's bond ratings and causing Bank Negara, Malaysia's central bank, to devalue the ringgit, or Malaysian dollar, by nearly 20 percent.

The balance of payments deficit, coupled with a sizable federal budget deficit, has created a dangerous savings-investment gap for Malaysia, too, although that has begun to turn around somewhat. Between 1981 and 1985, however, Malaysia had a net dissavings averaging 8.5 percent of GNP, a level that was clearly unsustainable. Though the savings rate has consistently been above 30 percent of GNP, that is not a very accurate statistic. In fact it may well be higher, since *bumis* are notorious underspenders, and the Chinese, who probably account for two-thirds of the total anyway, are traditional oversavers but apply much of their savings to flight capital.

"Unlike the public sector, the private sector has consistently been a significant net saver," Bank Negara's deputy governor, See Yan Lin, told me. "In the early 1980s, however, this surplus turned negative, reflecting the worldwide recession and poor agricultural commodity prices. But I think we have successfully turned things around through a combination of fiscal restraint and the higher public savings that reflect our better economic performance of late."

Shortly after he became prime minister in 1981, Mahathir made a concerted effort to turn Malaysia's economic attention from agricultural commodities to manufacturing. He proclaimed a "Look East" policy, by which he meant Malaysia ought to spend more time analyzing the industrial economies of Japan, Korea, and Taiwan, perhaps emulating some of their developmental strategies. One outcome of his policy was the creation of the Heavy Industry Corporation of Malaysia Berhad, or HICOM, a government agency that spearheaded the country's embryonic (and, to date, largely unsuccessful) efforts in manufacturing, including a barely profitable automaking venture and two big losers (one in cement, the other in steel, both now defunct).

In 1983 HICOM created an automobile venture with the Mitsubishi group, one of Japan's largest industrial conglomerates, to produce an indigenous Malaysian car. Assuming a dominant 70 percent ownership position, HICOM teamed up with minority partners Mitsubishi Motors and Mitsubishi Corporation (15 percent each) to invest $250 million in a new Malaysian automaker called Perusahaan Otomobil Nasional Sendirian Berhad—Proton for short. (Sendirian Berhad means "Private Limited" and is Malaysian for "Co., Inc.," abbreviated Sdn. Bhd.) By 1985 it had begun producing the Saga, a rather unimaginative four-door sedan based for the most part on outmoded Mitsubishi technology that had been popular in the late 1970s. Saga is a Malaysian word that means "strength and stability."

It took five years for the company just to break even. By August 1989 Proton had made (and sold) only about 150,000 Sagas in the domestic market, but it doubled its production capacity anyway, to 80,000 cars a year, utilizing two eight-hour shifts. (The Saga model has two-thirds of the domestic Malaysian market now, though barely 25,000 of the cars were sold in 1987 and very few more in 1988.) The company is managed by eighteen Mitsubishi Motors executives, but it employs more than 2,000 *bumis* at its big, noisy Shah Alam plant, about a fifth of whom have spent various periods of six to twelve months training in Japan. Malay workers make an average industrial wage of about $5 a day.

"When we started production, our local content was less than 20 percent," Aidi Rosli Khalim, a bright young *bumi* in Proton's general affairs department, told me as we toured the Saga assembly line. "Now we're up to 60 percent, though most of the more sophisticated components, like engines, are still imported from Japan, and all the cold rolled steel is too."

As you might expect, the machinery and equipment in the Proton plant were Japanese: Hitachi presses, Aida stamps and dies, Hitachi metal stampers, Kimura automatic welders, and spot welders from Mitsubishi Heavy Industries. But lower-value-added components like headlamp assemblies, taillights, wheel rims, hubcaps, alternators, tires, and trim were all locally made, mostly through joint ventures with other Japanese suppliers.

I asked Aidi if Proton had to observe the strict racial ratios for employment, and he said, "We don't have to maintain a precise sixty-thirty-ten ethnic balance here, because we're open to all Malaysians regardless of ethnicity. Worker loyalty is strong, though, and we'd like to make motorbikes too if we can." The only religious symbols I saw inside the plant were a small indoor mosque and several Islamic prayer rugs, which conveyed the distinct impression that *bumis* monopolized HICOM's work force.

Although HICOM's original agreement with Mitsubishi, euphemistically called a "transfer of friendship and technology," specified that Proton's entire production would be sold in the domestic market, Malaysia had begun to export Sagas to moribund overseas markets like Sri Lanka and Bangladesh. And when HICOM criticized its Japanese partners for transferring only outdated technology to the Malaysian venture, Mitsubishi reminded it that the Saga was intended to be for domestic consumption only.

The Saga is also available now in the UK, and is strangely popular there even though the early export models had no heater, a component that is needless to say not standard equipment in the tropics. Proton also had plans to enter the U.S. market, but chose as its distributor the same company that brought in Yugoslavia's ill-fated Yugo—Bricklin Industries, Inc. When it sank, so did Proton's plans for North America.

Foreign investment in Malaysia is coordinated by the Malaysian Industrial Development Authority (MIDA), a predominantly *bumi*-staffed, quasi-governmental body that creates the incentives necessary to attract new capital into the country and is used by foreign investors for their "one-stop shopping" (a term Malays detest). MIDA, like Singapore's Economic Development Board before it, gives "pioneer status" to foreign companies that qualify, which can include a five-year tax holiday that can be extended if their fixed assets total 25 million ringgit or if they employ 500 full-time Malaysian workers. In principle, as a throwback to the New Economic Policy, 100 percent foreign ownership is prohibited, but exceptions can be made in those cases in which a company exports 50 percent or more of its production or employs 350 Malaysian workers full-time.

That the NEP effort has largely failed is recognized as true by most thoughtful Malaysians, *bumi* and Chinese alike. But despite the poor results, the government is now considering an extension of the NEP for another ten years, through 2000, because it feels that two decades wasn't enough time for the policy to show results.

In a recent survey of American investment in Malaysia by the U.S. embassy in Kuala Lumpur, the NEP was cited by nearly half of the corporate respondents as the most serious disincentive to investing there. Twice as many nonmanufacturers as manufacturers cited the NEP as a major disincentive; in fact the NEP was the most frequently mentioned disincentive of all, ranking well ahead of the small size of the Malaysian market, the government relations climate, and the socioreligious environment. (This is a euphemism for fundamentalist Islam: as one of my American friends in Kuala Lumpur put it, "Malaysia is a NIC, all right—a Newly Islamicizing Country.").

The Federation of Malaysian Manufacturers, known locally as the FMM, is probably the best organized and most articulate advisory group in Malaysia's industrial policy formulation process. The federation's subcommittees prepare working papers on specific industry sectors that are fed into the relevant government ministries, but because they are Chinese their effect is understandably limited. Still, the FMM submitted an extensive memo to the National Economic Consultative Council on the NEP after 1990 called "New Policy Directions and Strategies."

"Dynamic and sustained economic growth . . . is a sounder basis for achieving [the objectives] of the NEP, rather than upfront equity holding percentages [ethnic quotas]," the FMM wrote. "To achieve the NEP's restructuring objective, the incentive approach should be used in place of licensing [or] direct government funding. The manufacturing sector plays a vital role because it is the leading sector in the Malaysian economy; it is a significant source of employment; its exports account for more than 40 percent of total receipts; and there is strong linkage between manufacturing and key service sectors such as finance and communications. Active measures should therefore be taken to ensure that Malaysia's manufacturing sector remains strong and continues to expand."

The FMM's focus on incentives reflects a sound, externally oriented developmental process. Its priorities strike a responsive chord that would resonate in any of the industrial policy ministries in Japan, Taiwan, or Singapore. The FMM wants to make Malaysia's manufacturing sector globally competitive, and its own statistical analysis has shown that political economies with a bias toward manufacturing enjoy appreciably higher rates of economic growth, higher productivity rates, and lower price inflation than those that don't. But its recommendations, however sound or rational, strike a blow at the heart of the NEP, which is a racially driven *political* vehicle that benefits the Malay elite.

"Clearly the one thing holding domestic investors back has been the NEP and its *bumiputra* ownership restrictions," Datuk Kamil Salih, the American-educated executive director of the Malaysian Institute for Economic Research (MIER), told me. "There is a distinct need, therefore, to relax these restrictions to create additional opportunities for investment. New domestic private investment jumped from $300 million ringgit to $900 million ringgit last year, though that was all primarily non-Malay."

When Malaysians use the term *non-Malay*, they usually mean Chinese. Salih suggested that Malaysia would have to shift toward a more growth-oriented plan, not equity-oriented as in the past. Recently the central bank and even his own institute had forecast a GNP growth rate averaging 9 percent over the next few years. I asked Salih how realistic he thought that was, given the domestic political environment and Malaysia's own historical averages.

"Nine percent may not be realistic," he admitted. "I think 6 percent may be more reflective of our actual potential. But whether or not we can even do that depends on how 'open' the world trading system remains, on regional developments already taking place, and of course on Japan. There is now a distinct division of labor occurring between Northeast and Southeast Asia as the Little Dragons upshift to higher-value-added production, so I think Malaysia will benefit because of this East Asian dynamism, coupled with faster growth in Japan."

Salih's own analysis of the results of Malaysia's NEP after twenty years showed that the original targets would not be met. While the incidence of poverty in peninsular Malaysia had fallen from about half the total number of households in 1970 to under 20 percent by 1989, the level of government subsidies remained high, and the more important question had become the growing inequality within and among ethnic groups. Overall employment roughly follows the ethnic breakdown, though sectoral representation is still skewed; *bumiputras* are underrepresented in skilled and higher-level occupations in the commercial and industrial sectors but overrepresented in the low-paying jobs. (Chinese make up most of the country's managers and engineers, while Indians dominate the professions, such as accounting, medicine, and law.) And even though *bumi* ownership of share capital had risen to 18 percent of the total, it was far below the official target of 30 percent, most of which was in the hands of the government's trust agencies, not individuals.

"These less-than-satisfactory results have prompted us to propose an income-doubling and distribution plan as the basic framework for the NEP after 1990," Salih told me. "We would like to see Malaysia's per-capita income double between 1990 and 2000 and achieve income parity for *bumis* by then, including the eradication of absolute poverty. The IDDP, in other words, is essentially a plan for accelerated growth with distribution."

But did the MIER want to have its cake and eat it too? To *double* Malaysian per-capita income from $2,000 to $4,000 in ten years assumes an average growth rate of 7 percent a year, based on simple mathematical compounding. But given Malaysia's population growth at 2.6 percent a year, the economy would have to grow at nearly 10 percent *every* year. And by Salih's own admission, actual growth will be nowhere near that fast, so, practically speaking, the IDDP may be more ideal than real.

If the NEP has not achieved either ownership equity or income parity for *bumis*, what has it done? Well, many believe it has dramatically increased the power of the federal government, its share of employment, and its share of the national wealth. Another recent study shows that a major impact of the NEP has been to legitimize the growth of a large central bureaucracy to manage Malaysia's ethnocentric capitalist state. From a total of 140,000 civil servants in 1970, federal employment ballooned to more than 500,000 by 1983, a nearly four-fold increase that produced jobs primarily for *bumis*. The government's share of GNP rose from 11 percent in 1970 to nearly 14 percent in 1983, growing at a rate half again as fast as the economy itself.

The central truth of the NEP is that the ruling Malay elite, in assuming the role of trustee, has emerged as a cartel. It has cornered the market for economic planning and decision making to enrich itself while giving good rhetoric to the elimination of poverty. Interracial income inequality, long a major source of ethnic conflict, has been replaced by an even wider *intra*ethnic inequality, particularly among Malays: mass poverty at the bottom of Malaysia's social pyramid has become a necessary condition for income and wealth concentration at the top. Not unlike in Thailand, income distribution favors the elite: the top 20 percent of Malaysian households control 53 percent of the wealth. The roots of this condition can be traced back to Malaysia's colonial past. When Malaysia was a British colony, its surplus wealth was siphoned off to London; today, after two decades of NEP-style affirmative action, it is drained off by the Malay elite.

What would one alternative to the NEP's affirmative action program be? High-speed industrial growth. Japan, Korea, Singapore, and Taiwan are the textbook cases of income-doubling plans actually achieved as a result of very rapid economic growth. Japan accomplished its original goal in the late 1950s and early 1960s, the Little Dragons in the 1970s. Singapore's example may be the most analogous since it, too, is a multiracial society, and Malays there will tell you that, no matter how little they may like Lee Kuan Yew or his authoritarian system of government, there has been more economic opportunity and greater individual achievement for them there than in their own country. As the ethnic minority, Malays are also the "immigrant" group in Singapore and accordingly must fight for survival, which hones the competitive instincts, as any American immigrant, from his or her own experience, can confirm. Because of its racist practices, Malaysia is called—only partly in jest—the world's greatest producer of Singaporeans.

Immigrant experience also refutes the theory of some scholars who suggest Malays are somehow inherently lazy, resist innovation, and prefer to avoid the risk necessary to become entrepreneurs. Recent studies have shown how *bumi* fishermen on Malaysia's less-developed East Coast work longer hours for less pay, and overseas Malays are not only competitive but adapt well, Singapore again being the paradigm. In any case, the challenge of economic development policy for Malaysia in the years ahead is to achieve a more broadly based distribution of wealth through high-speed growth, not through the restrictive racial quotas it has tried to impose in the recent past. In other words, make the cake bigger instead of telling people how they must cut it.

Bumis get special privileges from the federal government—such as licenses and permits to operate certain businesses, like taxis and retail shops—but since they lack the capital to run them, they either sell the licenses to the more entrepreneurially experienced Chinese, in which case they become Malaysia's so-called "instant millionaires," or they go into partnership with them. These partnerships are called "Ali-Baba" ventures: the Malay represents himself as the proprietor in order to obtain government assistance (which the Chinese, because of his ethnicity, is not allowed to do), and his Chinese business partner provides the capital and then runs the business. The system has been designed perfectly for patronage, kickbacks, and corruption. (The motorcar of choice for Chinese in Malaysia today is the Mercedes, but wealthy Malays now drive the BMW, known locally as the Bumiputra Motor Works.)

Bumis also borrow money from the federal government to finance the acquisition of a home, and while Chinese and Indians can, too, *bumi* borrowing predominates. Under Malaysian law *bumis* are allowed to purchase a house at 80 percent of its market value. Many more Malay instant millionaires are created when they borrow the down payment from the government, buy a house at a 20 percent discount, then turn around and sell it to a non-Malay at the market, repay the down payment, and pocket the difference. Or, as a more cynical Malaysian friend suggested, they may not bother to repay the government at all. They won't be prosecuted, so voluntary bankruptcy is another way to create instant wealth.

Misron bin Yusof laughed when I cited these examples of Malay entrepreneurship. Yusof is the young, British-educated general manager of Federal Power and Telecoms Sdn. Bhd., a *bumi* enterprise created by the Malaysian government under the NEP.

"Well, we're just lazy, happy-go-lucky people, you see," he was telling me with just a hint of sarcasm as we toured his factory just south of Kuala Lumpur. "Malays always had life rather easy under the British, compared to the immigrant groups. You throw a seed, *any* seed, into the ground anywhere in this country, and it grows. But the British sheltered the Malays, left them alone with their religion and their local rulers, and never encouraged them to go into the commercial sector, where conditions are harsher and more competitive than in the *kampong*."

Federal Power and Telecoms makes electric cables for power generation and has a 30 percent share of the domestic market. As Yusof explained it to me, FPT is the largest of seven competitors in a three- or four-company market. A majority (51 percent) of FPT's equity is owned by Permodalan Nasional Berhad, the National Equity Fund; the National Electric Board owns 9 percent; Federal Cables, a local Malay group, owns 30 percent; and Fujikura Cable, a major Japanese manufacturer that is FPT's technical adviser, 10 percent. The National Electric Board is FPT's main customer; it makes concrete poles, transformers, and meters.

"Poles are doing well these days, a lot better than cables," he said with a smile. "The domestic Malaysian market is very small, and tariffs protect it from foreign competition. There is also a 15 percent price margin regulated by the government, so if we bid, say, 14 percent higher than a foreign competitor, we still get the business. Some foreign products are banned completely. But all the other *bumi* cable companies here have Japanese technical advisers, too."

FPT is a typical low-tech enterprise that is symbolic of Malaysia's attempt to build a managerial *bumi* class. The factory Yusof guided me through utilizes standard copper and aluminum wire-twisting machinery and simple rubber casing equipment. As a publicly owned company, FPT is required by the Ministry of Trade to maintain a strict sixty-thirty-ten racial balance on its staff and must regularly submit paperwork confirming the levels attained. At the time of my visit in mid-1989, 180 of its 260 employees were *bumis*, well above the minimum required.

"Companies in the private sector are supposed to respect these racial quotas too," said Paul S. K. Low, a Chinese entrepreneur who is chairman of Malaysian Sheet Glass Berhad, a joint venture with Nippon Sheet Glass Co., Ltd., of Japan. "And that's from the factory floor all the way up to senior management. So a *bumi* may be the titular managing director of a firm and perform well because he has two Chinese middle managers right below him who actually run the business. Then he thinks, 'Hey, there's really nothing to management. I think I'll go off on my own and give it a try.' So he borrows some money, sets up shop, and then goes bust because he really doesn't know how to make it work. The problem is not providing a supply of capital; it's experience—knowing how to gauge market demand. The government has set up a $500 million rescue fund to bail the *bumis* out. It's incredible."

Another enterprising Chinese businessman *cum* scholar is Paul Chan Tuck Hoong, executive director of the G-14 working committee on ASEAN economic cooperation and integration. A former professor of economics at the University of Malaysia, Chan, now in his mid-forties, runs an educational consulting operation called HELP, which is short for Higher Education Learning Programs. He and Paul Low are both members of the National Economic Consultative Council, a group of 150 prominent Malaysians who are trying to help the government decide what to do with the NEP after 1990. (Kamil Salih, head of MIER, is also a member.)

"The new NEP will depend more on the outcome of our 1990 national elections than it will on any underlying economic factors," he told me as we sat in his modest office in central Kuala Lumpur. "And the politicians can play it both ways, using it as an issue before or after the election. If the economy keeps expanding, they can afford to take a tougher posture. But there are contradictions inherent in the NEP, which the government doesn't realize. When you invite foreign investors from Hong Kong and Taiwan to come in, they will naturally tie up with non*bumi* Chinese. So we have a kind of prisoner's dilemma: if we offer no investment incentives, foreign investors will opt for Indonesia or Thailand, which do; but if we do offer them, we're still not sure they will come, because of the restrictiveness of the NEP. The more we open up the economy to foreign participation, to stimulate growth and competition, the more it goes against the grain of the NEP, which imposes racial quotas. It has successfully turned Malaysia into a nation of rentiers."

Dato' Abdul Rahim bin Mokhzani may symbolize what many *bumis* say they aspire to when they talk of running their own companies. Chairman of Innovest Berhad, a Malaysian venture capital company with substantial holdings in various industries, Mokhzani manages a corporate empire whose assets total nearly $300 million. Educated at the London School of Economics, he was formerly vice chancellor of the University of Malaysia, an executive director of United Motor Works, and a past president of the Malaysian Economic Association.

"The second generation of Malays is now coming into its own in these companies," Mokhzani told me. "They are becoming more modern and technical in their orientation, so there is more pride, more achievement, and more self-confidence among them."

Innovest owns the Malaysian franchise for Kentucky Fried Chicken, it is Malaysia's biggest poultry trader, and its outlet in Kuala Lumpur had the highest sales volume in the world for seven years running, believe it or not, until KFC opened a new franchise in Beijing. Begun as a company that made fishing nets, Innovest also has interests in engineering, manufacturing, and industrial chemicals as well as other fast-food operations—such as Shakey's Pizza, Sate Ria, and the White Castle hamburger chain. Fast foods are where Innovest makes most of its money.

Another enterprising *bumi* is Tengku Mohamad Azzman Shariffadeen, although it could be fairly said that he is where he is because of his elite connections. (Tengku means prince in Malay and denotes royalty.) Shariffadeen, a small, thin man who earned his Ph.D. at Manchester University in England, is director general of the Malaysian Institute of Microelectronic Systems, or MIMOS, a government-sponsored effort to conduct high-tech R&D and to support the creation of new information-intensive industries so as not to lag too far behind the Little Dragons.

"We will continue to have a resource-based economy, but one that has increasing application to information-based resources," he told me during a recent visit. "Information technology is the future, and Malaysia's future will be bright because it has both natural resources and human resources and can develop the best of both."

When he mentioned human resources, it became apparent that even Asia's least industrializing economy had picked up the latest buzzwords. Malaysia's literacy rate, at about 75 percent, is far lower than Thailand's, and a recent survey found that 38 percent of the Malays sampled spent less than two hours a week reading. What's more, one-tenth did not read even a single newspaper regularly, and 27 percent had no books at home. In comparison with UNESCO's book-reading rate of eighty pages a year for developing countries, Malaysians average *half a page a year*.

The striking thing about these statistics was that they had come from a paper written by Shariffadeen himself. When I asked him about the apparent discrepancy between his rhetoric and his research, he said, "I agree that the drag on our effort has been our political system. To the extent that the racist policies of the past continue to dominate domestic politics, it is an open question as to whether we can succeed in attaining our goals in microelectronic technology. The reason I can't find qualified Malay engineers is that they're practically all Chinese. But the Malay work force is very disciplined and displays a strong willingness to follow directions."

Shariffadeen may be right about Malaysia's future, but I for one remain highly skeptical. Again as in Thailand, more than 90 percent of Malay children are enrolled in primary school, but less than half of them go on to high school, and only 4 percent of the population receives any higher education at all —hardly the base for a national future in information technology. If the overwhelming majority of Malaysia's scientists and engineers are Chinese, and if the system continues to discriminate against them, what then?

After the 1969 riots Bahasa Malay became the language of instruction in all Malay schools, and many thoughtful Malays now agree this may have been a mistake, not simply because English fluency is worse today but also because English could have helped homogenize the society, whereas Bahasa keeps racial tensions raw. (The government has recently returned to the practice of teaching English in local schools, but only as a second language.)

Education is also a continuing political problem for the Chinese community. In 1978 the Chinese petitioned the government for permission to establish a privately funded Chinese-language university, but their request was rejected. Many Chinese have no recourse but to send their children out of the country for quality education. The government's ethnic quotas that regulate university admission also mean that more than 80 percent of the students in Malaysian universities are Malay. Two-thirds of the more than 40,000 Malaysian students studying abroad are Chinese, who must pay their own way because they do not qualify for their own government's scholarships; the balance are Malays who do.

"Unfortunately for us, the *bumis* will never realize they should change the system as long as the government gives them a roof over their heads and three meals a day," one elderly Chinese intellectual, a writer who has been censored frequently by the government, told me. "Islam is their official religion, which claims to be tolerant, but then just look at the Middle East. No, Buddhism is tolerant; Islam is dogmatic and very authoritarian, closed to other ideas. So I don't see much chance of high technology coming in and giving Malays much of a future."

What about the Chinese? What would their options be?

"We'll adapt and adjust as we always have," he said philosophically. "Assimilation is a fact of life for us in Indonesia and Thailand, but here it's different; we really don't know what to do. But we Chinese will survive, no matter what, because wherever we go in the world, we know one thing, and that's how to survive. We're like weeds: no matter where you plant us, we'll not only grow; we'll thrive."

Malaysia's political economy is plagued by racism. Without racial tension there would be no politics; without politics, the country would cease to exist. The Malays, Indians, and Chinese have been coexisting for centuries, but not under the divisive political pressures they are increasingly being subjected to today.

Malays are essentially an easygoing, come-what-may people whose cultural attitude is captured in the popular expression *tidak apa*, meaning "never mind," or "no matter"—mañana.

The Indians are hardworking, pragmatic, intense, technical, intellectual, professional, the women given to good food and fine dress.

And the Chinese are the world's quintessential money-makers—practical, disciplined, with a good mind for business and strong Confucian values of education and family. They are, as my Chinese informant confirmed, survivors.

But Malaysia's politicians—especially the Malay-controlled UMNO—maximize racial tension rather than try to eradicate it because it keeps them in power, helps the Malays "believe" in their future, gives the *bumis* special rights and privileges, establishes their power base, and preserves and protects narrow parochial interests at the expense of a broader national interest.

Racism *defines* Malaysia, and to assess the nation's future, one must understand how politics and racism have combined to corrupt the country.

MALAYSIA'S POLITICS:
INSTITUTIONALIZED CORRUPTION

As one seasoned expatriate with long years of experience in Asia put it recently, "All Asian countries are corrupt, but nowhere is the *system* so corrupt as it is here."

The best way to understand the bizarre drama called Malaysian politics is to study the actors and their roles. Let us therefore meet the major players and their questionable accomplishments over the past decade—deeds I have named Malaysia's dirty dozen—and conclude with a detailed round of interviews that should fill in the remaining gaps.

First, however, a note of caution: Of all the government leaders I interviewed in the three countries in this study, the politicians and bureaucrats of Malaysia proved to be the most obstinate and evasive. Appointments made with ranking ministers were canceled, then rescheduled, then canceled again. Few of them would go on the record. Most prefaced their comments by saying "Now, don't quote me on this, but. . . ." If I had a ringgit for every time they used that phrase, I could have upgraded my hotel room to a penthouse suite. For lack of anything documentable, gossip and rumor are the hard currencies of politics in Kuala Lumpur.

Given its small size and geopolitical irrelevance, Malaysia is an insignificant actor on the stage of international affairs. Consequently Malaysians don't really care much about what foreigners think of them or their country, and what's more, they don't go out of their way to ask them since they know the answer is more than likely to be critical anyway.

The Players

Datuk Seri Mahathir bin Mohamad has been Malaysia's prime minister since 1981, having been personally selected by his predecessor, Tun Hussein Onn, to succeed him. Mahathir is only the country's fourth prime minister; its "founding father" was Tengku Abdul Rahman, who served from independence in 1957 through 1971, when he was succeeded by Tun Abdul Razak. Tun Razak suffered a heart attack (a fate that befalls many Malays, given the local Islamic diet which is heavy in saturated fats from red meat, like lamb) and died in 1976. Hussein Onn, more administrator than politician, then took control.

Malaysian honorary titles are both ubiquitous and confusing. The most common, Datuk, and its equivalent Dato' represent honorary awards conferred by local sultans, and practically everybody has one. A woman Datuk is a Datin. Datuk Seri and Datuk Paduka simply signify higher ranks within the Datuk order. Tun is equivalent to a British earl, Tengku means prince, and Tan Sri is Malaysian for the English "Sir," signifying a kind of knighthood, an honor only the king may confer. (A Tan Sri can bump a Datuk from a crowded flight, for example, but not vice versa.) Years ago, when the titles were first being conceived, Tan was the title of choice for earl, rather than Tun, but linguistic difficulties ultimately eliminated it from consideration. Tan Tan, in the case of a common Chinese name, sounded rather silly, and Tan Das, for an Indian name, became an insult, since *tandas* was Malaysian for "toilet," so Tun became the title. Haji indicates the person has made the pilgrimage to Mecca—the *haj*—while Encik simply means "Mister."

Hussein's father, Dato' bin Ja'afar Onn, was UMNO's first secretary general and the first head of UMNO Youth. After an early military career he studied law in England, and his political career blossomed. He was minister of education, minister of trade and industry, and finally deputy PM in Razak's early cabinets, succeeding Razak as prime minister in 1976. Soft-spoken and kind, Hussein was known as a gentleman in the old Malay tradition. His strengths as an administrator earned him the reputation as a "red-liner," meaning someone who underlined key points in memorandums so as not to forget them. He very effectively defused racial tension during his tenure by amending the Societies Act to depoliticize Malaysia's thousands of ethnic clubs and associations and ordered the Islamic youth movement, ABIM (Angkatan Belia Islam Malaysia), to sever all ties with foreign Islamic groups. Hussein's five-year era was racially quiet and politically stable; when he chose Mahathir as his successor in 1981, he delivered an emotional half-hour speech that brought a nationwide audience to tears. "I pray that God has given me the wisdom to make the right choice," he said.

Mahathir is a medical doctor by training and is the nation's first (and only) political leader never to have been educated in England.

He is a product, pure and simple, of Malay schools, including university (in Singapore, of course, which at that time was part of Malaya). In his early years as a politician he had been chauvinistic, controversial, and provocative, saying things that his fellow Malays weren't accustomed to hearing, such as that maybe they *were* lazy and risk-averse and not up to competing with the Chinese. In short Mahathir brought racism out of the closet, and in so doing he violated a fundamental Malay principle of superficial harmony. He was rewarded for his bluntness by being booted out of UMNO by the party elders.

"If race differentiates citizens, then there must also be racial loyalty," Mahathir asserted in *The Malay Dilemma*, which he wrote while he was in the political wilderness following the 1969 violence in Kuala Lumpur. "Racial loyalty must involve privileges for one's race and denial of rights to others. Under these conditions, each member of a race must be instinctively guided by considerations of profit and loss for himself. Each member must therefore seek to enhance the position of his race so that he himself may gain in the long run. If this fact of race, race loyalty, and privilege are understood, then attitudes on race relations in Malaysia can be better appreciated."

Mahathir was born in 1925 in the northern state of Kedah. He first became involved in politics in 1945, when he joined several organizations that later merged into UMNO. After earning his medical degree in 1953, he went into private practice and didn't return to politics until a decade later, when in 1965 he was appointed as a delegate to the UN and made a member of UMNO's Supreme Council. Expelled in 1969, he was readmitted in 1972 and in 1975 became one of UMNO's three vice presidents—a position regarded as the traditional stepping-stone to the prime ministership. He had been chosen by Hussein Onn as deputy prime minister in 1976, paving the way for his succession at such time as Onn either retired or stepped down. Asked once how long he would like to be prime minister, Mahathir replied, "for life."

When Mahathir became prime minister in 1981, he chose as his deputy Datuk Musa bin Hitam, himself a former member of UMNO's Supreme Council, a former head of UMNO Youth, and of course a vice president of the party. In the previous Hussein Onn cabinet he had been minister of primary industries and minister of education. Born in 1925 in the southern peninsular state of Johore, across the causeway from Singapore, the son of a Chinese mother and a Malay father, Musa is a skilled orator and a consummate political gamesman. In addition to contributing a geographic balance, with Mahathir from the North and Musa from the South, he has complemented Mahathir's aggressive, no-nonsense style with his own reputation for politeness and courtesy. They worked so well together that they became known as Malaysia's "M&Ms." As deputy prime minister Musa was next in line to become PM until he abruptly resigned his post, citing personal differences, in 1986.

Tengku Tan Sri Razaleigh bin Hamzah, minister of finance in Mahathir's early cabinets, is a trained economist and lawyer, having studied in Belfast and London. Born in 1934 and never married, he is a member of the royal family of Kelantan, a northern state whose residents are said to be known for their lemminglike behavior. After his father died, Razaleigh became minister of state for Kelantan and chairman of its UMNO division. In 1970 he became the youngest-ever chairman of Bank Bumiputra, a national bank for *bumis*. As Malaysia's youngest minister of trade and industry in 1971, he led its first trade delegation to Beijing and was elected one of the three UMNO vice presidents in 1975. In 1974 *Time* magazine named him one of 150 people under the age of forty-five as a future leader of the world. Razaleigh has been described variously as brilliant, energetic, impatient, and exceedingly ambitious. He led a charge to unseat Mahathir as president of UMNO (and PM) in 1987, lost, and then promptly bolted UMNO to create a new political party, Semangat '46 (the Spirit of 1946), from which he is challenging Mahathir today.

Datuk Paduka Daim bin Haji Zainuddin, Malaysia's minister of finance until early 1991, is from the same state (Kedah) and attended the same schools as Prime Minister Mahathir. Born in 1938 and trained as a lawyer in London and at Berkeley, Daim came late to politics, having taught, practiced law, and been a businessman for many years. Mahathir broke with tradition in 1984 and brought his old friend into the finance ministry right from the private sector. In his seven years as finance minister Daim achieved many notable successes—reducing the personal tax rate, imposing stricter fiscal restraints, slowing the growth of foreign debt, and persuading Mahathir to abandon his pet HICOM projects—though critics have asserted that he was successful for two simple reasons: he is disciplined but thoroughly unprincipled, and he has a brilliant secretary general, Tan Sri Zain, Malaysia's former ambassador to the United States, as his top bureaucrat.

For Daim the phrase *conflict of interest* does not exist. As finance minister he froze new listings on the Kuala Lumpur stock exchange to boost the shares of his own holdings, purchased a controlling interest in United Malayan Banking Corp., Malaysia's third-largest bank, and continued to serve as chairman of UMNO's investment arm, which controls four major newspapers and the country's biggest TV station. Daim's personal assets are managed by his family or registered in their name; his publicly listed and private holdings are worth nearly $300 million. "There is no law which says a cabinet minister's family should not hold assets," he has said.

Encik Anwar Ibrahim is Mahathir's new minister of finance and his youngest cabinet officer. Born in 1947 in Chinese-dominated Penang, Anwar founded ABIM, the Islamic youth movement, in 1971, and was for many years its president. He is a Muslim fundamentalist, a brilliant intellectual, and a firebrand as an orator—the Tom Hayden of Malaysian politics. As head of ABIM he was perhaps the government's most outspoken critic, focusing on its corruption and its inability to relieve rural poverty, and in 1970 he was detained without trial for eighteen months under its strict Internal Security Act. But in 1982 Mahathir persuaded him to join UMNO, and he became president of UMNO Youth, shocking and stunning his friends. He was appointed minister of culture and sports in 1983, minister of agriculture in 1984, minister of education in 1986, and succeeded Daim as minister of finance in early 1991. He is one of UMNO's three vice presidents and is so frequently mentioned as a future prime minister that the question asked is always when; never if. Now that he is finance minister, he has emerged as the frontrunner to replace Mahathir.

These, then, are the principal actors in Malaysia's current political drama. There are other, minor players who shuffle constantly on- and offstage: Mahathir's present deputy, Ghafar Baba, who has himself had heart problems and plays a kind of caretaker role; Samy

Vellu, head of the Malaysian Indian Congress, and his number two, S. Subramaniam; Lim Kit Siang, the fiery leader of the opposition Democratic Action Party, and his capable deputy, Lee Lam Thye; Ling Liong Sik, who succeeded Tan Koon Swan as head of the Malaysian Chinese Association following Tan's arrest and conviction in 1986 for criminal breach of trust and fraud; and Goh Cheng Teik of Gerakan, the dominant party in Penang. We will meet many of these characters, as well as some of the leading figures, in the interviews presented later in the chapter but it is UMNO and UMNO alone that dominates Malaysian politics.

Malaysia's Dirty Dozen

The following synopsis of events describes, in roughly reverse chronological order, how the drama has unfolded and how incestuously corrupt Malaysia's political system has become.

1. The UMNO Split

Imagine the shock Americans would have felt at the resignation of Vice President George Bush during President Reagan's second term. In effect that is what Musa did to Mahathir in early 1986, upsetting Malaysia's M&M combination. A heartbeat away from the prime ministership if he had only waited his turn, Musa turned his back on it all and simply walked out. At a senior UMNO meeting Mahathir had questioned the loyalty of his Supreme Council members, some of whom had taken to calling him "corrupt, a dictator, and among the richest men in the world." Musa, confident he had Mahathir's complete trust, asked the PM if he included Musa in the lot, and to his complete surprise Mahathir said he did. Shocked and hurt, Musa abruptly resigned.

A year later, in early 1987, still in the party but with no rank, Musa teamed up with former minister of finance Razaleigh (Team B) to challenge Mahathir and Ghafar Baba (Team A) for UMNO's leadership. They lost by the hair-thin margin of forty-three votes out of more than 1,000 cast. Mahathir took immediate revenge and sacked *everyone* who had supported Razaleigh and Musa from their positions in government. Razaleigh countered by taking Mahathir to court and suing *him*, claiming the prime minister had obtained votes from more than fifty unregistered branches of UMNO, making his election illegal and Razaleigh the party president (and, by extension, prime minister).

The case kicked around in the courts for more than a year. In early 1988 a high court justice dismissed Razaleigh's suit but in so doing ruled that UMNO had indeed failed to register its branches properly and that *the whole party* had thereby become illegal. The irascible Mahathir responded by creating a brand new party called UMNO Baru (New UMNO), simultaneously kicking out all his rivals and their supporters. Razaleigh retaliated by incorporating Semangat '46 and organizing a new opposition to UMNO by collaborating with the DAP and PAS, the Islamic fundamentalists, to challenge UMNO Baru in local contests until the next national election, scheduled to be held no later than 1991. He figured if his sixteen MPs could combine with the DAP's twenty-four, PAS's one, and the MCA's seventeen, and the handful of opposition parties that were outside the Barisan (Alliance) anyway, he would have seventy-four seats and could destroy the two-thirds majority Mahathir needed to pass constitutional amendments and other important legislation.

For a time Mahathir held up an olive branch, saying he would welcome "back" into UMNO Baru without penalty any Razaleigh supporters who would be willing to leave Semangat '46. Few accepted the invitation. But Musa, who had grown increasingly uncomfortable with Malaysia's new, more abrasive politics, ultimately rejoined UMNO Baru in late 1988. As his reward he was appointed Malaysia's permanent representative to the UN in mid-1989. Undeterred, Razaleigh has pressed on, determined to unseat Mahathir. Though he has yet to win any local elections outside his home state of Kelantan, his defeats have been by very small margins. He figures he has at least half the Malay vote.

"The political hegemony of the Malay community," scholar Diane Mauzy wrote in a thoughtful article, "Malaysia in 1987: Decline of the 'Malay Way,' " "has led to an unfortunate, perhaps inevitable, by-product—the eruption of serious internal differences within the dominant party and the decline of the 'Malay way.' The 'Malay way' involves, among other elements, a method of problem-solving and conflict-avoidance that has [historically] helped to soothe political tempers. It emphasizes traditional courtesy and good manners, wide consultation, compromise, avoidance of direct confrontation, and a striving for consensus rather than imposing the will of a (sometimes narrow) majority. . . . Critics are wooed rather than repressed and defeated opponents are not pounded into complete submission, but openings are left for future reconciliation."

2. Castrating the Judiciary

The high court's ruling against Mahathir was just one of many decisions that did not go his way. Earlier the high court had granted an injunction against an UMNO-owned company's signing a lucrative contract with the UMNO-dominated government, four of whose ministers sat on the company's board; had upheld a challenge by the *Asian Wall Street Journal* against expulsion of its correspondents and revocation of its publishing license; and had ordered the home ministry to allow Aliran, a consumer-*cum*-human-rights group, to publish its newsletter in Bahasa. Then it ruled that UMNO Baru could not simply assume ownership of assets formerly belonging to the old UMNO; they would have to be purchased, not transferred.

This was all too much for Mahathir. In an unprecedented maneuver Mahathir petitioned the king to remove the head of the judiciary, Lord President Tun Mohamed Salleh Abas, pending a hearing by a tribunal of five judges. Tun Salleh said he was being called to account for not showing partiality in the court cases involving UMNO, and Mahathir responded by saying that in fact it was the *king* who had requested that Salleh be replaced, because Salleh had written the king complaining of interference from the executive branch in the affairs of the judiciary.

King Mahmood Iskandar suspended Tun Salleh and five other high court judges in May 1988, just days after he had decided that the Malaysian Supreme Court should hear an appeal by Razaleigh's UMNO dissidents regarding the outcome of the intraparty elections a year earlier. In 1977, when he was solicitor general, Salleh had successfully prosecuted the crown prince of Johore—now ironically the king—for manslaughter and sentenced him to jail. The crown prince's father, then the sultan of Johore, pardoned his son afterward, so there may have been more than a pinch of vengeance in the king's decision to sack Salleh. (In fact as crown prince the king had killed not one man, but two. He shot a fisherman who had got in the way of his waterskiing and later reportedly bludgeoned a man to death with a golf club.)

Two months after his suspension, the tribunal unanimously charged Salleh with misbehavior and misconduct and sacked him. Then it found the five high court judges guilty of improper behavior and sacked them, too. Three days later the Supreme Court simply dismissed the appeal by Razaleigh and his dissident faction. And shortly after *that* the UMNO Baru–dominated Parliament amended the Constitution to restrict the powers vested in the high court, removing its right to interpret the law and giving it the authority only to reach a verdict and hand down the appropriate punishment.

"The Mahathir government's actions against the judiciary are likely to have far-ranging effects on the rule of law in Malaysia," the U.S. Lawyers' Committee for Human Rights concluded in its 1989 report, *Malaysia: Assault on the Judiciary.* "Before mid-1988, the judiciary was able to provide a limited but important check on the power of the executive branch. Today, the restraint on government power provided by an independent judiciary is effectively eliminated. The parliament, the judiciary, and the royalty have been forced to surrender their powers gradually to the executive, which has emerged as the dominant group to which everything else in the country is [now] subservient."

3. United Engineers (Malaysia) Bhd.

Once Mahathir had succeeded in emasculating the courts, it was a simple process for Malaysia's Supreme Court to simply dismiss the case brought by the DAP's Lim Kit Siang charging that the UMNO-controlled government had unlawfully assigned to an UMNO-owned company, United Engineers (Malaysia) Bhd., its most lucrative public works contract ever. UEM thereby got the green light to proceed with a $1.5 billion project to link Singapore in the south with the border of Thailand up north via a new 600-mile expressway.

The contract also privatized Malaysia's main north–south highway under a consortium led by UEM, which would operate the highway and collect all tolls, and it paved the way for UEM to bid on a privatization project for Kuala Lumpur's sewers. UEM was controlled by Hatibudi Sdn. Bhd., all but one of whose shares were held by Halim Saad, the chairman of UEM and a business associate of finance minister Daim Zainuddin, who is also the treasurer of UMNO Baru. Hatibudi later reincorporated under UMNO Baru as Hatibudi Nominees Sdn. Bhd.

For his part Mahathir naturally brushed off objections to the deal. "I don't see why we shouldn't sign the contract," he said. "The DAP is just frustrated that after 30 years of independence it still can't form a government and that there is no other hard issue to champion." UMNO Baru badly needed the revenues from the contract to pay for its luxurious, $150 million Putra World Trade Center. But UMNO's secrecy about the project and the absence of any public debate created a serious image problem. "Sometimes the Malaysians are their own worst enemies," one critic said.

4. Operation Lalang

In October 1987 Mahathir's Ministry of Education, headed then by Islamic fundamentalist Anwar Ibrahim, promoted a hundred non-Mandarin-trained Chinese teachers as senior assistants in Chinese primary schools throughout Malaysia. The Chinese community took this as a serious affront, which it clearly was, and acted unanimously in opposition. They held a rally to protest the appointments and called for a boycott of classes at affected Chinese schools. A joint government committee was formed to investigate the issue.

In response 15,000 members of UMNO Youth held a demonstration to *support* Anwar's decision, and they planned a massive rally on November 1, when 500,000 Malays were expected to converge on Merdeka Stadium (whose seating capacity is only 40,000). Word got around that anti-Mahathir forces would try to crash the rally; Tengku Abdul Rahman urged that it be called off; racial taunts and slurs in Kuala Lumpur escalated; and the underground "Xerox" press wrote that Malays had begun practicing martial arts in anticipation of expected violence.

For Mahathir not to react would have been a clear sign of weakness and loss of face. But had he allowed the rally to take place, he would have risked the most serious riots in Malaysia since 1969. So he did what was most in keeping with his increasingly totalitarian style: he canceled the rally and invoked the Internal Security Act, recently strengthened to permit arrest and detention for up to two years without formal charges. Between mid-October and mid-December, Mahathir's ISA police arrested 112 key political opponents and detained them without trial, including Mahathir's chief nemesis, Lim Kit Siang (who had been similarly detained many times before), but conveniently excluding several UMNO leaders who had contributed to the escalation in tension. The sweep and detention effort was named Operation Lalang, *lalang* being a Malaysian word meaning a weed or grass that collapses easily in the soft wind.

The ISA comes under the authority of the minister for home affairs—none other than Mahathir himself, who holds that portfolio as well. But he didn't stop at emasculating the opposition; he bludgeoned the press, too. All three opposition newspapers—the *Star* (owned by the MCA), the Chinese-language *Sin Chew Jit Poh*, and the Malay biweekly *Watan*—had their publishing licenses revoked. The only major media remaining were the *New Straits Times*, the *Berita Harian*, *Utusan Malaysia*, and *Utusan Melayu*—all owned by UMNO—in addition to the unofficial press like the DAP's *Rocket*. By mid-1989, after average confinement of about six months, all of the political detainees had been conveniently released, in time for Mahathir to announce with a clean conscience that Kuala Lumpur would host the Commonwealth heads of government meeting that coming October.

When the foreign press criticized Operation Lalang, Mahathir in turn charged that the foreign media simply censored comments that weren't critical of the ISA arrests. "There is no free Western press," he said at the time. "The only free press is in Malaysia."

5. The Tornadoes

Having secured Kuala Lumpur as host city for the upcoming Commonwealth meeting, Mahathir's UMNO-controlled government concluded a huge $2 billion arms deal with London for the purchase of British Tornado jet fighters, artillery, and radar equipment. The basic price of an off-the-shelf Tornado, as paid previously by both the

RAF and Germany's Luftwaffe, was about $30 million. Mahathir agreed tö pay $50 million each for the same aircraft.

Sources in London and Kuala Lumpur pointed out that the higher price included an up-front payback of some $125 million to UMNO Baru plus another $80 million to Malaysian agents and ruling families. Mahathir was well aware that a bitter election fight with Razaleigh would be forthcoming, and UMNO needed to fill its campaign coffers in anticipation of higher prices for vote buying in the provinces. As one senior defense official put it, "Unusual people are involved in the deal, so we must expect unusual terms."

6. The Tan Koon Swan Scandal

UMNO was not the only Malaysian political party capable of perpetrating world-class scandals. The Malaysian Chinese Association (MCA) also made a try for the gold ring on its own.

In November 1985 Malaysian-Chinese entrepreneur and millionaire Tan Koon Swan ended a long and bitter struggle for party leadership when he was successfully elected president of the MCA. Tan's story was the stuff of fiction, the local equivalent of Horatio Alger: he was the son of an immigrant hawker who sold dumplings in the street, and he rose to become the most powerful Chinese in Malaysia at age forty-five. But by January 1986 Tan's empire had crashed, and the onetime tycoon faced a jail sentence in Singapore for criminal breach of trust.

Tan had been a board member of Multi-Purpose (Holdings) Bhd. (MPHB), MCA's investment arm, for some time. Court documents revealed that he had illegally plowed MPHB cash into his Singapore-based Pan Electric group (a hotel, property, and marine salvage company), a group that also owned the well-known Orchard Hotel there. By late 1985 Pan Electric's revenues had slowed, its debts had mounted, and it faced nearly $100 million in speculative forward purchases of stock-contract obligations (similar to calls). In mid-November, days after Tan had completed his political victory, Pan Electric defaulted on a scheduled installment of a syndicated loan, triggering a dominolike effect in the market. Despite Tan's injection of cash from MPHB, Pan Electric went bankrupt, closing the stock exchange of Singapore and causing an official investigation that landed Tan in jail, threw the MCA into total disarray, and precipitated the most serious unrest between Malaysia and Singapore since the 1969 riots.

By early 1986 MPHB, which had been created originally as a kind of cooperative, or mutual fund, for small Malaysian-Chinese investors, had run up debts totaling nearly $300 million and could no longer assure its shareholders a return on their investment. The Chinese community was furious that its hard-earned savings were at risk and MCA was again a ship without a captain, but it was all just business as usual for Malaysian politics.

Tan Koon Swan was released from Singapore's Changi jail after having served sixteen months and then promptly faced a jail term in Malaysia. But like other white-collar criminals, he had become a born-again Christian in prison. Asked about his mounting legal problems, Tan simply replied, "I leave it all to God. I have submitted myself to His will." But his fellow Chinese critics were less than Christian in their support. "The first wave was sympathy," an MCA official said when 12,000 Chinese demonstrated to protest Tan's unfair treatment by the Singapore government *before* he went to jail. "But the second wave has come and drowned him. He is still drowning."

7. UMNO *Baru* and *Multi-Purpose (Holding) Bhd.*

MPHB had to do something about its mountain of debt from the Tan scandal, so it began to cast about for a possible acquirer or a buyer for some of its assets, which ranged from plantations and gambling casinos to banking, real estate, and shipping. It took a while, but one finally emerged: Hume Industries (Malaysia) Bhd., a local construction firm that *itself* had been awarded a $200 million contract by the UMNO-controlled UEM to supply concrete products for the north-south highway project. Hume bid just over $400 million in mid-1989 to acquire MPHB.

The MCA was not amused; not only was the bid low (Price, Waterhouse was MPHB's court-appointed receiver), but it sensed an attempt by UMNO to exert indirect control over its party's investments as well and reacted bitterly—all the more so considering that Hume's controlling company was Hong Leong Co. (Malaysia) Bhd., whose boss was another young Chinese tycoon, Quek Leng Chan, who owned 51.3 percent of Hume and was eager to gain control of the bank owned by MPHB to round out his own holdings. "Would any commercial group bid for Multi-Purpose without assurances or backing from the authorities?" one Malaysian business consultant asked rhetorically.

By mid-1989 the plot had thickened when *another* company with close business links to then-finance minister Daim Zainuddin's family, Kamunting Corp. Bhd., one-fifteenth the size of MPHB, made a competing bid to acquire all the assets of an ailing cooperative that held a 28.9 percent controlling stake in MPHB, the value of which was estimated to be about a third higher than Hume's offer. Kamunting, once a moribund Malaysian company, had found new strength through the privatization contract its own affiliate, Seri Angakasa, had been awarded before. Earlier in 1989 Kamunting had also acquired a 32.5 percent interest in another MPHB affiliate, Malaysian Plantations, for $30 million.

One Malaysian-Chinese businessman summarized local sentiment when he said, "Kamunting looks like an off-white knight to me."

8. *Malaysian Overseas Investment Corp.*

In April 1983 one of Malaysia's highest-flying *bumi* businessmen, Mohammad Abdullah Ang, got Mahathir's blessing to set up a new company called Malaysia Overseas Investment Corp. Sdn. Bhd. (MOIC), whose share capital was funded by ten of the country's most prestigious firms and whose managing director would be Ang himself.

MOIC was modeled on the typical Japanese trading company, with a low capital base leveraged by high levels of short-term debt. Its aim was to act as an agent in countertrade transactions, to help local companies with their exports, and to become a conduit for Malaysian private investments overseas. Two of its first projects were construction of a hotel in Fuji and construction of the Malaysian consulate in Papua New Guinea. It also supplied wooden railroad ties to Bangladesh.

Under Abdullah Ang, MOIC's staff soared from thirty to more

than 400 in just a few months, with overseas offices in New York, Singapore, and Seoul. Whenever Mahathir made an official trip abroad, MOIC was the company in tow. But by year-end 1985 it had accumulated losses of $10 million with only $400,000 in collectible assets. When it went out of business, Abdullah Ang went to jail and had to give up both of his Rolls-Royce sedans—one oyster pink, the other powder blue.

9. Bankrupt Deposit-Taking Cooperatives

In January 1989 Bank Negara, Malaysia's central bank, announced that Cooperative Central Bank, the country's largest deposit-taking cooperative (like an S&L), would henceforth cease to exist and that its assets and deposit liabilities would be merged into a yet-to-be-named finance company. It had accumulated losses of nearly $300 million and liabilities of more than $400 million owed to some 250,000 depositors.

The collapse of CCB was part of a severe shakeout of Malaysian financial institutions that had forced Bank Negara to take over four banks, two finance companies, and more than *two dozen* deposit-taking cooperatives since 1986. What had these institutions been doing with their depositors' money? Lending to *bumis*, of course; financing speculative investments in the stock market; and making lots of real estate loans that went sour when Malaysia's economy slowed in 1985 and 1986. (In 1986 Finance Minister Daim, who himself owned a 41 percent controlling interest in Malaysia's third largest bank, United Malayan Banking Corp., had temporarily suspended business at twenty-three cooperatives with a total of more than 500,000 members and some $500 billion in assets.) The central bank bailouts simply confirmed most peoples' conviction that *bumis* could never go bankrupt.

Among the many powerful Malaysians in debt to CCB (and who were tentatively barred from leaving the country) were former information minister Adib Adam, the former chairman of the K.L. stock exchange; Tan Loon Swan, brother of the jailed Chinese tycoon Tan Koon Swan; the ex-chairman of Singapore's Sea Lion Hotels, Yap Yong Seong; and a mélange of other Malaysian politicians, civil servants, and businessmen.

10. Makuwasa, Malaysia's Mystery Firm

In 1984 finance minister Daim organized a plan to enable assets of the $10 billion national Employee Pension Fund, or EPF, to be channeled from public institutions into speculative stocks in an attempt to boost share prices on the slumping Kuala Lumpur stock exchange. Makuwasa, a private limited company wholly owned by the government, obtained shares from the EPF at no cost in what amounted to a "slush fund without accountability."

The government's capital issues committee, which rules on all new share issues, would direct a Malaysian company planning a public issue to allocate a specified percentage of new shares to the EPF at preferential prices. Then the EPF would subscribe to the issue using public funds and transfer 70 percent of the allotted shares—at the same preferential price—to Makuwasa; Makuwasa would then benefit from the (presumed) price appreciation once the shares traded publicly. (This technique is not uncommon in other Asian stock markets, but nowhere outside Malaysia is it used with foreordained government complicity.)

Five million Malaysians—80 percent of the work force—are contributors to the EPF, and when news of the Makuwasa scandal hit in mid-1986, several thousand of them picketed the EPF building in downtown Kuala Lumpur. Although only 3 percent of the EPF's assets had been invested in equities, the total amount involved— nearly $300 million—made the EPF (via Makuwasa) one of Malaysia's largest institutional investors. It lost $20 million in 1985 and $60 million in 1986 before its disgrace via public disclosure. UMNO's response, not atypical, was a combination of suppression and secrecy.

11. The Bank Bumiputra Scandal

Bank Bumiputra Malaysia Bhd., one of Malaysia's largest commercial banks, had been created by the government as part of the embryonic NEP to help small Malay businessmen. But the bank had not only made questionable loans; it had done so to Chinese businessmen overseas, a fact that shocked and stunned ordinary Malaysians.

The Bank Bumiputra scandal was a case involving "massive fraud." Through its wholly owned overseas subsidiary, Bumiputra

Malaysia Finance, it channeled fraudulent loans totaling nearly $150 million to the Hong Kong–based Carrian group, a property development concern owned by George Tan, and another $150 million to two other Hong Kong real estate firms, Eda Investments and Kevin Hsu—loans that represented two-thirds of BMF's total loan portfolio. The yarn began to unravel when Hong Kong's property market went sour following the announcement in 1982 that Britain would allow the colony to revert to China without incident in 1997.

In early 1983 an internal Bank Bumiputra auditor, Jalil Ibrahim, was sent to Hong Kong to investigate and was murdered for his efforts. Shortly thereafter, Malaysia's auditor-general, Tan Sri Dato' Ahmad Noordin Zakaria, headed a two-year investigation of the bank's troubles that resulted in a 1,000-page, two-volume report in early 1986. Bank Bumiputra ultimately had to be rescued by Malaysia's state oil company, Petronas, which assumed an 87 percent ownership position in the bank under a provision of the Petroleum Development Act that gives the prime minister control of Petronas and subjects it to his authority "as he sees fit." (Tengku Razaleigh, who was finance minister at the time, was never willing to discuss the case.)

"Bad bank loans for good oil money," one senior Petronas official admitted privately, citing a valid instance of Gresham's law in action.

12. Cornering the World Tin Market

The ink was hardly dry on Mahathir's confirmation as Malaysia's prime minister in 1981 when he created a plan, financed secretly and in part by loans from Bank Bumiputra, to corner the world market in tin.

The idea was put to Mahathir in 1980 by an Egyptian tin trader, David Zaidner, who worked for the commodities firm Marc Rich & Co. in Switzerland and traveled on a Swiss passport. Zaidner was obsessed with the thought of monopolizing trading in tin, much as Nelson Bunker Hunt had been at the time with the idea of controlling the world silver market. Zaidner approached the Indonesians first, but they smelled a rat and sent him packing. (Marc Rich was subsequently indicted, arrested, extradited to the United States, and convicted of massive tax fraud.)

Mahathir and his colleagues, including Tengku Razaleigh, proved to be more receptive. Mahathir had always felt that developing countries came out losers when trading their goods in global markets, so in December 1980 the state-owned Malaysian Mining Corp. Bhd. named Marc Rich its trading agent in a move that stunned the world commodities industry. Large, secret Malaysian tin purchases on the London Metal Exchange continued throughout 1981, inducing a worldwide price increase. Mahathir's strategy was cheap; the Malaysians had to pay only a 10 percent deposit against three-month forward purchase contracts.

But the scheme came unglued in late 1981 when other world producers, including the United States, started increasing production or selling from strategic stockpiles to take advantage of the Malaysian-induced price rises. Malaysia had amassed about 50,000 tons of tin and had to hold it off the market to keep prices up. Production continued to soar, obscure suppliers materialized from out of nowhere to cash in, the world went into the second oil shock–induced recession, and the tin market crashed.

Malaysia lost an estimated $250 million on its failure to honor forward contracts, and Bank Bumiputra lost another $1 billion in separate losses on loans it had made covertly out of its Hong Kong subsidiary, BMF. For five years Mahathir categorically denied that Malaysia had anything to do with the plan, but the outside pressure was unremitting. Mahathir finally revealed the details in 1986, but not before making a last-ditch cover-up attempt by using Malaysia's mystery firm, Makuwasa, to bury the losses.

Backstage with the Actors

"Money is *always* disappearing around here, *lah*," one young Chinese-Malay, a scholar at the University of Malaysia, told me in the lilting, singsong manner that characterizes Malay speech. "The striking thing about all these cases is that the funds just somehow seem to vanish. They may nail a few functionaries, but the seniors all get off the hook. As an old Malay proverb goes, 'The flesh and fat have gone to others; we are left with the bones and feathers.' Malaysia, quite simply, is a political system of the elite, by the elite, and for the elite."

Still, as a result of his efforts in unraveling the Bank Bumiputra debacle, Tan Sri Dato' Ahmad Noordin Zakaria, the former auditor-general, became Malaysia's "Man of the Year" in 1984. Now retired, he lives in Petaling Jaya, a quiet suburb just south of Kuala Lumpur, where I interviewed him about the systemic corruption that has become so pervasive in Malaysia. Slight of build, almost frail, with receding white hair, he was thoughtful and soft-spoken, a distinct personal symbol, it seemed, of the old Malay way.

"We've created a monster," Noordin told me, "and it's called money politics, the road to riches in this country. There's always been a certain conflict of interest that goes back to colonial times, but now there's a distinct departure from the norm."

I asked him if the NEP had been a contributing factor, and he said, "More money equals more votes—it's as simple as that. I suppose the NEP has forced the creation of business opportunities in the three major coalition parties—you know, you scratch my back and I'll scratch yours."

The Prime Minister and Possible Successors

The burden of this corrupt system, and Mahathir's personal role in it, prompted the *Far Eastern Economic Review* to redefine Malaysia's NEP as Mahathir's New Equation of Power:

$$NEP = Dr.\ M \times (UMNO\text{--}Tengku\ Razaleigh\ Hamzah) + ISA^2$$
$$+/\text{--}MCA +/\text{--}Musa\ \text{--}Judges\ \text{--}Media\ \text{--}DAP.$$

The prime minister had become not a victim but the prime instigator of the "decline of the Malay way."

"This man is deinstitutionalizing Malaysia," one foreign expatriate with long experience in K.L. told me recently. "Yet Mahathir himself is a bit of an enigma. I don't think he's personally corrupt, despite the people around him who are. Still, he's very strong-willed, authoritarian, and absolutely ruthless."

"He's a doctor, you see, not a lawyer, *lah*," another young Malay, a textbook publisher, suggested to me. "So he has no innate sense of justice and treats political problems as if they were simply medical ones. If your finger has cancer, you just cut it off. Therapeutic treatment is out of the question; power and control are the issues."

Another informant, a Chinese politician with no ax to grind,

had a slightly different perspective on the prime minister. "Mahathir's stubborn, to be sure," he told me, "but he can also be flexible
if tactics require. If he needs to be accommodating to ensure total
control, he'll be accommodating." To which a prominent Indian, a
young businessman, added, "He's a brilliant tactician, I'll admit, but
he's simply power-crazy."

I met with Raphael Pura, the author of so many well-docu-
mented and informed accounts of Malaysian political intrigue for the
Asian Wall Street Journal. A bright, still youthful-looking American
who had first come to Malaysia two decades earlier as a Peace Corps
volunteer, he is now the *Journal*'s ASEAN correspondent based in
Kuala Lumpur.

"Mahathir had a long honeymoon in 1981," Pura said as we sat
in his office overlooking the nearby Kuala Lumpur Hilton. "Then he
started to step on some toes and bruised a few egos and found he
could dish it out but not take it. He's not a magnanimous man, and
he does not take defeat lightly, so when some of the more experienced UMNO people got bypassed by their juniors, like Anwar and
Daim, they got angry and began forming factions. The big question
thus became, would the next-in-line ever get their turn in the driver's
seat? They thought by attacking Mahathir directly they might get him
to yield, but instead he became even more spiteful, arrogant, and
vengeful. A lot of his ideas were cockeyed, but some, like the Proton
venture with Mitsubishi, have worked. The point is, he's blocked off
all the major points of conflict or opposition, and the economy
continues to do relatively well—he has benefited politically by taking
credit for it, of course—and he has put his own health issue to rest.
His heart surgeon was Malay, and the operation was done here, not
in Singapore or London, a very nationalistic sign. So many Malays
think he's digging trenches now to position himself as PM for the
long haul."

Should anything happen to Mahathir, Deputy Prime Minister
Ghafar Baba would take over, but most agree he would merely be a
caretaker until UMNO elected its new president and, by extension,
Malaysia's next prime minister. (Baba was Mahathir's vote manager
in the 1987 UMNO elections. According to rumors, the going
reward for a Mahathir vote was $4,000 and the woman of your
choice.) Pura's point about the more experienced UMNO people

having been shunted aside brought Musa Hitam immediately to mind since he was clearly the nation's copilot until his abrupt resignation in 1986.

"Musa is a lot weaker, having mousetrapped himself as a result of stepping down," Pura said. "He's circuitous, likes the gamesmanship and the intrigue of politics rather than—as with Mahathir—the raw power. He also lacks the killer instinct."

Many feel that the traditional Malay process of consensus building needs to be restored before the next national elections, and some think Musa is the man best qualified to do just that. He has come back from the cold, rejoined UMNO, made his amends with Mahathir. Musa sits now in a kind of catbird seat as Malaysia's permanent representative to the UN pending his return as Mahathir's designated heir.

"There's no doubt that UMNO's major preoccupation up to the elections has to be compromise, not confrontation," another Chinese politician from one of Malaysia's smaller parties and a veteran of many political campaigns told me. "And Mahathir needs Musa's help to do this, although many consider Musa too indecisive. You can go to him a dozen times, for example, and get no decision. Looked at from afar, this may be rather dull stuff, but when you examine it more closely, Malaysia is the only Southeast Asian country that has any *real* politics going on."

But had confrontation now become the dominant characteristic of Malaysian politics, and was it here to stay, given the widely acknowledged decline of the Malay way?

"It may be a little late in the day to stop these confrontational tactics," Musa Hitam admitted. "It is clear Tengku Razaleigh won't be coming back to UMNO, so there seems to be no alternative to confrontation in terms of the political opposition."

Quiet and soft-spoken, Musa appeared relaxed and fit when I saw him, very much in a thoughtful mode, as if pondering his next move. This was just before Mahathir sent him to the UN. Many felt that Mahathir had cut a deal with Musa to bring him back into the party and that, if anything happened to the PM, Musa would be his designated successor—a sort of "least worst" scenario.

Meanwhile Tengku Razaleigh continues his broadside assault on UMNO from the trenches, in local elections, trying to chip away at

Mahathir's chokehold on the Malay vote. Some see him having limited success, but I found no one outside his inner circle of confirmed loyalists who felt he had any chance at all.

Anyone who meets with his senior political strategists, as I recently did, can't help feeling the moral intensity that rages within Semangat '46. The party sees its efforts as a kind of mini-*jihad*, a holy war to rid Malaysia of the scourge of money politics once and for all.

"When UMNO gives $2,000 to a village headman so he can fix his house, you know it's buying his vote," one of Razaleigh's lieutenants told me. "Others may get only $100 or $50, depending on their rank, but still, that's a lot of money to a poor family in the *kampong*. And roads get built, schools get fixed up, electricity is brought in, all as rewards for voting for UMNO. Therefore, to stay in power Mahathir has to play on their racial fears and at the same time keep the rural areas 'selectively' poor so he can continue to 'reward' their votes. He's definitely positioning himself to stay in power for at least another ten years if nothing happens to him. But if something does, the country's in trouble, because he has surrounded himself only with yes-men and incompetents."

When I suggested that pork barrel considerations tended to go with the franchise in most functioning democracies, I was abruptly reminded that Malaysia was no functioning democracy.

"Corruption, not democracy, is what runs this place. UMNO hands out all these commercial contracts to its own companies, and it's all done secretly so the local people don't know what's going on. They're simply told how to vote, and if they don't obey, they're told they'll lose their jobs. And Mahathir uses his Special Branch police under the ISA to intimidate voters at the polls. No, I don't think the present government is working on behalf of a multiracial society at all, because Mahathir is using a dangerous divide-and-conquer strategy. He's done it with UMNO, he's done it with senior bureaucrats—transferred them or moved them out—and now he's doing it with the people."

The local people are clearly not moved by principle, but neither do they accept either party at face value. "Which camp is better?" one Malay fisherman recently asked. "Both camps are crooks. How can I choose?"

Anwar Ibrahim, the young Islamic firebrand Mahathir brought

into UMNO and who was minister of education and is now minister of finance, remains quietly in the background. Some say he is brilliant; others maintain he is merely another Mahathir pawn, even those who agree he may be Mahathir's longer-term choice as successor.

"Anwar is more Islamic than the rest of us put together," one seasoned Malay observed at the time when Ibrahim was the minister of education. "He's not an administrator, he has no business experience, and he has mucked up the educational bureaucracy—he forces teachers and administrators to be UMNO loyalists or they lose their jobs. He can be impressive, sure, but he plagiarizes from others, and he is probably more extremist than will ever be good for the country. He's power-crazy, too, and I think he's even more ruthless than Mahathir."

On the Issue of Racism

The problem of succession in the Malaysian political economy is just one of several it will have to cope with during the last decade of this century. Another, of course, is the more critical issue of racial integration.

When I asked Musa Hitam whether he thought Malaysia could ever build a multiracial society, or UMNO a multiracial party, given the adversarial nature of its domestic politics today, his answer was as abrupt as it was truthful.

"No," he said simply. "Like the world becoming one, or Europe achieving unity in 1992, it will never happen."

Tun Hussein Onn, the red-liner who was Malaysia's former prime minister and chairman of the Institute for Strategic and International Studies, was somewhat elliptical on the subject. "I don't like to use the word *problem* when discussing race," he told me when I met him for a long, somewhat rambling interview at his office high atop the Petronas building in downtown Kuala Lumpur. "But even if you don't have a race problem in a multiracial society, you have a problem. People ask why you don't at least have a multiracial party, but that's just not possible under current conditions."

Nearly seventy when I saw him, Hussein appeared tired and his face drawn (he would succumb to a fatal heart attack just months later, in California, in early 1990, no doubt partly due to his meat-rich Malay diet, his active advisory functions, and his concern for a country that today is clearly not what it was when he was leading it). Quite tall for a Malay, Hussein was impeccably mannered, a trait befitting his aristocratic background. Hussein's unofficial role as mediator between Mahathir's UMNO Baru and Razaleigh's Semangat '46, enhanced his already unique perspective. Where *did* he think his country was heading?

"My concern is the division of Malays into factions," he said softly. "I think our people realize they have to live together, and I hope the lesson of 1969 will stay with us forever. The crux of the matter is fear—fear of the distribution of wealth. Malays always felt non-Malays had all the cards before, and even though the NEP has given those cards to the Malays now, they still feel disadvantaged. But part of the problem is a Malay tendency to exaggerate. We create all these wonderful economic statistics and then crow about them. As my father used to say, we lay one egg and we cackle like hell!"

Some thoughtful observers of the local scene have suggested that by not keeping English as the national language Malaysia has lost its best opportunity to create a truly integrated, multiracial society.

"Maintaining English as the official language might have helped defuse the communal problems," a Singaporean who spends considerable time in K.L. confided to me. "A multiracial society would still be workable, but you have to have the *will* to achieve it, and I don't see that there—with anybody. Their leaders, all of them, have pandered to the emotional, primordial fears of the Malays from early on, painting the Chinese and the Indians into a corner. I'm afraid they're going to make a rather large dent in the welfare of the Malay community in the long run as Mahathir executes his version of the Final Solution."

Datuk S. Subramaniam, deputy head of the Malaysian Indian Congress, agreed with that assessment.

"We are beginning to realize that maybe we did it wrong," he said when I spoke with him in Kuala Lumpur. "We formed parties to govern the country by cooperating, not by assimilating. Now some of us are beginning to think, 'How can we achieve the national unity that we have so far failed to bring about?' But the big question is, what is national unity?"

Subramaniam had just returned from the United States, having toured the country and visited Congress on a program sponsored by the Asia Foundation. He had also just lost by a narrow margin in his bid to unseat Samy Vellu as president of the MIC. Subramaniam is a member of the ASEAN Inter-Parliamentary Union, or AIPU, and on Friday every week he conducts "clinic days" with his constituents in nearby Hulu Selangor.

"I agree that English ought to be the national language," he said with a quick smile. "Unfortunately, we emphasized Bahasa for narrow communal and ethnic interests, not for the national interest. If, as a minority, we continue to lag behind, it is bad for the nation. Malaysian Indians could become the worst of the lot, and ten years from now the government might have to come out with an NEP for the sake of Indian economic progress."

Most UMNO politicians are adamant about keeping the party monoracial—that is, for Malays only. When I asked Datuk Leo Moggie, a linebacker-sized *bumi* from Sarawak who earned his M.B.A. at Penn State University and is now Mahathir's minister of works, whether UMNO would ever consider admitting non-Malays as party members, he said, "No, not in the near future."

The Democratic Action Party has been the most outspoken on the subject of interracial policy. It has also been the most criticized (by UMNO) for continually raising a subject that is, by most accounts, taboo. Its members, especially Lim Kit Siang, its intense leader, have been the most frequently persecuted for needling the UMNO leadership for its narrowness.

Lim Kit Siang was into his eighteenth month of detention from Operation Lalang when I was last in Kuala Lumpur, so I spoke with his deputy president, Lee Lam Thye, instead.

"UMNO talks all about social restructuring under the NEP," Lee said, "but this has not been carried out fairly in the public sector. There are more than 500 Chinese towns that were resettled by the government during the Communist emergency. More than 2 million people were relocated to help fight the insurgency, and yet to this day they have received no grants or privileges from the government. So we represent their grievances, because they have not gotten a fair deal under the NEP's poverty eradication program."

An energetic man in his mid-forties, Lee has been a member of Parliament since he was old enough to get elected—he has only a high school education. The DAP is Malaysia's only multiethnic party and has been since its inception as a branch of Lee Kuan Yew's PAP in 1966. Articulate and a skilled speaker, Lee more nearly resembles a university lecturer than a politician. We talked about Mahathir, about corruption, and about the future.

"Corruption has obviously become institutionalized now," he said, "and rampant. I think the prime minister will have to stay in power until he dies, because if he ever steps down, his opponents will drag all the skeletons out of his closet. Anwar was put in charge of one committee responsible for investigating corruption, but that was like putting a fox in the henhouse to guard the chickens. And there are serious problems that are not being addressed by the government, like education and capital flight. The brain drain will unavoidably get worse as more and more of our children realize they will have no real opportunity for advancement in their own country."

Goh Cheng Teik, a member of the minority Gerakan party, which governs the state of Penang and competes with the DAP for Chinese votes, concurred with Lee's assessment and took it one or two steps further.

"Mahathir's battle with Razaleigh is more like 'You bring the skeletons out of my closet, and I'll drag the skeletons out of yours,'" he said as we talked over lunch. "That's why there's been relatively little personal criticism between them, at least publicly, as they fight for Malay votes. But Mahathir is our 3D prime minister—dictatorial, doctrinaire, and dogmatic."

Goh is a Harvard-educated political scientist and the author of *Racial Politics in Malaysia*. His somewhat controversial book makes the point that a multiracial, more pluralistic political system should be adopted and suggests that the race-derived policies of the NEP should be allowed to lapse. When I suggested to him that, based on the successes of the Little Dragons, political authoritarianism was one fundamental ingredient for stability and economic takeoff, he nearly choked on his soup.

"In this country that is clearly subversive," he said, regaining his composure. "There is such a thing as giving Mahathir too much power. Malaysia is not a democratic country. If more than five people demonstrate, they need a police permit; otherwise they're illegal. And if they're convicted as charged, which is likely, sentencing is mandatory. UMNO rallies are the only ones that get police permits—one local agency arranges the buses, they throw in a free lunch, and they've got their rally. But what concerns me most is the tremendous waste that results from all the corruption. Since the late 1970s the government has stuck its hand into just about everything, and we've suffered tremendous losses—both economic and political—as a result."

Dato' Param Cumaraswamy, a young Tamil who studied law in the UK and is an attorney with Shook, Lin & Bok in Kuala Lumpur, was until recently the president of the Malaysian Bar Council (the equivalent of the American Bar Association). He has been outspoken about the need for the country to move away from the racial narrowness of its political past, an outspokenness that has not stood him in particularly good stead with UMNO's conservative leaders, despite his title.

"With its abundant natural resources and sparse population, Malaysia was the most richly endowed country in Asia," Param told me recently. "And yet we've squandered more opportunities than most countries can ever create. Why is this? Because our politicians make political capital for their own survival, which is used to suppress opposition in the name of quelling racial tension. But the racial element has been and will always be there to suppress more basic human and civil rights. In the name of democracy, they are destroying it."

Cumaraswamy received his Datukship from the sultan of Kelantan, who honored Param and five judges simultaneously. Some saw the honor as a way of "buying" his silence, but as he put it, "Every Tom, Dick, and Harry who supports the government gets a Datuk award."

He was instrumental in assisting the U.S. Lawyers' Committee for Human Rights when it investigated Mahathir's emasculation of the Malaysian judiciary. We discussed the discernible political shift that occurred as a result, and his surprising optimism for the future.

"Operation Lalang was bad enough," Param said, "but the real shock came when he tampered with the judiciary and sacked the judges. There is no habeas corpus now and no process of judicial review—not even for ministerial indiscretions. The sad thing about Malaysia in all this is that the people have not risen to the occasion.

After the Lalang arrests we expected widespread public protest, and there was *nothing*. But I still believe there is a great future here. Someday I think we'll see the emergence of a multiracial political party, which will be a historical event and a real signpost for the future."

But without inspired leadership and the will to change, Malaysia seems destined to a long future of racial politics. A Chinese-Malay who writes extensively about Malaysian politics told me a story that explained why.

Two Chinese, about to board the train from Singapore to Kuala Lumpur, bought just one ticket between them. Two Malays, each with a ticket, watched them carefully, curious to see what they would do. After the train left the station, the Chinese locked themselves in the lavatory. When the conductor passed by, he tapped on the door, and one of the Chinese men stuck his hand out with the ticket. The conductor took it, went on his way, and the Chinese had one free ride.

Not long thereafter the two Malays thought they would try the same trick. Purchasing just one ticket at the station, they boarded the train and waited for the conductor to enter their car. When he did, they rose from their seats and locked themselves in the toilet. A few minutes later there was a knock on the door. Opening it slightly, one of the Malays stuck his hand out with the ticket, and a Chinese man took it.

"Malaysia has in fact made some solid achievements despite all the ethnic tension," a senior Singapore government official said as we talked about Malaysia's problems. "But the point is, they should have done much better. Now they're trying to play down their economic nationalism and debating whether NIC status is really even worth pursuing."

FOREIGN AFFAIRS: A MODERN-DAY OXYMORON

Malaysia is the smallest nation in ASEAN, but with the exception of the tiny city-state of Singapore it has the highest ratio of armed forces per 1,000 population and, at 4 percent of GNP, the highest level of military spending per capita. In both 1986 and 1987 (the latest years for which figures are available), Malaysia spent an estimated $1 billion on defense, which kept 120,000 men in arms. To that sum must be added the recent $2 billion acquisition of Tornadoes from Great Britain.

Which prompts the obvious question: why does Malaysia need all this military hardware? The Communist insurgency has been defeated, Vietnam has withdrawn from Cambodia, the old policy of *konfrontasi* with Indonesia is long gone, Malaysia has no current border conflicts with its neighbors, and the primary challenge to Malaysia is economic, not military. But Malaysia does have a nagging territorial conflict with the Philippines, whose sultan of Sulu regards the Malaysian state of Sabah as having been ceded to him, and Malaysia has staked its own claim to the Spratly Islands in the South China Sea.

"The army is apolitical in Malaysia," a senior military official in Kuala Lumpur told me, "unlike in either Indonesia or Thailand. Though it is officially a nonaligned nation, as a Commonwealth country it is a signatory to the five-power defense agreement with the UK, Australia, New Zealand, and Singapore. They have some apprehension about the expansion of India's navy, and given the communal problems with the Chinese, there is always China to worry about."

But why a dozen new Tornadoes?

"There are two models, an air strike version and one for self-defense," my informant, an expatriate with many years in the region, said. "The Malaysians chose the attack version, and it might have had something to do with personnel. There used to be more Chinese and Indian troops here under British rule, but now they've all been replaced by *bumis*. The top officers are all Malay, and Malays are regularly promoted over other ethnic officers of greater experience and ability. Nobody asks why anymore; they just do it. So nationalism plays a role."

ASEAN remains Malaysia's major foreign policy preoccupation, and yet its tail-end position relegates it pretty much to creating reactive policies. In mid-1989, as Washington and Manila continued negotiations regarding the future of two U.S. military bases in the Philippines, Clark Air Field and Subic Bay Naval Station, Singapore's Lee Kuan Yew offered additional repair and refueling facilities to the U.S. Navy as a fallback position. Mahathir howled, saying he didn't want foreign bases in ASEAN (meaning he didn't want them next door, in Singapore, conveniently forgetting that they had been in ASEAN all along). But Indonesia rules the local sea lanes, and Thailand dominates the mainland; since Singapore is ASEAN's traditional spokesman, Malaysia more or less sits quietly at the back of the class.

"The most important feature of the Malaysian sociopolitical context is the tendency for every political issue to be transformed into a communal one," the Singapore-born Malay scholar Zakaria Haji Ahmad recently wrote in a perceptive essay called "Malaysian Foreign Policy and Domestic Politics: Looking Outward and Moving Inward?" "The issue of ethnicity accordingly is a predominant factor [in foreign policy]. With a heterogeneous population and a physically-divided territory, Malaysia has an arduous task establishing an international identity."

Malaysia's foreign policy has been personified by Mahathir himself, who has averaged seven overseas trips a year since he became prime minister in 1981. Since every other ASEAN country had a prestigious think tank, he decided Malaysia ought to have one too, so in 1983 he authorized the establishment of the Institute for Strategic and International Studies in Kuala Lumpur, ostensibly "private" but underwritten with government (read: UMNO) money. ISIS hosts a cadre of local scholars who research local political and economic policy issues and is on the circuit of regional conferences that belabor them.

"There was a time, a decade ago, when we thought we could do no wrong," Noordin Sopiee, the executive director of ISIS and a former editor of UMNO's New Straits Times, told me as we sat in his office at the think tank one day. "Those were the days of Malaysia, Inc., when we were sure we wanted to industrialize. Well, we still want to industrialize, I think, but I'm not sure we want to be called a NIC and lose the international advantages that come with staying as a developing country. We want to have a cheap currency and keep our UN contribution the same, but once we are officially labeled a NIC, the ringgit appreciates and our UN dues go up."

For all intents and purposes an international political midget, Malaysia appears fully content to continue playing with racial fire at home. As old suspicions and hostilities are fanned into new sources of friction by UMNO, the disappointments and inadequacies of the

Malays make the Chinese a convenient scapegoat. Absent faster industrial growth to enlarge the economic pie, resentment remains the operant emotion and racism the policy of choice.

On the basis of ASEAN's present leadership, as Singapore's brilliant prime minister Lee Kuan Yew recently said, you can rule out serious problems among member states. But Malaysia's racism has created a strong nationalistic orientation among its leaders, as indicated by the growing desire of the ruling Malay elite to be "more Muslim." Malaysia is thus being increasingly seen in global affairs as an Islamic state. Islam could well turn out to be Malaysia's bugbear, a curse on the corrupt political cartel that runs the country.

Malaysia's relationship with the United States is primarily an economic and commercial one, though more than 3,500 Peace Corps volunteers worked in Malaysia over a period of twenty years until the program was phased out in 1983. In 1988 the United States ran a trade deficit of $1.8 billion with Malaysia, some $600 million higher than in 1987. The issues of videocassette piracy and unauthorized public performances of copyrighted American material have dominated recent trade negotiations, but otherwise things are quiet, as one would expect of a country with such little strategic significance. There are some 20,000 Malaysian students at American universities today, making Malaysia the second-largest source of foreign students in the United States after Taiwan.

Malaysia continues to be an important foreign aid beneficiary of Japan. In 1985 and 1987 Malaysia received $126 million and $276 million, respectively, ranking number six on Tokyo's list of ODA recipients and accounting for just under 3 percent of Japan's total foreign aid. In 1986 and 1988, however, it did not make the top ten. Tokyo has traditionally had trouble living down its reputation of giving aid tied to its own trade, and Malaysian environmentalists on Sarawak have been protesting Japanese deforestation projects there; Japan buys virtually all of Malaysia's raw log and timber exports.

IS MALAYSIA'S FUTURE ALREADY HISTORY?

Malaysia will in all likelihood continue to be preoccupied with a number of domestic issues that could discourage new foreign investment and narrow its already slim chances of becoming a Little Dragon.

The NEP

The National Economic Consultative Council must decide in 1991 what to do with the NEP, make its recommendations to the prime minister, and then hope the government will act. It has three apparent options: to continue the NEP as is, to let it lapse, or to jigger it somehow to reflect changing economic circumstances. But the betting money in Kuala Lumpur is on a fourth option; namely, that Mahathir will successfully manipulate the elections and achieve control of Parliament for UMNO, thereby consigning the NEP as well as Alliance candidates to the dustbin of history. In short, he will act in the interests of UMNO and its ruling elite; the country will just have to make the necessary adjustments.

Elections

By law national elections had to be held by 1991. Mahathir saw his chance in October 1990; he called them once the Persian Gulf crisis had erupted and caused crude oil prices to explode, benefiting Malaysia's oil and gas exports (and UMNO's rule). The elections were the shortest in Malaysian history—they lasted only ten days. Mahathir, as most expected, won reelection to a third term and gained the two-thirds majority in Parliament he needed to assure passage of constitutional amendments. His National Front coalition won 127 of the 180 seats contested.

Tengku Razaleigh and his cunning band of Semangat '46 dissidents were able to win only forty-eight legislative seats, though they did inflict losses on UMNO Baru in Kelantan and Sabah, causing Mahathir's ministers from those two states to lose their seats. But outside Kelantan, Razaleigh's home state, the tengku was unable to assemble the multiracial coalition he had hoped for.

Ghafar Baba remained deputy prime minister in Mahathir's new cabinet, but Musa was noticeably absent from the ministerial lineup, having returned to New York as Malaysia's representative to the UN. For his efforts at corraling the *bumi* vote, Anwar Ibrahim was awarded a datuk seri title and retained his portfolio as education minister. Mahathir also announced the creation of a new cabinet-level minister for domestic trade and consumer affairs, in an attempt to blunt consumer opposition to the NEP—however misshapen that misguided economic plan might become.

Succession

The question of who will eventually become prime minister after Mahathir is still unresolved. UMNO will never turn to Razaleigh, Ghafar Baba is too old, and Anwar may still be too young. So with Musa back in UMNO, unless Anwar chooses to continue Mahathir's confrontational style (which has become the de facto Malay way), Musa could well be the front-runner. But Mahathir may die before that option becomes real.

Islam

Religion is at best a neutral element in all the Little Dragons. In Malaysia it is a serious problem. Islamic divorce rates are the highest in Asia, family stability the lowest. Unlike the tolerance of Buddhism, fundamental Islam preaches strict adherence to Allah's straight-and-narrow. If Anwar can subjugate his considerable personal ambition to the country's broader national interest, that might be one thing; but if the young firebrand uses Islam as a tactical tool to acquire greater political power, he could well fan the fires of Malay racism into an Islamic *jihad*.

Malaysia's future was perhaps best summed up by a young Malay scholar who told me, "Dr. Mahathir had heart failure, and a coronary bypass operation was his salvation, as it was for his predecessor, Tun Hussein. The question now is whether Malaysia itself may need a 'coronary bypass' in order to survive or whether it will succumb, if not by systemic collapse, then by Islamic infection."

NIC STATUS

Of the three NIEs examined in this book, Malaysia is the only one for which the question of imminent NIChood must be broken down into two subquestions: whether it *can* be a Little Dragon and whether it *wants* to be. "To be or not to be" is the issue being raised by the prime minister himself. Beginning in mid-1989, Mahathir started berating everyone who said Malaysia would be Asia's next Little Dragon. In a speech delivered to the Malaysian Technical Services Union that July the prime minister said that Malaysia's efforts to raise its head proudly would be futile, because every time it tried to do so it would be pushed back down by the industrialized nations of the West, who become resentful and vengeful when the developing countries start to succeed.

"If Malaysia achieves NIC status," Mahathir said, "it is very likely that we will be pressured to the point that we will collapse." The prime minister made a pointed reference to the United States, citing its abrupt termination of the Generalized System of Preferences for Singapore in early 1988 and for Thailand in early 1989 following the stalemate of negotiations on intellectual property rights and copyright law. "NIC—Status Symbol or Mere Trouble?" was the headline in the *New Straits Times* the next day.

As to whether Malaysia can become a NIC, Mahathir would clearly like to industrialize further, but Malaysia's political and social instability, its strident Islamic polemic, its woefully inadequate public education system, its worsening ethnic conflict, and widespread corruption are crushing handicaps. By the end of this century Malaysia will probably remain an outlying supplier to Japan's strategic manufacturing empire, while giant Indonesia nearby will have surged past it in the commodities markets. Ironically, this could benefit Mahathir and UMNO, too, since they thrive on hostility and can use the threat of foreign competition to win the Malay vote.

Again, Malaysia's bottom line is that it should have done much better. Its small population and strong resource base have created an abnormally high per-capita income, which has perpetrated the myth that Malaysia *is* on the verge of becoming a NIC, with Little Dragon status as a dynamic industrializing nation.

Based on the parameters of performance outlined at the beginning of this book, Malaysia is on the verge of doing no such thing. With its political system corrupt to the core, its people suppressed by a government that is moving ever closer to totalitarianism, and its social stability threatened by policies clearly racist in nature, Malaysia is a nation with an inferiority complex. It may be unfair to call Mahathir the Ferdinand Marcos of Malaysia, but to say that Malaysia is mainland Southeast Asia's equivalent of the Philippines may not be far off the mark. Over time Marcos and his Manila cronies became known as Ali Baba and the forty thieves; Malaysia may lack an Ali Baba, but Kuala Lumpur has more than its share of thieves.

5

IMPLICATIONS FOR U.S. FOREIGN AND ECONOMIC POLICY

That Japan's security depends on its economic strength is the main premise of Japanese foreign policy. So its broad aim in East and Southeast Asia is to sustain a stable and capitalist region that can provide raw materials, factories and, increasingly, markets for its industries. Part of what Japanese companies and their patron ministries, particularly MITI, are doing is to expand the Japanese economy beyond the country's geographic borders. Over the next decade, how Japan continues to do this will determine in large part the way the region develops.

The goal would be to integrate the economies of the [old] NICs and new NICs into something that would look a lot like a greater Japan, Inc. Its core would be Japan. Industrial policy would be coordinated from Tokyo. [It] would be done by something called the "Asian Brain," [which] would control the disposition of industrial investment throughout Japan and the region and coordinate the necessary policy support by the governments of those countries. The [cortex of the] "Asian Brain" is clearly intended to be the Japanese civil service, just as MITI was the brain behind Japan, Inc., in the 1960s.

—Paul Maidment
"The Yen Block: Together Under the Sun," *The Economist*

A KINDER, GENTLER CO-PROSPERITY SPHERE

The Cold War is over; conventional wisdom holds that America has won, hands down. But is the real winner in fact Japan?

In 1945 the United States emerged from the ravages of a global hot war as the only nation in the world with its industrial capacity

281

intact; the highest levels of accumulated savings and capital formation; the best-educated work force, including the largest per-capita
concentration of engineers; an unparalleled reputation for smooth
and close cooperation between government and business; and a
market itching to shift from making weapons to producing consumer
goods again.

Wartime, for America, galvanized the national consciousness,
forged a unity of purpose from what had been a pluralistic icono-
clasm, and then created the bipolar world of geopolitical reality that
followed—a global Pax Americana with the United States as its
dominant if not sole political leader.

In 1990, Japan was emerging from the constraints of a cold war
as the nation with the world's strongest and most advanced manufacturing capability; the highest levels of accumulated savings and
capital formation; unarguably the best-educated work force, including the largest per-capita concentration of engineers; an unparalleled
reputation for smooth and close cooperation between government
and business; and a political economy itching to expand its mutant
form of authoritarian, turbocharged capitalism well beyond its
shores.

Peacetime, for Japan, galvanized its national consciousness,
forged a unity of purpose that enabled it to win by economic means
what it couldn't win militarily, and helped create the multipolar
world of geoeconomic reality that exists today—signaling the end of
the old American century, with the United States no longer overwhelmingly dominant and Japan in many ways having become the
world's financial and industrial leader.

The story of Southeast Asia is, in part, another chapter in the
story of Japan. Beginning with Korea and Taiwan, its former colonies—the Asian countries it knew best and the ones that shared a
common cultural heritage—Japan helped create, in miniature, clones
of its own capitalist system.

In time these two nations formed the core of a group called the
Little Dragons, and their political economies mirrored the system
crafted so ingeniously by Japan: an authoritarian political structure;
harmony between the public and private sectors; an outward orientation to the economy, with world-class manufactured exports; massive incentives to boost savings and capital formation; a focus on

value-added production and applied R&D; the development of an industrial policy that targeted strategic industries and shielded them in their infancy from foreign competition, nurturing them to mature strength; and, above all, an unquestioned commitment to high-performance public education that has produced the best-trained human resources in the world.

Later, in response to a changing economic environment in which it saw its currency rise and its major trading partner, America, react petulantly to its successes, Japan expanded the sphere of its influence into Indonesia, Thailand, and Malaysia. Like an ever-widening band of concentric circles, Japan's regional economic, technological, and financial dominance now encompasses Southeast Asia. These nations have become a vital cog in Japan's global industrial machine, supplying the lower-value-added components for Japan's own manufactured goods exports, serving as launchpads for exports of indigenous products manufactured with Japanese technology, and gradually developing into dynamic, prosperous, rapidly growing markets of their own.

What was denied Japan by means of military conquest a half-century ago—an integrated political and economic sphere of influence throughout Southeast Asia under Japan's leadership, guidance, and control, otherwise known as the Greater East Asia Co-Prosperity Sphere—has today become reality perhaps because the military component is missing. Through commerce, economic policy, trade, technology, and capital, Japan has succeeded in creating for itself a kinder, gentler co-prosperity sphere.

Mikhail Gorbachev has bet the farm on *glasnost* and *perestroika*, and in the past year the world has witnessed an unprecedented disassembling of the Warsaw Pact powers. As the U.S. economic presence in Asia continues to decline, beset by increasingly bitter trade disputes with the NIEs, Washington's foreign economic policy could become magnetized by the political gains it sees in promoting democracy in Eastern Europe. The likelihood therefore exists that a deficit-ridden and capital-deficient America may be persuaded to underwrite the resurrection of these dinosaur economies through the new European Bank for Reconstruction and Development (EBRD) and, in so doing, neglect its own economic interests in East Asia—by far the world's most dynamic and vibrant economic sector.

Then, too, as the superpowers focus on cooperation rather than confrontation, driven by economic necessity in failed central command systems like the Soviet Union, the potential for conflict between them may eventually subside. But as it does, the potential for greater political conflict among the ASEAN powers could increase, for it was the immense ideological rift between capitalism and communism that bound the ASEAN five (now six) together in the first place. Still, America's de facto economic withdrawal from Southeast Asia has created a noticeable commercial vacuum that Japan has moved in to fill. Japan could thus augment its economic power in the region—and at the same time enhance its political standing—by playing a mediating role in the context of any regional conflict that may ensue.

With the possible exception of Malaysia, the political economies examined in this book are now on the verge of becoming Little Dragons themselves. Considered separately, their economies are small and, from the point of view of the new geoeconomic reality, remarkably unthreatening. Taken together, however, as part of a regional Japan, Inc., they have meaningful roles to play, roles that Japan has helped create and assign. Indonesia has a particularly bright future, and Thailand's creative flexibility in adapting to external conditions should serve it well in the years ahead.

Especially notable are the high rates of economic growth created by Indonesia and Thailand—through 1989 the highest rates of growth not only in the region but anywhere in the world. And their skilled political leadership has helped foster and encourage that growth. Though for the most part educated in the West, the economic helmsmen of these two countries have increasingly turned to Japan for direction and guidance in implementing innovative industrial policies that not only promote that growth but also tend to shift it in favor of higher-value-added manufactured goods for export.

As recently as five years ago crude oil generated two-thirds of Indonesia's domestic economic revenues and 80 percent of its export earnings—unarguably the number-one source. Today nonoil merchandise exports generate a higher percentage of its overall export revenues than oil, a development virtually unheard of for a country so richly endowed in natural resources and a member of OPEC to boot. Who would have ever thought that such impressive incentives for manufacturing growth and development would have emanated from a country that a mere generation earlier had suffered the bloody national trauma of Communist insurrection and the demise of its charismatic postwar leader?

It is perhaps axiomatic to say this, but unlike Korea or Taiwan, Indonesia and Thailand will not be flooding the United States or European markets with their own manufactured goods. Indeed there is really no equivalent to Hyundai or Samsung in Jakarta, no parallel to Acer or Tatung in Bangkok. But what *will* increasingly be the case is a continued flow of competitive *Japanese* manufactured products throughout the world, because so many of those products are now either produced in or assembled from components of or made with the resources (human and otherwise) of the new Little Dragons of Southeast Asia.

Japan needs these nations as much as they need Japan, as buffers or shock absorbers for the abrupt impact of changes in currency rates or trade policies imposed by Washington on Tokyo. Products, like computer disks or videocassette tapes, that are indispensable in a knowledge-intensive age can perhaps be manufactured more cheaply in Jakarta or Bangkok, but it is the *information* they contain—their intellectual content—that comes from Japan and determines their value.

Nowhere has this relationship of interdependency become more apparent for Japan than in Thailand, today a country that in any other era would be called a Japanese colony (despite the irony that of all Southeast Asian nations, Thailand had never in its history been previously colonized). Unlike the more indigenous policies of the Berkeley Mafia in Indonesia, though, Thailand's growth strategy has depended more on Japanese capital, Japanese technology, and Japanese trade, to the point where Bangkok has clearly become Japan's primary production hub in Southeast Asia.

But Thailand's destiny may be tied *too* closely to Japan's own fortunes, which is one reason the kingdom's political leadership is so concerned about its position of growing overdependence on Japan. (One sign of this overdependence: in August 1990, in Bangkok, on the heels of a precipitous drop in the Tokyo stock market, the Stock Exchange of Thailand lost a full third of its value in less than two weeks.) And to the dismay of Japanese diplomats, former prime minister Chatichai has publicly stated that he wants his children to grow up speaking English, not Japanese—which is just another verbal symbol of Thailand's sense that Japan's position in the Thai economy has become too dominant.

Which itself is a veiled, indirect way of saying to America, Where are you now that we need you? You defended us from the threat of Communist aggression during the Vietnam War and prevented the domino theory from becoming reality. But the *new* reality now is that economic conflict has replaced military confrontation as the primary means of bilateral competition. As U.S. armed forces have withdrawn from the military bases at Udorn and Udon Thani, their commercial counterparts have not moved into Bangkok and Chiang Mai. In Thailand, America has been left behind in the wake of Japan's powerful inward investment thrust.

U.S. manufacturing firms like Seagate, the world's leading producer of computer disk drives, and American Standard, which commands a monopoly on vitreous china products in the Thai market, are two notable exceptions that prove the rule: American investment in Thailand has concentrated overwhelmingly on lower-value-added sectors like travel (airlines and shipping), construction (hotels and office blocks), and tourism. Not only are Japanese products increasingly made in Thailand; they are aggressively sold there as well. This is especially true, as we have seen, of Japanese production equipment on the factory floors of the many new joint-venture companies that have been multiplying in the industrial estates around Bangkok in recent years.

Only in Malaysia have American manufacturing firms been more typically assertive in their investment patterns. Firms like Texas Instruments, Seagate (again), Hewlett-Packard, and other household names in U.S. electronics have led the commercial charge into Malaysia's industrial estates around Kuala Lumpur and Penang. But these examples are once again exceptions to the rule that American investment in the region has not really been in manufacturing or production per se but in either the extractive or service sector. And they belie the fact that, were it not for the space constraints (and the higher wage components) in nearby Singapore, Malaysia might not have benefited from this surge in American manufacturing interest to the extent it has.

Indonesia and Thailand each suffer from shortcomings that

could stall their growth and development. In Jakarta the thorny problem of political succession for President Soeharto and the related issue of political openness for the New Order regime are constant concerns but ones the Indonesians are well aware of and prepared to confront. In Bangkok, as we have seen, social, religious, and national security problems (viz. Cambodia) loom large on Thailand's horizon, in addition to the gnawing problem of Japanese economic dominance and Bangkok's deteriorating physical infrastructure. Still, Thailand's reputation for flexibility and adaptation augurs well for its immediate future.

But alone among the three potential Little Dragons, Malaysia has some black clouds on its horizon. The deterioration of its political system into a virtual totalitarian dictatorship under Prime Minister Mahathir in recent years calls into serious question whether this newly Islamicizing state will be able to keep pace with its more durable competitors, Indonesia and Thailand. Its regressive affirmative action policies, characterized by the so-called New Economic Policy, have concentrated political power even more strongly in the hands of the Malay elite and continue to threaten the social fabric of the country. The uncertainty as to who will succeed Mahathir, and how competently, is also a negative factor. Japan remains Kuala Lumpur's number-one foreign investor and its number-one trading partner, but in light of the more attractive political economies in nearby Jakarta and Bangkok, one must ask whether subsequent Japanese (or even other foreign) investment here will grow.

For Japan remains the number-one foreign investor in *all* of these NIEs, as well as the number-one foreign lender to (and the number-one trading partner with) each of them. And, too, in each of these countries, Japan's focus remains centered on its own traditional sources of high-speed growth—manufacturing, value-added production, and exports—expanding the circle of its economic and industrial policies more widely throughout the region, as the opening quote from *The Economist* at the beginning of this chapter so aptly described.

DUAL IMPLICATIONS

There are two broad implications for both American public policy and private sector strategy stemming from these recent developments.

From a public policy viewpoint Japan has clearly and forth-rightly centered its economic and commercial attention on East Asia, just as the United States has focused its traditional sights on Europe (and, more recently, on Canada and Mexico, via new free-trade agreements). But there is one major difference: Japan has not ne-glected Europe or Canada to the extent America has neglected South-east Asia.

In an increasingly global market, with "borderless economies" the new watchword and growing commercial interdependence the new economic reality, America can no longer afford to pay minority attention to the fastest-growing region of the world. Washington must shift its attention from an obsession with yesterday's concern for military and security concepts (as symbolized by Cambodia, China, and the Philippines) to today's preoccupation with economic growth and commercial development (as symbolized by Indonesia, Thailand, and Malaysia).

For America's private sector the process of globalization must invariably have an impact on strategy. Firms once content simply to shift their manufacturing capability to countries like Taiwan, or to just move across the border and establish manufacturing pods in Mexico's *maquiladoras*, will find these countries (and their surro-gates) increasingly less attractive—Taiwan because of its accelerating currency realignment and rising wage rates, Mexico because of the coming free-trade agreement with the United States that could elim-inate many of its previous advantages.

America's private companies also need a more aggressive pres-ence in Southeast Asia for two additional reasons.

One, they will find themselves at a growing competitive disad-vantage vis-à-vis their Japanese counterparts if they can't monitor closely what they are doing. This is a corollary of the Chinese military strategist Sun-Tzu, who said you must always know more about your enemy than he knows about you.

And two, they will find it more and more difficult to sell into these rapidly expanding Southeast Asian markets if they are not on the ground with a direct manufacturing capability themselves, whether wholly owned or jointly managed with local partners.

In recent years too many of America's corporate managers have been blinded by China, on the one hand, and the elusive mystery of its massive "market"—if we can get every Chinese to buy just one widget or gadget or doohickey, the reasoning goes, we'll coast into executive heaven. Or they have been distracted by Eastern Europe, on the other, with the allure of its pristine "markets" that have such pent-up consumer demand. But it took Western Europe more than a decade after the war to establish hard currencies, implement commercial trading mechanisms, and integrate its economies with the United States and the UK, so how much longer is it likely to take the dinosaur economies of COMECON to achieve even vaguely similar results?

THEN AND NOW

The external conditions that existed two decades ago, when the Little Dragons began their ascent, have rather obviously changed. The question now is whether the would-be Little Dragons can continue their very high rates of economic growth in the face of a much less receptive (and clearly more distracted if not pluralistic) external environment. An America that for years has symbolized the magnet market for Japan is becoming increasingly inhospitable to the aggressive market-penetration strategies of its East Asian competitors, so Japan is now having to play the role of shepherd to the Asian flock.

Twenty-five years ago the United States was the dominant economic power in East Asia. Today Japan is. Then the United States controlled the regional economic agenda. Now Japan does. At a time when military and political aspects of foreign policy are receding into the background, financial, economic, and technological issues dominate. But the United States no longer commands East Asia's undivided attention on these new issues; Japan does.

Twenty-five years ago the United States was waging a bitter land war on the Indochinese Peninsula. Although it ultimately lost that war, it served notice that the totalitarian forces of communism would be held in check, and it created a security umbrella for the region that enabled ASEAN to come into being. Today the totalitarian threat of communism has been eliminated, and the nations of ASEAN can either build on two decades of cooperation or let the historical forces of intraregional hostility and divisiveness return to throw them into disarray. This is precisely why, if the NIEs return to a bygone era of bilateral political conflict, they may be unable to fulfill their economic potential.

Twenty-five years ago American products held their own in these East Asian markets. The automobile of choice was from Detroit, the most visible tourists were from America, and the U.S. dollar was the marker currency. Today virtually the only automobiles on East Asian roads are Japanese, the richest tourists are from Tokyo, Osaka, and Nagoya, and the region's marker currency is becoming the yen. The Ugly American is becoming the Ugly Japanese; economic success creates its own fear and loathing.

Twenty-five years ago the world was bipolar and frozen in a cold war between the two nuclear superpowers, the United States and the Soviet Union. Political and military priorities defined national security, and America controlled the agenda. Today the Cold War is thawing quickly, and the world has become more multipolar. Economic issues are the new realities underlying national security, and Japan is beginning to set the economic agenda.

Twenty-five years ago the United States market, still the world's biggest and most vibrant, was open to all foreign goods. America was the leading champion of free trade, and Japan took relentless advantage of it. Today, with two-thirds of Japan's manufactured exports under some form of voluntary export restraint or orderly marketing agreement, international trade with Japan has become progressively "managed." But Japan increasingly dominates the rhetoric on free trade, while America tries to come to grips with the new realities of competing in a multipolar world.

Twenty-five years ago the United States encouraged Japanese exports into the American market, in part to help keep its strategic political ally in Asia strong. As a result the region was unanimously pro-American. Today, frustrated by its inability to curb that sorcerer's apprentice in Tokyo, the United States lashes out with protectionist tactics against other nations in East Asia. As a result the region is becoming increasingly anti-American.

Twenty-five years ago America was the model. Its schools set the standard for scholastic achievement, its traditional two-parent family was the symbol of stability, and New York was the commercial and financial epicenter of the world. Today, for the developing world, Japan is increasingly the model of choice. Its public schools now set the highest international academic standards, its stable two-parent family system has become the cultural norm, and Tokyo has replaced New York as the symbolic hub of finance, manufacturing, urban planning, and design.

In 1980 America's trade across the Pacific about equaled its trade across the Atlantic. But by 1988 U.S. trade with East Asia was 50 percent higher than its trade with Europe. By the end of this century America's total trade with Asia-Pacific will *double* that of its trade with the European community, and the Asia-Pacific region will have a combined GNP of some $6.5 trillion in the year 2000—and will be the fastest-growing—compared to $7.2 trillion for North America and $6 trillion for a unified Europe. But the primitive economies of Eastern Europe are coming out of their half-century slumber and preoccupying Washington politically at precisely the time it ought to be paying more attention to the economic dynamism of East Asia.

The largest economies of East Asia together now account for about 24 percent of the world's GNP—roughly equivalent to the current U.S. share itself. Regional economic interdependence has also grown: the share of intraregional trade among the major East Asian economies expanded from about half of the total to nearly two-thirds by 1987. (ASEAN *alone* now sends a third of its total exports to Japan.) Asia-Pacific trade now comprises more than a third of America's total trade, and the region accounts for about 80 percent of the total U.S. global trade deficit.

These intraregional statistics demonstrate that the Asia-Pacific region is the world's fastest-growing trading area, now number three in terms of its share of total world trade, accounting for nearly 10 percent (by value) of the global total in 1988. This regional dynamism is also helping to wean these economies away from their dependence on the United States as Japan plays a more dominant role. The General Agreement on Tariffs and Trade (GATT) calculations showed a slowing of world trade growth to 7 percent in 1989, down from 8.5 percent growth in 1988. But growth in Asia-Pacific trade remains above the world average.

Even if global economic growth slows, as it shows signs of doing, East Asia will still be the world's most active market region. The International Monetary Fund (IMF) has projected that GNP growth in Europe and the United States will slow to 3 percent and 2.1

percent a year, respectively, through 1991. By comparison the dozen economies of East Asia will grow at 5.5 percent a year through 1991, still below the 6.1 percent growth they registered in 1989 and lower than the robust 8.4 percent achieved in 1988. But relative to the rest of the world, the region's rates remain higher, with exports the engine of growth.

Living standards, too, with the exceptions of those in China and the Philippines, continue to rise throughout the region. Whether measured in terms of per-capita income, infant mortality, literacy rates, or libraries and hospitals per 1,000 of population, virtually every social indicator continues to show the highest rates of improvement in the world. Again with the notable exception of China, East Asian political systems also are starting to shift from their single-party, authoritarian rule to a more pluralistic, representative style of democratic government. The process of privatization and deregulation, as we have seen, is also well ahead in most of these political economies, proving the proposition that economic development must precede political change.

TOWARD FORMAL REGIONAL INTEGRATION

Over the years a number of proposals have been put forth suggesting that the East Asian nations create a more formal regional organization. In 1968 a number of private-sector executives from countries throughout the region established the Pacific Basin Economic Council (PBEC), opened an office in San Francisco, and began holding regular annual meetings to discuss trade and investment issues. In 1980 the prime ministers of Australia and Japan launched the concept of a Pacific Economic Cooperation Council (PECC), a semiofficial association of government officials, businesspeople, and academics from fifteen Asia-Pacific countries, with the Soviet Union in attendance as an observer. It, too, conducts an informal meeting each year.

Then, in January 1989, concerned about the possible effects a united Europe might have on his country, Bob Hawke, the prime minister of Australia, proposed the creation of an East Asian OECD called the Asia-Pacific Economic Council (APEC; including also the United States and Canada) that would establish a formal secretariat and serve to monitor a broad agenda of economic, trade, and investment issues. Not to be outdone, Secretary of State James Baker then called for a "new Pacific partnership" (undefined), which would continue America's involvement in regional affairs, foster a more creative sharing of global responsibilities with Japan, and create a mechanism for increased economic cooperation.

Finally, in early 1991, not to be outdone, Malaysia's paranoid prime minister, Mohamad Mahathir, made yet another pitch for a more aggressive Asian economic alliance. But his arbitrary grouping includes only the ASEAN six plus Vietnam, Burma, Taiwan, Hong Kong, and South Korea, pointedly *excluding* Japan, China, the United States, Canada, Australia, and New Zealand. It even lacks an acronym. Understandably, the U.S. reaction is unenthusiastic and Japanese government officials are skeptical about a concept which, because of its capricious nature, is not likely to go anywhere. Thailand, and especially Indonesia, despite their ASEAN status, have dismissed the idea out of hand.

The problem with all these proposals to create an official Asia-Pacific body is that they immediately encounter a number of difficulties that do not exist in Europe.

First, any Asia-wide group ought to include China, but it must also include Hong Kong and Taiwan, two of the region's most dynamic free-market economies. China is (so far) opposed to that.

Second, ASEAN members fear that their regional grouping may be weakened by the existence of any broader, more formal organization and want assurances that it will remain intact.

Third, an official secretariat would need to be established, and every country in the region could easily justify its capital city as the appropriate (and only reasonable) location.

Finally, the extreme geographic distances, not to mention the linguistic and cultural differences, among the many countries in the region are not easily bridged; they create informal obstacles to the harmonious functioning of any such group.

So it is highly unlikely that any formal organization will surface anytime soon, although APEC had one initial meeting in Canberra in summer 1989, met again in Singapore in mid-1990, and was scheduled next for Seoul in 1991. What is likely, however, is that the process of formal integration will take a full decade or more to evolve before any final organizational decisions can be reached. In the meantime the world trading system may move into three distinct blocs, or zones—a process that is already under way—as it shifts from the postwar free trade era to a *post*postwar era symbolized by a global, borderless economy:

- An East Asian zone, headquartered in Tokyo, with the yen as its marker currency, symbolized by Japan's kinder, gentler co-prosperity sphere and characterized by broader regional economic integration;
- A North American zone, dominated by New York and the U.S. dollar, symbolized by the Canada/U.S. free trade agreement and characterized by broader economic integration between North and South America;
- A European zone, centered in Berlin, with the deutsche mark as its core currency, symbolized by the reunification of Germany and characterized by both economic integration with the former COMECON countries of Eastern Europe and greater economic domination of Africa and the Middle East.

So before a truly borderless global economy arrives, it may pass briefly through a stage in which some artificial borders are being redrawn as a temporary, interim step.

THE U.S.-JAPAN GLOBAL ECONOMIC RIVALRY

In the meantime, while Washington bureaucrats noisily produce vapid political rhetoric, Japan is quietly generating solid economic results. Japanese corporate investors continue to move forward with new plant and equipment commitments throughout the region, securing their manufacturing bases, strengthening their strategic alliances, solidifying their presence. For example, Toyota has established a complementary, integrated production network throughout ASEAN to manufacture automotive components, committed to investing $125 million a year in each of four core markets. Mitsubishi Motors has a comparable scheme, as does Komatsu, both heavy industries manufacturers. For Japan there is no alternative to globalization in the new era.

Japanese firms overseas are now exporting more than $10 billion worth of manufactured goods back to Japan each year, representing nearly 15 percent of its manufactured goods imports. Two-thirds of these imports now originate from offshore Japanese producers in other Asian countries. There are now 1,500 Japanese manufacturers operating throughout Asia. From 1976 to 1985 an average of fifty Japanese companies a year set up operations overseas. Since 1985 that number has doubled to more than a hundred. Japan is the top export market for these firms, needless to say, with 17 percent of their total production going to Japan, 12 percent to other Asian markets, and just 8 percent to the United States.

American manufacturers have yet to understand what it means to go up against Japanese competitors that have more invested in plant and equipment, spend more on R&D, and are content to accept lower profit margins in the near term in order to reap higher market shares over the long term. On an aggregate basis, as a percentage of GNP, Japan now spends more than the United States on R&D. As a result it has a higher ratio of R&D-intense industries in its total manufacturing output than America does. And Japan also has five times the number of industrial robots in place.

Twenty-five of the one hundred largest international corporations outside the United States are now Japanese, and the top ten international banks in the world are headquartered in Tokyo. In 1989, for every dollar invested by American firms in new plant and equipment, Japanese firms invested two; they increased their capital base by five times the amount U.S. firms did.

The top ten Japanese trading companies—with familiar names like Mitsubishi, Sumitomo, and Mitsui—today ship nearly half the country's total exports and handle more than three-quarters of its total imports. The same ten companies now account for more than 15 percent of America's own international trade. Of the major industrialized nations in the world Japan's rates of savings and capital formation are still the highest, at more than 18 percent of GNP. Until very recently, following a precipitous decline in early 1990, the Tokyo Stock Exchange had the highest market capitalization in the world; and Osaka, not New York, was number two. Japan is now the number-two contributor to the UN and is negotiating to become the second-largest shareholder in the World Bank and the IMF; it has dominated the Asian Development Bank for years.

Recent global developments—political in Eastern Europe and

military in the Middle East—could well alter the U.S.-Japan relationship further, possibly for the worse. It is axiomatic that citizens
of these former COMECON countries are expressing the desire, long
repressed, for freedom, for liberty, for freer markets and higher
standards of living. These principles, while universal, have been
promoted proudly and defended stoutly by America throughout the
Cold War, and America has won the battle of ideas with communism
hands down.

But the rapid collapse of communism has accelerated the pace of
demands by the peoples of Eastern Europe. While their political
leaders now try to articulate American political ideals and capitalist
economic goals, it has become increasingly clear that it will take them
an enormously long time to fulfill those ideals or realize those goals.

So they may find Tokyo's policies more relevant in the short
run, for Japan could conceivably serve as their interim political and
economic role model: the substitution of communism by an authoritarian, single-party system (such as the LDP) that would keep their
leaders in command, and the implementation of industrial policies
that could manipulate their currencies, add value to their production
process, and grow exports, all at a faster rate than comparable
American approaches would otherwise allow.

For years all the major Japanese banks and the top Japanese
trading companies with household names like Sumitomo and Mitsubishi and Mitsui have had branches or representative offices in the
COMECON capital cities and in Moscow. They are well positioned
to take advantage of the growing need these countries have for
capital, for technology, and for trade. When Prime Minister Kaifu
made his historic visit to Warsaw in early 1990, Polish leader Lech
Walesa perhaps summarized the feelings of his neighboring counterparts best when he said that Poland wanted to be the new "Little
Japan" of Eastern Europe.

More recently, in the Middle East, as the United States has led
an international consortium of countries in opposing Saddam Hussein through the tactics of both a worldwide economic blockade and
an allied military buildup, Japan alone among the major capitalist
powers has declined to share a proper burden of this coordinated
military exercise.

Japan constitutes a whopping 25 percent of the combined GNP

of Europe, the United States, and Japan but contributes only 4 percent of the group's combined defense costs. Accordingly the United States could be justified in presenting Japan with a bill for one-fourth of the total costs of defending Western interests in the Middle East against Iraq if Japan is not prepared to contribute more substantially—either ships or defensive weapons systems, which clearly would be permissible under its postwar peacetime constitution—to these multinational efforts. Otherwise the growing antagonism toward Japan and its aggressive (if one-dimensional) commercial strategies may explode unavoidably into outright hostility. The prognosis is not good. "America started the Gulf War," one Japanese observer recently noted. "Let America finish it."

THE COMING TRENDS

As a result of Japan's commercial strength and the inherent dynamism of the East Asian political economies, combined with the broader potential for political conflict between Japan and the United States, there appear to be five basic trends that could tend to dominate a new era characterized by structural interdependence, faster information flows, and somewhat slower economic growth.

Heightened Competition

As our multipolar world grows more complicated, our old allies are capable of being new adversaries at one and the same time. Japan, long America's political ally, has already become its most formidable economic adversary. It is not yet certain how this new world will best be managed. The critical issue is not *protection from* the Japanese economic challenge but *adaptation* to it. Those who speak of a natural interdependence between the United States and Japan—Japan needs the U.S. market, for example, while America needs Japanese capital—miss the point that interdependence is often largely used as a smoke screen to hide increasing bilateral friction.

Structural interdependence spells *more* competition and conflict, not less—especially as the familiar bipolar world recedes into memory. As communism continues to disintegrate, it may not give birth to a new kind of international harmony, as many believe, but could more likely bring back what the British philosopher John Gray has called the classical terrain of history—antagonism between the great powers, covert espionage (both economic and military), and outright war.

And on that terrain the two great capitalist systems of the twentieth century—Japan and the United States—could well compete for economic dominance. In the future, Tokyo may replace Moscow as America's number-one foreign policy problem, because its mutant form of authoritarian, strategically targeted, turbocharged capitalism could clash increasingly with America's democratic, free-market, free-enterprise model. Japan's primary political values of duty, loyalty, and obligation could unavoidably do battle with America's deeply held values of freedom, liberty, and justice.

The proving grounds for this new ideological confrontation could well be the developing economies of the world, including both Southeast Asia and Eastern Europe. Two-thirds of Americans recently polled rightly cited Japan as a more serious long-term economic threat to American security than the Soviet Union. The problem is that America's politicians have yet to catch up with their constituents.

Still, just as America's stout defense of its proud values against the totalitarian threat of communism produced a victory in the Cold War, so will America's promotion of those principles continue to drive the new information age and ultimately succeed against the narrower value system of Japan. Yet Japan has seemingly done a better job of marketing its economic value system in Southeast Asia than America has.

The big question in this bubbling cauldron of changing geopolitical circumstances is whether dominance by any one power really matters. Can't the United States maintain its high standard of living, some ask, without dominating the global political agenda? Look at Switzerland, for example, or Sweden—two modern European political economies whose per-capita incomes are among the highest in the world but whose governments control neither markets nor political ideology.

But the United States is no Switzerland or Sweden. Homogeneous nations with small markets and a history of political neutrality, which live by no ideology or principle other than simply protecting economic gain, cannot serve as beacons of freedom and liberty for people seeking a better life. Such nations may provide well for their own, but they are not and can never be role models for the rest of the world.

So globalism and interdependence may imply three things: an escalation of competition, both political and economic; global standards against which national performance is judged; and a shifting focus of nationalism from military confrontation to economic competition as a means of resolving bilateral conflict.

Techno-nationalism

As Japan puts increasing emphasis on higher-value-added technology through its strategic industrial targeting process, the likelihood of "technological friction" with the United States becomes even greater. The bitter dispute between Tokyo and Washington in 1989 over coproduction and codevelopment of Japan's next-generation fighter jet, the FSX, may be the beginning of more technological conflict to come. The United States has a full agenda of issues needing prompt attention, from raising its anemic capital formation and investment rates to thinking more strategically about its own high-technology manufacturing sector and linking its commercial trade to these strategic issues.

A New Global Order

The world is on the threshold of political change every bit as significant today as that which occurred in 1945: Japan has emerged as the world's number-one creditor nation, and the two Germanies are now one. The difference is, America has not emerged from the cathartic experience of war and is not putting into place the policies or incentives necessary to strengthen its competitive position for the new era.

A world that the United States can easily dominate (and has easily dominated) no longer exists. The question now is whether America can remain primus inter pares in a world of powerful economic rivals or whether it could decline, as Britain and France before it, to a kind of permanent second-rate status. The end of the

American century does not have to mean the end of the American dream, predicated on the pessimism of decline. But the creation of a new American century, based on the optimism of renewal and revitalization, does mean new policies, new strategies, and new priorities.

Isolationism

The United States has a dangerous history of turning inward at times of pronounced external pressure, as it did in the 1890s and then again in the 1920s and 1930s. Its national political agenda is now overwhelmingly domestic in nature: fighting the war on drugs, restructuring public education, solving the child-care problem, building affordable housing, restoring a deteriorating physical infrastructure, helping the homeless.

These pressing needs demand America's attention precisely when its position in the external world is no longer imperious, when the financial resources available to confront these issues are improbably inadequate, and when the forces of the new era are driving toward economic integration and commercial interdependence, not isolationist separation.

Revitalization and Renewal

Despite the beauty and simplicity of the argument about the rise and fall of the great powers, though, America is *not* like the other great powers before it. Because it is a vigorous, healthy, functioning democracy, it has the power of restoration, reinvigoration, and renewal. America has the potential to release an even greater burst of entrepreneurial energy than it has yet seen, *if* it can demonstrate a creative adjustment to these external competitive pressures.

Some predict the next century will be an Atlantic century, symbolized by "Fortress Europe" and its reunification with the former dinosaur economies of Eastern Europe, anchored by a unified Germany. But that ignores the role Japan will (and must) play in revitalizing those Eastern European economies.

Others predict the next century will be a Pacific century, created by the economic dynamism that now drives East Asia. But a Pacific century without a revitalized America is inconceivable, and a new

American century that cannot incorporate East Asian dynamism is simply another modern-day mirage.

JAPAN'S HIDDEN LIABILITIES

No one today needs any reminder of Japan's formidable economic power or the cultural vitality that has nurtured it. In the eyes of many the Japanese competition is now invincible, a giant ten feet tall. But commercial strength makes Japan a "flat" power because it is simply one-dimensional. It also hides a litany of liabilities and masks some fundamental cultural weaknesses because below that façade of Japanese industrial domination lies a massive iceberg of potential problems.

For starters, Japan lacks a broader, more universal political ideal; the desire of its corporations to dominate overseas commercial markets is derived solely from a hierarchical culture that thrives on control. While Japan's primary values—loyalty, duty, and obligation—may resonate in a narrower, more insular culture, they fall flat when measured against the broader Western values of freedom, liberty, and justice that have legitimized the postwar global system.

Japan's authoritarian single-party political system has proved itself incapable of providing strong leadership at times of critical urgency. It took Tokyo more than a month to respond appropriately to the Persian Gulf crisis in mid-1990, and then only after persistent prodding by Washington to up the ante of its financial support. The Liberal Democratic Party continues to self-destruct through its internal factional disputes, as the neonationalists battle the regionalists, who fight the internationalists. And the opposition parties—led by the Socialists and their popular figurehead, Takako Doi—have become impotent if not irrelevant. What can Socialists (or Communists) possibly offer a post–Cold War world that is accelerating into the information age?

Japan's powerful central bureaucracy, symbolized by its vaunted Ministry of Finance and the feared MITI, played a key role throughout the past era of high-speed industrial growth. But it may prove increasingly powerless in a knowledge-intensive era whose driving forces are decentralization, individual autonomy, and personal choice. The nearly 50 percent drop in the Tokyo stock exchange in

1990 is prima facie evidence of the bureaucracy's waning power. MOF can no longer tell the Big Four to simply "buy the market."

Japan's impressive public education system may get high marks for behavioral control but can't stimulate either creativity or innovation in the classroom because of its heavy hierarchy. Constitutional revision, too, is badly overdue—especially Article 9, which defines Japan's military role solely in terms of an outdated 1945 era and which created a "free ride" for its national defense.

Electoral redistricting is also long past due. Japan's rural districts far outweigh its urban areas politically, and this is contributing to widespread voter anger and hostility. Soaring land prices in Japan's cities have put home ownership practically out of reach for the average Japanese family. Consumer empowerment has become a modern-day oxymoron in Japan, where the popular phrase "rich country, poor Japanese" reflects a wealthy mercantilist state with an impoverished citizenry that pays twice as much for consumer goods as Americans or Europeans.

The U.S.-Japan Security Treaty, written in 1952 and amended for perpetuity in 1960, is another important document urgently needing revision. While it commits America to Japan's defense, it obligates Japan in no mutual way whatsoever, unlike the agreement with NATO that provides for reciprocity between Europe and the United States.

These dozen hidden liabilities put a somewhat different spin on Japan's arrogant swagger of late. They suggest that the Land of the Rising Sun may now be undergoing a transition from its insular, mercantile protectionism to a fuller participation in the international community—a transition not unlike the one it experienced more than a century ago, when it lurched in the 1870s from the medieval feudalism of Tokugawa to the industrial modernization of Meiji.

As that earlier transition was marked by political instability, urban unrest, frequent riots, and severe social dislocation, the present transition may be punctuated by similar disturbances. Municipal riots in Osaka in October 1990 protesting police corruption bring to mind Tokyo's famous rice riots of 1918, when impoverished tenant farmers rebelled against their monopolistic landlord elites, and imply that Japan's nagging problems may put America's own difficulties in quite another light. They suggest that Japan may have a very long way to go yet in solving them and that the one-dimensional Japanese competitive threat of the 1990s may not be as ominous as the pessimists fear.

THE NEW ECONOMIC REALITIES

"For almost two centuries," management guru Peter Drucker writes in his latest book, *The New Realities*, "we hotly discussed what government *should* do. We almost never asked what government *can* do. Now increasingly the limits and function of government will be the issue."

Drucker himself confirms the powerful geopolitical shift that is taking place today from military to economic priorities as the bedrock of national security. This shift, which is fundamental, encompasses a powerful move toward decentralization, embracing more pluralistic forces in society. It tracks on a macro level what has been happening at the micro level since about the mid-1970s as private firms, regardless of nationality, have been decentralizing, downsizing, and eliminating unnecessary layers of management.

"The death in the belief of salvation by society," Drucker concludes, "which for two hundred years had been the most dynamic force in the politics of the West . . . creates a void. The emergence of fundamentalist Islam is [one] attempt to fill this void. It is the result of disenchantment alike with the welfare state of the 'democratic' West and with Communist Utopia."

So the implications for America's public and private sectors are becoming clear.

U.S. firms must move forward with global strategies that make greater leverage out of East Asia's dynamism. In turn this means a more aggressive manufacturing presence in their markets and a greater number of strategic alliances in the region. Software and hardware products as well as manufacturing and marketing strategies must be globalized.

For its part Washington must abandon the overused and counterproductive tactic, though politically advantageous at home, of bashing its Asian trade partners. A more positive, mutually profitable process must replace the negativism of the recent past. America has amassed a generation's worth of goodwill in East Asia, but current policies are quickly eroding it and giving our regional trading partners little choice but to ally themselves even more closely with Japan.

"No country has an entitlement to prosperity," Staffan Buren-stam Linder, Denmark's former economics minister, recently wrote. "No region has special privileges. There must be adjustment without tears, and Asian-Pacific competition now underscores this reality. It demonstrates dramatically that staleness is not tolerable."

The value of the demonstration effect of East Asia's economic dynamism is that it shows the need for vitality and the necessity to ask how we can adapt to the future rather than why we still cling to the past. If you want to guide the ship of state through the uncharted waters that lie ahead, you can't do it by lounging about on the stern, gazing back over its disappearing wake.

America has great underlying strengths as it moves toward the new century: an uncompromising commitment to representative democracy; an incredibly diverse and resilient society capable of unmatched entrepreneurial energy, vitality, and skill; a market second to none in responsiveness, flexibility, and size; an unparalleled inventiveness; a dynamic ethnic heterogeneity symbolized by new waves of immigration that are infusing the United States with its most vital source of national power; still the most feared "hard" power in the world, with the largest single economy and the most sophisticated integrated defense system; and clearly the strongest "soft" power in the world, with more authority and influence stemming from its superb higher educational system and an entertainment industry that generates a greater level of information, innovation, and ideas than anyone else.

George Gilder captures this American spirit best in *Microcosm: The Quantum Revolution in Economics and Technology.* "Once seen as a physical system tending toward exhaustion and decline," he writes, "the world economy has clearly emerged as an intellectual system driven by knowledge. [American] capitalism—supremely the mind-centered system—finds the driving force of its growth in innovation and discovery. In the age of the microcosm, value added shifts rapidly from the extraction, movement, manipulation, and exhaustion of mass to the creative accumulation of information and ideas."

The trick will be to harness these underlying assets and strengths more effectively in order to strengthen America's competitiveness in the new information era now unfolding. Conventional wisdom, which clings to the past, suggests we look to the federal government for leadership. But a contrarian view, more in tune with the emerging reality, says Washington is the last place we ought to be looking.

Why? Because the information revolution has rendered centralized, inflexible bureaucracies—whether public or private—obsolete and inoperative. Decentralization, individual autonomy, and personal choice have become the driving forces of this new era, and America—not Japan, not Germany—can once again be the leader provided we recognize the importance of these trends. So it will be more important to watch what is happening in Sacramento and Austin and Trenton, the state capitals around this country that are leading the charge back to federalism. Their decentralized decisions and policies are already shaping and influencing the direction of the new information age, from the high-tax/low-growth mentality in America's Northeast to the low-tax/high-growth approach of the Sunbelt.

Again Gilder: "The real target of bureaucracy is the entrepreneurial freedom conferred by quantum technology. Rather than a New Industrial State, this [new] era will disclose the impotence of the state. . . . Systems of national command and control will wither away. Systems of global emancipation will carry the day. The dismal science of the economics of aggregates—capital, labor, and land—will give way to a microeconomics of liberty. The beggar-thy-neighbor strategies of mercantilism—of trade as a weapon of state—will collapse before the strategies of global wealth creation under the leadership of entrepreneurs. The economics of scarcity and fear will surrender to the economics of hope and faith."

As pragmatic examples of Gilder's perceptive trend analysis for the future, imaginative forms of what I call complementary strategic alliances in the private sector are gradually emerging to create new competitive strategies for this new era. They are all being created by pressures unique to their own autonomous environments, not commanded by fiat from Washington.

- "Tiering" is a cross-border concept that merges strength with weakness in a cooperative way. Intel, a first-tier American manufacturer of microprocessors, has allied with NMB Semicondutors, a second-tier Japanese memory chip maker, for new generation DRAMs: NMB makes, Intel markets. Such alliances as this are the best way of disarming Washington policymakers, who still pursue a mindless mercantilism and treat Japan as the new enemy.

- Non-Japanese *Asian* alliances are an innovative way for American firms to compete with their Japanese counterparts in the home market. GE has tied up with Korea's Samsung to manufacture medical imaging equipment and is exporting its systems back to the United States to blunt Hitachi's market-penetration moves here.
- U.S.-European ventures are emerging from a similar strategic construct: witness IBM's recent alliance with Siemens AG to research next-generation megabit memory chips. New R&D efforts in sophisticated technologies are both expensive and redundant when carried out separately by independent firms; cooperative ventures such as IBM/Siemens point the way toward the future.
- Domestic alliances between U.S. firms in their own domestic market can also provide new synergies, as with the recent tie-up between IBM and Texas Instruments to create automated industrial control processes called computer-integrated manufacturing (CIM). A ripple effect of the "borderless economies" concept is the elimination of artificial barriers at home that restrict American competitiveness in the global marketplace.

None of these strategies is directly dependent on either leadership or control from Washington. While American proponents of industrial policy would have the federal government emulate the Japanese model and create a national economic strategy on the grounds that America could thus compete better against its formidable German and Japanese rivals, that concept is mired in the old industrial era, which was bureaucratically driven and rooted at the center. It also makes about as much sense as imitating totalitarian methods of political organization would have been while we were fighting the Cold War with Russia.

So for all the talk about the need for Washington to provide new leadership for the new age, we ought to be looking instead to places *outside the center*, where America's dynamic, pluralistic leadership is currently being forged. The old cultural image of one wagon train with a single driver forging ahead into the wilderness has been overcome by historical events. America now has thousands of wagon trains with countless leaders, all showing healthy signs of adaptation and adjustment to the new age.

Which should provide a hint for new and more relevant public sector strategies as well. These strategies are no longer based solely on increased federal spending and expanded bureaucratic control but rather on the creation and implementation of broad *incentives* as a more practical (and efficient) way to change.

In the past Americans have debated about what the federal government *should* do about public education, family policy and social welfare, crime and drugs, infrastructure improvement, urban redevelopment, health care, the environment. But in the future the debate will center more on what a central bureaucracy realistically *can* do about these critical areas, given the many claims on our resources and the acknowledged (and unarguable) inefficiencies of the public sector.

Far from over, the new battle of ideas has really just begun. Traditional, liberal solutions simply call for larger government, more spending, and a bigger bureaucracy—solutions more appropriate perhaps to the old era that is now being ushered out. Conservatives would argue that the forces of decentralization, individual autonomy, and personal choice are now driving the new age, so public policy must benefit from a more pragmatic, results-oriented, incentive-based approach.

While we are beginning to learn that there are limits to what centralized governments can do, we are also slowly realizing there are limits to what government money can buy. Government spending, far from solving our problems, too often simply makes them worse. So we should more often be looking to government as a mechanism for creating incentives that favor production over consumption, work over leisure, savings over spending, but that then gets out of our way so we can respond appropriately to them:

- Incentives, through higher levels of tax-exempt interest and dividends, can raise our levels of savings and capital formation—U.S. personal savings today as a percent of GNP are still the lowest in the OECD;
- Incentives, through lower individual income tax rates, can generate higher rates of economic growth, wealth creation, and job production—but they must be combined with realistic spending cuts that reduce the size and inefficiency of the federal bureaucracy;

- Incentives, through lower capital gains taxes, can and will drive higher levels of investment—in 1989 Japan invested $520 billion (20 percent of GNP) in new plant and equipment, compared to $490 billion (just 10 percent of GNP) for U.S. firms, a two-to-one per capita advantage;
- Disaggregated incentives in the tax code, through more aggressive depreciation benefits, higher R&D tax credits, and restoration of the Investment Tax Credit, can strengthen manufacturing capabilities in the critical information technologies;
- Incentives, through higher personal deductions, can shelter larger portions of two-parent incomes and help stabilize America's traditional family unit—instead of the current $2,000 deduction, a more realistic $5,000 figure is needed;
- Incentives, through greater competition and choice that flow from institutional restructuring and innovative policies like tuition tax credits, can sharply raise the performance levels of our public schools—experiments with school-based autonomy in Dade County, Florida, with interdistrict choice in Minnesota, and with tuition tax credits in Wisconsin are symbols of both this new incentive-based approach and the powerful forces of decentralization;
- Skill-based (as opposed to family-related) incentives can generate even higher levels of skilled and trained immigrants— America would suffer a serious deficiency of health-care professionals today were it not for open immigration;
- Incentives, through public funding of national elections and reasonable limitations on congressional terms, can rejuvenate our political system and revitalize the legislative branch of government, which has become what many feared it would: the politburo of America's welfare state.

There is arguably no more pressing public policy issue for the United States today than the implementation of new and more refined tax policies that will have the effect of encouraging much higher rates of economic growth than we have seen in recent years, in effect creating these very incentives by applying more finely tuned supply-side tax cuts and results-oriented policies to the needs of the nineties. If America continues to grow at a real rate of 1 percent per annum while Germany and Japan and the East Asian economies grow at real rates of three or four or five times that, the longer-term implications become quite clear.

"We have gained the skill and learned the details," Lawrence Lindsey writes in his brilliant book, *The Growth Experiment*. "What we need now is the political courage and perseverance to create a tax system that liberates economic energy, not enervating envy; a tax system that puts people before political pandering; a tax system that will keep America great in the 1990s and beyond."

With the collapse of the central command economies and the death of communism as an ideological alternative to democracy, Japan's politically authoritarian, strategically targeted mutant of capitalism will unavoidably move into this vacuum to compete head-to-head against America's democratic, free-market, free-enterprise model in the information age.

But the new American variant, based on the decentralized, autonomous examples cited, will not be the centrally controlled, welfare-state capitalist model inspired by John Maynard Keynes, dominated by a bloated bureaucracy, and linked to the pessimism of decline.

Instead it will be a more vigorous and vibrant entrepreneurial capitalism, inspired by Joseph Schumpeter's concept of creative destruction, based on America's innovative genius, driven by an indigenous spirit of American optimism and renewal, and much more appropriate to the demands of the new age.

This is the America that can respond to the challenge of East Asia's economic dynamism.

Perhaps Gilder put it best in *Microcosm*: "This is not a world in which the gain of one nation can only come at the expense of another," he writes. "All the world will benefit from the increasing impotence of imperialism, mercantilism, and statism. In this new economy of freedom, Americans must hope for the prosperity and freedom of Russians and Chinese. We must celebrate the successes of Koreans and Japanese. We must hail the increasing wealth and power of the Third World. Depending on an altruistic spirit, the microcosm requires not only a technological renaissance, but also a moral renewal."

And America will lead that moral renewal, in the future as in the past.

APPENDIX

COUNTRY-SPECIFIC STATISTICAL SUMMARY
(All Data as of 12/31/88 Unless Otherwise Specified)

Country	GNP ($billion)	GNP Growth (% p. a., '84–'88)	Population (million)	Pop. Growth (% p. a.)	Per Cap. Income	% GNP Def.
Indonesia	100	11.9	190	2.0	$ 500	1.5
Thailand	60	7.0	60	1.7	1,000	3.6
Malaysia	35	2.9	17	2.6	2,000	3.0
Philippines	35	2.9	65	3.5	450	2.2
Singapore	25	8.5	2.5	1.3	10,000	4.8
ASEAN (5)	250	—	334.5	—	750	—
Korea	200	17.5	45	1.3	4,500	4.4
Taiwan	100	9.7	20	1.1	5,000	4.8
Hong Kong	50	8.4	5.5	0.9	9,500	N/A
Japan	3,000	4.5	125	0.5	24,000	1.0
China	350	11.0	1,200	1.5	300	1.7
Germany	1,200	3.6	60	0.0	20,000	3.5e*
France	950	2.3	55	0.3	17,500	3.5e
Britain	825	2.3	57	0.2	14,500	3.5e
Italy	825	3.0	57	0.2	14,500	3.5e
Holland	225	4.0	15	0.5	15,000	3.5e
EC (12)	4,850	2.5	325	0.3	14,900	3.5e
U.S.A.	5,000	2.0e	250	1.3	20,000	5.5
Latin America	1,000	2.5	415	3.0	2,400	N/A
U.S.S.R.	2,675	1.0	290	0.7	9,225	17.5e
World	18,500	2.5e	5,250	1.8	3,500	N/A

*e = estimated figure

% GNP Mfg.	% GNP Total Trade	Exports ($billion)	Imports ($billion)	% Trade w/Japan	% Trade w/USA	Foreign Debt ($billion)	Country
13.9	32.4	19.2	13.2	25.6	13.1	60.0	Indonesia
24.4	60.0	15.8	19.9	23.3	16.4	20.0	Thailand
25.6	100.0	20.6	14.8	19.9	17.5	17.0	Malaysia
25.0	43.0	7.1	8.1	18.6	27.5	30.0	Philippines
30.1	326.0	39.0	42.5	15.6	24.0	0.1	Singapore
—	80.0	101.7	98.5	20.6	19.7	—	ASEAN (5)
31.6	56.0	60.7	51.8	25.0	31.0	30.6	Korea
37.8	110.0	60.6	50.0	14.5	38.7	0.0	Taiwan
21.7	254.0	63.2	63.9	12.0	17.0	0.0	Hong Kong
25.2	15.0	264.9	187.5	—	29.1	0.0	Japan
34.0	29.0	47.5	55.3	5.4	2.8	40.0	China
35.0	46.0	315.0	235.0	EC52.7	10.0	0.0	Germany
33.3e	33.0	153.6	162.4	EC53.0	7.4	0.0	France
22.0	35.0	130.0	159.1	EC48.1	14.2	0.0	Britain
36.0	32.0	128.6	138.5	EC56.0	10.0	0.0	Italy
25.0	82.0	93.0	91.3	EC74.9	4.7	0.0	Holland
30.2	21.0	495.0	530.0	—	—	0.0	EC (12)
23.2	15.0	322.2	440.9	21.8	—	N/A	U.S.A.
22.3	29.0	175.0	115.0	N/A	>50.0	600.0	Latin America
N/A	8.0	110.0	107.0	>50.0	w/COMECON	N/A	U.S.S.R.
N/A	26.0	2,400.0	2,400.0	—	—	1,000.0	World

Sources: *World Factbook* 1990 (CIA); *Asia Yearbook* 1990 (FEER).

NOTES

CHAPTER 1: INTRODUCTION: OF DRAGONS OLD AND NEW

Page 1. Opening quote from Nicholas Valéry, "Japanese Technology: Thinking Ahead," *The Economist*, December 2, 1989.

Pages 1–2. Growth Rates for the Little Dragons: Two of the best and most cogently argued summaries of both the economic and the cultural factors behind these East Asian success stories are a speech by Hong Kong University Professor of Economics Edward K. Y. Chen entitled "The Economics and Non-Economics of Asia's Four Little Dragons," delivered on January 26, 1988, in Hong Kong; and a paper by the Australian economist (and Hong Kong resident) George Hicks titled "Explaining the Success of the Four Little Dragons: A Survey," presented at the Convention of the East Asian Economic Association, Kyoto, Japan, October 29–30, 1988. Probably the best single source on the dynamics of growth in Northeast Asia (Japan, Korea, and Taiwan) is *The Political Economy of the New Asian Industrialism*, edited by Frederic C. Deyo, 1987. My last book, *The End of the American Century*, 1990, detailed the political and cultural background of the four Dragons' successes, citing Deyo among other recent scholarly contributions.

Page 2. Growth rates 1983–88: See *Far Eastern Economic Review, Asia Yearbook 1990*, pp. 6–7.

Page 2. Foreign exchange reserves: See "Japan and the NICs: The Political Economy of Rising Interdependence," an excellent account of growing regional interrelationships between Japan and the Little Dragons, presented by Kent Calder of Princeton University, Fifth U.S.–ASEAN Conference, Singapore, June 11–15, 1989.

Page 2. Exports and intraregional trade: *Asia Yearbook 1990*, pp. 6–7, and Calder, *op. cit.*

Page 3. Critics: See Robin Broad and John Cavanagh, "No More NICs," *Foreign Policy*, fall 1988, pp. 81–103, and the report of the Atlantic Council's Policy Working Group, Richard Kessler, ed., *The Role of the Newly Industrializing Economies in the World Economy* (Washington, 1989).

Page 3. Broad and Cavanagh, *op. cit.*, p. 103.

Page 3. Runway analogy attributed to former Japanese foreign minister Saburo Okita in Broad and Cavanagh, *op. cit.*, p. 103.

Page 5. Table: *Asia Yearbook 1991*, pp. 6–9, and *World Factbook 1990* (CIA, 1990).

Page 7. Political authoritarianism: Probably the best recent sources on the political background of the Little Dragons are Bruce Cumings, "The Origins and Development of the Northeast Asian Political Economy: Industrial Sectors, Product Cycles, and Political Circumstances," and Hagen Koo, "The Interplay of State, Social Class, and World System in East Asian Development: The Cases of South Korea and Taiwan," both in Deyo, *op. cit.*

Page 7. Authority: See Samuel P. Huntington, *Political Order in Changing Societies*, 1968, pp. 6–8.

Page 8. Industrial policy: See Chalmers Johnson, *MITI and the Japanese Miracle*, 1982, a detailed analysis of the background on Japan's economic growth and its historical and institutional underpinnings. See also my *Trade War*, 1984, and Johnson's chapter "Political Institutions and Economic Performance: The Government-Business relationship in Japan, South Korea, and Taiwan," in Deyo, *op. cit.*

Page 8. Capitalist developmental economics: see Johnson, *MITI and the Japanese Miracle*, especially Chapter 2, "The Economic Bureaucracy," and Chapter 3, "The Rise of Industrial Policy." See also "The Dynamics of Turbocharged Capitalism" in Schlossstein, *The End of the American Century*.

Page 9. Japan's domestic economic growth: The two best sources are Kazushi Ohkawa and Henry Rosovsky, *Japanese Economic Growth: Trend Acceleration in the 20th Century*, 1973, and Edward F. Denison and William K. Chung, *How Japan's Economy Grew So Fast* 1976.

Page 9. Export orientation of the Little Dragons: See Hicks, *op. cit.*, pp. 3–5.

Page 9. 1978–82 export composition and GNP growth rates: See *Far Eastern Economic Review, Asia Yearbook 1984*, pp. 6–9.

Page 10. 1983–88 GNP growth and export composition: See *Asia Yearbook 1990*, pp. 6–9.

Page 10. Korean debt: *Ibid.*, p. 8.

Pages 10–11. Japanese savings and postal system: See Johnson, *MITI and the Japanese Miracle*, especially Chapter 6, "Institutions of High-Speed Growth."

Page 11. Singapore's CPF: See Schlossstein, *The End of the American Century*, pp. 55–59.

Page 11. Capital formation figures: See *Asia Yearbook 1990*, p. 6.

Page 12. Student achievement: See the National Science Board's *Science and Engineering Indicators: 1987*, pp. 44, 201. For a broader discussion of East Asia's public education systems, especially at the secondary school level, see Schlossstein, *The End of the American Century*, Part III, Chapters 10 and 11.

Pages 12–13. Japanese R&D: See Jon Choy, "Research and Development in Japan: 1989 Update," *Japan Economic Institute* Report No. 24-A, June 23, 1990, pp. 2, 9–10. A more complete description of the incremental approach to Japanese R&D can be found in Schlossstein, *The End of the American Century*, Chapter 5.

Page 13. Technology exports to Asia from Japan: See Choy, *op. cit.*, pp. 12–15.

Page 13. Singapore R&D: See *Singapore 1987*, pp. 80, 86.

Pages 16–17. The individual vs. the group: for a detailed analysis of social systems in East Asia, see Schlossstein, *The End of the American Century*, Part IV, "The Family as Society's Fortress," especially Chapter 14, "Social Stability in East Asia: Withstanding the Winds of Change." A complete listing of bibliographic citations is appended.

Page 18. Table: see *Asia Yearbook 1991*, pp. 6–9; Bank Indonesia *1987–88 Report*, pp. 75–77 and *World Factbook 1990* (CIA, 1990).

Page 19. The brief comments on Indonesia, Thailand, and Malaysia that follow here are derived primarily from more than 200 background interviews conducted in Jakarta, Bangkok, and Kuala Lumpur over a three-month period, June through August, 1989, during my stay as a visiting fellow at the Institute of Southeast Asian Studies in Singapore. More complete citations and full interview details are presented in the text below (Chapters 2–5).

Page 20. For a good overview of Indonesia's historical background, see Frederica Bunge's *Indonesia: A Country Study*, 1983.

Page 20. See Bunge's comparable *Thailand: A Country Study*, 1981.

Page 20. Bunge also edited *Malaysia: A Country Study*, 1985. These country studies are an outgrowth of the older Area Handbooks, which had previously been prepared in cooperation with the U.S. Army and the Central Intelligence Agency. See also James Clad, *Behind the Myth: Business Money and Power in Southeast Asia*, 1989.

Page 21. There is a large number of excellent scholarly studies on the subject of ethnic minorities in Southeast Asia, especially regarding the assimilation of the Chinese into Indonesia by Leo Suryadinata of the University of Indonesia. These are cited in detail in the full text below. This brief material is drawn principally from personal interviews in Jakarta, Bangkok, and Kuala Lumpur, summer 1989.

Page 22. See Bunge, country studies for each country, *op. cit.*

Page 22. Foreign debt figures: see *Asia Yearbook 1990*, pp. 6–9.

Page 23. Personal interviews, June–August 1989.

Page 23. Reference to literacy: See *Asia Yearbook 1990*, pp. 6–7.

Page 24. National expenditures on education: See *Asia Yearbook 1990*, pp. 8–9.

Page 24. Japanese technology exports to Asia: See Choy, *op. cit.*, pp. 13–14.

Page 24. Asian university students: See *Asia Yearbook 1990*, pp. 6–7.

Page 26. Reference to Thai and Malaysian manufactured goods: See *Statistical Handbook of Thailand: 1988*, p. 172, and N. Balakrishnan, "Malaysia: the Next NIC," *Far Eastern Economic Review*, September 7, 1989, p. 97.

Page 26. Reference to Indonesian manufactured goods: personal interviews, Jakarta, August 1989.

Page 30. Archipelagic states: See Phiphat Tangsubkul, *ASEAN and the Law of the Sea*, 1982, p. 113.

Pages 30–31. Regional conflict: Lee Yong Leng's thoughtful book, *The Razor's Edge: Boundaries and Boundary Disputes in Southeast Asia*, published by ISEAS in 1980, provides valuable historical perspective on the background to conflict in the region.

Page 33. The death of communism: See John Gray, "The End of History—or of Liberalism?" *National Review*, October 27, 1989, p. 35.

Page 34. Japanese national economic interests: See Ezra Vogel, "Japan as Number One: Revisited," speech delivered at ISEAS, Singapore, July 17, 1985.

CHAPTER 2: INDONESIA: UNITY IN DIVERSITY

Page 37. Opening quote from Clifford Geertz, *Agricultural Involution: The Process of Ecological Change in Indonesia*, 1971, pp. 130–31.

Page 38. Indonesia in the first person: Some of the most vivid and effective "thought experiments" have been devised by Charles Murray in *Pursuit of Happiness and Good Government*, 1988, especially regarding empathy with the poor (pp. 73–79), orphaned childhoods (pp. 79–82), and parents hiring teachers (pp. 224–31).

Pages 39–49. Historical background: For a detailed account of Indonesia's early history, see Bunge, *Indonesia: A Country Study*, Chapter 1, "Historical Setting," pp. 11–62, and Chapter 2, "Society and Environment," pp. 63–118. See also Hamish McDonald, *Suharto's Indonesia*, 1980, Chapter 1, "Java," pp. 1–23; Harold Crouch, *The Army and Politics in Indonesia*, 1988, Chapter 1, "The Army as a Social-Political Force," pp. 24–43; O. G. Roeder, *The Smiling General: President Soeharto of Indonesia*, 1970, pp. 81–96; and former ambassador Howard Palfrey Jones, *Indonesia: The Possible Dream*, 1971, especially Part I, "Toward Understanding Indonesia," pp. 1–64, and Part IV, "Back from the Brink," pp. 369–423.

Page 49. Indonesia's *jihad* against the Communists: While it is generally acknowledged that the United States played a role in identifying many Communist leaders for Sukarno's opponents (namely Soeharto), it seems inappropriate, as some have done, to conclude that the United States was therefore responsible for the bloodbath that followed the PKI's attempted coup. It is difficult to recall today just how strained political tensions were in 1965 at the peak of the Cold War. Washington was understandably worried about the potential fall of the world's fifth-most-populous nation (and one of its geopolitically most important) to communism as the PKI grew in size and influence, openly aided and abetted with money, arms, and ideology by Beijing. This is by no means to excuse immoral actions that may have been committed by the CIA in the aftermath of the coup (or excesses committed later in Vietnam in its politically flawed Phoenix program). But press reports that criticized the CIA for furnishing "as many as 5,000 names" of suspected Communists to Soeharto may have overstated the CIA's role, for two reasons: (1) it is unlikely that Soeharto himself did not know who most of the suspected Communist leaders were, and (2) they represented a small fraction (1 percent) of the total killings estimated to have been committed by the Indonesians. So when one account suggests that "the people of Indonesia deserve to have their history back," it ignores the important fact that the Indonesian people were in fact *creating* their own history through their long-recognized historical tradition of amok behavior. See "Notes and Comments," *The New Yorker*, July 2, 1990.

Page 49. National income: See Bunge, *Indonesia: A Country Study*, pp. 55–56.

Page 50. Statistics on Indonesia's economic achievements from the World Bank, *Indonesia: Strategy for Growth and Structural Change*, 1989, pp. 1 (poverty), 13 (budget deficits), 94 (education), 96 (population), and 174 (rice production).

Pages 52–53. Personal interview with Dr. Mohammed Sadli, Jakarta, July 19, 1989. See also Bunge, *Indonesia: A Country Study*, p. 166, re Indonesia's impressive satellite communications network.

Pages 53–55. Personal interview with Dr. Anwar Nasution, Jakarta, July 17, 1989. References to external borrowings and industrial restructuring from his unpublished paper, "Structural Adjustment for Sustainable Growth: The Case of Indonesia in the 1980s," presented at a conference, Structural Adjustment for Sustainable Growth in Asian Countries, Tokyo, November 7–8, 1988. For a discussion of Indonesian domestic incentives and industrial policy reforms, see also the World Bank report, *op. cit.*, pp. 57–84, especially Chapter 3, "Promoting Private Sector Development," Sections B, "Trade Policy," pp. 58–68, and C, "Domestic Incentives and Regulatory Framework," pp. 69–75.

Page 56. Indonesia's intraregional trade with Asia: See the World Bank report, *op. cit.*, pp. 150–51.

Page 56. Projected growth rates: See the World Bank report, *op. cit*, Introduction, p. x.

Pages 56–57. Personal interview with Willem van der Wall Bake, Jakarta, July 18, 1989.

Page 57. Taxes and tax collection: see the World Bank report, *op. cit.*, pp. 24–25 and 44–46.

Pages 57–58. Personal interview with Minister of Industry Hartarto, Jakarta, July 22, 1989.

Page 58. Personal interview with Jim Castle, Jakarta, July 19, 1989.

Page 59. Reference to developmental functions of government: See Johnson, *MITI and the Japanese Miracle*, p. 19. See also *The End of the American Century*, especially Chapter 2: "Turbocharged Capitalism: The Dynamics of Japanese Economic Development."

Pages 59–60. Personal interview with Dorodjatun Kuntjorojakti, Jakarta, July 22, 1989.

Page 61. Background data on Dr. Habibie and IPTN from "The Extended Family: A Survey of Indonesia," *The Economist*, August 15, 1987. Personal interview with Dr. Wardiman by telephone, Jakarta, July 24, 1989. See also Habibie's recent speech, "Human Resources are Key to Prosperity," reprinted in the *Jakarta Post*, August 30, 1989.

Pages 61–62. References to CSIS: See McDonald, *op. cit.*, pp. 30, 99–103, 130–31. See also *Who's Who in Indonesia*, 2nd Ed., 1980.

Pages 61–62. Reference to CSIS and Roman Catholics: See McDonald, *op. cit.*, p. 101, and Leo Suryadinata, *Eminent Indonesian Chinese*, 1981, pp. 116–17, 164–65.

Page 62. Soesastro and deregulation: See M. Hadi Soesastro, "The Political Economy of Deregulation," unpublished paper presented at the Association of Asian Studies annual meeting, Washington, D.C., March 19, 1989, p. 23.

Pages 62–63. Personal interview with Hadi Soesastro, Jakarta, July 25, 1989. Banking Reforms: See Michael Vatikiotis and Adam Schwarz, "Free to Fly: Indonesia's Financial Sector," *Far Eastern Economic Review*, October 12, 1989, pp. 72–77, and "The Indonesian Economy: Reform and Resurgence," a speech by Minister of Finance Johannes Sumarlin given at the Asia Society, New York, September 21, 1989.

Page 63. Sumarlin's remarks from comments made at the Asia Society, New York, September 21, 1989.

Page 63. Personal discussion with D. E. Setiyoso, New York, November 6, 1989.

Page 65. Personal interview with Soedradjat, Jakarta, July 25, 1989. The *beçak* controversy stems from a decision made a decade ago to clear the old pedicabs from central Jakarta, a decision the pedicab drivers disliked intensely, as it meant significantly lower incomes for them if they had to scour the relatively pedestrian-free back roads for passengers. Still, most of them converted to the motorized *bajaj*, and others among them became street-corner vendors under a government-financed retraining program. In 1988, of 500 *beçak* drivers who opted to participate in this program, only twenty-five decided to become vegetable vendors; the remaining 475 converted to other professions, such as becoming licensed *bajaj* operators. During 1989 1,000 of the 1,750 *beçak* drivers taking part in the program decided to become bread vendors because they had been promised better-paying jobs by the Jakarta bakers' cooperative. The question then is whether Jakarta will become inundated by a surfeit of bakery goods, necessitating retraining for bakers. *Jakarta Post*, July 20, 1989.

Page 66. Background on Sofjan Wanandi: Personal interview, Jakarta, July 19, 1989. See also Suryadinata, *op. cit.*, pp. 164–65.

Pages 66–67. Personal interview with Sofjan Wanandi, Jakarta, July 19, 1989.

Pages 67–73. For additional background on the Chinese ethnic community in Indonesia, see Leo Suryadinata, *Pribumi Indonesians, the Chinese Minority, and China*, 1978, especially pp. 1–7 and 78–109. See also George McTurnan Kahin, *The Political Position of the Chinese in Indonesia*, Stanford University master's thesis, 1946, pp. 7–17. For biographical data on Liem Sioe Liong, published accounts of which are few, see Suryadinata, *op. cit.*, pp. 107–108, and McDonald, *op. cit.*, pp. 118–122. An excellent and highly readable summary of the Malari affair is in McDonald, *op. cit.*, pp. 134–141. By far the best account of anti-Chinese ethnic conflict in Indonesia (and the factional disputes in domestic politics underlying it) is J. A. C. Mackie, ed., *The Chinese in Indonesia*, especially his own chapter, "Anti-Chinese Outbreaks in Indonesia, 1959–68," pp. 77–138. Mackie quote from p. 130.

Pages 73–76. Background on the creation and development of ABRI: see McDonald, *op. cit.*, pp. 13–23, and Crouch, *op. cit.*, Chapters 1 and 11. Crouch quote from pp. 273–274. Additional data from confidential background interviews, Jakarta, July 1989.

Page 77. Javanese concept of power: See Benedict R. O'G. Anderson, "The Idea of Power in Javanese Culture," in Claire Holt, ed., *Culture and Politics in Indonesia*, 1972, pp. 1–9.

Pages 77–78. Javanese concept of power: See Anderson, *op. cit.*, pp. 4–9, 25, 65. See also his *Mythology and the Tolerance of the Javanese*, published in the Monograph Series of the Modern Indonesia Project at Cornell University, 1974, and McDonald, *op. cit.*, pp. 2, 57–8.

Some of Anderson's other monographs are also especially insightful. His *Notes on Indonesian Political Communication*, 1974, relates Javanese tradition to Indonesian politics, and an unpublished paper, "American Values and Research on Indonesia," presented at the annual meeting of the Association for Asian Studies in 1971, shows the problems inherent in trying to interpret Javanese cultural practices and traditions through unsympathetic and untrained Western eyes.

The Dutch scholar Niels Mulder has also written extensively on Javanese mysticism. See his *Mysticism and Everyday Life in Contemporary Java*, 1980, which was originally published as a monograph at the University of Amsterdam entitled "A Cultural Analysis of Javanese Worldview and Ethic as Embodied in Kebatinan and Everyday Experience," in 1975, which itself was an outgrowth of an earlier paper, "A Comparative Note on the Thai and the Javanese Worldview as Expressed by Religious Practice and Belief," published in *The Journal of the Siam Society*, Part 2, July 1970.

Page 78. Hardjijo quote: Personal interview with Brigadier General Bantu Hardjijo, Third U.S.-Indonesia Bilateral Conference, Bali, August 29, 1989.

Statistics on Indonesian defense spending from International Institute for Strategic Studies (IISS), *The Military Balance, 1988–1989*, pp. 162–164.

Pages 78–80. Background on the new generation of ABRI officers from Crouch, *op. cit.*, pp. 353–59. Moerdani quote from remarks he made at the Third U.S.-Indonesia Bilateral Conference, Bali, August 28, 1989.

For additional background material, see Chin Kin Wah, ed. *Defense Spending in Southeast Asia*, 1987, especially Chapter 5, "Indonesia: Defense Expenditures in the Period of the New Order," by Dorodjatun Kuntjorojakti. See also Soedjati Djiwandono, "The Military and National Development in Indonesia," Harold Crouch, "The Military Mind and Economic Development," in Crouch, *op. cit.*, and Donald Emmerson, "The Military and Development in Indonesia," in Soedjati Djiwandono and Yong Mun Cheon, ed., *Soldiers and Stability in Southeast Asia*, 1988.

Statistics on Indonesia's defense spending from *The Military Balance 1988–1989*, pp. 162–164, and Chin Kin Wah, *op. cit.*, pp. 142–145, 310–311, and 322–323.

Page 81. Three-stage pattern of relationship development: See James Scott, "Corruption, Machine Politics, and Political Change," Southeast Asia Development Advisory Group, Discussion Paper No. 52, December 6, 1968, pp. 8–11.

See also Raymond Vernon's thoughtful cost-benefit analysis of foreign investment in this context, "Multinational Enterprises in Developing Countries: An Analysis of National Goals and National Policies," Harvard Institute for International Development, Discussion Paper No. 4, June 1975, p. 7.

Page 82. Reinvestment of political income: See Edward S. Mason, "Corruption and Development," Harvard Institute for International Development, Development Discussion Paper No. 50, December 1978, p. 36. The classic case of a developing country in Asia with extraordinary high rates of capital flight (rather than income reinvestment) is the Philippines.

Page 82. Anderson quote re perquisites: See Benedict R. O'G. Anderson, "The Idea of Power in Javanese Culture," *op. cit.*, p. 33.

Pages 83–85. Background to Pertamina and Sutowo: The best account of this era is McDonald, *op. cit.*, Chapter 6, "The Feudal State," pp. 113–141, and Chapter 7, "The Rise and Fall of Ibnu Sutowo," pp. 143–165. See also Harold Crouch, *The Army and Politics in Indonesia*, especially Chapter 11, "The Army's Economic Interests," pp. 273–303.

Page 86. Stolen car account: See Ray Bonner, "The New Order," *The New Yorker*, June 13, 1988, Part 2, p. 83. (Part 1 of the two-part series appeared in the June 6, 1988, issue, pp. 45–80.)

Page 86. Personal interview with Sarwono Kusuma-atmadja, Jakarta, July 20, 1989. A similar account with Sarwono, and the driver's quote, appear in Bonner, *op. cit.*, Part 2, p. 82.

Page 87. Arrests and convictions for corruption: See Crouch, *op. cit.*, p. 295.

Page 87. Suspension of principals from *Jakarta Post*, July 24, 1989. State electricity corporation account from Crouch, *op. cit.*, p. 298. Sarwono speech from *Jakarta Post*, July 22, 1989.

Pages 87–88. Personal interview, Jakarta; see also Crouch, *op. cit.*, p. 299.

Pages 88–90. Reference to Soeharto's family: See John Andrews, "Indonesia: The Extended Family," *The Economist*, August 15, 1987, p. 14.

Pages 90–96. Background on the Soeharto family's commercial interests: See Bonner, *op. cit.*, Part 2, June 13, 1989, pp. 80–82 (direct quote from p. 81). See also McDonald, *op. cit.*, pp. 121–122, 127 (segment of President Soeharto's speech from p. 127). See also Andrews, *op. cit.*, viz. his brief section "All in the Family." Personal interviews, on background, Jakarta, July 1989.

By far the most complete account of the Soeharto children's financial dealings and details of their many holdings was published by *Asian Wall Street Journal* in a three-part series several years ago. See Steven Jones and Raphael Pura, "Suharto-Linked Monopolies Hobble Economy," November 24, 1986; Steven Jones, "Suharto's Kin Linked with Plastics Monopoly," November 25, 1986; and Raphael Pura, "Suharto Family Tied to Indonesian Oil Trade," November 26, 1986. A related piece by the *Journal*'s Jakarta correspondent, Richard Borsuk, entitled "Jakarta's Steel Mill Rescue Sparks Debate," appeared on July 5, 1989.

Pages 96–97. Background on Indonesian politics: See Bunge, *Indonesia: A Country Study*, Chapter 4, "Government and Politics," pp. 175–217, especially pp. 189–205. See also Crouch, *op. cit.*, viz. Chapter 1, "The Army as a Social-Political Force," and Chapter 11, "The Army and Politics"; and David Jenkins, *Suharto and His Generals*, 1984.

Pages 98–99. Personal interview with Rachmat Witoelar, Jakarta, July 25, 1989.

Pages 99–100. Comments on Soeharto's succession from personal interviews, all on background, Jakarta, July 1989. Details on the *Tempo* poll from a discussion with government officials, Jakarta, July 20, 1989, and on the *Editor* poll from *Straits Times*, Singapore, July 6, 1989.

Page 101. Reference to political openness: See R. William Liddle, "Development or Democracy: An Indonesian Dilemma?" for an excellent background analysis of these issues. This unpublished paper was presented at the Third Indonesia–U.S. Bilateral Conference, Bali, August 27–31, 1989. See also his *Cultural and Class Politics in New Order Indonesia*, "The 1977 Indonesian Election and New Order Legitimacy," and *Power, Participation, and the Political Parties in Indonesia*.

Page 102. Looking at Indonesia through Western eyes: See Harry J. Benda, "Democracy in Indonesia," and Herbert Feith, "History, Theory, and Indonesian Politics," in Benedict Anderson and Audrey Kahin, eds., *Interpreting Indonesian Politics: Thirteen Contributions to the Debate*, 1982, for two excellent contributions to the problem of interpreting Indonesia's political developments empathetically.

Page 103. Background on student demonstrations: See Bonner, *op. cit.*, Part 1, June 6, 1988.

Page 104. Makarim quote from Nono Anwar Makarim, *The Indonesian Press: An Editor's Perspective*, 1974, p. 9. See also Benedict R. O'G. Anderson, *Notes on Indonesian Political Communication*, 1974.

Page 105. Background on *Sinar Harapan* from Bonner, *op. cit.*, Part 1, June 6, 1988, pp. 74–76, and personal interviews, Jakarta, July 24, 1989.

Page 107. Background on the Nahdlatul Ulama and NGOs: see Bonner, *op. cit.*, Part 1, June 6, 1988, pp. 68–72, and Michael Vatikiotis, "Lobbying the Donors," *Far Eastern Economic Review*, August 24, 1989, p. 23. Personal interview with Abdurrahman Wahid, at the Third U.S.–Indonesia Bilateral Conference, Bali, August 29, 1989.

In a recent international forum for NGOs, a confrontation ensued between organization representatives and government officials, both of which represented Indonesia. It was prompted by a letter sent by the NGOs to the World Bank, complaining about the resettlement of some 1,500 families from a World Bank–financed dam project in central Java with inadequate compensation.

When the World Bank sent a special mission to Indonesia to investigate, it proved embarrassing for the New Order government. Soeharto was concerned that further NGO lobbying might pressure not only the World Bank but also the Japanese government to insist on stricter human rights conditions prior to disbursing additional development funds. In July 1989 Soeharto ordered action against the NGOs, saying their actions had harmed Indonesia's national interests, but Commander-in-Chief Sutrisno said he was reluctant to reprimand them, preferring to maintain a friendly dialogue rather than to curtail their activities. However, the NGOs could well represent the next stage of domestic opposition, taking up where student demonstrators had left off.

Page 108. Reference to retired Army generals: See David Jenkins, *op. cit.*, p. 183.

Page 108. Reference to mysterious killings from Bonner, *op. cit.*, Part 1, June 6, 1988, p. 65.

Page 109. As an example of *beçak* drivers running amok, the *Jakarta Post* ran this brief story in its August 26, 1989, issue:

"An angry mob attacked and killed a man in a slum area in West Jakarta late Thursday after the man badly injured a police sergeant.

In an unrelated incident, residents of Sukaraja village in Chjeruk district, Bogor, assaulted and killed two local residents late Wednesday evening. The attackers threw the bodies of the two victims into the office of the local village administration and told officials that the two had often extorted money from them. . . .

Vigilante justice in Sukaraja Wednesday claimed the lives of Hari bin Harya, 30, and Misna bin Said, 35, residents of Tajurhalang village. The two had just three months ago completed jail terms for theft at the Pledang county prison."

Pages 110–11. Anderson quote from Benedict Anderson, "The Idea of Power in Javanese Culture," pp. 28–29.

Page 111. Personal interview with Dr. Mochtar Kusuma-atmadja, Jakarta, July 20, 1989.

Pages 111-17. Background on the Japan-Indonesia relationship: personal interviews in Ciawi (PT Unitex), July 21, 1989, and in Jakarta, July 18 (JETRO) and July 19 (Toto), 1989.

Details of Japan's foreign investment in Indonesia are from the World Bank report, *op. cit.*, pp. 148–55. See also *Indonesia: A Guide for Investors*, 1986, and two excellent reports from the Japan Economic Institute in Washington: Eileen Doherty, "Japan's Foreign Direct Investment in Developing Countries," Report No. 31A, August 11, 1989, pp. 3, 4, 9–10, and Gretchen Green, "Japan's Foreign Aid Policy: 1989 Update," Report No. 41A, October 27, 1989, pp. 6, 9, 12-13. Additional statistics are from *Japan 1989: An International Comparison*, 1989, pp. 53–58.

Japanese publications cited include MITI's *ASEAN-Go-ka-koku ni miru Nikkei Seizogyo no Jittai Chosa (Substantive Analysis of Japanese Manufacturing [Industries] in the five ASEAN Countries)*, Part 2, (Indonesia), pp. 63–134, 1988; "Saikin no Indoneshia no Keizai Kankyo" ("Indonesia's Recent Economic Environment"), July 25, 1989; and *Indoneshia ni kan suru Kikkei Seizogyo Toshi (List of Japanese Investment Projects in Indonesia)*, 1988, as well as the 1988 annual reports of PT Unitex and PT Surya Toto.

Background on the yen bloc is from Paul Maidment, "The Yen Block: Together Under the Sun," *The Economist*, July 15, 1989; Kenji Dobashi, "Changes in Japanese Corporate Strategy: In Search of Real Globalization," June 1989; Akira Ogino, "The Importance of Capital Market Developments and Recycled Funds from Japan," June 1989; Kent Calder, "Japan and the NICs: The Political Economy of Rising Interdependence," *op. cit.*, pp. 27–32; and Tsunehiko Watanabe, "Improvement of Labor Quality and Economic Growth: Postwar Japan's Experience," October 1970.

Page 118. Reference to Japanese logging: see *The Nation*, Bangkok, June 21, 1989.

Page 122. Personal interviews with Indonesia's foreign minister, Ali Alatas, Jakarta, July 26, 1989; with former ambassador Hasnan Habib, Jakarta, July 21, 1989; with U.S. Ambassador John Monjo, Bali, August 29, 1989; with Kernial Sandhu, ISEAS, Singapore, July 29, 1989; with Dr. Mochtar Kusuma-atmadja, Jakarta, July 20, 1989.

Page 124. Personal interviews with foreign minister, Ali Alatas, Jakarta, July 24, 1989; the late Husni Pane, secretary general of ASEAN, Jakarta, July 22, 1989. Background on ASEAN and Cambodia from various sources, including Kusuma Snitwongse and Sukhumbhand Paribatra, eds., *Durable Stability in Southeast Asia*, 1987; Sheldon Simon, *The Future of Asian-Pacific Security Collaboration*, 1988; Hans H. Indorf, *Impediments to Regionalism in Southeast Asia: Bilateral Constraints Among ASEAN Member States*, 1984; and Donald Weatherbee, *Southeast Asia Divided: The ASEAN-Indochina Crisis*, 1985. For a broader treatment of ASEAN economic issues, see C. Y. Ng, R. Hirono, and Narongchai Akrasanee, eds., *Industrial Restructuring and Adjustment for ASEAN—Japan Investment and Trade Expansion*, 1988, and C. Y. Ng, et al., eds., *Effective Mechanisms for the Enforcement of Technology and Skills in ASEAN*, 1988.

Page 125. Personal interview with Dr. Mochtar Kusuma-atmadja, Jakarta, July 21, 1989.

Pages 126-27. Background on East Timor from McDonald, *op. cit.*, especially Chapter 9, "War and Diplomacy: The Timor Case," pp. 189–215, and Bonner, *op. cit.*, Part 2, June 13, 1988, pp. 84–89. Leifer quote from Michael Leifer, *Indonesia's Foreign Policy*, 1983.

Page 129. General Simatupang quote from Bonner, *op. cit.*, Part 2, June 13, 1988, p. 89. Personal interviews with Gordon Hein, Jakarta, July 18, 1989; foreign minister, Ali Alatas, Jakarta, July 24, 1989; Rachmat Witoelar, Jakarta, July 25, 1989; and Jusuf Wanandi, Bali, August 29, 1989. See also Jusuf Wanandi, "Indonesian Domestic Politics and Its Impact on Foreign Policy"; Hasnan Habib, "Security and Political Aspects of U.S.–Indonesia Bilateral Relations"; and Steven Erlanger, "Security and Political Aspects of Indonesia–U.S. Bilateral Relations"; all papers presented at the Third Indonesia–U.S. Bilateral Conference, Bali, August 27–31, 1989.

Page 130. Reference to educational attainment: See Biro Pusat Statistik, *Statistik Indonesia: 1988*, 1989, pp. 102–103, and *World Development Report: 1988*, 1989, pp. 268, 280. See also Bruce Fuller, "Raising School Quality in Developing Countries: What Investments Boost Learning?", World Bank Discussion Paper, 1986, and Dov Chernichovsky and Oey Astra Meesook, "School Enrollment in Indonesia," World Bank Staff Working Paper No. 746, 1985.

Pages 130-31. Personal interviews with Sarwono Kusuma-atmadja, Jakarta, July 20, 1989; Dorodjatun Kuntjorojakti, Jakarta, July 22, 1989; and Soedradjat, July 25, 1989. See also the *Jakarta Post* editorial, "Occasion for Introspection," August 15, 1990, and Steven Erlanger, "Oil Surge Disrupts Southeast Asian Economies," *New York Times*, November 15, 1990. See also Donald K. Emmerson, "Indonesia in 1990," *Asian Survey*, February 1991.

Page 132. Geertz quote from *Geertz*, *op. cit.*, p. 130.

CHAPTER 3: THAILAND: THE BANGKOK CONNECTION

Page 135. Opening quote from Somsakdi Xuto, ed., *Government and Politics in Thailand*, Chapter 1, "Political History," by Chai-Anan Samudavanija, p. 33.

Pages 137-43. Cultural and historical background: See Frederica M. Bunge, ed., *Thailand: A Country Study*, 1981, Chapter 1, "Historical Setting," pp. 1–47, for a brief overview. For by far the best historical account of Thailand, see David K. Wyatt, *Thailand: A Short History*, 1984. See also John L. S. Girling, *Thailand: Society and Politics*, 1981, especially Chapter 1, "Past and Present," and Chapter 4, "Political Structure"; David J. Steinberg, ed., *In Search of Southeast Asia*, 1987, Chapter 29, "Siam," and Chapter 35, "The Kingdom of Thailand"; G. Coedès, *The Making of South East Asia*, 1966, Part V, Chapter 1, "Siam or Thailand"; and U.S. Department of State, "Thailand: Background Notes," March 1988.

Page 145. Background on Bangkok: See Geoffrey Murray, "Saving Asia's Sinking Cities," *Asia Technology*, October 1989. See also Tim Hindle, "Thailand: Tropical Balance," *The Economist*, October 21, 1987, and various articles from *The Nation* and the *Bangkok Post*, dated June 17, 19, 26, and 27, 1989.

Page 145. Japanese statistics from Shoichi Ikuta, *Thai Koku Keizai Gaikyo, 1988–89 (An Overview of the Thai Economy, 1988–89)*, 1989, pp. 262–271. Japanese direct investment figures from personal interviews with Board of Investment personnel, Bangkok, June 1989, and Government of Thailand, *Statistical Handbook of Thailand: 1988*, 1989. See also Shoichi Ikuta, *Boeki Shijo Shiriizu: Thai (Foreign Trade Market Series: Thailand)*, May 31, 1989, Section 5, "Toshi Doko, Toshi Kankyo" ("Investment Trends, Investment Environment"); James Sterngold, "Japan Builds East Asia Links, Gaining Labor and Markets," *New York Times*, May 8, 1990; and Eileen Doherty, *op. cit.*, p. 3. A related study is Patcharee Thanamai, *Patterns of Industrial Policymaking in Thailand: Japanese Multinationals and Domestic Actors in the Automobile and Electrical Appliance Industries*, doctoral thesis, University of Wisconsin, Madison, 1985.

Pages 146–48. Foreign investment approvals from Board of Investment representatives, Bangkok, June 1989. See also *Thai Koku Keizai Gaikyo (1988–89)*, pp. 410–23. Nava Nakorn figures from *Boeki Shijo Shiirizu: Thai*, Section 5, and BLC Publishing Co., Ltd., *Setting Up in Thailand: A Guide for Investors*, 1988, pp. 101–104.

Pages 148–51. Personal interviews with Shoichi Ikuta, First Secretary, Embassy of Japan, Jakarta, June 21, 1989; Noboru Isowa, Director, International Division, Tomy (Thailand) Ltd., June 22, 1989; and Yukata Kuroda, Managing Director, Royal Thai Citi Co., Ltd., June 22, 1989.

Page 153. Statistics on Japanese industrial restructuring and overseas production: See Kenji Dobashi, "Changes in Japanese Corporate Strategy: In Search of Real Globalization," June 1989.

Page 153. Thai economic statistics: See National Economic and Social Development Board, "Selected Economic Indicators," June 1989; Economist Intelligence Unit, *Thailand Country Report*, No. 2, 1989; *Asia Yearbook 1990*, pp. 6–9; Government of Thailand, *Statistical Handbook of Thailand: 1988*, 195–203; and Bunge, *op. cit.*, Chapter 3, "The Economy," pp. 119–69.

Page 155. Thai-Japan export-import data: See Shoichi Ikuta, *Saikin no Thai no Boeki Doko (Recent Trends in Thailand's Trade)*, June 1989. See also *Asia Yearbook 1990*, pp. 8–9.

Page 156. Background on Japanese investment in the Thai textile industry: See Daniel Unger, "Growth in Thai Textile Exports as a Response to Currency Realignment," a paper presented at the annual meeting of the Association for Asian Studies (AAS), Washington, D.C., March 17–19, 1989, pp. 5, 8, 9, 15, 16. See also Richard F. Doner and Ansil Ramsay, "Thailand as a Case of Flexible Strength," a paper presented at the same meeting, pp. 5–9.

Page 156. Prime minister's quote from the *Bangkok Post* (Weekly Review), November 24, 1989.

Pages 156–57. Personal interview with Minister of Industry Banharn Silpa-archa, Bangkok, June 28, 1989.

Pages 157–58. Personal interview with Subin Pinkayan, Minister of Commerce, Bangkok, June 23, 1989. See also USTR, *1989 National Foreign Trade Estimate Report on Trade Barriers*, pp. 169–173.

Page 159. Personal interview with Michael Parrott, General Manager, Glaxo (Thailand), Bangkok, June 26, 1989.

Pages 159–60. Infrastructure and external debt statistics: See Preyaluk Dona-vanik, "Infrastructure Shortage," Bangkok Bank *Monthly Review*, April 1989, and National Economic and Social Developmental Board, "Selected Economic Indicators."

Page 161. Personal interview with General Chamlong Srimuang, Bangkok, June 21, 1989. Chamlong was overwhelmingly reelected mayor of Bangkok in early 1990 with 83% of the vote.

Pages 161–62. Logging and forestation: See Norani Visetbhakdi, "Deforestation and Reforestation in Thailand," Bangkok Bank *Monthly Review*, June 1989.

Pages 162–63. Personal interview with Dr. Staporn Kavitanon, BOI, Bangkok, June 20, 1989. See also the Economist Intelligence Unit, *op. cit.*, and the Board of Investment, Government of Thailand, *A Guide to Investing in Thailand*, 1989, for details on BOI incentives and the Map Ta Put petrochemical project.

Page 164. Skilled manpower development: See Thailand Development Research Institute, *The S&T Manpower Situation in Thailand: An Analysis of Supply and Demand Issues*, 1988, pp. 27, 28, 30, 34–35. See also *Statistical Handbook of Thailand: 1988*, pp. 87–98, and two related papers: "Thailand into the 1990s: The Emergence of Asia's Fifth Tiger," by Amnuay Viravan, executive chairman of the Bangkok Bank, Ltd., presented at the University of Michigan, March 15, 1988, and Vachiratith Viraphong et al., "What It Takes to Be a NIC," Bangkok Bank *Monthly Review*, March 1989.

Page 165. Personal interview with Dr. Narongchai Akrasanee, TDRI, Bangkok, June 20 and 23, 1989. Background data on the institute from the Thailand Development Research Institute *1988 Annual Report*, 1989.

Page 166. Personal interview with Dr. Phisit Pakkasem, NESDB, Bangkok, June 28, 1989. See also National Economic and Social Development Board, "Resolution of the Council of Economic Ministers on Adjustment of the Sixth National Economic and Social Development Plan," NESDB, June 1989, pp. 11–13.

Pages 167–68. Background on Thailand's savings-investment gap: See the World Bank, *Indonesia: Strategy for Growth and Structural Change*, *op. cit.*, 1989, p. 44; *Asia Yearbook 1990*, p. 7; NESDB "Resolution," *op. cit.*, p. 13; and Banyong Lamsam, "Bridging the Investment and Savings Gap," speech delivered at the Euromoney conference Thailand: Prospects for a Fast-Emerging Newly Industrializing Country, Bangkok, June 19–20, 1989.

Pages 168–69. Background on Chinese commercial interests: see Krirkkiat Phi-patseritham and Kunio Yoshihara, *Business Groups in Thailand*, 1983, pp. 3–9, and corporate annual reports. See also Paisal Sricharatchanya, "Chinese in Thailand: Happy Together," *Far Eastern Economic Review*, February 18, 1988.

Pages 169–70. Personal interview with Dr. Amaret Sila-On, Senior Vice President, Siam Cement Group, following his speech, "Development of Professional Management in Thailand," delivered at the Euromoney conference Thailand: Prospects for a Fast-Emerging Newly Industrialized Country, Bangkok, June 21, 1989.

Pages 171–72. Thai politics as a moving equilibrium: William H. Overholt, "Thailand: A Moving Equilibrium," *Pacific Review*, Vol. 1, No. 1, 1988, p. 7.

Pages 172–75. Background on Thai politics and recent coups: see Overholt, *op.*

cit., pp. 8–13; Hindle, *op. cit.*, pp. 5–6; and Wyatt, *op. cit.*, Chapter 10, "Development and Revolution, 1957–1982," pp. 277–307. See also Bunge, *op. cit.*, Chapter 4, "Government and Politics," pp. 171–211, and Likhit Dhiravegin, *Social Change and Contemporary Thai Politics*, 1984. For more recent updates, see also Larry Niksch, "Thailand in 1988," *Asian Survey*, February 1989, pp. 165–173; Clark Neher, "Thailand in 1987: Semi-Successful Semi-Democracy," *Asian Survey*, February 1988, pp. 192–301; and the *Far Eastern Economic Review*, issues for August 4, 11, 18, and 25, 1988.

Page 175. Riggs quote from Fred W. Riggs, *Thailand: The Modernization of a Bureaucratic Polity*, 1967, p. 387.

Page 176. Personal interviews with M. R. Sukhumband Paribatra, Singapore, June 15, and Bangkok, June 21 and 26, 1989.

Page 177. Background on the king: See Barbara Crossette, "King Bhumibol's Reign," *New York Times*, May 25, 1989, and Wyatt, *op. cit.*, pp. 306–7.

Page 177. *Lèse-majesté affair*: See Hindle, *op. cit.*, p. 5.

Page 178. Crown Property Bureau: see Paisal Sricharatchanya, "The Jewels of the Crown," *Far Eastern Economic Review*, June 30, 1988.

Page 178. Overholt quote: See Overholt, *op. cit.*, p. 20.

Page 179. Thailand defense spending: See ISIS, *The Military Balance, 1988–1989*, pp. 179–180.

Page 180. Prime Minister Chatichai's background: See Krirkkiat Phipatseritham and Kunio Yoshihara, *op. cit.*, p. 25, and Vanvalai Yenbumroong, *Who's Who in Thailand: 1987*, p. 149.

Page 180. Chumphon typhoon and Chatichai's problems: See Paul Handley, "Eye of the Storm," *Far Eastern Economic Review*, November 23, 1989.

Page 181. Background on Thai political parties: See Shoichi Ikuta, *Thai Koku Keizai Gaikyo, 1988–89*, Chapter 3, "Seiji" ("Politics"), pp. 13–29. See also the four issues of the *Far Eastern Economic Review* following the 1988 elections, dated August 4, 11, 18, and 25, 1988, and Erlanger, *op. cit.*

Page 182. Personal interviews with Governor Chamlong Srimuang, mayor of Bangkok, and Boonyakit Tansakul, Chief, Foreign Relations, Bangkok Metropolitan Administration, Bangkok, June 21, 1989.

Pages 183–84. Background on General Chaovalit: See Hindle, *op. cit.*, p. 5; Niksch, *op. cit.*, p. 169; and Rodney Tasker, "Rebel Clowns?", *Far Eastern Economic Review*, June 15, 1989.

Pages 185–86. Personal interview with Dr. Amnuay Viravan, Bangkok, June 23, 1989. See also his speech, "Privatization Reconsidered," delivered to the Thai-Canadian Business Club, Bangkok, July 12, 1989, and Overholt, *op. cit.*, p. 16.

Page 186. Interview with Dr. Maruey Phadoonsidhi, Bangkok, June 20, 1989. Background on Thai International from Hindle, *op. cit.*, p. 10.

Pages 186–87. Personal interview with Akira Ogino, Bangkok, June 20, 1989.

Page 188. Prime Minister Chatichai's policy advisory council: See Tan Lian Choo, "The Bright Boys from Bangkok," Singapore *Straits Times*, April 2, 1989, and "Shadow of the Army," *The Economist*, August 12, 1989. Personal interview with Sukhumband Paribatra, Bangkok, June 26, 1989.

Page 189. Background on Thai Buddhism: see Hindle, *op. cit.*, p. 7. Somboon quote from Somboon Suksamran, *Buddhism and Politics in Thailand*, 1982, p. 1.

Pages 190–91. Thai Buddhism and Phra Bodhirak: See Richard Martin, "Thai Rebel with a Buddhist Cause," *Insight*, August 21, 1989; Rodney Tasker, "Busting a Bronze," *Far Eastern Economic Review*, June 15, 1989: "Bodhirak Freed on 20,000 Baht Bail," *Bangkok Post*, June 22, 1989; "Not So Tolerant," *The Economist*, July 1, 1989; John Berthelsen, "A Sectarian Dispute Roils Thai Buddhism," *Asian Wall Street Journal*, August 21, 1989; and Steven Erlanger, "Ban on Journal Erodes Thais' Tolerant Image," *New York Times*, November 19, 1989.

Page 192. Xuto quote from Somsakdi Xuto, *op. cit.*, pp. 197ff.

Pages 193–96. Background on Thai corruption: See Paisal Sricharatchanya, "Interest in a Conflict," *Far Eastern Economic Review*, March 10, 1988, and Paul Handley, "Back to Business," *Far Eastern Economic Review*, August 25, 1988. *Bangkok Post* editorial, "A Harvest Worth One Trillion Baht," June 21, 1989. Other data obtained from confidential interviews, Bangkok, June 1989. See also Steven Erlanger, "Thai Prime Minister Shakes Up His Cabinet," *New York Times*, August 28, 1990.

Page 198. Background on Thai prostitution: See Marjorie Muecke, "Mother Sold Food, Daughter Sells Her Body: Transformations in Thai Femininity," paper presented at the annual meeting of the Association for Asian Studies, Washington, D.C., March 17–19, 1989, which also supplies the deputy prime minister's quote. Reference to American naval visits at Pattaya from the *Bangkok Post*, June 23, 1989.

Page 198. Mulder quote from Niels Mulder, *Everyday Life in Thailand: An Interpretation*, pp. 80–1. See also Benedict Anderson, and Ruchira Mendiones, eds., *In the Mirror*, 1985, and Niels Mulder, *Java-Thailand: A Comparative Perspective*, 1983.

Page 199. Pira Sudham quote from *Monsoon Country*, 1988, p. 69. See also his *People of Esarn*, 1987, for a touching description of Thailand's poverty-stricken Northeast. For statistics on Bangkok bars and AIDS, see Paul Handley, "The Lust Frontier," *Far Eastern Economic Review*, November 2, 1989. Reference to Red Wing tours from Singapore *Straits Times*, August 31, 1989.

Pages 200–203. Personal interview with Mechai Viravaidya, Bangkok, June 29, 1989. See also Cimi Suchontan, "Mechai Viravaidya: From Condom King to Deputy Minister," *World Executive's Digest*, February 1986, and the Population and Community Development Association 1988 annual report.

Pages 203–4. Background on Thai violence: See Rodney Tasker, "The Wild East," *Far Eastern Economic Review*, September 21, 1989, and *Statistical Handbook of Thailand*, 1988, pp. 62–3 (national divorce statistics on pp. 36–9). See also Mulder, *op. cit.*, p. 74; Overholt, *op. cit.*, p. 18; and a fascinating monograph by Purachai Piumsombun, "Violent Crimes in Thailand: Trends, Characteristics, and Solutions," *Thai Journal of Development Administration*, April 1984.

Pages 205–6. Personal interviews with Nopphong Bunyajitradulya, June 21, 1989, and with Dr. Charoen Kanthawongs, June 24, 1989, both in Bangkok. Visit to Vajiravudh School, Bangkok, June 27, 1989. Mulder quote from Mulder, *op. cit.*, pp. 189, 196.

Pages 206–7. Background on Thai nationalism: See Likhit Dhiravegin, "Nationalism and the State in Thailand," Thammasat University, Faculty of Political Science monograph, March 1985.

Pages 207-8. Personal interviews with Sukhumband Paribatra, Bangkok, June 21 and 26, 1989. See also David Chandler, "The Khmer Rouge and Internal Politics in Kampuchea," a paper presented at the Sixth Regional Security Conference on International Security in Southeast Asia: Current Problems and Prospects for Resolution, Chiang Mai, Thailand, July 4-6, 1989. See also Russell Watson, "Cambodia: Asia's Next Flash Point," *Newsweek*, June 26, 1989; Chandran Jeshurun, ed., *Governments and Rebellions in Southeast Asia*, 1985; and Sukhumband Paribatra, "Thailand: Defense Spending and Threat Perceptions," pp. 75-79.

Pages 208-9. ASEAN relations: Personal interviews, Bangkok, June 17-30, 1989. See also Likhit Dhiravegin, *ASEAN and the Major Powers: Today and Tomorrow*, Thammasat University, Faculty of Political Science monograph, May 1984, and Donald Weatherbee, "International Security and ASEAN in the 1990s," a paper presented at the Sixth Regional Security Conference on International Security in Southeast Asia: Current Problems and Prospects for Resolution, Chiang Mai, Thailand, July 4-6, 1989.

Page 209. Background on Burma: See William H. Overholt, "Burma: Disintegration, Drugs, Democracy"; David I. Steinberg, "Crisis in Burma: Stasis and Change in a Political Economy in Turmoil"; and Overholt, "Burma: Disintegration or Revival," papers presented at the Sixth Regional Security Conference on International Security in Southeast Asia: Current Problems and Prospects for Resolution, Chiang Mai, Thailand, July 4-6, 1989. See also Stan Sesser, "A Rich Country Gone Wrong," *New Yorker*, October 9, 1989.

Pages 210-11. Personal interviews with Prasert Chittiwatanapong, Bangkok, June 23 and 26, 1989, and with Sukhumband Paribatra, June 21 and 26, 1989. See also his series of papers on the Thai-Japan relationship: "Japan's Role in the Asia-Pacific Region: A Political Dimension," presented at a conference on the Pacific century organized by the Japan Institute of International Affairs, Tokyo, March 3-4, 1988; "The Problem of Japanese Official Development Assistance to Thailand," Thammasat University mimeo, December 1988; "Anti-Japanese Movements in Thailand," presented at a symposium on Thai-Japan relations at Thammasat University, Bangkok, January 15-16, 1987; and "International Conflict and Japanese Decision-Making: Perspectives from Thailand," presented at a conference at Dokkyo University, Japan, December 18-19, 1987. Additional analysis is contained in "Thai-Japan Economic Conflicts," published by the Thailand Development Research Institute (TDRI), Bangkok, April 1986. Background data on Japanese foreign aid to Thailand from Gretchen Green, "Japan's Foreign Aid Policy: 1989 Update," pp. 12-13. See also Leszek Buszynski, "New Aspirations and Old Constraints in Thailand's Foreign Policy," *Asian Survey*, November 1989, and Randall Purcell, ed., *The Newly Industrializing Countries in the World Economy*, 1989.

Page 213. Personal interview with Professor Kernial S. Sandhu, Singapore, June 30, 1989.

Page 214. Personal interview with foreign minister Siddhi Savetsila, Bangkok, June 28, 1989. See also Leszek Buszynski, *op. cit.*

Pages 214-16. Personal interviews with Narongchai Akrasanee, Virasak Futrakul, and Sukhumband Paribatra, Bangkok, June 28-30, 1989.

CHAPTER 4: MALAYSIA: QUINTESSENTIAL AFFIRMATIVE ACTION
Page 221. Opening quote from Ian Buruma, *God's Dust: A Modern Asian Journey*, 1989, p. 111.
Pages 223-29. Cultural and historical background: See Frederica M. Bunge, ed., *Malaysia: A Country Study*, 1985, Chapter 1, "Historical Setting," pp. 1-65; Richard Winstedt, *The Malays: A Cultural History*, 1981, pp. 176-87; Richard Winstedt, *A History of Malaya*, pp. 267-71; R. S. Milne and Diane K. Mauzy, *Malaysia: Tradition, Modernity, and Islam*, 1986; R. S. Milne and Diane K. Mauzy, *Politics and Government in Malaysia*, 1978; Kua Kit Soong, ed., *National Culture and Democracy*, 1985; Mohd. Taib Osman, ed., *Malaysian World View*, 1985; William R. Roff, ed., *Islam and the Political Economy of Meaning*, 1987; Heng Pek Koon, *Chinese Politics in Malaysia*, 1988, Chapter 1, "Historical Background," pp. 9-33, and Chapter 9, "Epilogue: From Indigenization to Marginalization," pp. 251-77; William R. Roff, *The Origins of Malay Nationalism*, 1967, pp. 1-31, 248-56; S. Husain Ali, *The Malays: Their Problems and Future*, 1981; R. S. Milne, *Politics in Ethnically Bipolar States*, 1981, pp. 40-59, 201-13; Mahathir bin Mohamad, *The Malay Dilemma*, 1970, Chapters 3, 4, and 8; A. C. Milner, *Kerajaan: Malay Political Culture on the Eve of Colonial Rule*, 1982, Chapters 1 and 2; and Karl von Vorys, *Democracy Without Consensus: Communalism and Political Stability in Malaysia*, 1975, Chapter 1, "A Society Dominated by Communal Cleavages," and Chapter 2, "The Failures of Extreme Designs."
Pages 230-31. Background on Malaysia's economy: See Bunge, *op. cit.*, Chapter 3, "The Economy," pp. 129-83; Keith Colquhoun, "At Bay: A Survey of Malaysia," *The Economist*, January 31, 1987; Economist Intelligence Unit, *Malaysia*, EIU Country Report No. 2, 1989, pp. 12-19; *Asia Yearbook 1990*, *op. cit.*, pp. 6-9; Tan Bok Huat, "Malaysia as a NIC?", paper prepared for the Institute of Strategic and International Studies, Kuala Lumpur, August 1989; and Karim Gulrose, ed., *Information Malaysia:1989 Yearbook*,1989, pp.290-307, 422-27.
Page 231. Naipaul quote from V. S. Naipaul, *Among the Believers: An Islamic Journey*, 1981, p. 215.
Pages 231-33. Japanese investment in Malaysia: Personal interview with Sadahiro Sugita, Kuala Lumpur, August 8, 1989; *Mareeshia Handobuku 1989* (*Malaysia Handbook 1989*), published by the Japanese Chamber of Trade and Industry in Malaysia (JACTIM), Kuala Lumpur, pp. 52-4, 68, 177-93, 449-76; and Eileen Doherty, "Japan's Foreign Direct Investment in Developing Countries," *Japan Economic Institute*, Report No. 31A, 1989, pp. 3-4. See also *Mareeshia Keizai, Boeki Hokoku* (*Report on Malaysia's Economy and Foreign Trade*), 1989.
Page 234. Balance of payments deficits and the savings-investment gap: Personal interview with See Yan Lin, Kuala Lumpur, August 10, 1989; Bank Negara Malaysia, *1988 Annual Report*, pp. 21, 79, 164-66, 214-17; and Economist Intelligence Unit, *op. cit.*, statistical appendices. See also See Yan Lin, "The Savings-Investment Gap: The Case of Malaysia," paper presented at a symposium sponsored by the Institute of Developing Economies, Tokyo, July 25-27, 1989, pp. 6, 9-10, and See Yan Lin, "Malaysia: Issues in Capital Market Development," paper presented at a conference on the Malaysian economy after 1990, Kuala Lumpur, August 7-9, 1989, p. 6.

Page 236. Background on Proton Saga: Personal visit to Proton plant, Shah Alam, and interview with Aidi Rosli Khalim, August 9, 1989. Data from *Nashionaru Kaa Purojekuto "Puroton Saga"* (*National Car Project "Proton Saga"*), furnished by the Embassy of Japan, Kuala Lumpur. Proton may be a semi-successful HICOM project so far, but Perwaja Terengganu, a $500 million steel plant, clearly was not. It was closed by the government in 1987 following several consecutive years of operating losses. And Kedah Cement Sdn. Bhd., a HICOM project in Mahathir's home state, proved to be the least efficient producer of cement in Malaysia. Both have been divested to private owners and are now ironically managed by Chinese entrepreneurs. Had HICOM not ceded management of the Proton plant to Mitsubishi Motors, it probably would have had to bail out of that too. See Raphael Pura and Steven Duthie, "Mahathir Forced to Salvage State Firm," *Asian Wall Street Journal*, June 27, 1988; Alasdair Bowie, "The Business of Development in Malaysia: Business Associations and Industrial Policy Formulation, 1957–1989," paper presented at the Association for Asian Studies annual meeting, Washington, D.C., March 19, 1989, pp. 5, 31; and Carl Goldstein, "Saga of Recovery," *Far Eastern Economic Review*, August 3, 1989.

Page 236. Investment incentives: See Malaysian Industrial Development Authority (MIDA), *Malaysia: Investment in the Manufacturing Sector*, pp. 11–13, and Gulrose, *op. cit.*, pp. 408–17.

Page 237. Federation of Malaysian Manufacturers: See "FMM Memorandum on National Economic Policy after 1990: New Policy Directions and Strategies," Kuala Lumpur, March 21, 1989, pp. 1, 2, 4, and 5, and Shiew Wang Shing, "The Manufacturing Sector: Malaysian Experience and Outlook," paper prepared for the Malaysian Economic Association conference on the Malaysian economy beyond 1990, Kuala Lumpur, August 7–9, 1989, pp. 2, 4, 13.

Pages 238–39. Personal interview with Dr. Kamil Salih, Kuala Lumpur, August 1, 1989. See also Kamil Salih, *The New Economic Policy After 1990*, monograph presented at the MIER 1988 National Outlook Conference, Kuala Lumpur, November 29, 1988, pp. 1–3; Kamil Salih and Zainal Aznam Yusof, *Overview of the New Economic Policy and Framework for the Post-1990 Economic Policy*, monograph presented at the National Conference on Post-1990 Economic Policy, Kuala Lumpur, August 1, 1989, pp. 1, 2, 20, and 21–22; and Lim Mah Hui, "Reflections on the Implementation and Consequences of the New Economic Policy," paper presented at the Association for Asian Studies annual meeting, Washington, D.C., March 19, 1989, pp. 7–8.

Pages 239–40. NEP as cartel: See Ozay Mehmet, *Development in Malaysia: Poverty, Wealth, and Trusteeship*, 1988, preface and pp. 3–17; Ozay Mehmet, "Malaysian Development Alternatives Beyond 1990," paper presented at the annual meeting of the Association for Asian Studies, Washington, D.C., March 19, 1989; and Bunge, *op. cit.*, p. 299. See also S. Jayasankaran, "The New Economic Policy: Where Now?", *Malaysian Business*, August 1–15, 1989, pp. 11–14, and an earlier study by Donald Snodgrass, "Summary Evaluation of Policies Used to Promote *Bumiputra* Participation in the Modern Sector in Malaysia," Harvard Institute for International Development, February 1978. The Malaysian government's most recent analysis of the NEP is contained in its own "Mid-Term Review of the Fifth Malaysia Plan, 1986–1990," Kuala Lumpur, July 1989.

Page 242. Visit to Federal Power and Telecoms Sdn. Bhd., and personal interview with Misron bin Yusof, Shah Alam, August 9, 1989.

Pages 242–43. NEP as an investment disincentive: See *Survey of American Investment in Malaysia*, U.S. Embassy, Kuala Lumpur, April 1989, p. 2. For background on Japan's high-speed growth and income doubling, see Kazushi Ohkawa and Henry Rosovsky, *Japanese Economic Growth: Trend Acceleration in the 20th Century*, 1973, and Edward F. Denison and William K. Chung, *How Japan's Economy Grew So Fast*, 1976.

Pages 242–43. Personal interview with Paul S. K. Low, Kuala Lumpur, August 8, 1989.

Page 243. Personal interview with Paul Chan Tuck Hoong, Kuala Lumpur, August 9, 1989.

Page 244. Personal interview with Dato' Mohkzani, Kuala Lumpur, August 11, 1989. Additional data contained in Innovest Berhad's 1988 annual report.

Pages 244–45. Personal interview with Dr. Tengku Mohammad Azzman Shariffadeen, Kuala Lumpur, August 11, 1989. See also his paper, *Microelectronics, Information Technology, and Society*, presented as the Raja Tan Sri Zainal Lecture, Kuala Lumpur, September 17, 1988, and the Malaysian Institute of Microelectronic Systems (MIMOS) 1989 information booklet. According to Dr. Shariffadeen, the U.S. market for computer hardware and software combined in 1987 was just under $100 billion, that of Japan about $65 billion. By comparison the Malaysian market included $120 million worth of hardware and $7 million worth of software, all imported from foreign suppliers, and the industry's five-year compound growth rate in Malaysia for 1983–87 was an anemic 4 percent.

Page 245. Education: See Bunge, *op. cit.*, pp. 118–23.

Page 248. Malaysian titles: Personal interviews, Kuala Lumpur, August 1–15, 1989, and Gulrose, *op. cit.*, pp. 31–33. Perhaps as a legacy of their British colonizers, Malaysians are so in love with titles that their daily newspapers contain full-page spreads publicizing the awards. My favorite title is Datuk Paduka, because of the alliteration, but in Sarawak, in eastern Malaysia, the front-runner is Sentinggi-tinggi Tahniah. The honors list is endless.

One recent honor in the *New Straits Times* read, "Heartiest Congratulations to Tuan Yang Terutama, Yang Dipertua Negeri Melaka, Tun Datuk Seri Utama, Syed Ahmad Al-Haj bin Syed Mahmud Shahabudin" (followed by his ten previously awarded titles) "on being conferred the title Darjah Seri Paduka Mahkota Selangor by Sultan Salahuddin Abdul Aziz Shah Alhaj Ibni Almarhum Sultan Hishamuddin Alam Shah Al-Haj" (followed by his *fifteen* previous awards). A full page is frequently necessary just to fit them all in.

Page 249. Direct quote from Mahathir bin Mohamad, *The Malay Dilemma*, 1970, p. 175.

Pages 249–52. Personal background data on Malaysia's leading politicians from confidential background interviews, Kuala Lumpur, August 1989, and *Who's Who in Malaysia, 1982* (the most current edition available at the time), pp. A22–23 (Mahathir), A24 (Musa) A33 (Razaleigh), A62 (Hussein Onn), and

59 (Anwar). See also Bunge, *op. cit.*, pp. 208–10; Suhaini Aznam, "Mahathir's DileMMa," *Far Eastern Review*, March 13, 1986; Nick Seaward, "The Daim Stewardship," *Far Eastern Economic Review*, September 1, 1988; Philip Bowring, "Power to the Center," *Far Eastern Economic Review*, April 14, 1988; Ismail Kassim, "The Man Most Likely to Succeed," Singapore *Straits Times*, May 3, 1987; and Anthony Rowley, "Lull Before the Storm," *Far Eastern Economic Review*, December 19, 1985.

Pages 252–54. Background on UMNO split: See Suhaini Aznam, "The Gathering Storm," *Far Eastern Economic Review*, October 13, 1988, and Stephen Duthie and Raphael Pura, "Battle for UMNO Faces Legal Quagmire," *Asian Wall Street Journal*, March 15, 1988.

Pages 253–54. Mauzy quote from Diane K. Mauzy, "Malaysia in 1987: Decline of the 'Malay Way,' " *Asian Survey*, February 1988, p. 213. See also K. S. Nathan, "Malaysia in 1988: The Politics of Survival," *Asian Survey*, February 1989, pp. 129–39.

Page 255. Castrating the judiciary: Direct quote from James Ross, et al., *Malaysia: Assault on the Judiciary*, 1989, p. 82. See also four excellent articles by Suhaini Aznam in the *Far Eastern Economic Review*: "The Tilt of Power," March 31, 1988; "Sending Off the Umpire," June 9, 1988; "Objections Overruled," July 21, 1988; and "Judgment Week," August 18, 1988. See also Bowring, *op. cit.*

Pages 255–56. United Engineers: See Stephen Duthie, "UMNO Regains Party Assets, Adds Holdings," *Asian Wall Street Journal*, July 26, 1989; Raphael Pura, "Malaysian's Daim Tied to Contract Award," *Asian Wall Street Journal*, May 31, 1988; and Raphael Pura and Stephen Duthie, "Malaysian Court Allows Highway Award," *Asian Wall Street Journal*, January 18, 1988. See also Bowring, *op. cit.*

Pages 256–57. Operation Lalang: See Diane Mauzy, "Decline of the 'Malay Way,' " pp. 218–20; Raphael Pura, "Two Detainees Freed in Malaysia Ask for Release of More Activists," *Asian Wall Street Journal*, and *Far Eastern Economic Review*: "The Language of Politics," October 29, 1987, and "Taming the Guerillas," November 12, 1987. See also Malaysia's *Federal Constitution*, 1989, Part XI, "Special Powers Against Subversion, Organized Violence, and Acts and Crimes Prejudicial to the Public and Emergency Powers," Sections 149–51, pp. 137–42.

Pages 257–58. Tornadoes: See Adam Raphael, "Kickbacks for UMNO Baru?" *The Observer*, reprinted in *The Rocket*, Vol. 22, No. 4, 1989, p. 2.

Page 259. Tan Koon Swan: See Suhaini Aznam, "Trapped in a Storm," *Far Eastern Economic Review*, February 6, 1986; "The Tan Shock," *Asiaweek*, February 2, 1986; and Raphael Pura and Stephen Duthie, "Tan Faces New Misery After Jail Release," *Asian Wall Street Journal*, December 28, 1987. For an excellent account of the background on Tan's intraparty struggle, see Ho Kin Chai, *Malaysian Chinese Association: Leadership Under Siege*, 1984.

Pages 259–60. UMNO and MPHB: See three related *Asian Wall Street Journal* articles for background: Stephen Duthie, "Takeover Offer Sparks Row in Malaysia," April 17, 1989; Raphael Pura and Stephen Duthie, "Malaysia's Quek Aims to Expand Empire," May 8, 1989; and Raphael Pura, "New Bidder Rolls Fight for Multi-Purpose," May 12, 1989.

Page 261. MOIC and Abdullah Ang: See John Berthelsen, "MOIC's Ruin Seen as Blow for Mahathir," *Asian Wall Street Journal*, August 29-30, 1986.

Page 261. Deposit-taking co-ops: See two *Asian Wall Street Journal* articles by Raphael Pura: "Malaysia's Daim Tied to Private Bank Deal," April 30, 1986, and "Receiver Sought for Cooperative," January 30, 1989. See also John Berthelsen, "Cooperatives' Suspension Jolts Malaysia," *Asian Wall Street Journal*, August 11, 1986.

Page 262. Makuwasa and EPF: See "Mystery State Firm Puzzles Malaysians," *Asian Wall Street Journal*, July 10, 1986.

Pages 262-63. Bank Bumiputra scandal: See a series of articles from the *Far Eastern Economic Review* beginning with K. Das, "The Embattled Bank," August 4, 1983; James Clad, "The Buck Stops Here," September 27, 1984; Lincoln Kaye, "Reaping the Whirlwind," December 20, 1984; and Suhaini Aznam, "A Rough Ride Ahead," January 2, 1986. Ranjit Gill's summary of the Hong Kong chicanery called *The Carrian Saga*, 1985, is a convenient source for those interested in further detail. See also Syed Hussein Alatas, *The Problem of Corruption*, 1986, pp. 113-22.

Pages 263-64. Cornering the tin market: See Raphael Pura, "Malaysia Plan to Control Tin Led to Disaster," *Asian Wall Street Journal*, September 22, 1986.

Pages 264-65. Personal interview with Ahmad Noordin Zakaria, Petaling Jaya, August 10, 1989.

Pages 266-67. Personal interview with Raphael Pura, Kuala Lumpur, August 7, 1989.

Page 267. Personal interview with Datuk Musa Hitam, Kuala Lumpur, August 11, 1989.

Page 268. Fisherman quote from Fan Yew Teng, *The UMNO Drama: Power Struggles in Malaysia*, 1989, p. 8.

Page 269. Personal interview with Tun Hussein Onn, Kuala Lumpur, August 14, 1989.

Page 270. Personal interview with S. Subramaniam, Kuala Lumpur, August 8, 1989.

Page 271. Personal interview with Datuk Leo Moggie, Kuala Lumpur, August 10, 1989.

Pages 271-72. Personal interview with Lee Lam Thye, Kuala Lumpur, August 15, 1989. A collection of Lim Kit Siang's earlier speeches was published by the DAP under the title *Time Bombs in Malaysia*, 1978.

Pages 272-73. Personal interview with Dr. Goh Cheng Teik, Kuala Lumpur, August 14, 1989. His *Racial Politics in Malaysia* was published in early 1989.

Pages 273-74. Personal interview with Param Cumaraswamy, Kuala Lumpur, August 15, 1989.

Page 275. Defense spending: see International Institute for Strategic Studies, *The Military Balance, 1988-1989*, pp. 170-71, and Kusuma Snitwongse and Sukhumbhand Paribatra, eds., *Durable Stability in Southeast Asia*, 1987, pp. 143-45, 310-11.

Page 276. Direct quote from Zakaria Haji Ahmad, "Malaysian Foreign Policy and Domestic Politics: Looking Outward and Moving Inward?", draft monograph, undated (1989), pp. 7, 10.

Page 276. Personal interview with Noordin Sopiee, Kuala Lumpur, August 10, 1989.

Page 277. U.S. relationship: see Office of the U.S. Trade Representative, *1989 National Trade Estimate Report on Foreign Trade Barriers*, pp. 125–27. Relations with Japan: See Gretchen Green, "Japan's Foreign Aid Policy: 1989 Update," pp. 8, 10, 12–13.

Page 278. Elections: See Steven Erlanger, "Malaysian Prime Minister Wins by Margin He Sought," *New York Times*, October 22, 1990.

Pages 279–80. Background on NIC status: see Tan Bok Huat, "Malaysia as a NIC?", draft monograph, Institute for Strategic and International Studies, Kuala Lumpur, August 1989. Tan measures Malaysia by the conventional statistical yardsticks and concludes that the country is on its way to achieving NIC status by virtue of its per-capita income, percentage of GNP in manufacturing, and industrial employment as a percentage of the total. That argument alone is both weak and unrigorous, but his political analysis reveals how blind Malaysians have become to the reality of Mahathir's cutthroat politics.

"The ability of leaders to harness the set of converging factors [i.e., economic growth, manufacturing, and manufacturing goods exports] and to counteract and reduce the strength of diverging forces [i.e., racism and Islam] is a crucial test. If they can achieve this, Malaysia can be a NIC before the year 2000. Malaysia is likely to graduate to NIC status during the period 1996–2000." (p. 35) That is one monstrous "if"; like fiction, it requires a temporary suspension of belief.

See also N. Balakrishnan, "Malaysia: The Next NIC," *Far Eastern Economic Review*, September 7, 1989, and various press clips from the *New Straits Times*, *Star*, and the Singapore *Straits Times* dated July 16, July 25, and August 6, 1989.

CHAPTER 5: IMPLICATIONS FOR U.S. FOREIGN AND ECONOMIC POLICY

Page 281. Opening quote from Paul Maidment, "The Yen Block: Together Under the Sun," *The Economist*, July 15, 1989.

Page 291. In this chapter various references to "East Asia" or "Asia-Pacific" as an economic grouping (or combined GNP) include a dozen nations: Japan, of course; China; Australia and New Zealand; the four original Little Dragons of Korea, Taiwan, Singapore and Hong Kong; and ASEAN (minus Singapore)—Indonesia, Thailand, Malaysia, and the Philippines. For political reasons (and for reasons related to the size and influence of their trade and investment flows across the Pacific), the United States and Canada must be included in any formal regional organization or association, but their GNPs are excluded from referenced "East Asia" or "Asia-Pacific" totals.

Page 297. More detailed implications of these trends were spelled out in my last book, *The End of the American Century*, 1990. William Pfaff analyzed these issues from a European perspective in *Barbarian Sentiments: How the American Century Ends*, 1989.

Page 301. Statistical references and background data are from Barbara Wanner, "Pacific Economic Cooperation: Washington's New Asian Strategy?", Japan Economic Institute *Report* No. 44A, November 17, 1989, pp. 3–7; Kent Calder, "Japan and the NICs", p. 31; a series of four excellent articles by Steven Jones in *Asian Wall Street Journal*: "Growth Slows, but Asia Still Sets the Pace," October 23, 1989; "Rise in Imports Is a Boon for Much of Asia," October 24, 1989; "Asia Living Standards to Continue Rising," October 26, 1989; and "Democracy Advances Unevenly in Asia," October 27–28, 1989; Kenji Dobashi, "Changes in Japanese Corporate Strategy," "Offshore Japanese Firms Exporting Back Home," JETRO *Monitor*, October 1989, p. 3; *Japan 1989: An International Comparison, op. cit.,* pp. 24, 26, 27, 30, 46, 76, 86, 92, 94; and several recent speeches of my own: "The U.S. and Japan in Indonesia: Sharpening Our Competitive Edge," Washington D.C., May 22, 1990; "New Strategies for the New Era," Princeton, April 29, 1990; "The New McCarthyism," Dallas, April 19, 1990; "Beyond 'Revisionism': Being Realistic About Japan," New York, April 11, 1990; "Asia's New Little Dragons," Madison, Wisconsin, March 30, 1990; "Beyond the Cold War: Being Realistic About Japan," St. Louis, March 27, 1990; "The U.S. and Japan: Unhappy Marriage or Inevitable Divorce?", Princeton, March 1, 1990: "Beyond the Cold War: Coping with Japan," Chicago, February 12, 1990; "America's New Manufacturing Strategies in East Asia," Boca Raton, February 10, 1990; "Looking Back from the Year 2001: Reflections on the New Century," Grand Rapids, November 28, 1989; "Globalization of Research and Development: Heightened Competition in an Era of Interdependence," Princeton, October 31, 1989; and "The Hundred Years' War," Orlando, Florida, November 17, 1987. Japan quote on p. 297 from the *New York Times*, February 10, 1991.

Page 303. Drucker quote from Peter Drucker, *The New Realities*, 1989, p. 59.

Page 303. Drucker quote: *Ibid.,* p. 16.

Page 304. Quote from Staffan Burenstam Linder, *The Pacific Century: Economic and Political Consequences of Asian-Pacific Dynamism*, 1986, p. 118.

Page 304. Gilder quote from George Gilder, *Microcosm: The Quantum Revolution in Economics and Technology*, 1990, p. 378.

Page 305. Gilder quote: *Ibid.,* p. 369. See especially chapters 17 ("The New Balance of Power," pp. 220–32), 24 ("The New American Challenge," pp. 319–30), and 27 ("The Eclipse of Geopolitics," pp. 353–70). Gilder's new book and Drucker's *The New Realities* are two of the best guidebooks to the emerging information age.

Page 309. Lindsey quote from Lawrence B. Lindsey, *The Growth Experiment*, 1990, p. 236.

Page 309. Closing quote from George Gilder, *op. cit.,* p. 370.

BIBLIOGRAPHY

BOOKS

Ahmed, Sadiq. *Indonesia: Strategy for Growth and Structural Change*. Washington, D.C.: The World Bank, 1989.

Akamatsu, Chu, et al., eds. *Thai Koku Keizai Kankyo, 1986-87 (The Economic Environment in Thailand, 1986–87)*. Bangkok: Japanese Chamber of Commerce, 1987.

Anderson, Benedict R. O'G. *American Values and Research on Indonesia*. Unpublished monograph presented at the annual meeting of the Association for Asian Studies, March 1971.

Anderson, Benedict R. O'G., and Ruchira Mendiones, eds. *In the Mirror*. Bangkok: Editions Duang Kamol, 1985.

Anderson, Benedict R. O'G. *Mythology and the Tolerance of the Javanese*. Ithaca, NY: Cornell University, Southeast Asia Program, 1974.

Anderson, Benedict R. O'G. *Notes on Indonesian Political Communication*. Cambridge, MA: Massachusetts Institute of Technology, Center for International Studies, 1974.

Anon. *Who's Who in Indonesia*, 2nd ed. Jakarta: Gunung Agung, Ltd., 1980.

Arbhabhirama, Anat, et al. *Thai-Japan Economic Conflicts*. Bangkok: Thailand Development Research Institute, 1986.

Arief, Sritua. *Foreign Capital, Foreign Debt Burden, and the Indonesian Economy*. Jakarta: Institute for Development Studies, 1987.

Asia Foundation. *1987 Annual Report*.

Badan Koordinasi Penamaman Modal (BKPM). *Indonesia: A Guide for Investors*. Jakarta: BKPM, 1986.

Bandhyopadhyaya, Kalyani. *Burma and Indonesia: Comparative Political Economy and Foreign Policy*. New Delhi: South Asian Publishers, 1983.

Bank Indonesia. *1987–88 Report*. Jakarta: Bank Indonesia, 1988.

Bank Negara Malaysia. *1988 Annual Report*. Kuala Lumpur: Bank Negara Malaysia, 1989.

Bank Negara Malaysia. *Money and Banking in Malaysia*. Kuala Lumpur: Bank Negara Malaysia, 1989.

339

Bank of Thailand. *Annual Economic Report*, 1988. Bangkok: Bank of Thailand, Department of Economic Research, 1989.

Benda, Harry J. *The Crescent and the Rising Sun: Indonesian Islam Under the Japanese Occupation, 1942–45.* Dordrecht, Netherlands: Foris Publications Holland, 1983.

Benda, Harry J. *Japanese Military Administration in Indonesia.* New Haven, CT: Yale University, Southeast Asia Studies, 1965.

Biro Pusat Statistik. *Report on Modelling: The Indonesian Social Accounting Matrix, Static Disaggregated Model.* Jakarta: Central Bureau of Statistics, 1986.

Biro Pusat Statistik. *Statistik Indonesia 1988.* Jakarta: Central Bureau of Statistics, 1989.

BLC Publishing Co., Ltd. *Setting Up in Thailand: A Guide for Investors.* Bangkok: Amarin Printing Group, 1988.

Bunge, Frederica M., ed. *Indonesia: A Country Study.* Washington, D.C.: Government Printing Office, 1983.

Bunge, Frederica M., ed. *Malaysia: A Country Study.* Washington, D. C.: Government Printing Office, 1985.

Bunge, Frederica M., ed. *Thailand: A Country Study.* Washington, D.C.: Government Printing Office, 1981.

Buruma, Ian. *God's Dust: A Modern Asian Journey.* New York: Farrar, Straus, Giroux, 1989.

Calder, Kent E. *Crisis and Compensation.* Princeton, NJ: Princeton University Press, 1988.

Calder, Kent E., and Roy Hofheinz, Jr. *The Eastasia Edge.* New York: Basic Books, Inc., 1982.

Central Intelligence Agency. *World Factbook 1990.* Washington, D.C.: Government Printing Office, 1990.

Chin Kin Wah, ed. *Defense Spending in Southeast Asia.* Singapore: Institute of Southeast Asian Studies, 1987.

Chopra, V. D., ed. *Mikhail Gorbachev's New Thinking: Asia-Pacific, A Critical Assessment.* New Delhi: Continental Publishing House, 1988.

Clad, James. *Behind the Myth: Business, Money & Power in Southeast Asia.* London: Unwin, Hyman, 1989.

Clapham, Ronald. *Small and Medium Entrepreneurs in Southeast Asia.* Singapore: Institute of Southeast Asian Studies, 1985.

Clapham, Christopher. *Third World Politics: An Introduction.* Madison, WI: University of Wisconsin Press, 1985.

Cline, Ray S. *U.S.–ASEAN Relations: Prospects for the 1990s.* Kuala Lumpur: Institute for Strategic and International Studies (ISIS) Conference Report, 1987.

Coedès, G. *The Making of South East Asia.* Berkeley, CA: University of California Press, 1966.

Crouch, Harold. *The Army and Politics in Indonesia.* Rev. ed. Ithaca, NY: Cornell University Press, 1988.

deJonge, Nico, et al., eds. *Indonesia in Focus.* Meppel, Netherlands: Edu'Actief Publishing Company, 1988.

Denison, Edward F., and William K. Chung. *How Japan's Economy Grew So Fast.* Washington, D.C.: The Brookings Institution, 1976.

Department of Information, Republic of Indonesia. *The 1945 Constitution and the Republic of Indonesia.* Jakarta: Government of Indonesia, 1980.

Deshpande, Jayashri. *Indonesia: The Impossible Dream.* New Delhi: Prachi Prakashan, 1981.

Deyo, Frederic C., ed. *The Political Economy of the New Asian Industrialism.* Ithaca, NY: Cornell University Press, 1987.

Dhiravegin, Likhit. *ASEAN and the Major Powers: Today and Tomorrow.* Bangkok: Thammasat University, Political Science Research Center, 1984.

Dhiravegin, Likhit. *Nationalism and the State in Thailand.* Bangkok: Thammasat University, Political Science Research Center, 1985.

Dhiravegin, Likhit. *Social Change and Contemporary Thai Politics.* Bangkok: Thammasat University, Political Science Research Center, 1984.

Dhiravegin, Likhit. *Thai Politics: Selected Aspects of Development and Change.* Bangkok: Tri-Sciences Publishing House, 1985.

Djiwandono, J. Soedjati, and Yong Mun Cheong, eds. *Soldiers and Stability in Southeast Asia.* Singapore: Institute of Southeast Asian Studies, 1988.

Drake, Christine. *National Integration in Indonesia: Patterns and Policies.* Honolulu: University of Hawaii Press, 1989.

Drucker, Peter. *The New Realities.* New York: Harper & Row, 1989.

Duangtip Somnapan Surintatip. *Thai Proverbs and Sayings.* Bangkok: National Identity Board, 1985.

Economist Intelligence Unit. *Country Report: Indonesia 1989.* London: The Economist, 1989.

Economist Intelligence Unit. *Country Report: Malaysia/Brunei 1989.* London: The Economist, 1989.

Economist Intelligence Unit. *Country Report: Thailand/Burma 1989.* London: The Economist, 1989.

Economist Intelligence Unit. *Indonesia.* London: Business International, 1989.

Economist Intelligence Unit. *Malaysia.* London: Business International, 1989.

Economist Intelligence Unit. *Thailand.* London: Business International, 1989.

Embassy of the United States of America. *Economic Trends Report: Malaysia.* Kuala Lumpur: U.S. Embassy, 1989.

Embassy of the United States of America. *Survey of American Investment in Malaysia.* Kuala Lumpur: U.S. Embassy, 1989.

Emmerson, Donald K. *Indonesia's Elite: Political Culture and Cultural Politics.* Ithaca, NY: Cornell University Press, 1976.

Fan Yew Teng. *The UMNO Drama: Power Struggles in Malaysia.* Kuala Lumpur: Egret Publications, 1989.

Far Eastern Economic Review. Asia Yearbook 1984. Hong Kong: Review Publishing Company, Ltd., 1984.

Far Eastern Economic Review. Asia Yearbook 1990. Hong Kong: Review Publishing Company, Ltd., 1990.

Far Eastern Economic Review. Asia Yearbook 1991. Hong Kong: Review Publishing Company, Ltd., 1991.

Friend, Theodore. *The Blue-Eyed Enemy: Japan Against the West in Java and Luzon, 1942–45.* Princeton, NJ: Princeton University Press, 1988.

Gamer, Robert E. *The Developing Nations: A Comparative Perspective.* Boston: Allyn & Bacon, Inc., 1976.

Geertz, Clifford. *Agricultural Involution: The Process of Ecological Change in Indonesia.* Berkeley, CA: University of California Press, 1971.

Geertz, Clifford. *The Development of the Javanese Economy: A Socio-Cultural Approach.* Cambridge, MA: Massachusetts Institute of Technology, Center for International Studies, 1956.

Geertz, Clifford. *The Interpretation of Cultures: Selected Essays.* London: Hutchinson, 1975.

Gilder, George. *Microcosm: The Quantum Revolution in Economics and Technology.* New York: Simon & Schuster, 1989.

Gilks, Anne. *China and the Arms Trade.* New York: St. Martin's Press, 1985.

Gill, Ranjit. *The Carrian Saga.* Kuala Lumpur: Pelanduk Publications, 1985.

Girling, John L. S. *Thailand: Society and Politics.* Ithaca, NY: Cornell University Press, 1981.

Goh Cheng Teik. *Racial Politics in Malaysia.* Kuala Lumpur: FEP International Sdn. Bhd., 1989.

Government of Singapore. *Singapore 1987.* Singapore: Ministry of Communications and Information, 1988.

Government of Thailand. *A Guide to Investing in Thailand.* Bangkok: Board of Investment (BOI), 1989.

Government of Thailand. *Statistical Handbook of Thailand: 1988.* Bangkok: National Statistical Office, 1989.

Gulrose, Karim, ed. *Information Malaysia: 1989 Yearbook.* Kuala Lumpur: Berita Publishing Sdn. Bhd., 1989.

Haji Ariffin Siri, ed. *Who's Who in Malaysia and Singapore.* 14th ed. Singapore: Taylor & Francis, 1983.

Harned, Joseph W., and Bruce R. Magid. *The Role of the Newly Industrializing Economies in the World Economy.* Washington, D.C.: The Atlantic Council, 1989.

Heng Pek Koon. *Chinese Politics in Malaysia.* Singapore: Oxford University Press, 1988.

Ho Kin Chai. *Malaysian Chinese Association: Leadership Under Siege.* Kuala Lumpur: Chee Leong Press, 1984.

Hobohm, Sarwar. *ASEAN in the 1990s.* London: Economist Intelligence Unit, Special Report No. 113, February 1989.

Holt, Claire, ed. *Culture and Politics in Indonesia.* Ithaca, NY: Cornell University Press, 1972.

Hornick, Robert N., and Mark A. Nelson. *Foreign Investment in Indonesia.* Handbook reprint by the *Fordham International Law Journal,* Vol. 11, No. 4, summer 1988.

Hoskin, John. *A Guide to Bangkok.* Bangkok: Asia Books, 1989.

Huntington, Samuel P. *Political Order in Changing Societies.* New Haven, CT: Yale University Press, 1968.

Huntington, Samuel P., and Clement H. Moore, eds. *Authoritarian Politics in Modern Society.* New York: Basic Books, Inc., 1970.

Huntington, Samuel P., and Joan M. Nelson. *No Easy Choice: Political Participation in Developing Countries*. Cambridge, MA: Harvard University Press, 1976.

Husain bin Ali, Syed. *The Malays: Their Problems and Future*. Kuala Lumpur: Heinemann Asia, 1981.

Ikuta, Shoichi. *Saikin no Thai no Boeki Keiko (Recent Trends in Thailand's Trade)*. Bangkok: Government of Japan, Ministry of International Trade and Industry, 1989.

Ikuta, Shoichi, et al. *Boeki Shijo Shiriizu: Thai (Foreign Trade Market Series: Thailand)*. Bangkok: Government of Japan, Ministry of International Trade and Industry, 1989.

Ikuta, Shoichi, et al., eds. *Thai Koku Keizai Gaikyo, 1988–89 (An Overview of the Thai Economy, 1988–89)*. Bangkok: Japanese Chamber of Commerce, 1989.

Indorf, Hans H. *Impediments to Regionalism in Southeast Asia: Bilateral Constraints Among ASEAN Member States*. Singapore: Institute of Southeast Asian Studies, 1984.

International Institute for Strategic Studies (ISIS). *The Military Balance, 1988–89*. London: ISIS, 1989.

Jackson, Karl D., and Lucian W. Pye. *Political Power and Communications in Indonesia*. Berkeley, CA: University of California Press, 1978.

Japan External Trade Organization (JETRO). *List of Japanese Investment Projects in Indonesia*. Jakarta: JETRO, 1988.

Japan External Trade Organization (JETRO). *Mareeshia Keizai, Boeki Hokuku (Report on Malaysia's Economy and Foreign Trade)*. Kuala Lumpur: JETRO, 1989.

Japan Institute for Social and Economic Affairs. *Japan 1989: An International Comparison*. 2nd ed. Tokyo: Keizai Koho Center (Keidanren), 1990.

Japan Trade Association. *Substantive Analysis of Japanese Manufacturing [Industries] in the Five ASEAN Countries*. Tokyo: Overseas Economic News Center, 1988.

Japanese Chamber of Trade and Industry of Malaysia (JACTIM). *Mareeshia Handobuku: 1989 (Malaysia Handbook: 1989)*. Kuala Lumpur: JACTIM, 1989.

Jenkins, David. *Suharto and His Generals: Indonesian Military Politics, 1975–83*. Ithaca, NY: Cornell University Press, 1984.

Jeshurun, Chandran, ed. *Government and Rebellions in Southeast Asia*. Singapore: Institute of Southeast Asian Studies, 1985.

Johardin, H., ed. *Indonesia: 1989*. Jakarta: Republic of Indonesia, Department of Information, 1989.

Johnson, Chalmers. *MITI and the Japanese Miracle*. Stanford, CA: Stanford University Press, 1982.

Jones, Howard Palfrey. *Indonesia: The Possible Dream*. Singapore: Gunung Agung (S) Pte. Ltd., 1971.

Kahin, George McTurnan. *Nationalism and Revolution in Indonesia*. Ithaca, NY: Cornell University Press, 1952.

Kahin, George McTurnan. *The Political Position of the Chinese in Indonesia*. Stanford, CA: Stanford University, master's thesis, 1946.   —

Kamil Salih. *The Malaysian Economy in the 1990s: Alternative Scenarios*. Kuala Lumpur: Malaysian Economic Association, 1989.

Kamal Salih. *The New Economic Policy after 1990*. Kuala Lumpur: Malaysian Institute for Economic Research, 1988.

Kamal Salih and Zainal Anzam Yusof. *Overview of the New Economic Policy and Framework for the Post-1990 Economic Policy.* Kuala Lumpur: Malaysian Institute for Economic Research, 1989.

Kessler, Richard, ed. *The Role of the Newly Industrializing Economies in the World Economy.* Washington, D.C.: Atlantic Council Policy Working Group, 1989.

Kindleberger, Charles P. *The 1930s and the 1980s: Parallels and Differences.* Singapore: Institute of Southeast Asian Studies, 1989.

Koh Boon Hwee, et al., eds. *Singapore 1987.* Singapore: Ministry of Communications and Information, 1987.

Kritayakirana, Kopr, et al. *The Science and Technology Manpower Situation in Thailand: An Analysis of Supply and Demand Issues.* Bangkok: Thailand Development Research Institute (TDRI), 1988.

Kua Kit Soong, ed. *National Culture and Democracy.* Kuala Lumpur: Kersani Penerbit-penerbit Sdn. Bhd., 1985.

Landon, Margaret. *Anna and the King of Siam.* New York: The John Day Company, 1943.

Lazard Frères et Cie, et al. *The Republic of Indonesia.* Information prospectus prepared as background for investor interest in Indonesia, July 1988.

Lee Yong Leng. *The Razor's Edge: Boundaries and Boundary Disputes in Southeast Asia.* Singapore: Institute of Southeast Asian Studies, 1980.

Legal Research Board. *Federal Constitution* [of Malaysia]. Kuala Lumpur: International Law Book Services, 1989.

Leifer, Michael. *Indonesia's Foreign Policy.* London: Unwin, Hyman, 1983.

Liddle, R. William. *Culture and Class Politics in New Order Indonesia.* Singapore: Institute of Southeast Asian Studies, 1977.

Liddle, R. William, ed. *Political Participation in Modern Indonesia.* New Haven, CT: Yale University Monograph Series, 1973.

Liddle, R. William. *Power, Participation, and the Political Parties in Indonesia.* Cambridge, MA: Massachusetts Institute of Technology, Center for International Studies, 1974.

Liem Yoe-Sioe. *Die Ethnische Minderheit der Überseechinesen im Entwicklungsprozess Indonesiens (The Ethnic Minority of the Overseas Chinese in the Developmental Process of Indonesia).* Frankfurt: Breitenbach, 1980.

Lim Kit Siang. *Time Bombs in Malaysia.* Kuala Lumpur: Democratic Action Party, 1979.

Linder, Staffan Burenstam. *The Pacific Century: Economic and Political Consequences of Asian-Pacific Dynamism.* Stanford, CA: Stanford University Press, 1986.

Lindsey, Lawrence B. *The Growth Experiment.* New York: Basic Books, 1990.

Lubis, Mochtar. *Twilight in Jakarta.* Singapore: Oxford University Press, 1968.

Mackie, J. A. C., ed. *The Chinese in Indonesia.* Honolulu: University of Hawaii Press, 1976.

Mackie, J. A. C. *Konfrontasi: The Indonesia-Malaysia Dispute, 1963–1966.* Kuala Lumpur: Oxford University Press, 1974.

Mahathir, Mohamad. *The Challenge.* Kuala Lumpur: Pelanduk Publications, 1986.

Mahathir, Mohamad. *The Malay Dilemma.* Singapore: Asia Pacific Press, 1970.

Martin, Patricia, ed. *Indonesia–U.S. Relations: Opportunities, Obstacles, Options.* Jakarta: Center for Strategic and International Studies (CSIS), 1987.

May, Brian. *The Indonesian Tragedy*. Singapore: Graham Brash (Pte.) Ltd., 1978.

McDonald, Hamish. *Suharto's Indonesia*. Sydney: Fontana/Collins, 1980.

McKinlay, Robert O. *Aid and Arms to the Third World:. An Analysis of the Distribution and Impact of U.S. Official Transfers*. Singapore: Institute of Southeast Asian Studies, 1984.

Mehmet, Ozay. *Development in Malaysia: Poverty, Wealth, and Trusteeship*. Kuala Lumpur: Institute of Social Analysis, 1988.

Milne, Robert S. *Politics in Ethnically Bipolar States*. Vancouver, BC: University of British Columbia Press, 1981.

Milne, Robert S., and Diane K. Mauzy. *Malaysia: Tradition, Modernity, and Islam*. Boulder, CO: Westview Press, 1986.

Milne, Robert S., and Diane K. Mauzy. *Politics and Government in Malaysia*. Singapore: Federal Publications, 1978.

Milner, A. C. *Kerajaan: Malay Political Culture on the Eve of Colonial Rule*. Tucson, AZ: University of Arizona Press, 1982.

Ministry of Finance, Malaysia. *Economic Report, 1988–89*. Kuala Lumpur: National Printing Department, 1989.

Mitsubishi Motors Corporation. *Nashionaru Kaa Purojekuto "Puroton Saga" (National Car Project: "Proton Saga")*. Tokyo: MMC, 1988.

Mohd. Taib Osman, ed. *Malaysian World View*. Singapore: Institute of Southeast Asian Studies, 1985.

Mulder, Niels. *Everyday Life in Thailand: An Interpretation*. Bangkok: Editions Duang Kamol, 1979.

Mulder, Niels. *Individual and Society in Contemporary Thailand and Java*. Bielefeld, Germany: University of Bielefeld, 1981.

Mulder, Niels. *Java-Thailand: A Comparative Perspective*. Yogyakarta, Gadjah Mada University Press, 1983.

Mulder, Niels. *Mysticism and Everyday Life in Contemporary Java: Cultural Persistence and Change*. Singapore: Singapore University Press, 1980.

Murray, Charles. *In Pursuit of Happiness and Good Government*. New York: Simon & Schuster, 1988.

Naipul, V. S. *Among the Believers: An Islamic Journey*. London: A. Deutsch, 1981.

Nasution, Anwar. *Structural Adjustment for Flexible Growth: The Case of Indonesia in the 1980s*. Tokyo: Economic Planning Agency of Japan, 1988.

National Science Board. *Science and Engineering Indicators: 1987*. Washington, D.C.: U.S. Government Printing Office, 1987.

Ng, C. Y., R. Hirono, and Narongchai Akrasanee, eds. *Effective Mechanisms for the Enforcement of Technology and Skills in ASEAN*. Singapore: Institute of Southeast Asian Studies, 1988.

Ng, C. Y., R. Hirono, and Narongchai Akrasanee, eds. *Industrial Restructuring and Adjustment for ASEAN-Japanese Investment and Trade Expansion*. Singapore: Institute of Southeast Asian Studies, 1988.

Ng, C. Y., R. Hirono, and Narongchai Akrasanee, eds. *Industrial Restructuring in ASEAN and Japan: An Overview*. Singapore: Institute of Southeast Asian Studies, 1988.

Ng, C. Y., R. Hirono, and Robert Y. Siy, Jr., eds. *Technology and Skills in ASEAN: An Overview*. Singapore: Institute of Southeast Asian Studies, 1988.

Noer, Asril. *The Agglomeration of Manufacturing Industries in Indonesia's Largest Cities*. Ann Arbor, MI: University Microfilms International, 1987.

Nono Anwar Makarim. *The Indonesian Press: An Editor's Perspective*. Cambridge, MA: Massachusetts Institute of Technology, Center for International Studies, 1974.

Office of the United States Trade Representative (USTR). *1989 National Trade Estimate Report on Foreign Trade Barriers*. Washington, D.C.: USTR, 1989.

Ohkawa, Kazushi, and Henry Rosovsky. *Japanese Economic Growth: Trend Acceleration in the 20th Century*. Stanford, CA: Stanford University Press, 1973.

Orentlicher, Diane F. *Human Rights in Indonesia and East Timor*. Washington, D.C.: Asia Watch, 1988.

Ozawa, H., et al. *Malaysia Economic and Trade Report*. Kuala Lumpur: Japan External Trade Organization (JETRO), 1989.

P. T. Gemala Kempa Daya. *1988 Annual Report*.

P. T. Surya Toto. *1988 Annual Report*.

P. T. Unitex. *1988 Annual Report*.

P. T. Yuasa Battery. *1988 Annual Report*.

Palmier, Leslie. *Understanding Indonesia*. London: Gower Publishing Co., Ltd., 1985.

Pfaff, William. *Barbarian Sentiments: How the American Century Ends*. New York: Hill and Wang, 1989.

Phipatseritham, Krirkkiat, and Kunio Yoshihara. *Business Groups in Thailand*. Singapore: Institute of Southeast Asian Studies, 1983.

Potter, Sulamith Heins. *Family Life in a Northern Thai Village*. Berkeley, CA: University of California Press, 1977.

Prime Minister's Department. *Mid-Term Review of the Fifth Malaysia Plan, 1986–1990*. Kuala Lumpur: National Printing Department, 1989.

Prizzia, Ross. *Thailand in Transition*. Honolulu: University of Hawaii Press, 1985.

Purcell, Randall B., ed. *The Newly Industrializing Countries in the World Economy*. Boulder, CO: Lynne Rienner Publishers, 1989.

Rajendra, Cecil. *Bones and Feathers*. Kuala Lumpur: Heinemann Asia, 1982.

Ramsay, Ansil, and Wiwat Mungkandi. *Thailand–U.S. Relations: Changing Political, Strategic, and Economic Factors*. Berkeley, CA: University of California, Institute of East Asian Studies, 1988.

Reid, Anthony, ed. *The Japanese Experience in Indonesia*. Miami, OH: Ohio University, Center for Southeast Asian Studies, 1986.

Riggs, Fred Warren. *Thailand: The Modernization of a Bureaucratic Polity*. Honolulu: East-West Center Press, 1967.

Roeder, O. G. *The Smiling General: President Soeharto of Indonesia*. Jakarta: Gunung Agung Ltd., 1970.

Roeder, O. G., and Mahiddin Mahmud. *Who's Who in Indonesia*. Singapore: Gunung Agung, Ltd., 1980.

Roff, William R., ed. *Islam and the Political Economy of Meaning*. London: Croom, Helm, 1987.

Roff, William R. *The Origins of Malay Nationalism*. New Haven, CT: Yale University Press, 1967.

Ross, James, and George Schenck, et al. *Malaysia: Assault on the Judiciary*. New York: U.S. Lawyers' Committee for Human Rights, 1989.

Schlossstein, Steven. *The End of the American Century.* New York: Congdon & Weed, 1990.

Schlossstein, Steven. *Trade War: Greed, Power, and Industrial Policy on Opposite Sides of the Pacific.* New York: Congdon & Weed, 1984.

Scott, James C. *Weapons of the Weak: Everyday Forms of Peasant Resistance.* New Haven, CT: Yale University Press, 1985.

Securities Exchange of Thailand. *Securities Market in Thailand: 1989.* Bangkok: Securities Exchange of Thailand, 1989.

Shaplen, Robert. *Time Out of Hand: Revolution and Reaction in Southeast Asia.* New York: Harper and Row, 1969.

Shaplen, Robert. *A Turning Wheel.* New York: Random House, 1979.

Simon, Sheldon W. *The Future of Asia-Pacific Security Collaboration.* Lexington, MA: Lexington Books, 1988.

Siwaraksa, Sulak. *Siam in Crisis.* Bangkok: Komol Keemthong Foundation, 1980.

Siwaraksa, Sulak. *Siamese Resurgence.* Bangkok: Asian Cultural Forum on Development, 1985.

Sjahrir. *Basic Needs in Indonesia: Economics, Politics, and Public Policy.* Singapore: Institute of Southeast Asian Studies, 1986.

Snitwongse, Kusama, and Sukhumband Paribatra, eds. *Durable Stability in Southeast Asia.* Singapore: Institute of Southeast Asian Studies, 1987.

Steinberg, David Joel. *In Search of Southeast Asia.* Honolulu: University of Hawaii Press, 1987.

Sternstein, Larry. *Portrait of Bangkok.* Bangkok: Bangkok Metropolitan Administration, 1982.

Sudham, Pira. *Monsoon Country.* Bangkok: Shire Books, 1988.

Sudham, Pira. *People of Esarn.* Bangkok: Shire Books, 1987.

Suksamran, Somboon. *Buddhism and Politics in Thailand.* Singapore: Institute of Southeast Asian Studies, 1982.

Sumantoro. *MNCs and the Host Country: The Indonesian Case.* Singapore: Institute of Southeast Asian Studies, 1984.

Sundhaussen, Ulf. *The Road to Power: Indonesian Military Politics, 1945–67.* Kuala Lumpur: Oxford University Press, 1982.

Suryadinata, Leo. *Eminent Indonesian Chinese: Biographical Sketches.* Singapore: Gunung Agung, Ltd., 1981.

Suryadinata, Leo. *Pribumi Indonesians, the Chinese Minority, and China.* Singapore: Institute of Southeast Asian Studies, 1978.

Syed Hussein Alatas. *The Problem of Corruption.* Singapore: Times Books International, 1986.

Szende, Andrew. *From Torrent to Trickle: Managing the Flow of News in Southeast Asia.* Singapore: Institute of Southeast Asian Studies, 1986.

Tan, S. H. *Malaysian Potpourri.* Kuala Lumpur: Aspatra Quest, 1984.

Tan Loong Hoe and Narongchai Akrasanee, eds. *ASEAN–U.S. Economic Relations: Changes in the Economic Environment and Opportunities.* Singapore: Institute of Southeast Asian Studies, 1988.

Tangsubkul, Phipat. *ASEAN and the Law of the Sea.* Singapore: Institute of Southeast Asian Studies, 1982.

Tempo. *Apa & Siapa Sejumlah Orang Indonesia: 1983–1984 (Who's Who in Indonesia: 1983–1984).* Jakarta: *Tempo* magazine, 1984.

Tengku Mohd. Azzman Shariffadeen. *Microelectronics, Information Technology, and Society.* Kuala Lumpur: Malaysian Institute of Microelectronics (MIMOS), 1989.

Thailand Development Research Institute (TDRI). *1988 Annual Report.* Bangkok: TDRI, 1989.

Thailand Development Research Institute (TDRI). *The S&T Manpower Situation in Thailand: An Analysis of Supply and Demand Issues.* Bangkok: TDRI, 1988.

Thanamai, Patcharee. *Patterns of Industrial Policymaking in Thailand: Japanese Multinationals and Domestic Actors in the Automobile and Electrical Applicance Industries.* Madison, WI: University of Wisconsin, doctoral dissertation, 1985.

Thanamai, Patcharee, and Yos Santasombat. *A Survey of Development Policies and Strategies Implemented in Thailand, 1977-1987.* Bangkok: Thammasat University, Thai Khadi Research Institute, 1987.

Thoolen, Hans. *Indonesia and the Rule of Law: Twenty Years of "New Order" Government.* London: Frances Pinter (Publishers), 1987.

Tilman, Robert O. *The Enemy Beyond: External Threat Perceptions in the ASEAN Region.* Singapore: Institute of Southeast Asian Studies, 1984.

Unakul, Snoh. *Social Indicators, Thailand: 1986.* Bangkok: Development Studies and Information Division, Office of the National Economic and Social Development Board (NESDB), 1988.

Unakul, Snoh. *Thailand's Development Strategies.* Bangkok: Development Studies and Information Division, Office of the National Economic and Social Development Board (NESDB), 1988.

U.S. Lawyers' Committee for Human Rights. *Worker Rights Under the U.S. Trade Laws.* New York: Lawyers' Committee for Human Rights, 1988. Project Series, No. 2, 1989.

Vogel, Ezra F. *Japan as Number One: Revisited.* Singapore: Institute of Southeast Asian Studies, 1986.

von Vorys, Karl. *Democracy Without Consensus: Communalism and Political Stability in Malaysia.* Princeton, NJ: Princeton University Press, 1975.

Ward, Robert Spencer. *Asia for the Asiatics: The Techniques of Japanese Occupation.* Chicago: University of Chicago Press, 1945.

Weatherbee, Donald. *Southeast Asia Divided: The ASEAN-Indochina Crisis.* Boulder, CO: Westview Press, 1985.

Winstedt, Richard O. *A History of Malaya.* Kuala Lumpur: Marican & Sons (Malaysia) Ltd., 1968.

Winstedt, Richard O. *The Malays: A Cultural History.* Singapore: Graham Brash (Pte) Ltd., 1981.

World Bank. *Annual Report 1988.* Washington, D.C.: The World Bank, 1988.

World Bank. *Indonesia: Strategy for Growth and Structural Change.* Washington, D.C.: The World Bank, 1989.

World Bank. *World Development Report: 1988.* Washington, D.C.: The World Bank, 1989.

Wyatt, David K. *Thailand: A Short History.* New Haven, CT: Yale University Press, 1984.

Xuto, Somsakdi, ed. *Government and Politics of Thailand.* London: Oxford University Press, 1989.

Yenbumroong, Vanvalai. *Who's Who in Thailand: 1987.* Bangkok: D & S Bangkok Ltd., 1988.

Yoshihara, Kunio. *The Rise of Ersatz Capitalism in Southeast Asia.* Singapore: Oxford University Press, 1988.

Zach, Paul, and Mary Jane Edleson. *Jakarta.* Singapore: Times Editions, 1987.

ARTICLES

Two of the most dependable and most frequently cited sources of hard news in the East Asian region are the *Far Eastern Economic Review,* a weekly, and the *Asian Wall Street Journal,* published daily. Given the large number of citations from these two publications, they are identified simply by their abbreviations, *FEER* and *AWSJ* respectively.

Akrasanee, Narongchai. "Trade and Industry Reforms in Thailand: The Role of Policy Research." Thailand Development Research Institute *Quarterly Newsletter,* June 1989.

Anderson, Benedict R. O'G. "The Idea of Power in Javanese Culture." In Claire Holt, ed., *Culture and Politics in Indonesia.* Ithaca, NY: Cornell University Press, 1974.

Anderson, Benedict R. O'G. "Perspective and Method in American Research on Indonesia." In Benedict Anderson and Audrey Kahin, eds., *Interpreting Indonesian Politics: Thirteen Contributions to the Debate.* Ithaca, NY: Cornell University Southeast Asia Program, Modern Indonesia Project, 1982.

Andrews, John. "Indonesia: The Extended Family." *The Economist,* August 15, 1987.

Anon. "Japan's Link in Tropical Forest Destruction." *The Nation* (Bangkok), June 21, 1989.

Anon. "Mystery State Firm Puzzles Malaysians." *AWSJ,* July 10, 1986.

Anon. "Not So Tolerant." *The Economist,* July 1, 1989.

Anon. "Notes and Comment." *The New Yorker,* July 2, 1990.

Anon. "Occasion for Introspection." *Jakarta Post* editorial, August 15, 1990.

Anon. "The October 14 Uprising Revisited." *The Nation* (Bangkok), June 28, 1989.

Anon. "Shadow of the Army." *The Economist,* August 12, 1989.

Anon. "The Tan Shock." *Asiaweek,* February 2, 1986.

Aznam, Suhaini. "The Gathering Storm." *FEER,* October 13, 1988.

Aznam, Suhaini. "Judgment Week." *FEER,* August 18, 1988.

Aznam, Suhaini. "The Language of Politics." *FEER,* October 29, 1987.

Aznam, Suhaini. "Mahathir's DileMMa." *FEER,* March 13, 1986.

Aznam, Suhaini. "Objections Overruled." *FEER,* July 21, 1988.

Aznam, Suhaini. "A Rough Ride Ahead." *FEER,* January 2, 1986.

Aznam, Suhaini. "Sending Off the Umpire." *FEER,* June 9, 1988.

Aznam, Suhaini. "Taming the Guerillas." *FEER,* November 12, 1987.

Aznam, Suhaini. "The Tilt of Power." *FEER,* March 31, 1988.

Aznam, Suhaini. "Trapped in a Storm." *FEER,* February 6, 1986.

Aznam, Suhaini, and Hamish McDonald. "Ethnic Economics." *FEER,* June 22, 1989.

Balakrishnan, N. "Malaysia: The Next NIC." *FEER*, September 7, 1989.

Bangkok Bank, Ltd. "Commercial Banks in Thailand, 1989." Economic Publications Section, Research Office, Bangkok Bank, Ltd., 1989.

Benda, Henry J. "Democracy in Indonesia." In Benedict Anderson and Audrey Kahin, eds., *Interpreting Indonesian Politics: Thirteen Contributions to the Debate.* Ithaca, NY: Cornell University Southeast Asia Program, Modern Indonesia Project, 1982.

Berthelsen, John. "Cooperatives' Suspension Jolts Malaysia." *AWSJ*, August 11, 1986.

Berthelsen, John. "MOIC's Ruin Seen as Blow for Mahathir." *AWSJ*, August 29–30, 1986.

Berthelsen, John. "A Sectarian Dispute Roils Thai Buddhism." *AWSJ*, August 21, 1989.

Bodden, Robert Clark. "Thailand." A presentation at the Asia-Pacific Business Outlook Conference, UCLA. Los Angeles, February 27–March 1, 1989.

Bonner, Ray. "The New Order." *The New Yorker*, June 6 (part I) and June 13 (part II), 1988.

Borsuk, Richard. "Jakarta's Steel Mill Rescue Sparks Debate." *AWSJ*, July 5, 1989.

Bowie, Alasdair. "The Business of Development in Malaysia: Business Associations and Industrial Policy Formulation: 1957–1989." Unpublished paper presented at the 1989 annual meeting of the Association for Asian Studies, Washington, D.C., March 17–19, 1989.

Bowring, Philip. "Power to the Center." *FEER*, April 14, 1988.

Broad, Robin, and John Cavanagh. "No More NICs." *FEER*, February 9, 1989.

Broad, Robin, and John Cavanagh. "No More NICs." *Foreign Policy*, Number 72, fall 1988, pp. 81–103.

Buszynski, Leszek. "New Aspirations and Old Constraints in Thailand's Foreign Policy." *Asian Survey*, November 1989.

Calder, Kent E. "Japan and the NICs: The Political Economy of Rising Interdependence." Paper presented at the Fifth U.S.–ASEAN Conference, Singapore, June 11–15, 1989.

Chandler, David. "The Khmer Rouge and Internal Politics in Kampuchea." Paper presented at the Sixth Regional Security Conference on International Security in Southeast Asia: Current Problems and Prospects for Resolution; organized jointly by the International Institute for Strategic Studies, London, and the Institute of Security and International Studies, Chulalongkorn University, Bangkok, July 4–6, 1989, at Chiang Mai, Thailand.

Chen, Edward K. Y. "The Economics and Non-Economics of Asia's Four Little Dragons." Speech delivered at the University of Hong Kong, January 26, 1988.

Chernichovsky, Dov, and Oey Astra Meesook. "School Enrollment in Indonesia." Washington, D.C.: World Bank, 1985.

Chittiwatanapong, Prasert. "Anti-Japanese Movements in Thailand." Paper presented at a symposium on Thai-Japanese relations, Thammasat University, Bangkok, January 15–16, 1987.

Chittiwatanapong, Prasert. "International Conflict and Japanese Decision-Making: Perspectives from Thailand." Paper presented at a conference at Dokkyo University, Japan, December 18–19, 1987.

Chittiwatanapong, Prasert. "Japan's Role in the Asia-Pacific Region: A Political Dimension." Paper presented at a conference on the Pacific century, Japan Institute of International Affairs, Tokyo, March 3–4, 1988.

Chittiwatanapong, Prasert. "The Problem of Japanese Official Development Assistance to Thailand: Impact on the Thai Construction Industry." Mimeo, December 1988.

Choate, Allen. "Private Enterprise in Development." Paper presented at a symposium on ASEAN–U.S. relations, Singapore, July 6–8, 1989.

Choonhavan, Chatichai. "Thailand in a Changing Southeast Asia." Keynote address presented at the Sixth Regional Security Conference on International Security in Southeast Asia, Chiangmai, Thailand, July 4–6, 1989.

Choy, Jon. "Research and Development in Japan: 1989 Update." *Japan Economic Institute*, Report No. 24-A, June 23, 1990.

Clad, James. "The Buck Stops Here." *FEER*, September 27, 1984.

Colquhoun, Keith. "At Bay: A Survey of Malaysia." *The Economist*, January 31, 1987.

Conboy, Kenneth J. "Dealing with U.S.–Thai Strains." The Heritage Foundation, *Backgrounder*, Number 98, May 3, 1989.

Crossette, Barbara. "King Bhumibol's Reign." *New York Times*, May 25, 1989.

Curtis, Gerald L. "America's Evolving Relationship with Japan and Its Implications for ASEAN." Paper presented at the Fifth U.S.–ASEAN Conference, Singapore, June 11–15, 1989.

Das, K. "The Embattled Bank." *FEER*, August 4, 1983.

Djalal, Hasjim. Unpublished paper presented at the Third Indonesia–U.S. Bilateral Conference, Bali, August 27–31, 1989.

Djiwandono, J. Soedjati. "ASEAN's Agenda for the Future." *Indonesian Quarterly*, Vol. XVII, No. 1, 1989.

Dobashi, Kenji. "Changes in Japanese Corporate Strategy: In Search of Real Globalization." Paper presented at the Euromoney Conference, Investing in Thailand, Bangkok, June 20–21, 1989.

Doherty, Eileen M. "Japan's Foreign Direct Investment in Developing Countries." *Japan Economic Institute*, Report No. 31A, August 11, 1989.

Donavanik, Preyaluk. "Infrastructure Shortage." Bangkok Bank *Monthly Review*, April 1989.

Doner, Richard F., and Ansil Ramsay. "Thailand as a Case of Flexible Strength." Unpublished paper presented at the annual meeting of the Association for Asian Studies, Washington, D.C., March 17–19, 1989.

Duthie, Stephen. "Takeover Offer Sparks Row in Malaysia," *AWSJ*, April 17, 1989.

Duthie, Stephen. "UMNO Regains Party Assets, Adds Holdings." *AWSJ*, July 26, 1989.

Duthie, Stephen, and Raphael Pura. "Battle for UMNO Faces Legal Quagmire." *AWSJ*, March 15, 1988.

Emmerson, Donald K. "Bureaucratic Alienation in Indonesia: The Director-General's Dilemma." In R. William Liddle, ed., *Political Participation in Modern Indonesia*. New Haven, CT: Yale University Monograph Series, 1973.

Emmerson, Donald K. "Does Indonesia Fit the Pacific-Asian Model of Economic Development?" Paper presented at Dynamism in Asia: Non-Economic Elements in Economic Development conference, Columbia, SC, February 11–13, 1987.

Emmerson, Donald K. "Indonesia in 1990." *Asian Survey*, February 1991.

Emmerson, Donald K. "Islam in Modern Indonesia." In Philip H. Stoddard, et al., *Change in the Muslim World*. Syracuse, NY: Syracuse University Press, 1981.

Emmerson, Donald K. "The Military and Development in Indonesia." In J. Soetdaji Djiwandono, *Soldiers and Stability in Southeast Asia*. Singapore: Singapore University Press, 1988.

Emmerson, Donald K. "Orders of Meaning: Understanding Political Change in a Fishing Community in Indonesia." In Benedict Anderson and Audrey Kahin, eds., *Interpreting Indonesian Politics: Thirteen Contributions to the Debate*. Ithaca, NY: Cornell University, Southeast Asia Program, Modern Indonesian Project, 1982.

Erlanger, Steven. "Ban on Journal Erodes Thais' Tolerant Image." *New York Times*, November 19, 1989.

Erlanger, Steven. "Malaysian Prime Minister Wins by Margin He Sought." *New York Times*, October 22, 1990.

Erlanger, Steven. "Oil Surge Disrupts Southeast Asian Economics." *New York Times*, November 15, 1990.

Erlanger, Steven. "Security and Political Aspects of Indonesia–U.S. Bilateral Relations." Unpublished paper presented at the Third Indonesia–U.S. Bilateral Conference, Bali, August 27–31, 1989.

Erlanger, Steven. "Thai Prime Minister Shakes Up His Cabinet." *New York Times*, August 28, 1990.

Feith, Herbert. "History, Theory, and Indonesian Politics: A Reply to Henry J. Benda." In Benedict Anderson and Audrey Kahin, eds., *Interpreting Indonesian Politics: Thirteen Contributions to the Debate*. Ithaca, NY: Cornell University, Southeast Asia Program, Modern Indonesia Project, 1982.

Feith, Herbert. "The Study of Indonesian Politics: A Survey and an Apologia." In Benedict Anderson and Audrey Kahin, eds., *Interpreting Indonesian Politics: Thirteen Contributions to the Debate*. Ithaca, NY: Cornell University, Southeast Asia Program, Modern Indonesia Project, 1982.

Fisher, Stephen H. "Malaysia." *Business Month*, September 1988.

Fuller, Bruce. "Raising School Quality in Developing Countries: What Investments Boost Learning?" Washington, D.C.: World Bank, 1986.

Geertz, Clifford. "Afterword: The Politics of Meaning." In Claire Holt, ed., *Culture and Politics in Indonesia*. Ithaca, NY: Cornell University Press, 1974.

Gillis, Malcolm. "Economic Growth in Indonesia: 1950–1980." Development Discussion Paper No. 146, Harvard Institute for International Development, Cambridge, MA, March 1983.

Goldstein, Carl. "Saga of Recovery." *FEER*, August 3, 1989.

Government of Malaysia. "Mid-Term Review of the Fifth Malaysia Plan, 1986–1990." Kuala Lumpur, Prime Minister's Department, July 1989.

Gray, John. "The End of History—or of Liberalism?" *National Review*, October 27, 1989.

Green, Gretchen. "Japan's Foreign Aid Policy: 1989 Update." Japan Economic Institute *Report*, No. 41A, October 27, 1989.

Habib, A. Hasnan. "Security and Political Aspects of U.S.-Indonesia Bilateral Relations." Unpublished paper presented at the Third Indonesia-U.S. Bilateral Conference, Bali, August 27-31, 1989.

Handley, Paul. "Back to Business." *FEER*, August 25, 1988.

Handley, Paul. "Eye of the Storm." *FEER*, November 23, 1989.

Handley, Paul. "The Lust Frontier." *FEER*, November 2, 1989.

Handley, Paul. "Thailand Hits the Wall." *FEER*, September 29, 1988.

Hein, Gordon R. "Indonesia in 1988: Another Five Years for Soeharto." *Asian Survey*, Vol. XXIX, No. 2, February 1989.

Hicks, George. "Explaining the Success of the Four Little Dragons: A Survey." Paper presented at the Convention of the East Asian Economic Association, Kyoto University, Kyoto, Japan, October 29-30, 1988.

Hindle, Tim. "Thailand: Tropical Balance." *The Economist*, October 31, 1987.

Horn, Robert C. "Southeast Asian Perceptions of U.S. Foreign Policy." *Asian Survey*, Vol. XXV, No. 6, June 1985.

Indorf, Hans H., and Ernest W. Porta, Jr. "ASEAN: The Association for Southeast Asian Nations After 20 Years." Asia Program, Woodrow Wilson Center for International Scholars, Washington, D.C., February 1988.

Jakarta Japan Club. "Saikin no Indoneshia no Keizai Kankyo" ("Indonesia's Recent Economic Environment"). Jakarta, Jakarta Japan Club, July 25, 1989.

Jayasankaran, S. "The New Economic Policy: Where Now?" *Malaysian Business*, August 1-15, 1989.

Jeshurun, Chandran. "Civil-Military Relations and National Security in ASEAN." Paper presented at a conference on political and military control in Asia, Seoul, Korea, August 4-7, 1989.

Jeshurun, Chandran. "Continuity and Change in the Political Development of ASEAN." *Indonesian Quarterly*, Vol. XVII, No. 1, 1989.

JETRO. "Offshore Japanese Firms Exporting Back Home." Japan External Trade Organization *Monitor*, October 1989.

Johnson, Chalmers. "The Problem of Japan in an Era of Structural Change." Speech delivered at an EC Ministerial Meeting in Brussels, Belgium, May 1989. Subsequently published as "Their Behavior, Our Problem," in *National Interest*, No. 17, fall 1989.

Jones, Steven. "Asia Living Standards to Continue Rising." *AWSJ*, October 26, 1989.

Jones, Steven. "Democracy Advances Unevenly in Asia." *AWSJ*, October 27-28, 1989.

Jones, Steven. "Growth Slows but Asia Still Sets the Pace." *AWSJ*, October 23, 1989.

Jones, Steven. "Rise in Imports Is a Boon for Much of Asia." *AWSJ*, October 24, 1989.

Jones, Steven. "Suharto's Kin Linked with Plastics Monopoly." *AWSJ*, November 25, 1986.

Jones, Steven, and Raphael Pura. "Soeharto-Linked Monopolies Hobble Economy." *AWSJ*, November 24, 1986.

Kahn, Joel S. "Ideology and Social Structure in Indonesia." In Benedict Anderson and Audrey Kahin, eds., *Interpreting Indonesian Politics: Thirteen Contributions to the Debate*. Ithaca, NY: Cornell University, Southeast Asia Program, Modern Indonesia Project, 1982.

Kassim, Ismail. "The Man Most Likely to Succeed," Singapore *Straits Times*, May 3, 1987.

Kavitanon, Sutaporn. "Foreign Investment Policy: Quality, Not Quantity." *Bangkok Post*, June 21, 1989.

Kaye, Lincoln. "Reaping the Whirlwind." *FEER*, December 20, 1984.

Klavymai na Ayudhya, Thongtor. "Profile of the Bangkok Metropolitan Administration." Bangkok: Department of Policy and Planning, Bangkok Metropolitan Administration, 1987.

Knapp, J. Burke, et al., eds. "Developing the Private Sector." Washington, D.C.: World Bank, 1989.

Ksemsan, Suwarnarat. "A City Slowly Drowning." *The Nation* (Bangkok), June 26, 1989.

Kuntjorojakti, Dorodjatun, et al. "Statement of Eight Indonesian Scholars and Writers." *Sinar Harapan*, January 25, 1972.

Lamsam, Banyong. "Bridging the Investment and Savings Gap." Speech delivered at the Euromoney conference, Thailand: Prospects for a Fast-Emerging Newly Industrializing Country. Bangkok, June 19–20, 1989.

Layman, Thomas. "The LDC Debt Problem, the Pacific Economic Cooperation Initiative, and Implications for Indonesia." Paper presented at the Third Indonesia–U.S. Bilateral Conference, Bali, August 27–31, 1989.

Leifer, Michael. "Cambodia Conflict: The Final Phase?" *Journal of Conflict Studies*, May 1989.

Lev, Daniel S. "Judicial Institutions and Legal Culture in Indonesia." In Benedict Anderson and Audrey Kahin, eds., *Interpreting Indonesian Politics: Thirteen Contributions to the Debate*. Ithaca, NY: Cornell University, Southeast Asia Program, Modern Indonesia Project, 1982.

Levine, David. "History and Social Structure in the Study of Contemporary Indonesia." In Benedict Anderson and Audrey Kahin, eds., *Interpreting Indonesian Politics: Thirteen Contributions to the Debate*. Ithaca, NY: Cornell University, Southeast Asia Program, Modern Indonesia Project, 1982.

Liddle, R. William. "Development or Democracy: An Indonesian Dilemma?" Paper presented at the Third Indonesia–U.S. Bilateral Conference, Bali, August 27–31, 1989.

Liddle, R. William. "Evolution from Above: National Leadership and Local Development in Indonesia." *Journal of Asian Studies*, Vol. XXXII, No. 2, February 1973.

Liddle, R. William. "Indonesia in 1987: The New Order at the Height of Its Power." *Asian Survey*, Vol. XXVIII, No. 2, 1988.

Liddle, R. William. "The 1977 Indonesian Elections and New Order Legitimacy." In *Southeast Asia 1978*. Singapore: Institute for Southeast Asian Studies, 1978.

Lim, Linda Y. C. "Financing Development into the 1990s: The Asian NICs and

ASEAN Countries." *Southeast Asian Business*, No. 16, winter–spring 1988.

Lim, Mah Hui. "Reflections on the Implementation and Consequences of the New Economic Policy (NEP)." Paper presented at the annual meeting of the Association for Asian Studies, Washington, D.C., March 17–19, 1989.

Lin See Yan. "Malaysia: Issues in Capital Market Development." Unpublished paper presented at a conference on the Malaysian economy after 1990, Kuala Lumpur, August 7–9, 1989.

Lin See Yan. "The Savings-Investment Gap: The Case of Malaysia." Paper prepared for Present and Future of the Pacific Basin Economy symposium, Tokyo, July 25–27, 1989.

Lyman, David. "Financial Law and the Foreign Investor in Thailand." Paper presented at the Euromoney conference, Investing in Thailand, June 20–21, 1989.

Mackie, Jamie. "Indonesia Since 1945: Problems of Interpretation." In Benedict Anderson and Audrey Kahin, eds., *Interpreting Indonesian Politics: Thirteen Contributions to the Debate*. Ithaca, NY: Cornell University, Southeast Asia Program, Modern Indonesia Project, 1982.

Maidment, Paul. "The Yen Block: Together Under the Sun." *The Economist*, June 15, 1989.

Malee, Traisawasdichai. "The Chao Phraya Needs Cleaning." *The Nation* (Bangkok), June 19, 1989.

Mangkusudondo, Suhadi. "Economic Aspects of Indonesia–U.S. Bilateral Relations: Prospects for Economic Growth and Trade Policy." Paper presented at the Third Indonesia–U.S. Bilateral Conference, Bali, August 27–31, 1989.

Martin, Richard. "Thai Rebel with a Buddhist Cause." *Insight*, August 21, 1989.

Mason, Edward S. "Corruption and Development." Development Discussion Paper No. 50, Harvard Institute for International Development, Cambridge, MA, December 1978.

Mauzy, Diane K. "Malaysia in 1987: Decline of the 'Malay Way.' " *Asian Survey*, Vol. XXVIII, No. 2, February 1988.

McBeth, John, and Paisal Sricharatchanya. "The Coup Mentality." *FEER*, November 28, 1985.

McVey, Ruth T. "The Beantenstaat in Indonesia." In Benedict Anderson and Audrey Kahin, eds., *Interpreting Indonesian Politics: Thirteen Contributions to the Debate*. Ithaca, NY: Cornell University, Southeast Asia Program, Modern Indonesia Project, 1982.

Moreau, Ron. "Cambodia: Asia's Next Flash Point." *Newsweek*, June 26, 1989.

Morris, Stephen J. "Thailand's Separate Peace in Indochina." *Wall Street Journal*, September 6, 1989.

Muecke, Marjorie A. "Mother Sold Food, Daughter Sells Her Body: Transformations in Thai Femininity." Paper presented at the annual meeting of the Association for Asian Studies, Washington, D.C., March 17–19, 1989.

Mulder, Niels. "A Comparative Note on the Thai and the Javanese Worldview as Expressed by Religious Practice and Belief." *Journal of the Siam Society*, Vol. LVIII, Part 2, July 1970.

Murray, Geoffrey. "Saving Asia's Sinking Cities." *Asia Technology*, Vol. 1., No. 1, October 1989.

Nasution, Anwar. "Structural Adjustment for Sustainable Growth: The Case of Indonesia in the 1980s." Paper presented at a conference, Structural Adjustment for Sustainable Growth in Asian Countries, Tokyo, November 7–8, 1988.

Nathan, K. S. "Malaysia in 1988: The Politics of Survival." *Asian Survey*, Vol. XXIX, No. 2, February 1989.

National Economic and Social Development Board (NESDB). "Resolution of the Council of Economic Ministers on Adjustment of the Sixth National Economic and Social Development Plan." Bangkok: NESDB, June 1989.

National Economic and Social Development Board (NESDB). "Selected Economic Indicators." Bangkok, NESDB, June 1989.

Neher, Clark D. "Thailand in 1987: Semi-Successful Semi-Democracy." *Asian Survey*, Vol. XXVIII, No. 2, February 1988.

Niksch, Larry A. "Thailand in 1988: The Economic Surge." *Asian Survey*, Vol. XXIX, No. 2, February 1989.

Ninomiya, Osamu. "Singapooru no Gaikyo" ("The Outlook for Singapore"). Singapore: Embassy of Japan, Internal Publication, January 1988.

Oetama, Jakob. "Socio-Cultural Aspects of Indonesia–U.S. Bilateral Relations: Education, Human Rights, and the Role of the Press." Paper presented at the Third Indonesia–U.S. Bilateral Conference, Bali, August 27–31, 1989.

Ogino, Akira. "The Importance of Capital Market Developments and Recycled Funds from Japan." Paper presented at the Euromoney conference, Investing in Thailand, Bangkok, June 20–21, 1989.

Overholt, William H. "Burma: Disintegration, Drugs, Democracy." Paper presented at the Sixth Regional Security Conference on International Security in Southeast Asia, Chiang Mai, Thailand, July 4–6, 1989.

Overholt, William H. "Burma: Disintegration or Revival?" Paper presented at the Sixth Regional Security Conference on International Security in Southeast Asia, Chiang Mai, Thailand, July 4–6, 1989.

Overholt, William H. "Thailand: A Moving Equilibrium." *The Pacific Review*, Vol. I, No. 1, 1988.

Ozay, Mehmet. "Malaysian Development Alternatives Beyond 1990." Paper presented at the annual meeting of the Association for Asian Studies, Washington, D.C., March 17–19, 1989.

Paribatra, M. R. Sukhumband. "Into the Third Decade: ASEAN and Issues of Peace and Security in Southeast Asia." *Indonesian Quarterly*, Vol. XVII, No. 1., 1989.

Piumsombun, Purachai. "Violent Crimes in Thailand: Trends, Characteristics, and Solutions." *Thai Journal of Development Administration*, Vol. 24, No. 2, April 1984.

Pongpisanupichit, Jeerasak. "Backward and Forward Linkages of Foreign Direct Investment." Paper presented at ASEAN–U.S. Economic Relations symposium, Singapore, July 6–8, 1989.

Prakorbpong, Panapool. "Heading Toward a Standstill." *The Nation* (Bangkok), June 19, 1989.

Pura, Raphael. "Malaysia Plan to Control Tin Led to Disaster." *AWSJ*, September 22, 1986.

Pura, Raphael. "Malaysia's Daim Tied to Private Bank Deal." *AWSJ*, April 30, 1986.

Pura, Raphael. "Malaysia's Daim Tied to Contract Award." *AWSJ*, May 31, 1988.

Pura, Raphael. "New Bidder Roils Fight for Multi-Purpose." *AWSJ*, May 12, 1989.

Pura, Raphael. "Receiver Sought for Cooperative." *AWSJ*, January 30, 1989.

Pura, Raphael. "Suharto Family Tied to Indonesian Oil Trade." *AWSJ*, November 26, 1986.

Pura, Raphael. "Two Detainees Freed in Malaysia Ask for Release of More Activists." *AWSJ*, June 6, 1988.

Pura, Raphael, and Stephen Duthie. "Mahathir Forced to Salvage State Firm." *AWSJ*, June 27, 1988.

Pura, Raphael, and Stephen Duthie. "Malaysian Court Allows Highway Award." *AWSJ*, January 18, 1988.

Pura, Raphael, and Stephen Duthie. "Malaysia's Quek Aims to Expand Empire." *AWSJ*, May 8, 1989.

Pura, Raphael, and Stephen Duthie. "Tan Faces New Misery After Jail Release." *AWSJ*, December 28, 1987.

Raphael, Adam. "Kickbacks for UMNO Baru?" *The Rocket*, Vol. 22, No. 4, 1989.

Rowley, Anthony. "Lull Before the Storm." *FEER*, December 19, 1985.

Sadli, Mohammad. "Perspective on Multilateral Issues: Trade, Third World Debt, and the Pacific Economic Cooperation Council." Paper presented at the Third Indonesian–U.S. Bilateral Conference, Bali, August 27–31, 1989.

Scalapino, Robert A. "Japan in Its International Role." Paper presented at the Fifth U.S.–ASEAN Conference, Singapore, June 11–16, 1989.

Schlossstein, Steven. "America's New Manufacturing Strategies for East Asia." Speech at the National Association of Manufacturers annual meeting, Boca Raton, FL, February 10, 1990.

Schlossstein, Steven. "Asia's New Little Dragons." Speech at the University of Wisconsin, Madison, WI, March 30, 1990.

Schlossstein, Steven. "Beyond 'Revisionism': Being Realistic About Japan." Speech at the Carnegie Council on Ethics and International Affairs, New York, April 11, 1990.

Schlossstein, Steven. "Beyond the Cold War: Being Realistic About Japan." Speech at the National Conference for Editorial Writers, Washington University, St. Louis, March 27, 1990.

Schlossstein, Steven. "Beyond the Cold War: Coping with Japan." Chicago Council on Foreign Relations, Chicago, February 12, 1990.

Schlossstein, Steven. "Globalization of Research and Development: Heightened Competition in an Era of Interdependence." Speech at the 1989 US–Japan R&D Management Forum, sponsored by the Japan Productivity Center and Princeton University's School of Engineering and Applied Science, Princeton, October 31, 1989.

Schlossstein, Steven. "The Hundred Years' War." Speech delivered at the 1987 annual meeting of the Construction Industry Manufacturers' Association, Orlando, FL, November 17, 1987.

Schlossstein, Steven. "Looking Back from the Year 2001: Reflections on the New

Century." Speech at the annual meeting of the Western Michigan Area Chamber of Commerce, Grand Rapids, MI, November 28, 1989.

Schlossstein, Steven. "The New McCarthyism." Speech for the Dallas Council on World Affairs, Dallas, April 19, 1990.

Schlossstein, Steven. "New Strategies for the New Era." Speech at the Nassau Club, Princeton, NJ, April 29, 1990.

Schlossstein, Steven. "The U.S. and Indonesia in Japan: Sharpening our Competitive Edge." Speech at a conference on Indonesia sponsored by Harvest International, Washingon, D.C., May 22, 1990.

Schlossstein, Steven. "The U.S. and Japan: Unhappy Marriage or Inevitable Divorce?" Speech at the Princeton Area Chamber of Commerce, Princeton, NJ, March 1, 1990.

Seaward, Nick. "The Daim Stewardship." FEER, September 1, 1988.

Scott, James C. "Corruption, Machine Politics, and Political Change." Southeast Asia Development Advisory Group Report No. 52, Asia Society, New York, December 6, 1968.

Sesser, Stan. "A Rich Country Gone Wrong." New Yorker, October 9, 1989.

Shiew Wan Shing. "The Manufacturing Sector: Malaysian Experience and Outlook." Paper presented at the Malaysian Economic Association Conference, Kuala Lumpur, August 7-9, 1989.

Simandjuntak, Djisman. "Instability of the Global Environment and ASEAN Economic Cooperation." Indonesian Quarterly, Vol. XVII, No. 1, 1989.

Simandjuntak, Djisman. "Promoting Investment: Institutional and Legal Infrastructures." Paper presented at a Symposium on ASEAN–U.S. Economic Relations, Singapore, July 6-8, 1989.

Smith, Charles. "Part Exchange." FEER, September 21, 1989.

Snitwongse, Kusama. "Trends in Southeast Asia: Towards Greater Stability?" Paper presented to the Sixth Regional Security Conference on International Security in Southeast Asia, Chiang Mai, Thailand, July 4-6, 1989.

Snodgrass, Donald R. "Summary Evaluation of Policies Used to Promote Bumiputra Participation in the Modern Sector in Malaysia." Development Discussion Paper No. 38, Harvard Institute for International Development, Cambridge, MA, February 1978.

Soesastro, M. Hadi. "A Brief Overview of the Indonesian Economy." Unpublished paper, Jakarta, July 1989.

Soesastro, M. Hadi. "The Emerging Pacific Regional Structure." Indonesian Quarterly, Vol. XVII, No. 1, 1989.

Soesastro, M. Hadi. "The Political Economy of Deregulation." Paper presented at the annual meeting of the Association for Asian Studies, Washington, D.C., March 17-19, 1989.

Sricharatchanya, Paisal. "Chinese in Thailand: Happy Together." FEER, February 18, 1988.

Sricharatchanya, Paisal. "Interest in a Conflict." FEER, March 10, 1988.

Sricharatchanya, Paisal. "The Jewels of the Crown." FEER, June 30, 1988.

Steinberg, David I. "Crisis in Burma: Stasis and Change in a Political Economy in Turmoil." Paper presented at the Sixth Regional Security Conference on International Security in Southeast Asia, Chiang Mai, Thailand, July 4-6, 1989.

Sterngold, James. "Japan Builds East Asia Links, Gaining Labor and Markets." *New York Times*, May 8, 1990.

Suchontan, Cimi. "Mechai Viravaidya: From Condom King to Deputy Minister." *World Executive's Digest*, February 1986.

Sumarlin, Johannes B. "The Indonesian Economy: Reform and Resurgence." Speech delivered by the finance minister, Republic of Indonesia, at a meeting of the Asia Society, New York, September 21, 1989.

Tan Bok Huat. "Malaysia as a NIC?" Unpublished paper prepared at the Institute for Strategic and International Studies (ISIS), Kuala Lumpur, August 1989.

Tan Keok Yin. "Federation of Malaysian Manufacturers Association (FMM) Memorandum on National Economic Policy after 1990: New Policy Directions and Strategies." Confidential memorandum prepared by the FMM, Kuala Lumpur, March 21, 1989.

Tan Lian Choo. "The Bright Boys from Bangkok." *Sunday Times*, Singapore, April 2, 1989.

Tasker, Rodney. "Busting a Bronze." *FEER*, June 15, 1989.

Tasker, Rodney. "Eye of the Storm." *FEER*, November 23, 1989.

Tasker, Rodney. "Rebel Clowns?" *FEER*, June 15, 1989.

Tasker, Rodney. "The Wild East." *FEER*, September 21, 1989.

Thailand Board of Investment. "A Guide to Investing in Thailand." Bangkok, June 1989.

Thailand Development Research Institute and International Development Center of Japan. "Thai-Japan Economic Conflicts." Bangkok, April 1986.

Tilleke and Gibbins, R. O. P. "Business and Investments in Thailand." Presentation made at the Euromoney conference, Investing in Thailand, Bangkok, June 20–21, 1989.

Train, John. "Investing in Emerging Countries." *Harvard Magazine*, Sept–Oct. 1989.

Uathavikul, Phaichitr. "Thailand: National Issues and Goals to the Year 2000." Thailand Development Research Institute, *Quarterly Newsletter*, December 1988.

Unger, Daniel H. "Growth in Textile Exports as a Response to Currency Realignment." Paper presented at the annual meeting of the Association for Asian Studies, Washington, D.C., March 17–19, 1989.

United States Department of Commerce. "Indonesia: Foreign Economic Trends." Washington, D.C.: Government Printing Office, 1989.

United States Department of Commerce. "Malaysia: Foreign Economic Trends." Washington, D.C.: Government Printing Office, 1989.

United States Department of Commerce. "Thailand: Foreign Economic Trends." Washington, D.C.: Government Printing Office, 1988.

United States Department of State. "Indonesia: Background Notes." Washington, D.C.: Government Printing Office, 1985.

United States Department of State. "Malaysia: Background Notes." Washington, D.C.: Government Printing Office, 1988.

United States Department of State. "Thailand: Background Notes." Washington, D.C.: Government Printing Office, 1988.

United States Department of State. "Thailand: Investment Climate Statement." Washington, D.C.: Government Printing Office, 1988.

Valéry, Nicholas. "Japanese Technology: Thinking Ahead." *The Economist*, December 2, 1989.

Vatikiotis, Michael R. J. "Indonesia's Financial Sector: Free to Fly." *FEER*, October 12, 1989.

Vatikiotis, Michael R. J. "Lobbying the Donors." *FEER*, August 24, 1989.

Vatikiotis, Michael R. J. "U.S.-Indonesian Relations: The Socio-Cultural Aspect." Paper presented at the Third Indonesian–U.S. Bilateral Conference, Bali, August 27–31, 1989.

Vernon, Raymond. "Multinational Enterprises in Developing Countries: An Analysis of National Goals and National Policies." Development Discussion Paper No. 4, Harvard Institute for International Development, Cambridge, MA, June 1975.

Viraphong, Vachiratith, et al. "What It Takes to Be a NIC." Bangkok Bank *Monthly Review*, March 1989.

Viravan, Amnuay. "ASEAN: Where Next? The Shape of Future Regional Cooperation." Speech delivered to the Asian-Pacific Bankers Club, Auckland, New Zealand, March 1, 1988.

Viravan, Amnuay. "Privatization Reconsidered." Speech delivered at the Thai-Canadian Business Club, Bangkok, July 12, 1989.

Viravan, Amnuay. "Southeast Asia: Turning a Battlefield into a Marketplace." Bangkok Bank *Monthly Review*, April 1989.

Viravan, Amnuay. "Thailand into the 1990s: The Emergence of Asia's Fifth Tiger?" Speech delivered at the Southeast Asian Studies Center, University of Michigan, Ann Arbor, MI, March 15, 1988.

Visetbhakdi, Norani. "Deforestation and Reforestation in Thailand." Bangkok Bank *Monthly Review*, June 1989.

Wanandi, Jusuf. "Indonesian Domestic Politics and Its Impact on Foreign Policy." Paper presented at the Third Indonesian–U.S. Bilateral Conference, Bali, August 27–31, 1989.

Wanandi, Jusuf. "Japan in Southeast Asia." *Japan Economic Survey*, May 1989.

Wanner, Barbara. "Pacific Economic Cooperation: Washington's New Asian Strategy?" Japan Economic Institute *Report*, No.44A, November 17, 1989.

Watanabe, Tsunehiko. "Improvement of Labor Quality and Economic Growth: Postwar Japan's Experience." Economic Development Report No. 164, Project for Quantitative Research in Economic Development, Harvard University, Cambridge, MA, October 1970.

Watson, Russell. "Cambodia: Asia's Next Flash Point." *Newsweek*, June 26, 1989.

Weatherbee, Donald. "International Security and ASEAN in the 1990s." Paper presented at the Sixth Regional Security Conference on International Security in Southeast Asia, Chiang Mai, Thailand, July 4–6, 1989.

Wong, Steven C. M. "ASEAN Cooperation: Problems and Prospects." *Indonesian Quarterly*, Vol. XVII, No. 1, 1989.

Wong, Steven C. M. "Japan in Search of a Global Economic Role." Paper presented at the Fifth U.S.-ASEAN Conference, Singapore, June 11–15, 1989.

World Bank. "The Development Data Book." 2nd ed. Washington, D.C.: International Bank for Reconstruction and Development (IBRD), 1989.

Zakaria, Haji Ahmad. "Malaysian Foreign Policy and Domestic Politics: Looking Outward and Moving Inward?" Draft monograph, unpublished, undated (1989).

INDEX